PERSONAL IDENTITY
AND BUDDHIST PHILOSOPHY

What does it mean to be a person? The philosophical problem of personal identity has been the subject of much debate in both Western philosophy and Buddhist philosophy. This book initiates a conversation between the two traditions showing how concepts and tools drawn from one philosophical tradition can help solve problems arising in another, particularly as regards the philosophical investigation of persons.

The recent controversy over personal identity has concerned reductionism, the view that persons are mere useful fictions. Mark Siderits explores the most important objections that have been raised to reductionism, and shows how some key arguments and semantic tools from early Buddhism can be used to answer those objections. Buddhist resources are used to examine the important ethical consequences of this view of persons. The second half of the book explores a new objection to reductionism about persons that originates in Mahayana Buddhist philosophy.

Ashgate World Philosophies Series

The Ashgate World Philosophies Series responds to the remarkable growth of interest among English-language readers in recent years in philosophical traditions outside those of 'the West'. The traditions of Indian, Chinese, and Japanese thought, as well as those of the Islamic world, Latin America, Africa, Aboriginal Australian, Pacific and American Indian peoples, are all attracting lively attention from professional philosophers and students alike, and this new Ashgate series provides introductions to these traditions as well as in-depth research into central issues and themes within those traditions. The series is particularly designed for readers whose interests are not adequately addressed by general surveys of 'World Philosophy', and it includes accessible, yet research-led, texts for wider readership and upper-level student use, as well as research monographs. The series embraces a wide variety of titles ranging from introductions on particular world philosophies and informed surveys of the philosophical contributions of geographical regions, to in-depth discussion of a theme, topic, problem or movement and critical appraisals of individual thinkers or schools of thinkers.

Series Editors:

David E. Cooper, University of Durham, UK
Robert C. Solomon, University of Texas, Austin, USA
Kathleen M. Higgins, University of Texas, Austin, USA
Purushottama Bilimoria, Deakin University, Australia

Other titles in the series:

An Introduction to Yoga Philosophy
An Annotated Translation of the Yoga Sutras
Ashok Kumar Malhotra

Knowing Beyond Knowledge
Epistemologies of Religious Experience in Classical and Modern Advaita
Thomas A. Forsthoefel

Mencius, Hume and the Foundations of Ethics
Xiusheng Liu

Comparative Approaches to Chinese Philosophy
Edited by Bo Mou

Personal Identity and Buddhist Philosophy

Empty Persons

MARK SIDERITS
Illinois State University, USA

ASHGATE

Published by
Ashgate Publishing Limited
Gower House
Croft Road
Aldershot
Hampshire GU11 3HR
England

Ashgate Publishing Company
Suite 420
101 Cherry Street
Burlington, VT 05401–4405
USA

Ashgate website: http://www.ashgate.com

British Library Cataloguing in Publication Data
Siderits, Mark, 1946–
    Personal identity and Buddhist philosophy : Empty persons.
    – (Ashgate world philosophies series)
    1. Philosophy, Buddhist 2. Identity (Psychology)–Religious
    aspects–Buddhism
    I.Title
    181'.043

US Library of Congress Cataloging in Publication Data
Siderits, Mark, 1946
    Personal identity and Buddhist philosophy : Empty persons / Mark Siderits.
        p. cm. – (Ashgate world philosophies series)
    Includes bibliographical references and index.
    1. Self (Philosophy) 2. Identity (Psychology) 3. Buddhism–Philosophy. 4. Analysis
    (Philosophy) I. Title. II. Series.
    BD438.5.S53 2003
    126–dc21   2002038378

ISBN 0 7546 3473 6

Typeset in Times Roman by N²productions

Printed by MPG Books Ltd, Bodmin, Cornwall.

For Esther

Contents

Preface

Analytic philosophy and Buddhist philosophy share a fundamental commitment to trying to attain complete clarity about the matters they investigate. One such matter is what it means to be a person. Both traditions contain long and complex debates over questions concerning their mode of existence and the properties that attach to them. In this work I have tried to bring the two traditions into dialogue with one another over some key issues in the philosophical investigation of persons. While I know that the results fall short of complete clarity, I hope I have made some progress toward that goal. If so, there are many people I must thank.

David Anderson and Kenton Machina have proven invaluable conversational partners over the years. I consider myself truly fortunate in having two such colleagues – analytic philosophers who are willing (sometimes even eager) to discover how a non-Western philosophical tradition might contribute to a current debate. Not only did I learn much from my interactions with them, but without their examples I might have despaired of the possibility of finding an audience for 'fusion' philosophy.

I have gained much from my many long philosophical conversations with Arindam Chakrabarti over the years, and I hope he will not be chagrined by the fruit these have borne here. Roy Perrett provided many valuable comments on earlier drafts of the first part of this book, as well as a great deal of extremely helpful bibliographic information. Chakraborti Ram-Prasad had useful things to say about some of the material in the second half. And special thanks must go to Amita Chatterji, who introduced me to some of the exciting work being done at Jadavpur University.

As this work developed, portions of it were presented to a number of philosophy departments, and I must thank them all for useful comments and general encouragement. Portions of Chapter 3 were the basis of talks at Otago University (Dunedin), at Massey University (Palmerston North), and at Rabindra Bharati University (Calcutta). Parts of Chapter 4 were presented at Canterbury University (Christchurch), Jadavpur University (Calcutta), and to the Philosophy of Religions program at University of Chicago. Parts of Chapter 5 were presented to the Friday Seminar, Calcutta, where Kalipada Bakshi, Tara Chatterjea and Shefali Moitra all raised important points. Finally, my colleagues and friends in the joint philosophy colloquium series of Illinois State University and Illinois Wesleyan University heard earlier versions of some of the material in Chapters 1, 3 and 7; I especially wish to thank Carl Gillett and Michael Gorr for useful discussion and feedback.

I should also like to take this opportunity to express my gratitude to my many students who over the years have demanded clarity in the presentation of philosophical ideas.

If persons are ultimately empty, then there is no person who is ultimately to blame for any mistakes in these pages. Mistakes were made nonetheless – despite all the helpful advice, comments and criticism made by those mentioned here and by others. The ultimate responsibility for those mistakes must rest with me alone.

Introduction

This is an essay in fusion philosophy. But what *is* fusion philosophy? The term 'fusion' is now applied to everything from cooking to styles of tattooing, but my first encounter with the relevant use of the term was in the area of music. Perhaps today the label 'fusion music' seems little more than a marketing device, but the original idea was that the musicians involved in such an undertaking (typically including representatives from each of two distinct musical traditions) were making a serious and sustained effort to use elements from one tradition in order to try to solve problems arising in another. The enterprise of fusion philosophy is meant to be a successor to the practice of what has been called comparative philosophy. It is the centrality of problem-solving to the original conception of a fusion in music that recommends the term to those seeking a new name for the philosophical enterprise. Comparative philosophy has always involved the comparison of elements drawn from two distinct philosophical traditions. (The comparison has usually been between the Western tradition and either the South Asian or the East Asian tradition.) But the point of the comparison has often seemed to be limited to bringing out similarities and differences that might be of interest to scholars of one or the other tradition. To those who see problem-solving as central to philosophy, and who also believe that the counterpoising of distinct traditions can yield useful results in this endeavor, the name 'fusion philosophy' seems appropriate.

The Reductionist view of persons espoused by Derek Parfit in *Reasons and Persons* (1984) has provoked a great deal of controversy. While it is difficult to count heads on such matters, it seems unlikely that most Anglophone philosophers working on the issue of personal identity today accept that view. Still, Parfit has not recanted. Now Parfit himself was well aware that the Buddha once held a view similar to his own. What neither Parfit nor his many critics seem to have realized, however, is that in the classical Indian controversy over the Buddha's view of persons, philosophical tools were forged that might help us adjudicate the dispute between Parfit and his many critics. I propose to use the present dispute as a kind of test case for the project of fusion philosophy. What I hope to show is that we can sometimes make progress toward solving philosophical problems by looking at what traditions distinct from our own have had to say about the issues with which we are concerned.

The problem that is taken up here is this: we think of ourselves as persons, and as such we take ourselves to be the kinds of things that can continue to exist for many years. What exactly is involved in the continued existence over time of a person? And what ethical consequences, if any, might follow from the correct understanding of the continued existence of persons? Parfit's Reductionism provides clear answers to both questions. In the first part of this book I shall seek to show that those answers can be defended against the many objections raised by Parfit's critics. This defense will come at a certain price, however: in order to mount a successful defense, the Parfitian Reductionist will need to become more like what I shall call a Buddhist Reductionist.

But, I claim, the price is not onerous, since Buddhist Reductionism should recommend itself to anyone committed to a broadly realist project. The use of certain Buddhist philosophical resources thus enables Parfit to answer his many critics. This does not, however, yield a definitive vindication of Reductionism. Buddhist Reductionism had its own critics within the Buddhist tradition. These critics held a position which I think may be fairly described as a kind of global anti-realism. In the second part of this book I shall present those of their views that have a bearing on the problem with which we are here concerned. I shall seek to show that certain key arguments of theirs help us arrive at a proper diagnosis of the real difficulty with Reductionism. I shall also claim that the kind of anti-realism on offer has advantages over what has generally gone under that label of late. We will then assess what if anything remains of the ethical stance that Reductionists sought to support with their own view of persons. I shall claim that the same view concerning the obligatoriness of benevolence remains defensible on the Buddhist anti-realist view.

I have written this work with two sorts of readers in mind. (But if you fit in neither category, do not worry!) This is reflected in the fact that there are both footnotes and endnotes. The footnotes contain the usual sorts of information concerning references, contextual matters, and the like – but only of a sort that might be found in other works in the area of analytic metaphysics. Virtually no information concerning the Buddhist philosophical tradition is contained in the footnotes; readers seeking such information must turn instead to the endnotes. This division is motivated by the following considerations. One sort of reader will be primarily interested to see if I can deliver the goods I promise, that is, new light on the current controversy concerning persons. Such a reader will come to this work with little or no background knowledge concerning the Indian Buddhist tradition, and may not be particularly interested in determining if I have accurately depicted those parts of that tradition that I make use of. For this reader, the information I present in the endnotes might prove to be an unhelpful distraction from the argument presented in the text. Such information will be of great interest to another sort of reader, however, namely those with a background in Buddhology. To those readers I apologize in advance for the fact that they must thumb through to the end of each chapter to find what they seek. As they well know, however, sometimes too much Sanskrit too prominently displayed puts off just those readers who might profit from exposure to a tradition other than their own.

I should like to say a few words to each set of readers about how I think they might best approach this work. The first set I shall call the A readers (perhaps for 'analytic'), and the second group will be referred to as the B readers (perhaps for 'Buddhologist'). The first point I wish to make clear to the A reader is that this is not intended to be a definitive introduction to Buddhist philosophy. While the two strains of thought that I have chosen to discuss are major components of the Buddhist philosophical tradition, they are not the only ones. Some of the information contained in the endnotes may be useful for those who wish to explore the tradition in greater detail. There are now generally reliable English translations available for some of the Sanskrit texts that I have used, and complete references to these are provided in the part of the Bibliography devoted to Sanskrit sources.

The second point I wish to make to the A reader concerns the accuracy of my representation of Buddhist philosophy. It may well be natural for readers to wonder about this. And for those who wish to further explore the tradition I have, where possible, provided references to English translations in those endnotes that cite Sanskrit sources. But I suggest that it would be most useful for the A reader to at least initially set such questions aside. There will no doubt be controversy among Buddhologists over some of my readings (as there is among scholars of any subject over just about everything). I am confident that my interpretations will, at least for the most part, stand up to critical scrutiny. But what the A reader can be assured of in advance is that what is here presented as Buddhist philosophy does have its genesis in the Buddhist tradition. What may be debated among scholars of that tradition is the extent to which my rational reconstruction of some of its key elements illegitimately goes beyond anything to be found there. What is beyond dispute is that it is a rational reconstruction that begins with that tradition. And this is what matters when it comes to the project of fusion philosophy. It is the claim of those who advocate such a project that progress can be made when distinct traditions enter into dialogue concerning specific issues. The A reader may rest assured that this is at least an instance of such a dialogue; the real question is whether any progress has been made on the issue.

Among the B readers there will be those who are already quite familiar with current work on personal identity, and the methods of analytic metaphysics in general. Such readers need no advice from me about how to approach this work. But to those Buddhologists who lack such familiarity, I would sound a note of caution. What I present here as elements of Buddhist philosophy may not be immediately recognizable as such to those who are accustomed to reading the tradition in other ways and for other purposes. But perhaps this analogy will help. We might see philosophical traditions as distinct houses within which there have developed distinctive ways of life. In each house there will then be tools that were developed by the members of that household to solve specific problems arising there. What I propose to do is borrow tools from next door to fix some things in this house. (I am now speaking as a resident of the house in which the present problem of personal identity has arisen.) Someone might complain that what I am using as a pipe wrench was never intended as such. Two questions might be raised in response. First, will such use warp the tool? That is, will using the tool in this way seriously distort our understanding of the role it plays in its home context? Second, must those who borrow their neighbors' tools first master and then recite the complete ethnography of the house next door before they may use their tools? That is, is the Buddhist philosophical tradition to be a museum diorama, or may selected pieces of that tradition sometimes be put to novel uses? It is doubtless true that those of us who wish to understand Buddhist philosophy need to see how a given concept or theory connects up with the full range of issues and themes in the tradition. What is not clear is that the only legitimate employment of such concepts or theories is to help represent the total context of their origin. The drawing of overly facile analogies between elements of distinct traditions can result in serious distortions (typically to the tradition marked as 'other'); but surely this does not mean that the Buddhist tradition must be kept hermetically sealed in the museum of the history of ideas.

I should also acknowledge that my use of the Buddhist philosophical tradition sometimes goes beyond anything explicitly said by Indian Buddhist philosophers, and goes into the terrain of rational reconstruction. For instance, in Chapter 4 I state that the position I call Buddhist Reductionism ought to embrace a degree-theoretic account of truth (along with the sorts of adjustments to classical logic that will require). Now to my knowledge no Indian Buddhist philosopher ever discussed anything like a degree-theoretic account of truth. But I am not there claiming that they did. Neither am I claiming that something like such an account is what they 'really had in mind'. All I am claiming is that this is a reasonable extrapolation from what they did say, that this is what someone who held their view and was also a party to present philosophical discussions ought to say. My experience leads me to suspect that some B readers may be inclined to level the charge of anachronism (or worse yet, 'Orientalism') at my representation of certain positions as Buddhist or as flowing from the Buddhist tradition. I would urge such readers to show patience, and to bear in mind the difference between philosophy and philology.

There will also be those who are inclined to wonder whether any meaningful 'fusion' of analytic philosophy and the Buddhist tradition is possible, given the soteriological aims of the latter. This question will be felt particularly keenly by those who understand Buddhism to espouse the attainment of a state of non-discursive, direct insight that is antithetical to rational analysis. But a similar worry may haunt those who make no such (in my view false) assumption about what Buddhism teaches. For it is widely thought that soteriological aims are *prima facie* incompatible with the analytic enterprise, and Buddhism does after all purport to teach a method for bringing about the state known as nirvana, which is the cessation of existential suffering. This claim about incompatibility may be put in either of two ways. One version has it that Buddhism is thereby made to sound 'too scientific' or 'too positivistic'. The other version amounts to the complaint that analytic philosophy's commitment to clarity and logical rigor will be lost sight of once one enters into the domain of the spiritual and mystical. It is, however, important to be clear about why the commitment to clarity and rigor that is central to the analytic enterprise might be thought incompatible with a quest for nirvana. I would submit that behind both versions of the claim stands the presupposition of a strong fact/value dichotomy, which is in turn a manifestation of the reason/faith dichotomy characteristic of modern Western culture. Only when we assume that rationality is incapable of resolving soteriological or existential concerns will it seem as if bringing the two projects together imperils values central to one or the other. And certainly the Buddhist tradition never made such an assumption. Quite the opposite: the Buddha takes it as obvious that we shall never resolve our existential concerns until we become genuinely clear about what it is that our existence consists in.

It is by now well known how it came to be thought that Asian cultures promoted soteriological aims to the exclusion of scientific rationality. This was a strategy of nineteenth-century apologists wishing to explain the material ascendancy of Europe: while the West might have perfected material technologies that conferred certain military and economic advantages, Asia had instead devoted itself to supposedly higher ends. This notion of a division of intellectual labor between a 'materialist' West and a 'spiritual' East was flawed from the outset by its unquestioning acceptance of a crudely positivist view of rationality. We now know that whole-hearted endorsement of the principle of non-contradiction does not inevitably lead to a thorough flattening and spiritual desiccation of the world. Yet the view persists that Asian cultures advocate the attainment of spiritual ends by abandoning reason. It is time to shed this misconception. It stands in the way of a potentially fruitful conversation between historically distinct traditions.

This work falls roughly into two parts. In the first five chapters I discuss the more important objections that have been leveled against Parfit's Reductionism, and explore ways in which the resources of Buddhist Reductionism can be used to answer them. In the succeeding four chapters I mount a new challenge to Reductionism, based on a Buddhist variety of global anti-realism. The book begins, in the first chapter, with a discussion of just what Reductionism amounts to. I argue that an ontological reductionism about any sort of entity is best understood as a kind of 'middle path' between the two extremes of non-reductionism (the view that entities of that sort are ultimately real) and eliminativism (the view that such entities are utter fabrications). Thus Reductionism, or ontological reductionism about persons, is best understood as situated between Non-Reductionism and Eliminativism. I claim that by replacing Parfit's dichotomous taxonomy (Parfit speaks only of Non-Reductionism and Reductionism) with the Buddhist trichotomy, we can become much clearer about what Reductionists are and are not committed to.

The second chapter takes up the simplest form of Non-Reductionism: the view that the continued existence of a person consists in the continued existence of a self. Some effort is made at clarifying just what a self might be like, and defending the claim that it should be distinguished from the various psychophysical elements such as the parts of the body and mental states. Several Buddhist arguments against the existence of a self are presented. The chapter ends with a discussion of the connection that Buddhists see between belief in a self and existential suffering.

Refuting the self is just one small part of the defense of Reductionism. In the third chapter I take up a variety of objections to Reductionism, coming both from Eliminativists and from those Non-Reductionists who do not believe in the existence of a self. A common theme in all these objections is that they somehow involve Reductionism's impersonal description thesis, according to which although persons may be said to exist, it is in principle possible to give a complete description of reality without either asserting or presupposing that there are persons. This *prima facie* puzzling claim is elucidated using the Buddhist Reductionist distinction between conventional truth and ultimate truth. Reductionism may then be understood as claiming that while ultimately there are no persons but only series of impersonal psychophysical elements, still persons are useful fictions and so may be granted a kind of conventional reality. This provides the Buddhist Reductionist with the resources necessary to answer objections based on the Extreme Claim. This is the claim that Reductionism entails that we have no reason for special concern about our own future states; it has the effect of making Reductionists out to be asserting that we should live only in the present. In answering objections based on the Extreme Claim, Reductionists commit themselves to the view that persons are socially constructed, and this gives rise to concerns about circularity. For instance, if there are ultimately no persons, it might be wondered how the conventions governing personhood came to be formulated. The Reductionist response to such objections turns out to involve the controversial claim that pain is impersonally bad. Additionally there are discussions of several objections based on a kind of foundationalism about egoistic concern, as well as objections stemming from a Kantian dual-aspect theory.

The Buddhist formulation of Reductionism is based on a thoroughgoing mereological reductionism. This is the view that no composite entity is ultimately real, that only impartite entities belong in our fundamental ontology. The fourth chapter takes up this view, looking first at the argument that Buddhist Reductionists use in its defense, and then at some objections to the view. One key issue here turns out to be whether there is reason to believe there are genuinely impartite entities. Buddhist Reductionists may defend their affirmative answer by claiming that their view yields the only plausible solution to the problem of vague predicates, that is, the problem of how we are able to use terms like 'heap' and 'bald' that allow of borderline cases. The upshot will be a two-tiered semantics, with a degree-theoretic account of truth at the conventional level but strict bivalence holding at the ultimate level of truth. A second important issue is whether there are any genuine cases of non-reductive mereological supervenience. Here I explore some interesting parallels between classic Buddhist controversies over the status of the person and the current dispute over the ontological commitments that follow from functionalist theories of the mind.

Having defended Reductionism against the major objections that have been leveled against it, in the fifth chapter I take up the ethical consequences of the view. Becoming a Reductionist is said to result in a diminished degree of existential dread, and a greater concern for the welfare of others. I examine and defend a Buddhist Reductionist argument for the second claim. A major objection to this argument is that taking up the moral stance that it recommends results in alienation from one's life-plans and projects. The response to this objection turns on the claim that irony need not be distancing: that we can take up an engaged stance while seeing through the fiction that requires it.

In the sixth chapter a new objection to Reductionism is presented, the objection that Buddhist anti-realists first developed against Buddhist Reductionism. As a form of metaphysical realism, Reductionism is committed to the existence of things whose natures are intrinsic to themselves. Here I examine a variety of arguments against the claim that there are things with intrinsic essences. The seventh chapter examines a further consequence of the resulting global anti-realism: that nothing is intrinsically a means of knowledge. This is shown to yield not skepticism but a kind of epistemological contextualism. An interesting consequence of this position is that a central realist thesis – that reality may outstrip knowledge – turns out to be incoherent. This suggests that the Buddhist critique of Reductionism is based on a form of global anti-realism that does not depend on such internalist assumptions as verificationism or the KK thesis (the thesis that knowledge requires knowing that one knows). This is of interest in that anti-realism is widely thought to be incompatible with the rejection of internalism.

Anti-realists are commonly accused of 'epistemologizing' truth – of making truth dependent on our ability to know. In the eighth chapter I take up the question whether this charge applies equally to the form of global anti-realism that emerges from the Buddhist critique of intrinsic essences. The argument proceeds by way of a survey of the available approaches to explaining the semantic competence of language users. I claim that when these are considered in the light of some important results of Buddhist anti-realism, what results is a kind of semantic non-dualism. In the Buddhist context, this amounts to the claim that there is no ultimate truth, only conventional truth. In the context of contemporary discussions, this view could be seen as a kind of middle path between an epistemologized truth and a deflationist approach to truth. One interesting result discussed here is that the distinction between deductive and inductive arguments turns out to be quite problematic.

The ninth and final chapter returns to the ethical consequences of the claim that persons are empty. Surprisingly, these turn out to stand unharmed by the anti-realist critique of Buddhist Reductionism. This means that the argument for an obligation to exercise altruism goes through even if we find implausible the Buddhist Reductionist requirement that there be ultimately real, impartite entities. Buddhist anti-realism does nevertheless have some distinctive ethical consequences, and these are explored. Finally, in a brief appendix I present the semantic theory that was developed by one school of Buddhist Reductionists to explain how we can master the use of general terms even though there are neither real universals nor mind-independent resemblances among the things that ultimately exist.

CHAPTER ONE

Situating Reductionism

This work concerns Reductionism and its consequences. A Reductionist (that is, a reductionist about persons) holds that the existence of a person is really nothing more than just the existence of certain other kinds of things.[1] In this respect it is not unlike saying that a pool of water is really just a mass of H_2O molecules, or that a bolt of lightning is really just a series of electrical discharges. Reductionism about persons is thus a type of ontological reductionism: it holds that a certain sort of thing that is ordinarily thought to exist turns out to be reducible to certain other sorts of things that are in some sense ontologically more basic. Before investigating the consequences of Reductionism, it is important to be clear about just what it might mean to say that something is reducible to other kinds of things. In this chapter we will first investigate a broad framework that is meant to shed some light on ontological reductionisms in general; then we will look at how this applies to the case of persons.

Ontological reductionism

Suppose that the users of a given discourse regularly refer to things of kind K. There are three possible views one might take with respect to the ontological status of Ks. One might be a non-reductionist about Ks, holding that things of this sort belong in our final ontology – that the Ks will be among the items that must be mentioned in any complete theory about the nature of reality. Or one might be an eliminativist about Ks, holding that belief in the existence of Ks within the discourse community is wholly the product of the acceptance of a false theory. Finally, one might be a reductionist about Ks, holding that while Ks may be said in a sense to exist (*pace* the eliminativist), their existence just consists in the existence of things of a more basic sort, things of which the Ks are composed, so that (*pace* the non-reductionist) Ks do not belong in our final ontology. Now it may not be immediately apparent that this third sort of view is a genuine option. Quine, for instance, denied that a distinction may be drawn between what is here called reductionism and eliminativism.[2] To see why the reductionist is not just a very diplomatic eliminativist, we must say more about what motivates first the non-reductionist, and then the eliminativist. This should help to clear the land between the two for possible occupation by the reductionist.

A non-reductionist about Ks believes that things of that kind are not mere fictions or mental constructions (like Santa Claus), but are ultimately real, that is, make up part of the furniture of the universe as it is, independent of our theorizing about its

---

[1] I shall follow Parfit (1984) in using 'Reductionism' to refer to a reductionist view of persons and personal identity.

[2] See Quine (1960: 265). My 'reductionism' corresponds to his 'explicative reductionism', 'eliminativism' to his 'eliminative reductionism'.

nature.[3] What sorts of reasons might be given for such a claim? Suppose someone were a non-reductionist about corporations. They would then hold that while our final ontology contains persons and inanimate objects (such as buildings and machines, or whatever might be the ultimate constituents of buildings and machines), any theory that only referred to persons and inanimate objects and did not also refer to corporations would be radically incomplete. They might, for instance, claim that being an officer of a corporation has certain characteristic effects on individual psychology that cannot be explained just in terms of the physical and psychological interactions of the individual with other members of the corporation. It might likewise be claimed that only in this way can we understand how an individual might come to be morally obligated to provide reparation for a past injustice that they were not a party to (because the injustice occurred at a time when they were not a member of the corporation).[4] The corporation must be granted admission to the ontological inner circle, they would claim, since it has genuinely autonomous causal and explanatory powers that cannot be reduced to the causal and explanatory powers of its members.

Other sorts of reasons might be given for non-reductionism about corporations. It might be claimed, for instance, that a corporation cannot be reduced to the persons who are its members and the physical objects that are its property, since a corporation can continue to exist through the replacement of all its original members and property by new members and property (provided the replacement process is gradual enough). As we shall see, however, the reductionist has a ready reply to this claim. Moreover, the non-reductionist will face a serious challenge concerning the seeming lack of empirical evidence for their ontological claim: when we observe what is called a corporation, we always seem to perceive individual persons and property and never this supposedly extra thing, the corporation. Given this difficulty, it seems best for the non-reductionist to rest the case for their ontological claim chiefly on the grounds that the corporation has genuinely autonomous causal and explanatory powers.

What sorts of reasons might be given for an eliminativist view about *K*s? Since no one is likely to be an eliminativist about the corporation,[5] let us consider instead the eliminativist about disease-causing demons – the supposedly non-corporeal entities that were once thought to be the agents of various human diseases. We may imagine that within a community that shares this medical theory, people regularly refer to such demons, and there are specialists who have learned to identify particular kinds of demons. Thus the appropriately trained specialists would agree that a patient with

---

[3] As use of the expression 'ultimately real' suggests, the non-reductionist subscribes to metaphysical realism; so, it will turn out, do the reductionist and eliminativist. Metaphysical realism is usually characterized as the view that there is one true theory about the nature of the world, with truth understood as correspondence to mind-independent reality. The difficulty with this formulation is that the subjective idealism of a Berkeley or a Yogācāra Buddhist could not count as a variety of metaphysical realism, since on such views everything is mind-dependent. The Buddhist Reductionist conception of the ultimately real as what is beyond all conceptual activity (*nirvikalpa*) suggests a better formulation: metaphysical realism is the view that there is one true theory about the world, with truth understood as correspondence to how things are distinct from all conceptual activity.

[4] This example is taken from Perrett (1998: 80–81), who puts it to quite different use.

[5] As opposed to being a reductionist about corporations. This is the view that is commonly expressed by calling the corporation merely a 'legal fiction'.

high fever and chronic coughing suffers from possession by the blue lizard-lipped demon, while one with a low-grade fever, chronic coughing, and blood in the sputum suffers from possession by the yellow pin-feather demon. Let us also suppose that various treatments have been fashioned, different ones depending on which sort of demon is thought to be responsible for the patient's malady, and that these are at least marginally effective.

The eliminativist about demons would obviously claim that demons do not exist. For we now know that diseases are caused by microbial infection, not demonic possession, and our only reason for supposing there to be demons had to do with the explanatory role they played in the now-discredited theory. But then what explains the ability of speakers to learn to refer to distinct kinds of demons, and of specialists to tailor (marginally) effective treatment to the identity of demon-type? If demons really were invented out of whole cloth, then these abilities may seem somewhat mysterious. Might it not be that the term 'demon' was actually this community's rather confused way of referring to microbial pathogens? The eliminativist will resist this last suggestion, on the grounds that demons are simply too unlike microbes for the identity to go through. Demons have malicious intent, for instance, while microbes do not. And while both theories agree that pathogens may be perceived and identified by means of specialist techniques, the techniques that are prescribed could not be more different: according to the demonic possession theory, ingestion of certain herbs by the specialist; according to the microbe theory, culturing of patient tissue, followed by staining and microscopic inspection. Now that we accept the microbial theory, belief in demons cannot be retained, even in the guise of a limited perspective on the truth. While talk of demons did perform a systematizing role that must have connected up, somehow or other, with the manifest effects of microbial infection, the theory in which such talk is ensconced is simply incompatible with the theory we now accept. Demons must be eliminated.

What happens, though, when the theories are not so clearly incompatible? We know of many episodes in the history of science in which one theory is neither wholly eliminated in favor of another, nor simply absorbed into the other. Let us look at one such case, that of the theory of the covalent bond and quantum mechanics. This is, of course, a classic case of intertheoretic reduction in the sciences, and for that very reason it may suggest requirements on successful reduction that prove too stringent. It is, though, at least a place to begin if we wish to see some daylight between non-reductionism and eliminativism.

When we say that organic chemistry may be reduced to quantum mechanics, we are making a certain claim about the relation between two theories: talk of covalent bonds may be systematically replaced (through the employment of so-called bridge laws) by talk of certain quantum mechanical states, in such a way that the latter theory is thereby shown to explain the predictive success of the former. Some caution is required in interpreting this result. It does not show that the covalent bond is a quantum mechanical state. For the covalent bond is a feature of certain molecules, and molecules are not among the objects of study of quantum physics. The relevant bridge laws do not simply take us from talk of covalent bonds to talk of quantum shifts and leave everything else unchanged. Instead they take us from the domain of organic chemistry to the very different domain of quantum physics, from talk of enduring molecules to talk of wave functions. The straightforward identification of the covalent bond with quantum phenomena does not seem to be an option. On the other hand, neither does outright elimination of one theory or the other seem to be in the cards. Since, however, quantum mechanics is a well-confirmed theory that has a wide variety of applications far beyond the case of the covalent bond, it appears to have the upper hand here. Given this, two questions arise: (1) Why not simply declare organic chemistry to be superfluous, and eliminate it in favor of quantum physics? Moreover, (2) why not 'lighten' our ontology by retaining quantum mechanical states (which will be needed in any event) and dismissing the covalent bond from our ultimate ontology?[6] That these are distinct questions calling for separate answers is important to reductionism. We begin with (1), and shall return to (2) later.

The successful reduction of organic chemistry to quantum physics shows the former to be in principle dispensable, but showing this is not the same thing as giving a positive reason for eliminating the first theory. For one thing, there is not the marked incompatibility between statements of the two theories that we saw in the case of the demonic-possession and microbial-infection theories of disease. While it seems to us incomprehensible how a multitude of germs could have malicious intent, we think we can see how the quantum shift could underlie some of the properties we attribute to the covalent bond. Observation conditions for the two types of states seem likewise compatible. And the systematizing functions of the two theories do not appear to conflict. In the medical case, we expect there to be instances where the microbe theory requires a classificatory scheme at odds with that of the demon theory: blue-demon possession turns out to be two distinct diseases, bacterial and viral pneumonia. Not only does this situation not arise in the case of organic chemistry and quantum mechanics, but coming to understand the latter may help us better understand the rationale behind the former theory's classificatory scheme. Apart from its apparent superfluousness, we do not find any positive reason to eliminate the theory of the covalent bond.

Most important, though, is the simple fact that quantum mechanics would prove an extraordinarily cumbersome tool for explaining and predicting the behavior of (those physical systems that we treat as) organic compounds. Since we have an interest in the behavior of these sorts of things, we would do well to retain the theory of organic chemistry. True, the theory turns out to be in principle dispensable. But there is no obvious bar deriving from quantum mechanics to its continued employment, and the theory appears to be virtually indispensable in practice. Thus there seems to be good reason to retain it.

To say this is not, however, to say that the covalent bond deserves a place in our ultimate ontology alongside quantum phenomena. Given that the relevant bridge laws render the truths of organic chemistry deducible from those of quantum mechanics, the entities and states referred to by organic chemistry turn out to lack autonomous explanatory and causal power. Since we can explain the facts of this entire domain and more with just the entities and states referred to by quantum physics, it would violate the principle of lightness to include the covalent bond in our ultimate ontology. Yet it seems odd to eliminate it from our ultimate ontology while at the same time

---

[6] What is known in the Western tradition as Ockham's Razor is referred to by Indian philosophers as the principle of lightness. Since this name is more nearly self-explanatory than 'Ockham's Razor', I shall use it hereafter. Of course, all the usual cautions apply in the application of the principle.

retaining the theory that posits it. Here the nature of our reasons for retaining and not eliminating the theory of organic chemistry gives us some guidance. These reasons were thoroughly pragmatic. This suggests that the covalent bond is really just how certain sorts of quantum phenomena will appear to us, given certain relevant facts about our perceptual capacities, for example, that our sense faculties are macroscopes and not microscopes; our cognitive capacities, for example, that much of our thinking is algorithmic; and our interests, for example, in technologies of material transformation. The physical world is fully and accurately described by the laws of microphysics. But for creatures like us, it will prove useful to treat certain portions of this world as conforming to the laws of organic chemistry. The reductionist about Ks typically claims that Ks just consist in something else, some 'more particular' sort of thing: heat just consists in mean molecular kinetic energy, lightning just consists in electrical discharges, etc. It would be misleading to claim that the covalent bond just consists in certain quantum phenomena – the situation is much more complex than this. Still, such a statement does convey the flavor of the reductionist approach here. The covalent bond is just how we see certain stretches of the physical world, given our limited discriminatory abilities and our unwillingness to look too closely.

The covalent bond is not, then, ultimately real. Are we to be eliminativists about the covalent bond after all? Not precisely, says the reductionist. It is not, they say, wholly false to claim that covalent bonds exist – although, they hasten to add, this is just because of the way that we talk and think. The covalent bond is not in our final ontology, but it is a posit of a theory that, while in principle dispensable, is in practice indispensable (for creatures like us). This is what reductionism about the covalent bond comes to. Many will no doubt find this intermediate ontological status – neither ultimately real nor utterly unreal – mysterious. We shall shortly describe a device that is designed to dispel some of the seeming mystery. But first we need to reflect on the strategy that was just used to distinguish between reductionism and eliminativism. This depends crucially on seeing the question of the ontological status of Ks as in part a semantic question. To say, for instance, that organic chemistry may be reduced to quantum mechanics is to make a certain claim about the relation between two theories: talk of covalent bonds may be systematically replaced by talk of certain quantum mechanical states, in such a way that the latter theory may be seen to explain the predictive success of the former.[7] By contrast, the demonic possession theory of disease does not reduce to the germ theory, for there is no way to systematically replace talk of being possessed by a certain demon with talk of microbial infection. Thus it is that we take a reductionist stance toward the covalent bond, but an eliminativist stance toward disease-causing demons. The term 'covalent bond' is now revealed to refer to certain distinctive sorts of quantum mechanical phenomena. So while a complete description of reality need not mention covalent bonds (whereas it

---

[7] It is important not to confuse this relation with synonymy. Since the terms of the theory undergoing reduction will derive their meanings in part from their relations with other terms in that theory, no such term is likely to be synonymous with any term in the base theory. For this reason the definability of concepts from the theory undergoing reduction in terms of the concepts of the base theory is likewise too strong a condition for reduction. (Putnam (1992: 56) attributes this view to Fodor and appears to endorse it himself.) *Sorites* difficulties are one major source of a block on this sort of definability. (This will be discussed in Chapter 4.)

would have to mention such things as quantum shifts), we may tolerate talk of such things just because the term is a useful way to refer to a certain class of quantum phenomena in which we take an interest.[8] With demons, though, things are quite different. When we come to accept the germ theory of disease, it becomes apparent that our former talk of being possessed by demons cannot be seen as just a rough and ready way of referring to microbial infection. Whereas the covalent bond is a posit of a useful though subsumed theory, the demon is a posit of a discredited theory, hence all talk of demons is to be eliminated.

Distinguishing between reductionism and eliminativism requires introduction of the semantic dimension. But this complicates matters significantly. For success at replacing the terms of one theory with those of another is something that admits of degrees. Consider the terms 'sunrise' and 'sunset', which are intermediate between the case of the covalent bond and that of the disease-causing demon. We might have thought, when we transferred allegiance from the geocentric model to the heliocentric model of the solar system, that these terms were ripe for elimination. Yet they survive. Had we expected otherwise, this would have derived from the fact that their meanings seemed inextricably bound up with the now discredited geocentric theory. Instead, these terms exhibited sufficient semantic flexibility that we could retain them while suppressing the implication that the astronomical phenomena are explained by the sun's motion around the earth. This semantic shift was not accompanied by a shift in supposed referent: we take the Ptolemaic astronomers to have been referring to the same thing we refer to with these terms. We can imagine circumstances under which something similar might have occurred with our talk of demons (and as did happen with 'humor'). What this suggests is that reductionism and eliminativism represent the ends of a continuum, with a middle range of cases in which it may be indeterminate whether the entities of the old theory are being reduced to, or eliminated in favor of, the entities of the new theory. But as is often the case with *sorites* phenomena, the existence of such an intermediate gray area need not count against there being a real distinction to be drawn between reductionism and eliminativism.

Characterized semantically, then, non-reductionism about *K*s will be the claim that *K*s will be mentioned in our final theory about the ultimate nature of reality. Both reductionists and eliminativists deny this claim, but they disagree over whether continued talk of *K*s will have any utility in the light of our final theory. The eliminativist proposes eliminating all talk of *K*s, both in our final theory and in its ordinary-language adjuncts. The reductionist says instead that while the term '*K*' is in principle eliminable from our language (since we can give a complete description of reality without mentioning *K*s), its continued use is both tolerable (because truths about *K*s are derivable from our final theory), and of some utility given our interests. If we distinguish between the property of being a *K*, and the predicate 'is a *K*', we may put the trichotomy as: the non-reductionist defends both the property and

---

[8] As has already been acknowledged, this is too simple a way of putting the relation between quantum mechanical states and the covalent bond. This approach works better with a term like 'mob', which we may think of as a useful device for referring to certain aggregates of individuals. In the case of 'covalent bond' it seems we need to ascend from the level of the term to the level of the theory, and speak of this as a useful device for referring to a class of microphysical entities and events. We shall return to this point below.

the predicate, the eliminativist rejects both the property and the predicate, and the reductionist denies the property but recommends retaining the predicate.

All of this may be expressed fairly straightforwardly if we follow the Buddhist Reductionist[9] in distinguishing between two sorts of truth, conventional and ultimate.[a] A sentence is said to be conventionally true if and only if it is assertible by the conventions of common sense, where these are understood as standards based on utility. A sentence is said to be ultimately true if and only if it both corresponds to the facts and neither asserts nor presupposes the existence of what is not ultimately real.[b] Buddhist Reductionists also claim that all partite entities (for example, chariots) are mere conceptual constructions and are not ultimately real. It then follows that any statement that either asserts or presupposes the existence of such things as chariots is ultimately false. Many such statements are, however, conventionally true, and this fact requires explanation, given that our conventional linguistic practices arise because of their utility: if chariots are ultimately unreal, then why should talk of chariots be any more likely to help us meet our ends than our ancestors' talk of demons? The explanation for this is said to lie in the fact that 'chariot' is a convenient designator for a set of parts assembled in a certain way. Thus while there are ultimately no chariots, there are those wholly 'im-chariotal' facts into which all chariot-talk may be reductively analyzed; it is these facts that explain the utility of our talk of the fiction. Given this utility, we may then say that while the chariot is ultimately unreal, it is conventionally real. This will be the reductionist view of chariots. The non-reductionist will claim that chariots are both conventionally and ultimately real – that in addition to the parts of which chariots are composed, ultimate reality also contains some sort of separately existing chariot-essence. And the eliminativist will claim that chariots are both ultimately and conventionally unreal – that our ordinary talk of chariots is misleading and should be replaced by some entirely new way of conceptualizing collections of chariot parts.

The Buddhist Reductionist view that all partite entities are ultimately unreal will strike many as an implausibly extreme form of reductionism. We shall look later (in Chapter 4) at some of the arguments that were given in its defense. But it is worth mentioning at this point what appears to have been an important underlying motivation – the notion that all aggregation involves mental construction. Consider the set of chariot parts: wheels, felly, axle, etc.[10] Now first consider the set when its members bear to one another the set of relations we might collectively dub the 'assembled chariot' relation: wheel attached to felly, felly to axle, etc. Second, consider the set when its members bear to one another what we might call the 'scattered across the battlefield' relation: a wheel beneath this tree, axle ten meters to the southeast of the tree, etc. We have a name for the set when its members are in the 'assembled chariot' relation, but we have no name for the set when its members are in the 'scattered across the battlefield' relation. It is obvious why this should be so: we have an institutionalized use – as a means of transportation – for the parts when assembled, but there is no institutionalized use for us of the parts when strewn across

---

[9] Buddhist Reductionists are those Buddhist philosophers who, in addition to being reductionists about chariots, forests, armies, villages and the like, take a reductionist line with regard to persons. As we shall see, not all Buddhists are Reductionists.

[10] These are, of course, partite themselves. For now, though, let us not worry about this.

the battlefield that way. Now consider that we tend to readily conceive of the set as a single entity when its members stand in the first relation, but not when they stand in the second relation. This makes it clear that our ontological intuitions are being guided by our institutionally arranged interests. And, claims the Buddhist Reductionist, if we wish to know the ultimate nature of reality, we would do well not to allow our views to be shaped by conventions that reflect our interests. The ultimate nature of reality is how things objectively are – independent of our subjective wants, needs and interests. In order to keep the ultimate truth free from contamination by mental construction, we should ban the use of all terms for partite entities. Of course this has the effect of making the ultimate truth concerning even the simplest matter appear impossibly prolix. But it is worth remembering that the source of this apparent impossibility lies in us, not in the matters we seek to accurately describe. Then when we do resort to the conventional truth, with its use of convenient designators, we will understand the seemingly substantial entities that we talk about to be of our own making.

Some will claim that in addition to the three possible views about *K*s that we have discussed so far, there is a fourth possibility: that *K*s non-reductively supervene on those more particular entities and events of which the *K*s are composed.^{c} (This might also be seen as a variety of non-reductionist view, a more modest one that does not require the superlative entities that our formulation of non-reductionism calls for.) Here non-reductive supervenience will be understood to consist in determination without explanation: all the facts about the supervening level are determined by facts at the base level, but there are no explanatory links between the two levels, so that the *K*s must be accorded genuinely autonomous explanatory powers. Here it matters what we take to count as an explanatory link. Suppose we say that only deducibility via bridge laws – what is found in such classic cases of reduction as organic chemistry to quantum mechanics, or thermodynamics to statistical mechanics – will count as genuine explanation. Then non-reductive supervenience will be a common form of intertheoretic relation, for example, between embryology and developmental molecular biology, cognitive psychology and neurobiology, aeronautical engineering and statistical mechanics, etc. But this will be so for the simple reason that in each of these pairs, the first theory is not typically formulated in terms of a set of laws – so there will be nothing at that end for bridge laws to connect up with.[11] And this seems unduly restrictive. The discoveries of molecular biology, for instance, seem to throw genuine explanatory light on the details of embryonic development, despite the fact that deducibility via bridge laws is unlikely.

Taking a more liberal line on what counts as explanation has an added benefit: it allows a more unified treatment of cases like the covalent bond on the one hand, and cases like the mob or the chariot on the other. It seems odd to suppose that the mob non-reductively supervenes on its members, or that the chariot non-reductively supervenes on its parts; these seem like ripe targets for reduction. But suppose we collect the set of core common-sense beliefs concerning chariots and treat this as a kind of folk theory of chariots. Here too we will find no laws. At this level of complexity, interesting and important nomic regularities are hard to come by. And

---

[11] Indeed in the first and second cases, the second member of the pair is also not much given to formulation in terms of laws. On this point see Brooks' (1994: 804–805) discussion of the case of biology.

since 'chariot' is a functional expression, there will be multiple realizations of the chariot-kind (the chariot made primarily of cedar planks, the aluminum-body chariot, etc.), each exhibiting relevantly different material properties and so demanding different treatment. Once more, if we take explanation to require deducibility via bridge laws, then our folk theory of chariots will turn out to have autonomous explanatory power. Yet it seems obvious that the facts about chariots are explained by facts about their parts, that the relation here is importantly similar to that between the covalent bond and quantum shifts. This intuition can be accommodated if we take explanation to consist in showing what is to be expected given the facts at the base level, plus facts concerning our perceptual and cognitive abilities and our interests. Then our folk theory of chariots is explained by classical mechanics in the same way in which the theory of the covalent bond is explained by quantum mechanics. The deducibility we find in the latter case is just a special feature of certain sorts of theories. Our folk theory of chariots and the theory of organic chemistry are alike parts of conventional truth; organic chemistry is just a more regimented part.

If we relax the standards for what is to count as an explanatory link, then the doctrine of the two truths becomes a powerful device in support of a reductionist agenda. Conversely, genuine instances of non-reductive supervenience will then prove hard to come by. We will later examine the view that persons non-reductively supervene on psychophysical elements. At that time we will take up again the question of what should count as a case of determination without explanation.

Reductionism about persons

Having developed a taxonomy of possible views concerning the ontological status of Ks, we turn now to a particular sort of K, the person. How does this taxonomy fare when mapped onto the dispute concerning persons and personal identity? Parfit's general account of Reductionism (1984: 210–14) provides a convenient starting point for this examination. Parfit characterizes Reductionism (that is, reductionism about persons) as the view that the existence of a person just consists in the existence of a brain and body, and the occurrence of a series of interrelated physical and psychological events. Given the reductionist force of this 'just consists in', all of the facts to which the existence of a person is here being reduced – the existence of a particular brain, the occurrence of a certain psychological event, the holding of causal relations between a particular psychological event and certain other physical and psychological events, etc. – will allow of a completely impersonal description, that is, a description that neither asserts nor presupposes that this person exists. Hence the Reductionist view of the identity over time of persons: that this just consists in more particular facts, facts that can be described in a thoroughly impersonal way. This general schematism is fleshed out by neo-Lockeans with purely psychological facts, by others with facts about the body or the brain; hence there are two possible Reductionist approaches to personal identity. Parfit prefers a neo-Lockean approach: he holds that personal identity over time just consists in non-branching psychological continuity. An example of the physical approach would be Unger (1992), who claims that personal identity over time just consists in the continued existence of whatever physically realizes a person's core psychological capacities (typically a brain). These two approaches disagree about the results of simple teletransportation. This (science fiction) procedure involves a scanner that destroys a person's brain and body while recording information concerning each molecule. The information is then transmitted to a distant receiving station, where a perfect replica of the brain and body are assembled out of new matter. According to the neo-Lockean approach, the Replica (the person who emerges from the receiving station) is the same person as the person who pressed the button in the teletransporter, since there will be full psychological continuity between the two; simple teletransportation is a way of traveling. On the physical continuity approach, however, this is not so; simple teletransportation is a way of dying and being replaced by a qualitatively identical but numerically distinct person.[d] Despite this and related differences, the two approaches share an important Reductionist commitment – that there may be cases where personal identity is indeterminate. The significance of this point will be considered later.

Parfit claims (1984: 211–12) that there are also two possible Reductionist views about what a person is:

> (1) a person just is a particular brain and body and a series of interrelated physical and mental events;

and

> (2) a person is an entity that is distinct from a brain and body and such a series of events.

Parfit himself clearly prefers (2) over (1), since (2) will prove important to the defense of his views concerning rationality and morality. This view appears to retain something to serve as a subject of rational and moral assessment, whereas the Eliminativist flavor of (1) seems to call the existence of such a subject into question. Both views are said to be consistent with the basic Reductionist claim that

> (3) a person's existence just consists in the existence of a brain and body, and the occurrence of a series of interrelated physical and mental events,

which may be contrasted with the Non-Reductionist view that

> (4) a person is a separately existing entity, distinct from their brain and body, and their experiences.

But Parfit is at some pains to show that (2) is compatible with (3), and not instead equivalent to (4). The key to this reconciliation is to be found in a later passage:

> Even Reductionists do not deny that people exist. And, on our concept of a person, people are not thoughts and acts. They are thinkers and agents. I am not a series of experiences, but the person who *has* these experiences. A Reductionist can admit that, in this sense, a person is *what has* experiences, or the *subject of experiences*. This is true because of the way in which we talk. [1984: 223]

But now if the subject of experiences turns out to be a mere *façon de parler*, we will wonder why this does not make the objectionable (1) the better description. One begins to have more sympathy for Quine's claim that eliminative and explicative reduction are really equivalent in the end.[12]

The doctrine of the two truths sheds some light here. The Buddhist Reductionist claims that the statement 'Persons exist' is conventionally true but ultimately false, and that this statement's being conventionally true may be accounted for in terms of statements of the wholly impersonal ultimate truth. Claim (2) may then be accepted as conventionally true: given our use of the convenient designator 'person', it is conventionally true that a person is something that *has* a brain and body, and various experiences, and that persons are the *doers* of their deeds. Both (1) and (3) use the convenient designator 'person', so neither can be ultimately true as they stand. But the objectionable use may be turned into a benign mention, yielding,

> (1') what is conveniently designated a 'person' just is a particular brain and body and a series of interrelated physical and mental events,

and

> (3') the existence of what is conveniently designated a 'person' just consists in the existence of a brain and body, and the occurrence of a series of interrelated physical and mental events.

These are then two ways of describing that ultimate state of affairs that helps explain the utility of (2).[13] The Reductionist need not choose between (1) and (2). Instead they should claim that while persons are ultimately unreal, they are conventionally real.

Parfit distinguishes between two versions of Non-Reductionism: the view that persons are separately existing entities (such as Cartesian Egos), and the view that while we are not separately existing entities, the existence of a person involves a further fact, over and above the 'more particular facts' of the existence of a brain and body and the occurrence of a series of interrelated physical and psychological events. The classic expression of the first version in the Western tradition is, of course, Descartes' conception of the 'I' as a thinking substance; Swinburne's formulation (in Shoemaker and Swinburne (1984)) represents a more recent statement of this view. This type of view is also well represented in the Indian tradition, for example, in the Nyāya theory of the *ātman* and the Sāṃkhya theory of *puruṣa*.[e] The basic idea here is that the human being (and possibly other life forms as well) is a complex system consisting not only of those things, such as body parts and mental events, that are ordinarily observable through sense perception and introspection, but also containing

---

[12] Cassam (1989: 77) expresses these misgivings. But he then goes on to demand that the Reductionist grant the concept of the person autonomous explanatory power in order to escape the charge of eliminativism. Since this appears tantamount to conceding that persons are ultimately real, it is not clear that Cassam's professed sympathies for reductionism are genuine.

[13] Of course 'brain' and 'body' are just as much convenient designators as 'person', so strictly speaking these statements cannot be ultimately true either. A more rigorous approach to the ultimate truth will be discussed below.

some one entity that constitutes the essence of the system, that one part the presence of which is required in order for the system to exhibit the properties that we ascribe to persons; it is the continued existence of this entity that constitutes personal identity over time.

While this type of view is relatively familiar, the 'further-fact' version of Non-Reductionism is more puzzling. Here we appear to have a reluctance like that of the Reductionist to posit extra entities, together with the insistence that certain key facts about persons cannot be accounted for in terms of more particular, wholly impersonal facts. In the Western tradition, Reid, Butler, and more recently Chisholm have put forward views that might be interpreted as of this sort. But in each of these cases there are also elements that seem to suggest belief in persons as separately existing entities.[14] And it is not difficult to see why clear-cut instances of this position might be hard to come by, since if it is true that persons exist and it is also the case that the concepts of person and personal identity are simple and unanalyzable, we should expect there to be some distinct entity the existence and the endurance of which explain these singular facts about persons and their identity over time. The Vātsīputrīyas (or Pudgalavādins) of the Buddhist tradition do, though, represent a clear instance of this type of Non-Reductionism; this is precisely the force of their claim that the person, while existent, is neither identical with nor distinct from the psychophysical elements.[f] This view may usefully be formulated as claiming that persons non-reductively supervene on the psychophysical elements. Not so another sort of view that Parfit also includes in the 'further fact' variety, however, namely the 'dual-aspect' view espoused by Shoemaker, Peter Strawson and others. On this Kantian view, the person, when considered in one way, just consists in a series of impersonal entities and events, but considered in another way the person must be thought of as conceptually prior to these entities and events; these two perspectives on the person, while irreconcilable, are equally necessary. The fact that the two aspects or perspectives are deemed irreconcilable is what makes it wrong to think of this as a view involving non-reductive supervenience. The promise of the non-reductive supervenenience approach is to bring base and supervenience levels into a single, unified system. A dual-aspect theory denies that this can be done. Both sorts of view can, though, be thought of as 'further-fact' versions of Non-Reductionism, since each claims there is more involved in the existence of a person than just the occurrence of a series of impersonal events, yet also denies that persons are 'something extra'.

When it comes to characterizing Eliminativism some care must be taken, since the label has become something of a term of abuse that Non-Reductionists are wont to hurl at Reductionists. Stone's (1988) account is helpful. Eliminativism is to be distinguished from Reductionism not in terms of the denial of a self (both agree that we are not 'something extra', existing over and above body and brain, etc.), nor in terms of the denial that persons are to be found in our ultimate ontology (both deny that persons have this privileged status), but rather in terms of the question whether the attitudes we ordinarily take toward ourselves and others are at all coherent. The Non-Reductionist claims that such things as prudential concern, anticipation, regret,

---

[14] Swinburne (Shoemaker and Swinburne 1984: 27) represents all three authors as further-fact theorists. Noonan (1989: 19) takes them as representative of what he calls the Simple View, which is a form of the separately-existing-entity thesis.

responsibility for past deeds, merit, and the like all require that there be something extra, over and above body and brain, etc. The Reductionist denies that there is this something extra, but holds that such attitudes may still be rational (even if their scope is somewhat altered when we come to accept Reductionism). The Eliminativist agrees with the Reductionist that we are not something extra, but also agrees with the Non-Reductionist that our attitudes toward persons are coherent only if we are something extra. Prudential concern, hopes, fears and regrets, judgments of responsibility, merit, praise and blame – all these are irrational. And since Locke is right to see the forensic elements as central to the concept of a person, it follows that all talk of persons is deeply incoherent. In place of the mildly dismissive Reductionist attitude toward persons – as 'mere constructions' out of more fundamental entities – we find in Eliminativism an outright rejection of all that persons are thought to be. Like the demons believed in by our ancestors, persons are posits of an utterly misguided theory.

Now an eliminativist may or may not have in mind some replacement for the theory that is, in their eyes, so thoroughly discredited. In the medical case, the eliminativist about demons proposes that that theory be replaced by the microbial infection theory. But in the philosophy of mind, the eliminative materialist, who advocates scrapping so-called folk psychology, has no concrete replacement theory to offer, and merely gestures in the direction of future neuroscience. So the Eliminativist need not propose any new account to replace our current manner of conceptualizing persons. But Eliminativism is often portrayed as involving the proposal that we replace our conception of persons with something far more ephemeral, the person-stage. On this proposal, which we shall call 'punctualism', conventional truth should be revised so that we each think of ourselves as a set of connected, coexisting body parts and mental states. Since a person-stage goes out of existence with the cessation of any occurrent mental state, what we now think of as the life of a single person is, according to punctualism, really a succession of very many distinct sentient beings, each existing for only a short while. Since such beings cannot experience such person-regarding attitudes as prudential concern, anticipation, and regret – attitudes that are partly constitutive of the forensic concept of the person – it follows that punctualism represents a radically revisionary theory.

The Buddha described his view of persons as a kind of 'middle path' between the two extreme views of eternalism and annihilationism. By eternalism he meant the view that the person has an eternally existing essence, the self. By annihilationism he meant the denial of an eternally existing self, together with the presumed consequence that the person goes out of existence after a relatively brief duration.[8] We may now say that eternalism is a variety of Non-Reductionism, and annihilationism is the punctualist variety of Eliminativism. Of course not all Non-Reductionists are eternalists, and not all Eliminativists are punctualists. Still it is a welcome discovery that our tripartite taxonomy should accommodate views from a variety of disparate sources. This gives some confidence that it is a fruitful way of looking at the matter. We may now safely proceed to our investigation of Reductionism and its competitors. This begins, in the next chapter, with an examination of that form of Non-Reductionism that claims that a person is a separately existing entity, a self.

Notes

^a By 'Buddhist Reductionism' I shall mean the view of persons systematically worked out in the Abhidharma schools (principally Theravāda, Vaibhāṣika, and Sautrāntika). The distinction between conventional truth (*saṃvṛtisatya*) and ultimate truth (*paramārthasatya*) grows out of the earlier distinction between 'drawn out' (*nītārtha*) and 'requiring drawing out' (*neyārtha*) texts that was formulated by early Buddhist exegetes to help interpret the Buddha's discourses. In trying to work out an orthodox account of the non-self thesis (the thesis that there is no self, no one thing corresponding to the sense of 'I' and 'mine'), the founders of the Abhidharma tradition were struck by the fact that in some *Nikāya* discourses the Buddha speaks quite promiscuously of persons, while in others he explicitly denies the existence of persons and uniformly substitutes talk of psychophysical elements (*skandhas*) instead. The early Buddhist exegetes sought to resolve this apparent conflict by bringing in the Buddha's skill at tailoring his message to the capacities of his audience. They thus distinguished between those discourses that can be taken as fully explicit expressions of the truth (*nītārtha*), and those that cannot be taken literally but require interpretation (*neyārtha*). The former occur in contexts where the audience is prepared for the full truth about persons, the non-self thesis, whereas in the latter the Buddha adopts popular forms of expression in order to communicate with a less philosophically advanced audience. This distinction was then generalized by Ābhidharmikas to yield the doctrine of two truths. See Warder (1970: 150–51).

^b These accounts are extrapolations from what is actually said about conventional truth (*saṃvṛtisatya*) and ultimate truth (*paramārthasatya*) in the Abhidharma literature. But at AKB VI.4 (Pradhan 334, Pruden 911), Vasubandhu says that the conventions for the terms 'pot' and 'water' having been made, the statement 'Pots and water exist' is conventionally true. And since he has made clear that the relevant conventions involve the aggregation of either spatial parts or atomic properties, it seems fair to say that these conventions, and thus conventional truth, reflect the pragmatic standards of common sense. He also explains that ultimate truths are those statements that accord with what is grasped in extraordinary (*lokottara*) cognition or in its mundane expression. And by extraordinary cognition he means a state (presumably attainable through advanced meditational practice) that directly apprehends all the individual *dharmas* constituting what is ordinarily taken for a single entity or event. So an ultimately true statement would be one that accurately describes a state of affairs wholly in terms of its atomic constituents and their relations.

^c Supervenience is standardly defined in terms of an asymmetrical determination relation between two sets of properties, the supervenient properties S and the base properties B: all the facts about S are determined by facts about B. Determination is in turn understood in terms of a kind of necessary covariance: no change in S without some change in B. Different sorts of supervenience relation result from different understandings of the kind of necessity involved. See Kim (1993), especially essays 4 and 5, for details. The concept of non-reductive supervenience will be discussed in more detail in Chapter 4 below. I shall there propose Pudgalavāda as a possible example of the position that persons non-reductively supervene on the psychophysical elements.

^d It is not entirely clear where Buddhist Reductionism falls in this debate. Since early Buddhism appears to maintain that the same body continues to exist over a lifetime, and uses this assumption to explicate psychological continuity over a single life, it might seem to be holding a version of the physical approach. But identity over rebirth clearly involves no physical continuants; rebirth linkage is understood entirely in terms of causal connections between psychological events. By the time of Abhidharma, belief in the body as a continuant has been replaced by an analysis into ephemeral but causally linked physical events, so that one can no longer speak of a body (or body-part) that endures a lifetime.

^e For an introduction to the Nyāya view see Chakrabarti (1982). For the Sāṃkhya view see Larson (1987: 73–83).

^f See KV pp. 1–71, AKB 9 pp. 462–63.

^g In the *Brahmajāla sūtra*, the Buddha describes the annihilationist as someone who believes we escape the karmic consequences of our deeds at death. In Early Buddhism, then, annihilationism is the view that the person endures for a single lifetime, but is annihilated upon death. (See also Jayatilleke (1963:

107–108).) It is only in Abhidharma that it comes to mean the denial of any enduring subject whatever. (See, e.g., VM 585.) This is likely the result of a deepened understanding of the doctrine of impermanence. Both early Buddhism and Abhidharma see the psychological constituents of persons (the *nāma skandhas*) as radically ephemeral. But the Buddha seems to have thought of the body as an entity that endures from birth until death. Abhidharma resolves the body into its constituent physical components (the *rūpa dharmas*), all equally ephemeral but participating in causal processes that ensure their replacement. This analysis of the body guarantees that even within a single lifetime, no enduring subject can be found among the ultimate constituents of persons. The Early Buddhist understanding of annihilationism might not seem to us to deserve the label 'punctualism'. But in the context of a culture that took the karma–rebirth complex quite seriously, the claim that we endure for just a single lifetime represents a significant challenge to the prevailing theory of persons.

CHAPTER TWO

Refuting the Self

The simplest version of Non-Reductionism claims that a person is a separately existing entity, distinct from the person's brain and body, and their experiences. According to this view, in addition to the various parts that make up the psychophysical complex, there is some one extra part that constitutes the core or essence of the system. Since we tend to use 'person' to refer to the system as a whole, we may call this special part the self. But calling it a self rather than a person does not change the fact that the theory of the self is a theory about the person. This is shown by the fact that one often speaks of the self as 'the true me', thereby distinguishing it from the other parts of the psychophysical complex, which are seen as more peripheral or incidental to one's existence as a person. Since most people believe in the self, the Reductionist would do well to start the defense of their position by trying to show why this view is false. But first we need to be clearer about just what a self might be like.

Galen Strawson gives the following characterization of the ordinary sense of the self that most people have:

> I propose that it is (at least) the sense that people have of themselves as being, specifically, a mental presence, a mental someone, a single mental thing that is a conscious subject of experience, that has a certain character or personality, and that is in some sense distinct from all its particular experiences, thoughts, and so on, and indeed from all other things. [1997: 407]

He goes on to explain that being a single thing involves both synchronic identity and diachronic identity. And to the property of being the subject of experiences he adds that of being the agent of actions. Also, that the self is construed as a mental thing is not meant to preclude the possibility that physicalism is true. The self might, for instance, be thought of as identical with something physical, or wholly supervening on something physical. All of this strikes me as a useful and accurate description of a widely held view of the self.

By the end of his phenomenological investigation, however, Strawson has concluded that diachronic identity, agency and personality are not core attributes of the self. There are many who would agree with Strawson that it is not necessary to something's being the self that it be the agent of our actions and the substrate of our character traits, and that being the conscious subject of our experiences is a necessary condition. But as we shall be using the term 'self', it simply will not do to deny diachronic identity, that is, to say that the self need not exist over stretches of time much longer than the specious present. For the theory of the self is meant to serve as a theory about the existence of persons, and persons typically exist for many years. According to the sort of Non-Reductionism we are currently investigating, the continued existence of a person just is the continued existence of a self. So on this view, what makes me today the same person as the person who had a certain bicycle accident many years ago is that the conscious subject of these thoughts is the very same entity as the conscious subject that felt those pain sensations. While there may be much to recommend Strawson's 'Pearl' view (1997: 424), this is not the place to begin a discussion of Non-Reductionism.[1]

If the self is the essence of the person, then the self is what, in some sense, 'makes me who I am, *me*'. This has led to some confusion over the aims of a philosophical theory of the self. Since persons are separate, the self is thought of as what distinguishes each person from every other. And since distinctness is often conflated with qualitative uniqueness, the self is then taken to be whatever makes a person the 'unique individual' they are thought to be.[2] Popular candidates range from one's DNA to, somewhat more plausibly, the (presumably unique) character that results from the intersection of one's (presumably unique) heredity and environmental history. Monozygotic twins show the difficulty with the first view, and Twin Earth *Doppelgängers* the difficulty with the second. But perhaps we should not be so quick to dismiss the notion that the existence of a person is somehow intimately connected with the nature of their personality. It is now something of a truism that the philosophical discussion of persons and personal identity does not use the term 'identity' in its more popular sense, the sense in which one may be said to have an 'identity crisis' (that is, a crisis concerning what kind of person one is). Some have thought this reflected a mistake on the part of philosophers, and have sought to rectify it.[3] Most philosophers, though, have persevered in their pursuit of the question of diachronic identity largely independent of considerations of personality formation and transformation. As we shall soon see, there is reason to divorce the theory of the self from considerations of one's personality and its distinctiveness (or lack thereof). But we would do well to at least keep in mind the possibility that there may be some reason for the popular identification of the phrase 'personal identity' with questions concerning one's character.

As Strawson points out, it is central to the concept of the self that it is, *qua* subject of experience, somehow distinct from all its experiences. This has led to a certain tension in attempts to characterize it, and this tension has in turn affected efforts at substantiating its existence. If the self is the experiencer, then it becomes difficult to see how it might become the object of introspection. For introspection is a mode of

---

[1]   The view is so called because it holds that the life of a human being consists of a series of successive selves, likes pearls on a string.

[2]   One might speculate that this focus on the 'unique individual' – this notion that the value of the individual lies in what sets them apart from others – is a product of late capitalism, with its emphasis on market positioning through product differentiation, and its construction of demand through ever-increasing market segmentation.

[3]   Schechtman (1996), for instance, distinguishes between two senses in which there might be said to be a question of personal identity: the reidentification question (is this the same person as that earlier person?), and the characterization question (what is this person like?). She holds that the reidentification question rests on a series of mistakes, and that philosophers should instead concern themselves with the characterization question. Glover (1988) is less dismissive of the reidentification question, but seeks to demonstrate that it is in some ways quite intimately connected with the characterization question.

experience, and the self is said to be the subject, not the object, of our experiences. Knives cut, but a knife cannot cut itself.[a] Thus it is widely held that the self may not be perceived, but only inferred. Of course it is true that a finger may point at other fingers, so the anti-reflexivity principle – that an entity cannot operate on itself – would seem to be no bar to the perception of one self by other selves. But here the fact that the self is thought of as a mental presence becomes relevant. If mental states are thought of as private, that is, directly observable only by their subject, then it is tempting to suppose that this subject should be similarly private, and so not amenable to direct observation by others. The anti-reflexivity principle would seem to rule out perception of the self by the self, and the alleged privacy of the mental is taken to rule out perception of one self by other selves.

Of course, that the self could only be cognized through inference would not by itself keep us from knowing its nature, for its properties might prove eminently inferable. The Nyāya school of orthodox Indian philosophy, for instance, claims to prove the existence of a self having desire, aversion, effort, pleasure, pain and cognition as properties, and Descartes seems to have had a similar conception of the self's nature. In this case, one could be said to have ample evidence for the existence of the self, for instance, whenever one were aware of pleasure or pain.[b] But pleasure and pain are transient states, so for this strategy to succeed we must first assure ourselves of some one enduring thing that might be identified as their underlying subject. And what might be the nature of this entity? It is difficult to avoid the conclusion that its nature is just that of being conscious or aware, and this for two reasons. First, we may agree with Descartes that this is common to all those transitory states, such as desiring and judging, that we are inclined to attribute to the self. Second, any candidate property that is merely empirically given seems also to be one that we can imagine our lives might have lacked. I might well have existed without my chronic back pain or my recurrent desire for chocolate. Indeed I would hope that I might continue to exist without my anal retentive character or my mildly reclusive tendencies. So none of these should be thought of as reflecting the inherent nature of the self. Thus in the end it is difficult to avoid agreeing with Descartes that the self's essence is to be conscious or aware. And now the anti-reflexivity principle will preclude one's being directly aware of one's own self itself: that whose nature it is to be conscious cannot be directly aware of its own consciousness.

At this point the self-theorist has a choice. One might invoke the distinction between essential and incidental properties, and hold that such episodic states as desire or pain represent incidental properties of the self, only the activity of being conscious being an essential property. (This was Descartes' view, and on one reading it is that of Nyāya as well.) Or one might relegate these episodic states to other parts of the psychophysical complex, making of the self something whose whole nature it is just to witness the empirically given states of the psychophysical complex. Each approach has its attendant difficulties. On the first, there is still the problem of explaining how something whose nature is to be conscious might be characterized by such things as pain or desire. For it is possible to dissociate oneself from the latter sorts of states, namely by intently focusing one's awareness on them to the exclusion of all else. Pain states, while still apprehended, thereby lose their hurtfulness. This is presumably because the process of intently focusing one's awareness on the pain sensation makes it come to seem utterly distinct from the conscious subject that takes it as the object of its witnessing.[4] The same technique may be used to make desire, aversion, pleasure and the like seem equally separate from the self.

This difficulty has led some to embrace the alternative view, that the sole property of the self is being conscious. The obvious drawback to this approach is that it makes the role of the self in such things as memory and agency appear utterly mysterious. If the self is identified as just pure sentience, then it cannot be said to remember, or to act, or even to choose; its contribution to these activities can consist in no more than just awareness, for it is purely spectatorial in nature.[c] This approach has the added difficulty that it requires that the self be conscious for as long as it exists.[d] It is hard to see how the self-theorist could find non-question-begging evidence for the contention that we are conscious during dreamless sleep or while in a reversible coma. Yet personal identity appears to persist over such episodes, so that the self would have to as well. This difficulty could be avoided by making consciousness an episodic property of the self, as the first approach does with such states as desire and pleasure.[e] But then it becomes unclear just what the self itself is like: if the self is the enduring substrate underlying episodes of consciousness as well as (possibly) desire, pleasure, etc., what accounts for its ability to manifest these properties and unify these distinct episodes into a single mental life?

Hume famously declared himself unable to find the self when he looked within; Parfit agrees (1984: 223). We can now see what might have led to this negative result. Assuming that we can somehow solve the above difficulties and find some basic characterization of the self on which all can agree, this is likely to involve, minimally, being the subject of one's mental states. And the anti-reflexivity principle appears to guarantee that no such entity will be found when we 'look within'. The self is simply not the sort of thing that could be directly cognized through introspection. This suggests that if there is a self, its existence can be known of only through inference. This should seem puzzling. If it is true that most people believe they have a self, it is unlikely that they arrived at this belief through reflecting on the observed features of their experience and concluding that the self is required to explain these features. And this is the general form of the inferences that are standardly given for the self. To account for the widespread belief in the self, we should expect to find evidence more readily accessible than that.

Martin suggests that the evidence is more accessible than that (1998: 130ff.). He maintains that most persons experience themselves most of the time as what he calls 'perceivers' (and we are calling selves): as fixed, continuous points of observation on the external objects and internal states of which they are aware. This fact is not typically remarked on because it is like a constant background hum, something that first becomes noticeable by contrast upon its absence.[5] Here the hum in question is the sense that one is something distinct from one's experiences. It is not uncommon for persons to lose this sense under conditions of total absorption in some activity: the skier becomes one with the interaction of body, skis and mountain; the musician loses all sense of self as the improvisation flows effortlessly on. This 'common no-self

---

[4]   See also Dennett (1978: 206). Martin (1998: 134) describes an extension of this technique whereby it may be used to distance oneself from such affective responses as embarrassment.

[5]   Tinnitus sufferers would disagree with the claim that a constant background noise typically goes unnoticed.

experience', as Martin calls it, dissipates upon reflection, however. Less common is the state achieved by practitioners of certain forms of meditation, wherein the absence of the sense of a separate self is maintained throughout periods of intensive introspection. This sense of self also becomes more visible when it is heightened, as when one deals with pain or some negative affective state by the dissociative technique described above: the state in question loses its sting just to the extent that one's intently focused awareness makes apparent its otherness from what is perceived as the true me, the observer. The suggestion is that this sense of our separateness from our experiential content is present, in less pronounced form, in most of us most of the time.

In this case perhaps there is, after all, evidence for the self's existence that is available through introspection; Hume may just have been looking the wrong way when he 'looked within'. Such evidence would hardly be conclusive. Still I think it is worth considering for a moment just what kind of evidence it might be. We have so far simply assumed the standard dichotomy between perception and inference as the two ways of coming to know of something's existence. The suggestion was made that widespread belief in a self would require evidence more direct than that typically used by philosophers in arguing for a self, that is, that introspective evidence was required. And introspection is generally classified as a kind of perception.[6] If I became aware, through introspection, of a sense of being something that is somehow distinct from my experiential content, would that act of awareness count as a case of perception? The anti-reflexivity principle seems, once again, to preclude this. And yet if this sense of separateness is indeed evidence for the existence of my self, it seems somehow too direct, and even intimate, for it to be classed as merely the basis of an inference. There is a long controversy, among Indian philosophers who affirm the self, over whether the self might perceive itself, with those who claim that it does, taking this as grounds for denying the anti-reflexivity principle. Such a response seems excessive: what one seems to be aware of is not the observer itself, but rather just its felt otherness from the object of awareness. Still this response now appears more comprehensible. And it will be important that the Reductionist be able to explain the phenomenon on which it is based, the sense that one can introspect the distinctness of the observer self.

The evidence of introspection is, then, at best equivocal. What sorts of arguments are there for the existence of the self? Descartes claimed that the existence of a thinking substance could be indubitably established through his *Cogito*. While Descartes did not want the *Cogito* to be construed as an inference (lest it prove vulnerable to demonic deceivers), if it is to succeed in establishing the existence of a thinking substance then it must be so construed. And when interpreted in this way the argument clearly fails. Suppose a certain mental event is now occurring: there is the awareness of a certain mental state, for example, a pain, or a doubt, or a desire. What follows from this? That this thought – the awareness of this content – now exists seems clear. Perhaps we can also say that there is now the thinking of this thought. May we conclude that there is, in addition, a thinker of this thought? This would require that we take the thinking to be the action of an agent. But it is also open to us to

---

[6] Of course there are reasons, deriving from Wittgenstein, to question this classification. We shall have more to say about this below.

deny that this thinking is an action. We might, for instance, hold that mental events of this sort are not actions because they do not typically involve antecedent desires. While a prolonged bout of deliberation might properly be called an action, awareness of a simple mental state would not qualify. Still, if the thinking is a mental event, must there not be something to which or in which this event occurs? Perhaps. But so far nothing has been said to rule out the possibility that that in which thinking events occur is not a (Cartesian) thinking substance but rather a (Cartesian) extended substance, specifically a set of neurons.[7] More importantly for our purposes, it may be questioned whether the occurrence of an event of this sort requires something in which or to which it occurs. True, we do say that mental events occur to or in experiencing subjects or persons, or that they occur in brains. But this felt need for a subject may reflect no more than the demands of syntax, as with the dummy subject of 'It is raining.' Indeed the Reductionist will maintain that the experiencing subject is a conceptual fiction that is constructed out of just such ultimately real entities as mental events. And nothing said so far would seem to rule out this alternative. So the *Cogito* will not do the job. The awareness of particular mental states is too thin an inferential base for proving a self.

A more promising place to look might be our awareness not of particular mental states, but of a multiplicity of such states as they occur over time. Such a diachronic strategy is also the basis of a common Kantian line of objection to Reductionism, but for now we shall confine our attention to its use in trying to prove a self. A simple example of such an argument would be one that appeals to experience-memory, our ability to recall 'from the inside' some earlier experience. Consider some simple but memorable experience that was had earlier in adult life, such as the first time one tasted a mango. (Ideally it should be an experience that one has not had occasion to recall previously.) To remember this experience is, in part, to have a presentation that resembles in relevant respects that initial taste perception. There is more to remembering than just the occurrence of a memory-image, however. To remember is to take oneself to be producing a memory-image that faithfully reproduces the original perception. Of course we may be wrong in this. But when one does have a veridical experience-memory, it counts as a case of genuine memory precisely because its content matches those aspirations. And, claims the self-theorist, for there to be the possibility of such a match it is required that there be something common to original perception and memory-image, namely a common subject to which both are given. For otherwise how can these two distinct presentations, given at separate times, be taken to be at all related, let alone relevantly similar?[f]

This demand for a subject to unify a multiplicity of distinct mental states has broader application. Kant's doctrine of the threefold synthesis of apprehension (about which we shall say more below) essentially claims that we could not apply concepts to our experience without such unification. A number of Indian self-theorists point to the common phenomenon of recognition as giving rise to similar demands: one could not claim to recognize this as the building one used to pass going to school, were one not to assume the subject of the present visual experiences to be identical with the

---

[7] And it clearly will not do to maintain (as Descartes does) that this is ruled out by the consideration that while I cannot doubt the existence of that which is thinking, I can doubt the existence of my brain.

subject of those past experiences. Likewise our ability to unify perceptions across distinct sense modalities is said to require not just a common object underlying the perceptions, but also a unifying perceiver. To construe my experience as one of tasting the mango that I just saw, I must suppose there to be an enduring object behind both my visual and my gustatory perceptions, for the common object is not itself given in either sensory experience.[8] And this unification in the object in turn requires that there be a common subject to which both sensory perceptions are given. But perhaps the most interesting use of this strategy is in the argument from desire. Suppose that as we stroll through the market I see a mango and am immediately consumed with desire. This we understand to be the result of an earlier encounter with another mango, an encounter that included both visual and taste perceptions and that yielded pleasure. The argument is that we can make no sense of any of this unless we supply an enduring self to serve as unified subject of the whole series of mental states. For now we must not only explain the unification across sensory modalities in my earlier encounter, when I first saw and then tasted the mango, and the unification across time involved in my recognizing the present visual presentation as relevantly similar to the earlier one. We must also explain the evident connection between the earlier pleasure and the present desire. The memory that enables me to identify what I now see as a mango may also foster recollection of the prior pleasure. And perhaps it just seems obvious that the resulting association – between present visual perception and past pleasure – will lead to desire. But my cognition of your pleasure upon eating broccoli does not fill me with desire for broccoli (unless you are a model in a well-crafted commercial from the Broccoli Producers' Association). Once again we must suppose there to be a single conscious subject uniting the past pleasure and the present desire.[h] In general, any behavior revealing a capacity to place two distinct mental states in relation will require that there be a single conscious subject that is able to take both as its objects. If I can compare and contrast past mental states with present ones, or put mental states derived from different modalities in relation to one another, then these mental states must all have been given to a single mental thing, the same thing that now observes them in relation. Or so argues the self-theorist.

Parfit disagrees. He follows Locke and Kant in pointing out that diachronic unification can be achieved without an enduring self, provided the relevant information states of the system are passed on from one impermanent component to its successor, like the baton in a relay race (1984: 223–24). A more up-to-date analogy would be serial distributed processing, wherein one computer processes data and then passes on the result to another computer for further processing. For those who take a neo-Lockean view of personal identity, simple teletransportation is the basis for an effective counter-example to the above argument. The Replica's desire for Martian mangos is explained by their experience of seeing and tasting a mango on earth, yet there is no entity that is shared by the Replica stage and the earthling stage.[8] The Buddhist Reductionist might point to rebirth as an equivalent counter-example,

---

[8]   Assuming, of course, that a self is not the sort of thing that could travel alongside the beam that carries the information from earth to Mars. It is, however, held by many Indian self-theorists that the self is all-pervasive. In this case effective simple teletransportation would not undermine the argument from diachronic unification: that my Replica was able to remember my experiences, etc. could be explained by the fact that my self was already there waiting on Mars as my Replica was being assembled.

though this is weakened considerably by the fact that rebirth without a transmigrating self is widely seen as highly counter-intuitive.[i]

Buddhist Reductionists take an important further step, however. They claim that this felt need for an observer self that fuels the diachronic unification argument is the product of a powerful illusion fostered by our use of the convenient designator 'person'. The key to their analysis is the notion of a causal series. They maintain that what is conventionally called a person is in fact a causal series of impersonal, impermanent psychophysical elements. Since many Buddhist Reductionist arguments are couched in terms of their theory of the psychophysical elements, a word should be said about that theory at this point, after which we shall return to the key notion of the causal series. The doctrine of the five *skandhas* or psychophysical elements originates in Early Buddhism, and thereafter becomes the standard means of classifying the constituents of the psychophysical complex. The five consist of one category containing all things physical, and four categories of basic psychological events: feelings (the hedonic states of pleasure, pain and indifference), perceptions, volitions and consciousnesses.[j] It is assumed that all phenomena related to persons can be fit into one or more of these categories. A complex emotion such as jealousy, for instance, might be analyzed into certain feelings occurring in conjunction with certain perceptions and a certain type of volition. That there are five categories, and not just one, suggests that Buddhist Reductionism is committed to dualism. But this is not necessarily the case – or at least if it is the case, the dualism might not be the sort widely considered problematic. In Early Buddhism the theory seems to have served just as a way of ensuring that one was not overlooking any important person-phenomenon in one's search for the self. Only in Abhidharma does the doctrine begin to look like a genuine system of categories with real ontological significance. It is crucial to note, however, that each of the four types of mental event is said to originate in dependence on certain physical events.[k] And most important for our purposes is the fact that the members of the psychological categories are understood as events, and not as enduring substances, nor as properties or states of enduring substances. There are no immaterial substances in this ontology. It is true that Buddhist Reductionism maintains a kind of causal interactionism: causation flows not just from the physical to the mental, but from the mental to the physical as well. While it is a change in my sense faculty that causes the feeling of pain, the occurrence of the pain in turn may initiate a series of mental events culminating in bodily movement. Commitment to a physicalist causal closure principle would thus stand in the way of reconciling the Buddhist Reductionist ontology with physicalism. But it is not clear that anything of significance to the topic of personhood turns on this. Parfit pointed out that a physicalist might hold the neo-Lockean version of Reductionism, despite the fact that that approach emphasizes psychological continuity over physical continuity (1984: 209). I would add that dualists may also be Reductionists – provided they are not Cartesian dualists. Indeed idealists may be Reductionists – provided they are not Berkeleyan idealists.[l] What matters is not whether there is a separate category of mental entities in one's ontology, but what sorts of mental entities are in that ontology. A Reductionist must deny immaterial souls, but need not deny immaterial pains and wishes.

The Buddhist Reductionist claims that 'person' is a mere convenient designator for a complex causal series of impermanent, impersonal psychophysical elements.

That is, ultimately there are no persons, only physical objects, feelings, perceptions, volitions and consciousnesses. And none of these things endures particularly long, certainly not as long as persons are thought to endure. But the going out of existence of one such entity may serve as the cause for the coming into existence of another, and the newly arisen entity may possess some distinctive nature because of the occurrence of some prior entity that served as its antecedent condition. The replacement of body parts is a clear example of this sort of process: the cutting of one's hair, or consumption of a high protein diet, stimulates the growth of new hair; the new hair typically resembles the old. But also the initial contact between tongue and mango causes a taste perception and a feeling of pleasure, as well as distinct consciousnesses to register both.[m] And these may in turn serve as causes or conditions for the later occurrence of a memory-image and a desire. At any given moment there will be a large number of psychophysical elements in proximity to one another. And from one moment to the next there will be many, many causal connections between earlier and later elements. The death of one cell serves as cause of the growth of a new cell. Present perceptions, conditioned by an earlier intention, bring about a bodily movement. The occurrence of a memory-image causes a desire. And so on. The term 'person' is our convenient way of referring to a series of causally connected sets of contiguous psychophysical elements.[9] Since partite entities are unreal, the series is unreal, indeed twice over: the series collects together many sets, each of which collects together many simultaneously occurring psychophysical elements. Still, given our interests, it is generally more convenient to use the one term for such a series, hence the conventional truth of such claims as that there are persons and that persons endure over time. But all such claims are ultimately false. Ultimately there are only impersonal psychophysical elements in causal relation.

This would explain why one person cannot remember the experiences of another, and why your past pleasure does not explain my present desire. There simply aren't the right sorts of causal connections between psychological events in the one series and those in the other. The truth that, for instance, we do not remember the experiences of others, turns out to be a relatively superficial conventional truth. It merely reflects the ultimate truth that we use the word 'person' to mark out longitudinal clusters of psychophysical elements containing, among other things, experience–memory causal connections.[n] This does not yet explain the need that is felt in such cases for unification in a common subject, however. To understand the source of these intuitions we must consider the behavior of other convenient designators as employed in conventional discourse. Consider, for instance, the term 'light' when used to refer to the illuminating element of a lit oil-lamp. Suppose it would be (conventionally) true to say that the light moved from room to room. What is the ultimate truth that makes this statement conventionally true? The source of illumination is a flame, but 'flame' is a convenient designator for a collection of incandescent gas molecules. One such molecule will radiate light for just an instant, and is then dispersed into the surrounding atmosphere. But it also radiates heat, which brings about first the vaporization and then the rapid oxidation of other molecules from the fuel source. Thus the enduring 'light' is actually a causally linked succession

---

[9]   This is admittedly not a fully adequate account. In the next chapter we shall take up the task of trying to formulate a way of constructing persons out of psychophysical elements that is completely impersonal.

of momentary 'flames', each of which is just a set of incandescent gas molecules in spatio-temporal contiguity. This means, however, that when we say the light moves from room to room, ultimately there is nothing that is in motion. What happens instead is that the incandescent gas molecules in region r_1 at time t_1 give rise to a successor set of incandescent gas molecules in region r_2 at time t_2. Ultimately nothing moves, yet it is conventionally true that the light moves. Through our use of the convenient designator 'light' we have constructed a conceptual fiction with a new property – a light that moves.[o]

Next, consider the case in which we would say that a tree bears fruit. The tree is, like the light, a conceptual fiction, something we only think of as existent because of our use of a convenient designator for a causal series of collections of elements. Ultimately there are just the impermanent cells that make up, at a particular time, the roots, trunk, branches, leaves and the fruit. Since the fruit is among the more particular entities that make up what we call a tree, we might expect that the convenient designator 'tree' should uniformly designate the fruit together with those other entities. So it may seem odd that we should split it off from the other constituents, and make of those other constituents collectively a subject that then serves as bearer or possessor of the fruit. Yet this is just what we do when we say that the tree bears fruit. This is, however, understandable when we recall that we take a special interest in these constituents, and that they are only periodically present through the duration of the causal series. Through our use of the convenient designator 'tree' we have constructed an enduring subject to serve as bearer or owner of some of its constituents. Notice that we may do the same thing with other constituents as well, for example, leaves, buds, or new root growth.[p]

Next, consider the fact that persons have some degree of control over all the psychophysical elements of which they are constituted – some degree of self-control. Obviously this control is not complete, but we are for instance able to evaluate the states of the various parts of our bodies, and to at least seek to change those that are found unsatisfactory. This is likewise true of the various psychological events and states making up what we call the mind. I may set about trying to change my current hedonic state of indifference, or my habitual desire to snack before bedtime; I may even seek to bring about the cessation of my present consciousness when it apprehends an unavoidable pain sensation. If we call this function of self-scrutiny, self-control and self-revision the executive function, we may then be tempted to ask who is the chief executive performing this function. Now in any exercise of the executive function, certain psychophysical elements will be the object of control, and certain other elements will be on the subject side, that is, will be involved in performing the evaluation and attempted alteration of what is in object position. And the anti-reflexivity principle ensures that a given element may not play both roles simultaneously. But notice that an element that is on the subject side on one occasion of self-control may well show up on the object side in some later occurrence of self-control. For instance, when I decide to try to curb my bedtime snacking I may be employing a particular standard of acceptable body-shape, which I may subsequently decide is politically problematic and medically questionable. This fact of universal potential objectification creates the powerful sense that the chief executive must somehow transcend all the empirically given psychophysical elements. For if each of them is a potential object of the executive function, and an entity cannot operate on itself, then it seems that none of them could be the one enduring subject that performs this function.[q]

This sense of a transcendent chief executive is just an illusion, though, more specifically the product of a process of hypostatization, according to the Buddhist Reductionist. For as in the case of the moving light, our use of the convenient designator 'person' for the causal series of psychophysical elements leads us to suppose there to be some one enduring entity underlying the observed alterations. And, as in the case of the tree that bears fruit, our interests lead us to construct the enduring subject on the basis of a subset of the constituents of the series. Thus arises the notion that the person has an essence – that some constituents are more central to the existence of the person than others. And finally, the fact that any constituent of the psychophysical complex may be cast in the role of object of the executive function leads to the overwhelming sense that this essence must be some one thing that is always subject and never object. Of course this conclusion is not warranted. For the phenomena of self-control are adequately explained by supposing that what actually plays the role of chief executive is always just a shifting coalition of psychophysical elements.[10] We have no grounds for supposing there to be a single enduring chief executive behind these shifting coalitions.[r] Still the illusion is extremely powerful.

Finally, we return to the kinds of phenomena that drive the argument from diachronic unification. Suppose that within a given causal series of psychophysical elements, empirical content x is given at t_1 and content y is given at t_2. Why does it seem as though there must be some one observer to which both contents are given? First there is the fact that our use of the convenient designator 'person' leads us to think of the causal series as one enduring entity. Then there is the fact that in the sort of case at issue, where we are pondering how to explain the facts about these contents, x and y seem to take on the status of items of introspection. For instance, when I enjoyed my first taste of mango I may not have explicitly noted my feeling of pleasure, but now when I appeal to that pleasure to explain my desire for a new mango I must, as it were, retroactively introspect the feeling. This I might put in terms of the claim that while I may not have remarked on it at the time, I must have been aware of the feeling. (In putting it this way I would, of course, be blurring the distinction between having a sensation and making a sensation the object of an act of introspection.) The result is that x and y, though constituents of the causal series, end up being assigned to the object side of the series, as with the fruit in the case of the tree, or the unwanted desire in the case of the person as self-controller. And since we are already inclined to treat the series as one enduring entity, this leads us to expect that whatever plays the subject role in the introspection of x will be the same thing as that which plays this role in the introspection of y. Our partition of the causal series into a subject side and an object side makes the former more central to the existence of the entity we take the series to be. It turns whatever plays the subject role into an essence. And since we have already come to think of the series as an enduring person, it is natural to suppose the essence to likewise be just one enduring thing. This feeling is only enhanced by the consideration that any empirical content whatever may be the object of introspection. Since this

---

[10] Dennett (1991: 228) explains how this arrangement can result in a *virtual captain*. The Buddhist Reductionist would agree with Dennett that this sense of a seeming chief executive can be wholly benign – provided it is not taken too seriously. But see the discussion of transparency in the next chapter.

places all possible empirical content on the object side, it gives rise to the impression that what is on the subject side is quite unlike anything that we ever observe, that it is in fact utterly devoid of empirical properties. Now in the introspection of x, what is involved in the performance of the introspection is not itself observed. Likewise for the introspection of y. When I have been led to believe that the subject of acts of introspection is devoid of empirical properties, the invisibility of the subjects of both introspections will look like further evidence for their identity.

Of course the Buddhist Reductionist claims this is all just as much an illusion as is the sense of an enduring, transcendent chief executive. For instance, that I do not take note of any of the factors responsible for my introspective awareness of the pleasure while I introspect this feeling is merely the result of the fact that it is this feeling that is the focus of my current attention. In reflecting on the episode a moment later, I may discern some of the factors that brought about the introspective awareness, such as a desire to understand the source of my sudden craving for a mango. As with control, so with awareness, a given psychophysical element may appear on the subject side on one occasion and the object side on another occasion. Every British citizen has been the subject of a British monarch, and the monarch is the subject of no one, yet the Queen is a citizen for all that. The Queen was the subject of King George.

The Buddha provides an interesting diagnosis of the problem involved here, giving, by way of counter-example, what we might call a kind of degrees-of-perfection proof of the existence of Miss Universe. The context is that the Buddha is instructing an aspirant in the practice and results of meditation. He describes a series of meditational states each of which involves a particular type of introspective cognition distinct from that involved in its predecessor meditational state. In each case he makes clear that the prior type of introspective cognition must cease before the next meditational state can be entered into. Yet when he has finished his presentation, his interlocutor asks him about the self that enjoys all these meditational states. The Buddha responds by asking whether we would deem rational a man who conceived a passion for the most beautiful woman in the world on the grounds that there surely must exist some one woman fairer than all others.[5] The analogy is admittedly imperfect. The would-be lover has constructed his beloved based on a number of mistaken assumptions, few of which are shared in by the Buddha's interlocutor. The lover, for instance, assumes that there are only finitely many women, and that beauty is one-dimensional, so that there can be no ties between women of different appearances. The seeker after the self makes no such assumptions about cognition. Still there is something important that both cases share, namely that the result is arrived at through a process of hypostatization; both involve the construction of a transcendent entity based on what is common to an empirically given plurality. And hypostatization is generally a mistake. From the fact that each meditational state involves introspective cognition, it does not follow that they are all the states of one enduring cognizer.

We have spoken so far about what a self might be like, and what sorts of considerations lead some to suppose there is such a thing. We have also discussed how the Reductionist seeks to refute the self, namely by trying to show that all the evidence can be explained without positing any such thing. The Reductionist thus employs a classic argument from lightness; the self is said to be simply superfluous. But Buddhist Reductionists also seek to account for the intuitions that underlie and motivate the self-theorist's arguments. We saw earlier that it is difficult to resist the sense that we are aware of the self as something distinct from all empirically given content. The Buddhist Reductionist would explain this phenomenon as resulting from a process of hypostatization. And this process is, they claim, induced by our use of the convenient designator 'person'. In the next chapter we shall discuss some of the reasons a Reductionist might give for retaining the concept of the person. But at this point we should perhaps say something about why Buddhist Reductionists think it important to refute the self. To believe in the self is to think that the person has an enduring, transcendent essence. We have just seen how Buddhists seek to show that this belief is false, the result of a logical error. But it is also, they claim, the ultimate source of human suffering.

Belief in a self has consequences for the believer that make this belief quite unlike belief in any other sort of fictitious entity. To believe in a self is to believe that there is some one ultimately existing thing that is *me*. And this, Buddhists claim, is the source of suffering. Belief in the self is commonly the result of the process whereby a causal series of psychophysical elements comes to think of itself as a person – whereby, that is, such a series comes to contain a disposition to identify with and appropriate the past and future states of that series. While it is possible to think of oneself as a person without believing in the self, the processes of socialization that lead to personhood typically bring this about. Socialization into personhood normally aims at turning a pleasure-seeking system (the small child) into a happiness-seeking system. The difference between the two kinds of goals has to do with more than just the difference between instant and delayed gratification. To seek happiness is to seek out states and situations that affirm the value of one's existence as a person with a connected past and future. Becoming a person who seeks happiness is not just a matter of internalizing the laws of the hedonic calculus (such as the principle of diminishing marginal utility) and using them to maximize overall pleasure within the series. To learn to seek happiness requires learning to take pleasure in one's situation even when it is not intrinsically pleasant – provided one's situation may be incorporated into the right sort of narrative, one that connects past and present with a future of promise. And here is where belief in a self connects up quite naturally with the task of constructing a person. Embarking on the happiness-seeking enterprise requires that one see one's life as the sort of thing that can have meaning, so that one will actively seek out those projects that will in turn confer on it the right sort of narrative structure. Belief in a self makes this simple and straightforward. First, it helps if this narrative is thought to have a narrator. The self fills this role quite nicely, since it may be seen as simultaneously the omniscient observer and the central character of the narrative. Second and more significantly, the sort of meaning in question requires that there be that for which these life-events have meaning, and that whose projects these are. This is not to deny that persons may see their lives as deriving value from the contribution they make to some larger purpose. But this is something in which persons are thought to take satisfaction: because one's current situation may be seen as contributing to this larger goal, one's present efforts confer value on this life, so that one is justified in deeming this a good life.[11] And all of this makes perfect sense if we suppose there to be

---

[11] This should not be mistaken for an endorsement of psychological egoism. Suppose I dedicate my life to the struggle to perpetuate the standard transmission or 'stick shift', a struggle that involves countless

a self to serve as both the source and the object of value: this life is a good life because its projects issue from this self, and their realization accords with its nature.

In order to see how such a belief in a self is implicated in suffering, it will be useful to first consider two claims that Nagel makes concerning the meaning of life and our response to our mortality. The first involves the point that one's life can sometimes come to seem meaningless or absurd, in that one's own projects, whatever they may be, can come to seem the product of a purely parochial endorsement and thus not of the sort that could possibly confer genuine meaningfulness. From this perspective, it can seem as if one is condemned to take on and become engaged in some ultimately trivial project or other – for how else can one go on? Nagel takes this sense of the absurd to be a result of our ability to entertain both an internal or subjective stance and an external or objective stance with respect to ourselves and the world (1986: 218). And since Nagel regards the ability to take on both stances as definitive of our humanity, he regards outbreaks of the sense of the absurd to be ineliminable.[12] Nagel's second claim is that the difficulty we have in comprehending our own mortality stems from our tendency to privilege the internal over the external stance. Viewed from without, one's life is seen to have determinate temporal boundaries. But to see this from the internal perspective one must somehow anticipate what it is like to be non-existent:

> It turns out that I am not the sort of thing I was unconsciously tempted to think I was: a set of ungrounded possibilities as opposed to a set of possibilities grounded in a contingent actuality. The subjective view projects into the future its sense of unconditioned possibilities, and the world denies them. [1986: 228]

There is truth in both claims. Indeed, concerning the first claim, the Reductionist will agree with Nagel that the possibility of all one's projects coming to seem absurd is built into the structure of personhood, given that self-control requires capacities for self-scrutiny and self-transformation.[13] But to fully understand the Buddhist account of suffering we need to bring the two points together, substantially transforming both.

---

others and will continue long after my demise. The present point is that this is most likely because I have found that involving myself in this project gives me some measure of happiness, since it confers value and dignity on my life. Suppose I also claim that my motive in embarking on this project is to benefit future generations of drivers. The psychological egoist would say that in this I am deluded, since all motivation is at bottom self-interested. But the present point about happiness does not support this claim of the psychological egoist. As Butler pointed out long ago, the fact that some activity benefits the agent does not show that this benefit was the agent's principal aim.

   [12] One possible solution that he considers and rejects is that one lose all sense of the individual self through absorption into a universal, transcendent self (1986: 218–19). It is unclear whether Nagel considers Buddhism to be among the 'certain traditions' that espouse this approach, but this understanding of Buddhist nirvana has not been uncommon. Belief in such a 'universal, transcendent self' (or Self) is, however, incompatible with the basic commitments of Buddhist Reductionism.

   [13] Such a system of self-control must have the ability to call into question the value of any particular project on which it has embarked. Hypostatization would then make it seem as though all such projects must lack intrinsic value. Nagel's sense of the absurd thus has its origins in the same process that gives rise to the sense of a transcendent self.

The Buddha claimed that all sentient existence is predominantly characterized by suffering, and that this fact is intimately bound up with another fact about us, that we are mortal. By suffering I take him to have meant the sense of frustration, alienation and despair that arises in response to seeing the consequences of one's mortality for the happiness-seeking enterprise on which one is embarked. Realizing one's own mortality radically undermines this enterprise. The difficulty is not just that my present projects come to seem parochial and thus trivial, as Nagel suggests. The difficulty is rather that such projects derive their point from the larger happiness-seeking enterprise in which we are engaged, and this requires that there be a self with an open future. And the difficulty we have in grasping our own mortality is not merely that we cannot imagine the blank nothingness that the internal stance seems to demand here. The difficulty is that the happiness-seeking enterprise requires that one 'project into the future [one's] sense of unconditioned possibilities', and fully grasping one's own mortality means coming to recognize that such projection depends on an illusion. We can grasp this fact. But doing so is profoundly threatening, in that it makes all that has gone before seem a cruel joke. Personhood held out the prospect of something better than mere pleasure, the happiness that comes from the sense that one's life has meaning. But happiness requires an open future: the events of my life can be held to have meaning only if they can be seen to say good things about where I seem to be going. The inherently telic character of the happiness-seeking enterprise means that in the long run it cannot be sustained. For in the long run there will be no such thing as this *me* on which it all depends.

On the Buddhist analysis, suffering will inevitably come to predominate in the life of any minimally reflective person. Suffering is not, however, inescapable. The key to the cessation of suffering lies, the Buddhist claims, in coming to see that there is no self. This is no simple matter. Belief in a self is deeply implicated in some of our most fundamental cognitive and affective structures. The Buddhist thus recommends a twin practice of philosophy and meditation: philosophy in order to come to see how it might be true of us that we are just complex causal series of impersonal, impermanent psychophysical elements, collected together under the convenient designator 'person'; and meditation in order to confirm this in one's own case through systematic, detailed observation.[1] But notice that the aim here is to dispel the powerful illusion of the self; the aim is not to rid ourselves of our sense of being persons. The Buddhist Reductionist claims that their notion of the causal series provides a middle path between the extremes of Non-Reductionism and Eliminativism. They claim that we can come to see the wholly impersonal ultimate truth about ourselves and yet still retain many practices central to our employment of the personhood concept. Critics of Reductionism commonly dispute this claim. They hold that while the Reductionist is right to reject the superlative self of simple Non-Reductionism, Reductionism goes too far when it claims that the ultimate truth about us is wholly impersonal. These critics contend that Reductionism thereby turns into a kind of Extremism, something virtually indistinguishable from Eliminativism. In the next chapter we shall examine these charges, and see how the Reductionist might respond to them.

Notes

ᵃ This anti-reflexivity principle was subscribed to by most, though not all, schools of the Indian tradition. See, e.g., Śaṅkara's *Vedāntasūtrabhāṣya* III.iii.54; Vācaspati Miśra's *Tattvakaumadī* on *Sāṃkhyakārikā* xii. Yogācāra denies it, and proposes as a counter-example the case of the fire that illuminates itself as well as other things. To this it is objected that an entity may not be said to be illuminated unless it may also occur in the unilluminated state, and fire (considered *qua* source of illumination) does not occur in the dark (see VV 34). Such seeming counter-examples as the case of the surgeon who performs (minor) surgery on herself are handled by analyzing the entity involved into distinct parts to play the agent and patient roles. Thus the hands, eyes and brain together perform the activity of cutting, while the big toe suffers the passion of being cut.

ᵇ It is this that leads some Naiyāyikas to claim that the self is perceived. While Gautama is silent on the subject, and Jayanta argues vociferously against the perceptibility of the self, Udayana and Uddyotakara, as well as the Navya-Naiyāyikas Laugākṣi Bhāskara, Keśavamiśra, and Viśvanātha, all hold the self to be perceptible by means of the inner sense (*manas*). Their view is that since one's own pleasure is introspectable, and pleasure is a quality (*guṇa*) of the self, in becoming aware of one's pleasure one is thereby perceiving the self in which that pleasure inheres, just as one perceives a tree when one visually apprehends the green color that inheres in it. Here it is important to bear in mind that introspection is understood as a kind of perception performed by the organ of the inner sense.

ᶜ This is the approach taken by Sāṃkhya and Vedānta. The former solves the problem of agency by claiming that the self is called an agent through a sort of synecdoche. The king is but one part of the apparatus of the martial state, and indeed one that takes no active military role. The army's victory is nonethelesss attributed to the king, for without the king there would be no army and no *casus belli*. Likewise though the self performs no deed, without its contribution of consciousness there could be no purposeful action. See Vācaspati Miśra on *Sāṃkhyakārikā* 62. Memory, personality and the like dispostions are invested in a sort of 'subtle body', made of the same sort of insensate but active stuff (*prakṛti*) as all the rest of the psychophysical complex save the self, but capable of accompanying the self through transmigration. See Vācaspati Miśra on *Sāṃkhyakārikā* 40–45.

For a sympathetic presentation and defense of the approach to the self common to Sāṃkhya, Yoga and Vedānta, see Kesarcodi-Watson (1994). His 'detachment test' (197ff.) for determining whether something is a suitable candidate for selfhood brings out nicely the role of the anti-reflexivity principle in the thought of these schools concerning what sort of thing a self might be. According to this test, something cannot be my self if it is something from which I can detach myself. The reasoning is that detachment involves observation, and an observer cannot perform the function of observation on itself.

ᵈ As does the first approach, which likewise makes consciousness essential to the existence of the self.

ᵉ This is the approach taken by Nyāya. Sāṃkhya, Vedānta and Bhāṭṭa Mīmāṃsā all maintain that the self is conscious in dreamless sleep. (Descartes concurs.) Nyāya denies this, as does Prābhākara Mīmāṃsā. Of course Nyāya agrees that being conscious is essential to the self – but only in the sense that consciousness is distinctive of the self, not in the sense that the self must manifest this property as long as it exists.

ᶠ See Śaṅkara's commentary on *Vedānta Sūtra* III.iii.54. This sort of argument from memory should not be confused with the very different argument for the self that simply demands some permanent repository for memory traces. Udayana gives an example of the latter sort of argument at *Ātmatattvaviveka* 800–801, where he claims that the Buddhist non-self theory cannot explain memory since only a permanent self could provide the sort of enduring locus required to preserve memory traces between the time of the experience and the time of the recollection.

ᵍ According to Nyāya, I do perceive the mango both by means of vision and by means of taste. But the visual cognition is of the mango as inhered in by the red color, and the gustatory perception is of the mango as inhered in by the sweetness. Neither sense faculty can inform me about qualities it is incapable of registering. This was Gautama's reason for distinguishing between the sense faculties and the self. See NS III.3.1. Chakrabarti (1982: 223) remarks on the affinities with Kant's argument for the transcendental unity of apperception.

ʰ See Uddyotakara's comments on NS I.1.10: 'The question to be examined is this: how is it that desire, etc., cause there to be knowledge of the unapprehended self? It is because of the sharing of a single object with memory, namely, because singularity of agency is established because desire, etc., have the very same objects as memory. For [otherwise] there is no unification of diverse agents, diverse objects and diverse stimuli. For the cognitions of form, taste, odor and texture are not united; for it is not the case that "what form I have seen, that is this texture, and what texture I have felt, that is the form I see." Neither is there found any unification with Yajñadatta, when it is Devadatta who has seen something. For it is not the case that what Devadatta saw, I, Yajñadatta, saw. Why so? Because of the determination of the objects of different minds. According to those who propound the non-self view, there can be no determinate objects whose forms are here and there differentiated, and thus there is no reason for unification. Therefore, that which unites is the self.'

ⁱ Of course ordinary experience-memory and other sorts of psychological continuity are not typically preserved over rebirth. Memories of prior lives can be recovered, though, through mastery of certain esoteric techniques. The special feature shared by rebirth and simple teletransportation – the absence of a single, enduring, material basis for psychological continuity – really holds true only for Early Buddhism, with its view that the body endures for a lifetime. Later Abhidharma formulations of Reductionism accept the thesis of radical momentariness. On this view, each part of the body exists for only an instant, but in going out of existence causes a (usually similar) replacement to come into existence. This would mean that one is constantly being teletransported – from the present moment to the next.

ʲ See Chapter XIV of VM for a survey and detailed discussion.

ᵏ Namely events in which a sense faculty comes in contact with an object of the appropriate sort. See *Majjhima-Nikāya* Sutta 38.

ˡ The Yogācāra (Cittamātra) school of Mahāyāna Buddhism is a clear-cut example of idealist Reductionism. Indeed Vasubandhu claims that the denial of external objects is required in order to complete the Reductionist program: only through the denial of objects distinct from this mental stream can there be full realization that this mental stream is not to be conceptualized as a subjectivity. See *Vijñaptimātratāsiddhi* 10. Vasubandhu thus in effect performs a *modus tollens* on the *modus ponens* of Kant's Refutation of Idealism.

ᵐ It is crucial to bear in mind that for the Buddhist Reductionist consciousness is just as impermanent an event as any other basic psychological state, like a pain sensation. There are two distinct consciousnesses involved in registration of the taste perception and the feeling of pleasure. This follows from the fact that consciousness, like the other psychological elements, is caused by sense–object–contact events. The consciousness that registers the taste perception stems from contact between the faculty of taste and the mango, while the consciousness that registers the pleasure involves the inner sense. Since the sense–object–contact events are therefore distinct, so must the consciousnesses that are their effects be distinct.

ⁿ Uddyotakara explains well this part of the Buddhist Reductionist program in his comments on NS I.1.10: 'From the distinctions of ever earlier mental events, other, successively later, mental events come into being endowed with the whole mass of potencies in conformity with the potencies of the earlier mental events. Hence, even though there is diversity, there is unification owing to there being cause-and-effect, as in the case of a seed, etc. Thus, the shoot becomes manifest immediately after the rice-grain. Its conformity with the potency of rice is established by its precedent [that is, the rice-grain]. Thereafter, being involved with the elements, a further rice-grain is generated, not a barley-grain; for that was not its precedent. Just so, in the present case, the unification of mental events belonging to a single series, is due to the establishment of cause-and-effect, and excludes the mental events belonging to another series, because they are not the precedent [of the present mental events of the series in question]. But the unification is not due to there being a unique agent, because that is not perceived. This unification being otherwise [that is, explicable by other than the posit of an irreducible self], it cannot establish the being of the self.'

ᵒ The example of the moving light is used by Vasubandhu in his (Chapter 9) discussion of subjectless cognition at AKB p. 473 (Duerlinger 168–69).

ᵖ The example of the tree that bears fruit is discussed by Buddhaghoṣa at VM XVII.171–72, in connection with his discussion of karma and rebirth.

[q] This is one of the standard Sāṃkhya arguments for the existence of the self. See Vācaspati Miśra's commentary *Tattvakaumadī* on *Sāṃkhyakārikā* XVII.

[r] Chapter 6 of the *Mahāvagga* contains an argument for non-self that could be construed in this way. There the Buddha gives two different sorts of reasons for claiming that none of the *skandhas* could be the self. The first is the usual point that each of the *skandhas* is impermanent, while the self would have to endure. But the second is that if a given *skandha* were the self then one would have complete control over it, whereas our control over each of the *skandhas* is incomplete. Now the apparent violation of the anti-reflexivity principle in this argument is puzzling. But one might interpret the passage as claiming that since the self would be the part of the person that performs the executive function, it could never be the case that one sought to perform the executive function on that part of the psychophysical complex, that is, deemed it unsatisfactory and sought to change it. That is, application of the anti-reflexivity principle would yield the *appearance* of complete control over that one part of the person. And since there is no psychophysical element that we might not deem unsatisfactory and seek to change, it follows that there is no self to be found among the *skandhas*.

[s] See Poṭṭhapāda Sutta, in the *Dīgha Nikāya*. The example of the hypostatizing lover is actually not the Buddha's first reply to Poṭṭhapāda's query. His initial response is just to repeat the argument for non-self from the impermanence of the psychophysical elements. This leads to the ten indeterminate questions (the *avyākṛta*), which are all unanswerable precisely because each involves some presupposition that is a product of hypostatization. The case of the would-be lover is then used to illustrate the problem with all the indeterminate questions.

[t] Martin gives an extremely persuasive account not only of why both techniques might be necessary, but also of why philosophers who agree that the self is an illusion might fail to recognize the importance of meditation. See Martin (1998) Chapter 6, especially pp. 144–45.

CHAPTER THREE

Getting Impersonal

Our aim in this chapter is to determine if Reductionists can adequately answer the many criticisms that stem from their impersonal description (ID) thesis, the claim that we can give a complete description of reality without either asserting or presupposing that persons exist. But there is another aim as well. Some of the objections that we shall consider do not involve commitment to any particular alternative view about the nature of persons. Other objections, though, are based on what was earlier called the dual-aspect view, a kind of Non-Reductionism that agrees with Reductionism in rejecting the self, yet still maintains that the concept of the person is unanalyzable and in some sense primitive. If the arguments of the previous chapter are correct, then there are good reasons to reject the claim that the existence of the person involves the existence of a self. Proponents of the dual-aspect view claim that we still have good reason to take persons as existing over and above psychophysical elements. As we examine objections that are based on this view, we shall seek to give it the careful scrutiny it deserves.

Buddhist Reductionism and the ID thesis

Before we can start our investigation of these important objections, though, we need to say something more about how the Buddhist Reductionist deploys the distinction between conventional and ultimate truth in explicating their position. A good example of this is to be found in one part of a dialogue between the Buddhist monk Nāgasena and a king, Milinda by name, who has sought out Nāgasena in order to question him concerning the teachings of Buddhism.[1] At this point in their discussion, Nāgasena has succeeded in persuading the king that belief in a self should be rejected, but now the king wonders about the consequences of this for diachronic personal identity. He thus asks whether infant Milinda and adult Milinda are the same person, or distinct persons. The monk responds that the adult is neither the same person as the infant, nor is he a distinct person.[a] The king understandably finds this odd, and volunteers that he is now inclined to say (no doubt because he has come to believe that there is no self) that adult and infant are distinct persons. That is, the king makes the common assumption that the denial of the self entails some form of annihilationism, the view that what we think of as one enduring person is actually a series of successive persons,

---

[1] Milinda has been identified with the Indo-Bactrian king Menandros, whose reign in northern India c. 150 BCE was part of the legacy of the Alexandrian conquest. It is not known whether Nāgasena represents a historical personage. While it is not unlikely that discussions took place between the king and one or more representatives of Buddhism, the dialogue cannot be taken as the record of an actual conversation. It is available in English translation, as *The Questions of King Milinda*, translated by T.W. Rhys Davids (London: Pali Text Society, 1890; reprinted Delhi: Motilal Banarsidass, 1965).

each existing only as long as some set of core psychophysical elements continues to exist. The monk then sets out to refute this view through a series of *reductios*. If it were true then there would be no such thing as a mother, since a (biological) mother is a person who bears a fetus from conception to birth, and the psychophysical elements making up the woman at conception are distinct from those making up the woman bearing the third-trimester fetus. Likewise there could be no educated persons, since one is entitled to be called educated only if one underwent an earlier course of study, and the elements making up the student are distinct from those making up the would-be diplomate. Similarly it would never be just to punish a criminal for a crime committed earlier, for given the intervening replacement of psychophysical elements, such punishment would always be inflicted on some person other than the one who committed the crime. Instead one should say that adult and infant are the same person. The monk adds, however, that this diachronic identity is to be understood in terms of the notion of a causal series of psychophysical elements: the elements constituting the adult are effects of an earlier set, which were in turn caused by an earlier set, etc., so that the present ones are related to the elements constituting the infant through the ancestral of the causal relation.[b]

The monk Nāgasena has now made three claims:

1 It is neither true nor false that adult and infant are the same person.
2 Adult and infant are the same person.
3 These present psychophysical elements are related to those earlier elements through the ancestral of the causal relation.

The text has the king asking for an explanation at this point, and his confusion is understandable. The bivalence failure incurred in (1) seems bad enough by itself, but this is compounded by the fact that the second conjunct of (1) appears to be contradicted by (2). This can all be sorted out, though, with the help of the doctrine of the two truths. Claims (1) and (3) are both intended as ultimate truths, whereas (2) is merely conventionally true and is ultimately false. The bivalence failure in (1) is simply a dramatic way of making the point that ultimately there are no persons. In effect it states that the question whether these two sets of psychophysical elements are the same or different persons has a false presupposition – at least if we wish to speak strictly in terms of our ultimate ontology. Claim (3) tells us something more positive concerning our conventional use of the convenient designator 'person': it says that this use is grounded in a complex chain of causal connections. And this in turn explains why (2) should be conventionally true. It is useful for us to connect past and present elements in this way because of the causal connections that obtain in this series. The utility is illustrated by the examples of the mother, the student, and the criminal that Nāgasena uses in refuting the king's claim that adult and infant are distinct persons (a claim that Nāgasena would say is both ultimately and conventionally false). Delivering maternal health care to the set of body elements bearing the zygote will help promote the health of those later body elements that bear the fetus. Delivering math instruction to one set of psychophysical elements will promote the later occurrence of subsequent sets exhibiting valuable numeracy skills. And while inflicting punishment on the present set of elements will not undo the past crime, this will reduce the likelihood that successor elements of this causal series will bring about similar undesirable states of affairs. To collect together psychophysical elements into causal series enhances our ability to promote the good and prevent the bad, to maximize pleasure and minimize pain. Our use of the convenient designator 'person' is justified by the enhanced control its employment confers.

It is worth reflecting on one important feature of the strategy that is being used by the Buddhist Reductionist here. We ordinarily say that the student deserves to have the degree conferred, and that the criminal deserves to be punished. And desert is a property that would seem to pertain solely to persons; while we may often wish to punish our cars and our computers, in our calmer moments we recognize these to be irrational impulses. This means, though, that desert must disappear when we seek to describe the world in terms of the wholly impersonal ultimate truth. Were judges to speak the ultimate truth, they would say that the collection of psychophysical elements before them for sentencing is neither the same person as, nor a distinct person from, the collection that caused the crime; so it would be odd for the judge to say that this collection deserves punishment. This does not, however, make punishment unjustifiable, for desert may still be said to be conventionally real. That is, given the ultimate facts about causal connections among psychophysical elements, plus our interest in minimizing overall suffering, the institutionalized practice of causing certain sorts of suffering in those series that have caused significant suffering in other series can be shown to have utility. And to say that the practice is institutionalized is to say that pro-attitudes toward the punishment of criminals are routinely instilled as part of the socialization process: we come to view such punishment as deserved. The property of desert is no more ultimately real than is the entity to which it attaches, the person. To think otherwise is to allow our interests an unwarranted role in determining our ultimate ontology. But it does not follow that we should be eliminativists about desert. The property, like that of being a covalent bond, still has a useful role to play in the conceptual resources of beings like ourselves.

The Extreme Claim and the objection that Reductionism entails punctualism

With this in mind, we turn to our survey of objections to Reductionism's ID thesis. A number of these involve the allegation that this thesis entails what has come to be called the Extreme Claim, the claim that four central features of our present person-regarding practices cannot be rationally justified: interest in one's own survival, egoistic concern for one's future states, holding persons responsible for their past deeds, and compensation for one's past burdens.[2] One such objection is that of Schechtman (1996: 60), who argues that Reductionism is committed to punctualism, the view that the experiencing subject is not an enduring person but rather an ephemeral person-stage. Since the four features require an enduring subject, it follows

---

[2] What Parfit calls the Extreme Claim (1984: 307) is the thesis that if Reductionism is true then egoistic concern for one's future states is never rationally justifiable. While he also discusses analogous views concerning the other three features, it is Schechtman (1996: 51) who identifies the four features as central to our concept of personhood, deletes the antecedent of the conditional, and uses the term for the claim that all four features lack rational support. I shall follow her practice.

that Reductionism entails abandoning our commitment to the four features. Special egoistic concern for one's future, for instance, requires that one identify future stages as stages of oneself, an enduring person, something that is clearly irrational if there are no enduring persons. Schechtman's strategy for convicting Reductionism of punctualism is quite simple. Reductionism maintains that the continued existence of a person just consists in the occurrence of a series of appropriately related physical and psychological entities and events, all of which allow of completely impersonal description. Schechtman takes this to mean that on the Reductionist view the person is an abstract entity, something merely constructed out of person-stages, and thus not the sort of thing that can serve as the subject of such features as egoistic concern or responsibility. How, Schechtman wonders, might a person be said to anticipate certain future states as its own, and so feel the special sort of concern for the subject of those states, when the person is no more than a logical fiction? Thus the Reductionist must, Schechtman believes, hold the person-stage – the set of psychophysical events that exist together at any one time – to be the subject of the central personhood features. But a person-stage is necessarily ephemeral, and so cannot anticipate any future states as its own. Since the central features all require that the subject be able to anticipate certain future states as its own, Schechtman concludes that Reductionism entails rejecting these features, adopting instead the punctualist view that we live our lives wholly in the present. Thus she sees the Reductionist as advocating that we transfer our person-regarding attitudes and practices to the person-stage. Hence one could rationally feel special egoistic concern only for the presently existing set of psychophysical elements and not for any future set in the series.

Given the way that I have characterized Reductionism, a Reductionist must reject the Extreme Claim. So where is the flaw in Schechtman's argument? The first Reductionist response will be to point out that the argument involves what looks like a covert repersonalization of the ultimate truth, in contravention of the ID thesis. While the Reductionist would agree that the person, being constructed out of more particular entities, cannot be ultimately real, they would also insist that this holds equally for the person-stage. It is only at the conventional level that we may speak of such things as (enduring) persons or (ephemeral) person-stages. Ultimately there are just individual psychophysical elements and their myriad causal connections. A person-stage is an aggregate of co-present psychophysical elements, something partite, just as much a conceptual fiction as the person. So punctualism could not be ultimately true. Might it be conventionally true? This is one way of understanding the counsel of the Eliminativist: that we should replace a discredited theory of persons with one that better accords with the ultimate truth. But which theory we adopt at the conventional level is determined by considerations of utility. And so we must ask, which would bring about greater maximization of utility: aggregating psychophysical elements under the concept of the person, or under the concept of the person-stage? The first option would involve encouraging the occurrence, within a set of co-present psychophysical elements, of identification with and appropriation of past and future elements within the causal series to which they belong.[3] The second option would involve discouraging the occurrence of such identification and appropriation. Thus,

---

[3] For a careful analysis of the attitude of appropriation see Martin (1998).

for instance, occurrences of what we commonly call grossly imprudent acts – acts causing minor present pleasure but significant future pain within the causal series – would be less frequent on the first option than on the second. Likewise punishment could be expected to have a significant deterrent effect on the first option but not on the second. In general, the Reductionist will claim, there is a considerable advantage on the side of adopting the theory of the person.[4] Of course a Buddhist Reductionist will want to add that this practice also typically leads to hypostatization, clinging and suffering. And perhaps suffering would be less likely to occur were we to adopt the convention of thinking of ourselves as person-stages rather than persons. But even so the Reductionist claims that there is greater overall utility to be had in retaining our concept of the person – particularly if it is possible to remove those elements in our current personhood practices that lead to hypostatization, clinging and suffering.

Schechtman might respond that her punctualist reading of Reductionism is not the result of a covert repersonalization of the ultimate truth, but of a judicious application of the principle of interpretative charity. The Reductionist denies that persons ultimately exist, but affirms the existence of such psychological events as pains. Since, Schechtman might assert, no sense can be made of the claim that there are subjectless pains, the Reductionist must have some subject or other in mind when they speak of reducing the person to such states. And since it is manifestly not the person that they have in mind, it seems plausible to suppose that they intend the person-stage to serve as the subject of pains and other experiences.

The Reductionist will, of course, agree that it is conventionally true that pains require subjects: we say that twinges, aches and other such noxious sensations are had by persons (and other sentient beings – though we shall ignore those here). What the Reductionist disputes is that this consensus represents anything more than the result of our adopting a useful form of discourse. To see why, let us consider how one might set about trying to prove that there can be no subjectless pains. We may take it as a given that pain has as its essential nature being hurtful. The question may be raised whether this essential nature is intrinsic to pain – whether it is primitive and unanalyzable, something that cannot be accounted for in terms of the natures of other things – or whether this nature is something that pain has only by virtue of its relations to other entities. To use the terminology of Buddhist Reductionism, one may ask whether pain bears its own essential nature, or instead borrows its essential nature from other entities. We shall not attempt to answer this question here. Rather, we shall attempt to show that on neither possibility can it be demonstrated that pains require subjects.

When Buddhist Reductionists claim that pain sensations are ultimately real (that is, are in the domain of discourse for the ultimate truth), they are asserting that pain sensations bear their own essential nature.[c] For this tradition, something is ultimately real if and only if it bears its own essential nature. The Buddhist Reductionist will ground their claim about pain's ultimate reality by identifying its essential nature of hurtfulness with its phenomenal character, that distinctive 'what-it-is-likeness' that immediately announces pain's presence. Here the resort to the quasi-demonstrative expression 'what-it-is-likeness' as a way of indicating the *quale* in question suggests

---

[4] The basic strategy here parallels that of Parfit (1984: 289–93) in responding to Nagel's view that I am essentially my brain.

precisely that this nature is primitive and unanalyzable, something known only by acquaintance, hence that pain sensations do indeed bear their own essential nature. And on this point many will agree with them. Far more controversial is their claim that while there are (ultimately) pain sensations, there are (ultimately) no persons who feel them. It is important to understand that in claiming this, they are not denying that the occurrence of a pain sensation is typically brought about by some distinctive sense–object–contact event, is typically accompanied by the occurrence of a consciousness episode taking the sensation as object, and typically causes the occurrence of such mental forces as, for example, attentiveness or desire for cessation. They are not, in other words, claiming that pains somehow float freely about in the air, devoid of connection to any other physical or mental events.[d] They are simply claiming that there are no intrinsic connections between the existence of a pain and the occurrence of these other physical and mental events, that such connections as do obtain are wholly contingent and not implicated in the very natures of the entities involved. How, then, might one show their hypothesis to be absurd? Simply to insist that pains are adjectival on persons – that to speak of a pain is to presuppose a subject who feels it – is no argument. The Reductionist has proposed an account according to which our talk of persons as owners of pains is just a shorthand way of referring to a set of discrete but causally connected psychophysical elements. If we agree that pain bears its own essential nature, it is difficult to see how to rule out this conception of pain as something that is discrete but contingently connected to other psychophysical elements.[e]

In order to rule out this alternative, it seems one must show that it is part of the nature of pain that it be the state of some larger system. This is just what a functionalist analysis of pain does. On such an account, something's being a pain sensation necessarily involves its playing a certain functional role in a certain sort of complex system. Pain's hurtfulness will then be understood to be tied to pain's role in alerting the system's monitoring and control subsystem to potentially damaging situations. This approach guarantees that pains require a subject: something could not be said to be a pain, that is, be hurtful, unless it were hurtful for some system of which it was a part or state. But this would also make pain something that borrows its essential nature from other things, that is, not something that is ultimately real. Moreover, it is not clear that the required subject of pain states would itself be ultimately real. A Buddhist Reductionist would, in any event, deny that the sort of system in question here could be any more ultimately real than the chariot. Only a real self could, in their eyes, serve to make the requisite subject ultimately real. And if neither pain nor its subject is ultimately real, then the most that could be said about pain is that it is conventionally true that it requires a subject – something to which the Reductionist has already agreed.

That pain is not itself ultimately real does, as Shoemaker points out (1985: 446–47), have consequences for the Reductionst ID thesis. For Reductionists frequently treat pains as among the atomic primitives out of which persons are to be constructed, and this requires that they be ultimately real. So even if the opponent cannot prove that pains necessarily require subjects, still adopting a functionalist analysis of pains will call into question at least one common way of formulating the ID thesis. But a Reductionist might evade this result by distinguishing between different levels of analysis at which persons and pains disappear. They might, that is, claim that while the ultimate truth will contain references to neither persons nor pains, there is a level of analysis intermediate between ultimate truth and conventional truth at which we may speak of pains but not of persons. So then impersonal descriptions that make reference to pains, while not ultimately true, will be closer approximations to the ultimate truth than are conventional attributions of pains to persons.

To see how this might be, we must first note one important respect in which Shoemaker seems to be wrong. He claims that on a functional analysis, pains will turn out to be ontologically dependent on persons. But, strictly speaking, all that follows from such an analysis is that something cannot be a pain unless it plays a certain sort of (functionally specified) causal role in a certain sort of system. The point here is not that among such systems there might be some that we would not be inclined to call persons (which is no doubt true – many would be reluctant to call bats persons). The point is rather that when we speak of pain's role in such a system we have already descended to a sub-personal level of analysis. We are no longer thinking of the system as a single, unified subject of experiences and agent of actions. It has instead become a collection of interrelated sub-systems, each with its own (functionally specified) causal role. Of course functional specifications are often expressed in terms of characterizations of the system as a whole: something's being a factory whistle might be explained through reference to the factory's use of shift labor. But there is no reason to believe that such talk may not likewise be discharged through functional analyses of other parts of the system. Pain, we say, signals potential damage, something that the system will seek to avert. But if someone's having a hurtful sensation can be unpacked as something's playing the causal role of alerting the monitoring and control subsystem, why cannot that subsystem and its functions likewise be understood in terms of a range of causal connections with other parts of the system?[5]

At this level of analysis, persons seem to have already slid from view. Pains, however, have not. Granted, pain can no longer be thought of as bearing its own essential nature. Pain's hurtfulness is now seen as not intrinsic to the sensation itself, but as the result of pain's role of mediating between system-damaging input and aversion output. From this vantage point we can see that pain may itself disappear upon further analysis. For if pain's hurtfulness depends upon its causal role, then it may well turn out that what actually realizes the role lacks this property, that hurtfulness supervenes on very different sorts of base properties. (This is the grain of truth behind the claim that an inverted pleasure–pain spectrum is possible.) At the level of systems analysis, though, we still have a use for talk of pain as hurting. So a Reductionist with functionalist inclinations with respect to mental states might still claim that pains are more fundamental than persons. If Shoemaker (1984: 101) is correct to suspect that such a Reductionist must in the end reduce all mental events to purely physical states, then the Buddhist Reductionist is wrong about what belongs in the ultimate ontology. Still the sort of approach they and many other Reductionists favor is not thereby shown to be incompatible with a functionalist analysis of pain.

---

[5] Kim (1998: 82) makes what I think is the same error. He says that what he calls a second-order property (such as a functional property) and its realizers are at the same level in the micro–macro hierarchy. But while it is the sleeping pill that has the property of dormitivity, it is its constituent molecules that have the property of binding to certain neuroreceptors. Being a sleeping pill is not a kind recognized in neurochemistry. The question of the micro–macro hierarchy will be discussed in more detail in Chapter 4.

A circularity objection

To sum up the results of the preceding section: the Reductionist claims that our considering ourselves persons is the result of our having adopted a set of conventional practices whereby a given set of psychophysical elements learns to identify with and appropriate past and future elements in the causal series of which it is a part.[6] This convention has been adopted because it is better at minimizing overall occurrence of pain than the other possible conventions, such as punctualism (the convention that only spatio-temporally contiguous elements should form aggregate identities), the *Weltgeist* convention (that identification should involve aggregation over distinct causal series of elements), and the like. In stating this, the Reductionist is assuming that there can be impersonal pains: the property of minimizing pain cannot explain our adopting the personhood convention unless pain is in some sense ontologically prior to persons. I have argued that the notion of impersonal pains is not conceptually incoherent. But this gives rise to a new worry: when the Reductionist speaks of the personhood convention having been adopted over other possible conventions, are they not already presupposing the existence of persons? For what else might be said to have done the adopting of this convention if not persons?[7]

One possible strategy the Reductionist might employ to answer this question is suggested by the claim, commonly made in the Buddhist Reductionist tradition, that belief in a self is the result of 'beginningless ignorance'.[f] So it might be claimed that there was no time at which humans (or other sentients) first adopted the personhood convention; instead, each new generation was socialized into conformity with the convention by its predecessors.[8] In this case, while each generation might be said to endorse the adoption of the convention, we need not suppose that there was some initial generation of hominid psychophysical elements somehow intentionally constituting themselves as persons by formulating and adopting the convention. But for this strategy to succeed, we obviously must assume that there is no first generation of sentients – that sentient life forms have always existed. And while such a view is not unknown among cultures subscribing to the ideology of karma and rebirth, it is clearly controversial, and it would be better if Reductionism were not to be hostage to its acceptance.

A better strategy might invoke the concept of evolution – but of the cultural, not the biological sort. The earliest proto-hominids, while social, lacked language, and thus did not employ the sorts of linguistic conventions that lead to belief in mere conceptual fictions. So these creatures did not consider themselves persons – since in one important sense they did not consider themselves at all. But tool use created selection pressures favoring the rise and spread of language use (which was also facilitated by the plastic brain of our highly altricial but large-brained species). And with the rise of language use there would grow a need for some way to conveniently

---

[6] For the individual, this is not a 'natural' event but rather an achievement coming at the end of a long process of socialization. And in some cases even the best child-rearing practices have but indifferent results.

[7] The difficulty here is analogous to one common criticism of social contract theory when that theory is understood as describing a historical occurrence: how could humans living in the 'state of nature' have developed the social skills required to negotiate and ratify a social contract?

designate aggregates of the psychophysical elements constituting the hominid organisms themselves. For it would obviously be in the interests of such organisms to control and predict the behavior of these elements, and this task is facilitated by some shorthand way of referring to aggregates of elements. So ways of conveniently designating aggregates of psychophysical elements will have arisen among the language conventions of early hominids. (At the same time, of course, conventions will also have arisen governing convenient ways to designate those aggregates of elements that make up our comon-sense ontology of middle-sized objects; use of such conventions obviously facilitates control of the external environment.) But early hominids lived in many different social groups, each with its own distinctive set of customs and conventions. And there is no reason to suppose that the personhood convention would have arisen among all such groups as the one correct solution to the problem of aggregating psychophysical elements. Other such conventions, such as the punctualist convention and the *Weltgeist* convention, will have arisen among some groups. Here is where cultural evolution enters into the account. One basis for cultural selection is maximization of overall welfare, and the personhood convention simply proved better at this than the alternatives, so that the culture of those groups in which it arose prevailed in the long run. For instance, the personhood convention clearly yields far fewer instances of gross imprudence, such as blithely eating all one's seed corn, than does the punctualist convention. And while the *Weltgeist* convention might better facilitate group coordination than does the personhood convention, the former also has the crucial defect of stifling individual initiative. This is why we today consider ourselves to be persons, and not mere person-stages or superordinate *Weltgeists*. Our own culture is a descendant of those cultures in which the personhood convention arose.[8]

A second circularity objection

The circularity objection we have just considered was in response to the Reductionist claim that the personhood convention prevails due to its better promotion of overall welfare, which sounds to the opponent like the claim that at some time in human history this convention was chosen on rational grounds. The second claim is circular, since only those aggregates of psychophysical elements that consider themselves to be persons (or person-stages, or *Weltgeists*, etc.) may be said to deploy standards of practical rationality. The Reductionist can, I claim, avoid this charge of circularity by appealing to the impersonal processes of cultural evolution. Even if this strategy succeeds, however, there still awaits another sort of circularity objection. In characterizing Reductionism I have been making liberal use of the notion of a causal series of psychophysical elements. It might be wondered whether it is possible to assign all the elements of the Reductionist's basic ontology to one or another of these so-called

---

[8] It might still be objected that the notion of culture being employed here presupposes the existence of persons, so that the charge of circularity has not been avoided. But all that the Reductionist means by a culture is a stable pattern of talking and thinking among a set of interacting systems. Where the systems in question are learning systems, such stable patterns are readily accounted for. (I owe this point to Kenton Machina.)

causal series without implicitly employing our concept of a person – thereby making the account circular. This charge of circularity may be put more precisely. Consider what Perry (1975) calls the unity relation for diachronic personal identity, the relation that obtains between temporally separate elements just in case they are part of the history of the same person. The Reductionist's ID thesis requires that it be possible to formulate the unity relation in purely impersonal terms. The Reductionist will claim that this can be done through an analysis of the unity relation into certain causal relations holding among psychophysical elements. The charge is that any attempt to actually specify just those causal relations that might constitute the unity relation will inevitably presuppose the concept of a person and its associated criterion of diachronic identity. According to this objection, Reductionist gesturing in the direction of a purely impersonal 'causal series' is just so much hand-waving.

One simple version of this objection concerns the use of experience–memory connections to unpack the unity relation. Parfit has a satisfactory response to this objection, but it is worth reviewing both the objection and Parfit's reply before going on to more complex formulations. A Reductionist might claim that the unity relation is made up of experience–memory connections, which may be understood as a causal relation between two psychological events: I now seem to remember the earlier experience because my having that experience at the earlier time caused a memory trace that was retained and is currently being activated. And, such a Reductionist might claim, my being the same person over time just consists in there being many such experience–memory causal connections. But, comes the objection, it is part of the meaning of the word 'remember' that we can only be said to remember our own experiences. So this attempt to unpack the unity relation in terms of causal connections violates the ID thesis. Parfit's response uses the concept of quasi-memory, which is just like our concept of memory but without the presupposition of personal identity. So if it proved possible to transfer several memory traces from A's to B's brain, then B might be said to quasi-remember experiences had by A. It is important to note that this need not make B the same person as A, even for the Reductionist who claims that the unity relation is made up of quasi-memory connections. When we try to imagine what it would be like for B to seem to remember these experiences 'from the inside', it is tempting to suppose that B must somehow become A. But this is only because, as things currently stand, we can only quasi-remember our own experiences. Were memory-trace transfer to become possible, we might come to be able to know 'from the inside' how it was for someone else to have a certain experience. And since quasi-memory does not presuppose personal identity, a Reductionist might use this in their analysis of the unity relation without violating the ID thesis.[h]

That B may be said to quasi-remember the experiences of someone else, A, is meant to show that the experience–quasi-memory connection is a truly impersonal causal connection, and thus that it can be part of a Reductionist analysis of the unity relation. But notice that according to the Reductionist there may also be conditions involving quasi-memory transfer under which B does come to be the same person as A. Now most Reductionists who give a strictly psychological analysis of the unity relation agree that other sorts of psychological connections besides quasi-memory connections are involved in the continued existence of the same person. Suppose, though, that it is possible to transfer not just several but most of A's memory traces to

B's brain, but that this process requires that B's brain first be wiped of all memory traces caused by B's past experiences. Suppose that this is done, and that B's brain is simultaneously reconfigured so as to reproduce such other of A's dispositions as A's cognitive skills, values, character traits, and the like. Finally, suppose that at the end of this transfer process A were to die. Then, according to a Reductionist who accepted the psychological approach to the unity relation, it might be the case that B now is the same person as A earlier.[9] If so, this would be because there are now enough of the right kinds of causal connections between A earlier and B now (plus the fact that B now has no competitor for the role of being A). In the case where B quasi-remembered just a few of A's experiences, we would not say that B now is the same person as A earlier (even if the A-body were destroyed in the memory-trace transfer). But in this new case, where B's psychological makeup duplicates A's, and this is no mere coincidence but rather the result of hugely many causal connections, we might say that B is A. The important general point here may be put by saying that for the Reductionist, diachronic personal identity is *all in the numbers*. My being the same person as some earlier person just consists in there being sufficiently many of the right kinds of causal connections between the present set of entities and events and the earlier set.[10] And, claims the Reductionist, given the massive complexity of all these entities and events and all their causal connections, it is no wonder that we should have devised a convenient way to designate them all with a single term.

But now the more sophisticated formulation of the circularity objection may be stated: Reductionism cannot explain in a non-question-begging way the construction of persons out of wholly impersonal psychophysical elements. For consider all the psychophysical elements occurring at moment t_n, all the elements occurring at t_{n+1}, etc. The construction of persons requires that certain of the elements that occurred at t_n be associated with certain ones occurring at t_{n+1}, and how are we to know which go with which? The Reductionist will, of course, appeal to causal connections here: the person-series is constructed out of psychophysical elements by associating a given simultaneously occurring set with its prior causes. But this, says the critic, cannot be right, since events in (what we intuitively consider) one person-series can cause later events in another: my sneeze causes your startlement, your witty repartee causes my amusement, etc. The Reductionist's glib appeal to causal connections 'of the right sort' merely masks a covert appeal to persons as continuants: we could know which causal connections are the 'right' ones only if we already knew what it means for a person to continue to exist over time.[11]

The Reductionist response to this objection is that persons are constructed out of sets of psychophysical elements exhibiting the property of *maximal causal connectedness*. To see how such a construction works, consider the set of elements at

---

[9] For some of those Reductionists who take a strictly physical approach to the unity relation, a similar result might come about through the successful implant of enough of A's brain in B's body, or by the implant in B's body of a new brain that was gradually grown from A's brain cells in such a way as to duplicate the configuration of A's brain.

[10] Or rather, overlapping chains of causal connections; a Reductionist analysis of the unity relation will make use not only of the causal relation but also of the ancestral of the causal relation. See Parfit (1984: 206) for a sample formulation.

[11] See Williams (1998: 130–37) for a somewhat different formulation of this objection.

t_1, including a certain nose-state, that collectively give rise to a sneeze at t_2, which in turn causes a feeling of startlement at t_3, but also to a feeling of relief at t_3. The nose-state that is among the conditions of the sneeze is likewise a condition of the feeling of relief (it is a feeling of relief from that very state). And the feeling of startlement has as one of its conditions a certain faculty of hearing. In order for the feeling of startlement to have occurred at t_3, the nose whose nose-state that is, and the ear whose faculty of hearing that is, must be in proximity to one another at t_2. But as we track this nose and this ear at subsequent moments, we shall find them moving out of proximity to one another, so that the states of one can no longer cause events in the other. The ear will, though, remain in relatively close proximity to the hand that was caused by the feeling of startlement to drop the cup at t_4. And the nose and the feeling of relief may together directly give rise to further psychological states. And so on. Including the feeling of startlement in the set containing the sneeze would thus diminish the degree of overall causal connectedness. Including the feeling of relief in this set, on the other hand, would increase the degree of overall causal connectedness of the set. The goal of the construction is to include as many elements as possible consistent with the maximizing of causal connectedness.

The first task in constructing person-sets will be to assign body parts to the right set. Mere proximity will not do, since at any given time the body parts of what we consider two persons may be in quite close proximity. The key is to look for the possibility of reciprocal causal interaction between body parts (or their successors[i]) over time. A state of this ear causes a train of events leading to the state of this hand that causes the shattering of the cup. If at some later time the ear should fill with seawater, this hand can restore its auditory function by facilitating the draining of the seawater. We cannot count on the same sort of causal interaction between this ear and that nose. Of course body parts may get reassigned to different sets, as in cases of blood or kidney donation. But this is because after the donation, the tissue is no longer reliably available for causal interaction with other parts in the original set, and instead comes to be in causal interaction with parts in the new set. This blood no longer supplies oxygen to this ear, and will no longer be flooded with adrenaline when this ear registers explosive sneeze sounds; instead this blood supplies oxygen to that nose, and its oxygenation level will decrease when that nose is immersed in water. So looking for maximal causal connectedness over time allows us to sort body parts into the right sets. The next task will be to assign psychological events to sets. This should be fairly easy to do if psychological events supervene on or are reducible to bodily events and states. If the feeling of relief just consists in or supervenes on the binding of certain neurotransmitters to certain neurons, then its assignment can proceed straightforwardly on the basis of the set of body parts with which that brain event is in causal interaction. But a dualist about mental events (like the Buddhist Reductionist) can say something similar, provided they are interactionist about bodily and mental events. So the Buddhist Reductionist would say that the feeling of relief, while itself ultimately real (because it is itself causally efficacious), is the effect of a physical event (the sneeze), and can serve as the cause of physical events (the sigh that increases the volume of air in the nose). So once again the event can be assigned to one or another set based on maximal causal connectedness over time.

That the Reductionist can give a recipe for constructing the person out of impersonal elements does not, however, prove that the construction is not circular in the critic's sense. For it is possible that this recipe was arrived at in total reliance on our pre-theoretic intuitions about persons and personal identity, so that it does after all smuggle in the concept of a person. The Reductionist needs to give some independent reason, formulatable in impersonal terms, why this construction should have been adopted. This the Reductionist can do, once we grant that the point of the construction of persons is the maximization of overall utility. For systems with the capacities of self-scrutiny, self-control and self-revision turn out to be quite effective at local maximizing. And such systems can only be constructed out of sets of elements exhibiting maximal causal connectedness. The construction of the person as a series of psychophysical elements with maximal causal connectedness has what I shall call a Consequentialist justification.

A consequentialist holds that our reasons for action are based on the consequences of actions. A Consequentialist holds that the consequences that count are thoroughly impersonal in nature.[12] For instance, when the Buddhist Reductionist claims it is ultimately true that pain is bad, this might serve as the foundation for a Consequentialist account of our reasons for action. Not all consequentialists would agree with this claim; many might say, for instance, that the very idea of ownerless pain is incoherent. This would include many of those consequentialists who hold that the consequences of an action give rise to agent-neutral reasons for action, as well as many of those who assert that the consequences can only give rise to agent-relative reasons. What separates Consequentialists from other consequentialists is not what separates those who espouse agent-neutral reasons from those who espouse only agent-relative reasons. Indeed a Consequentialist might hold either view about what kinds of reasons we have for action – provided it is understood that these reasons represent merely conventional truths.[13] What sets Consequentialists apart from other consequentialists is their view that welfare is constituted by purely impersonal states and events, and that it is these that ought to be considered in determining what to do. (In Chapter 5 I shall sketch the kind of ethics that I think flows from Buddhist Reductionist Consequentialism.)

To see in greater detail how this Consequentialist justification of the person construction goes, more needs to be said about the the capacities of self-scrutiny, self-control and self-revision mentioned above. Self-scrutiny and self-control are clearly connected. For a system S to be said to control an object x, it must be the case that S has the ability to drive x into whichever of x's normal range of states S desires. Control thus requires that the controlling system S be able to represent to itself the states of x. And where x is S, this will mean that S must be able to be informed about its own states, hence the need for self-scrutiny. Moreover, for S to be said to have the capacity for self-control, it must have preferences concerning its own states, and be able to

---

[12] Roy Perrett pointed out to me the need to distinguish this from the more familiar varieties of consequentialism. He also suggested the typographical device I shall use to set it apart from its cousins.

[13] The distinction between agent-neutral and agent-relative reasons concerns which persons acquire reasons for action through the occurrence of certain states and events. It is difficult to see how this distinction could be formulated at the thoroughly impersonal level of the ultimate truth. Indeed it could be argued that the notion of a reason for action is unavailable at that level – that reasons are the sorts of things that only persons could be said to have. The Reductionist would, however, hasten to add that facts at the ultimate level explain how it comes to be conventionally true that we have reasons for action.

drive itself into certain of those states. Assuming that S's preference-formation were connected in some way to its interests (e.g., through S being a learning system), these abilities would clearly enhance the capacity of S to maximize its own welfare. But they also might seem to run afoul of the anti-reflexivity principle, the principle that an entity cannot operate on itself. How can the scrutinizer be the very thing that is scrutinized, the controller be the very thing that is controlled? This seeming paradox is resolved, of course, by noting that S is a complex system the parts of which may be partitioned into two distinct sets, a 'subject' set and an 'object' set. Members of the former set constitute a subsystem of S that performs the operation (scrutiny, preference formation, etc.) on members of the latter set. But this opens up a potential weakness in the ability of S to maximize its own welfare. Particularly where conditions in its environment are subject to wide variation, it might be that changes in the 'subject' set would improve S's performance. For instance, more frequent or more finely grained bouts of self-scrutiny might better enable S to catch potentially damaging conditions early on. And it might be that adjusting the rankings among the members of its preference-set in response to changes in the environment would enhance S's long-term welfare. Indeed a system without these sorts of meta-control capacities would seem to run a substantial risk of falling under the control of some competing system (by 'falling into a rut' that its competitor could then exploit), to its distinct disadvantage. So a capacity for self-revision would seem to confer a decided advantage on a system with the capacities of self-scrutiny and self-control.

This, though, makes the air of paradoxicality surrounding such a system seem quite genuine. True, we saw in the last chapter how each part of a system might be subject to the system's control without violation of the anti-reflexivity principle: by having the control sub-system consist of a shifting coalition of members, so that any given part might be in the 'subject' position on one occasion and the 'object' position on another. So if self-revision were merely a species of self-control, there would be no new paradox involved. But it is not. An effective self-controller will exhibit a certain stable character, for instance in its strategies for information-gathering and in the rankings it assigns to kinds of preferences. This is necessary both because of constraints on the resources it can devote to these activities, and because learning cannot happen if the activities are carried out in a wholly random way. So we may think of these as features of the control sub-system. Self-revision is a sort of meta-control that is carried out on this sub-system. So another partition seems in order, to separate off elements of the control sub-system from elements of the meta-control or self-revision sub-system. And this raises the prospect of an infinite regress of navel-gazing: if the controller's performance can be enhanced by a meta-controller, then surely the performance of the latter could be improved by a meta-meta-controller, etc. The paralysis that would clearly result suggests quite the opposite of an improvement in the system's welfare.

So invoking a separate meta-control sub-system will not do, and yet the capacity for self-revision that is wanted here must be thought of as involving a kind of meta-control. The solution is to see self-revision as a function that gets carried out by the control sub-system through strategic manipulation of the 'shifting coalitions' feature. Suppose this system has, as part of its character, five standing preferences, $P_1 \ldots P_5$, each of which generates various short-term preferences and subsidiary goals. The system obviously cannot subject all five to review and possible revision simultaneously without some separate set of (perhaps second-order) preferences, and this leads to the infinite regress of navel-gazing. What the system can do, though, is subject one to review and possible revision while holding the other four constant. And this might come about in the following way. It might be a feature of the system that conflicts among the short-term preferences and subsidiary goals of the system, when they exceed a certain threshold level, lead to a search for the one standing preference the deletion of which would yield the greatest diminution of intra-system conflict.[14] If one such preference is identified, it is then placed in the 'object' position for review and possible revision by the control sub-system. This is but one of a number of conceivable strategies that might be employed, and it is unlikely that any evolutionarily successful system will use just one. The important point is that the advantages of a capacity for self-revision can be realized while avoiding the paradoxes that threaten when the system seems to 'go meta-'.

The Reductionist claims that psychophysical elements can be assigned to distinct sets without reliance on the concept of a person, based wholly on the criterion of maximal causal connectedness. This criterion is said to be thoroughly impersonal because of its purely Consequentialist justification: assignment of psychophysical elements to maximally causally connected sets yields greater overall welfare than alternative assignments. Why is this? We have just seen that systems with capacities for self-scrutiny, self-control and self-revision will prove to be better maximizers than systems lacking them. And these capacities all require reciprocal causal connections among the elements of the system. For the flow of information and the flow of control both proceed through causal pathways. So assignment of psychophysical elements to causal series based on maximal causal connectedness will yield greater overall welfare.

The Consequentialist grounding of the construction of causal series helps explain some features that might otherwise seem puzzling. A critic might raise questions about the fact that a series must be constructed longitudinally: in order to assign an element to a series one might have to look at its causal connections over some significant stretch of its history. This does not mean, however, that one cannot say which parts made up which persons until their lives were over. At any given time in the history of a causal series there will be enough causal connections among past and present elements so that based on known regularities we may safely assign most present elements to either this or some other series. And of course known regularities are features that such systems are designed to exploit: self-control and self-revision require the ability to make reliable predictions about the future states of the system. Since such regularities will figure prominently in the control and meta-control strategies such systems employ, we should not be surprised to discover that assignment of elements to one or another system should depend on them.

Another question that has not yet been addressed concerns how such a series could ever come to an end. While the elements making up a series at one moment all go out of existence at some future time, in going out of existence each might give rise to some new entity or event. The cells making up the liver of my corpse will, when they cease,

---

[14] Notice, incidentally, that one possible source of intra-system conflict might be inter-system conflict. It might, that is, be the case that control sub-systems are designed to be sensitive to 'criticism' from other systems. And various heuristics can be imagined that seek to balance demands for inter-system coordination with the value of individual initiative.

give rise to the tissue of some worm. And these causal connections might prove to then be the pathway of maximal causal connectedness for this series. Indeed we can imagine that the pathway might travel through a small heap of dust for thousands or even millions of years. But for the fact that at some point there might be a tie between two competitors for maximally connected continuer (about which more below), it seems such a series should go on at least until the heat death of the universe. Yet surely persons do sooner or later cease to exist.[j] The Reductionist will thus want to claim that there is a threshold level of causal connectedness below which a series cannot continue. That is, given that at t_i a set P of psychophysical elements belongs to causal series S beginning at t_h, set P' at t_{i+1} is a member of S only if there obtain at least n causal connections between the members of P and the members of P'. While this will block the threat of a too-cheap immortality, it may seem *ad hoc*. What could motivate stipulating such a threshold other than desire to ward off an objection? The answer is that beneath a certain level of causal interrelatedness, a set of entities and events cannot function as a system of control and self-control. Death is just dis-integration.

Stipulation of a threshold level of causal connectedness allows for the introduction of a distinction Parfit draws between continuity and connectedness (1984: 206). Connectedness is a measure of the number of causal connections between the members of two sets of psychophysical elements P and P' occurring at different times. Continuity is the relation obtaining between P_i at t_i and P_k at (non-adjacent) t_k just in case there are, for each moment between t_i and t_k, sets $P_{i+1}, P_{i+2} \ldots P_{k-1}$, each bearing causal connectedness of at least measure n (the threshold number) with its immediate predecessor and successor sets.[k] (Where P_i and P_k are immediately temporally contiguous, there must be at least n causal connections between their members.) That is, between P_i and P_k there must be overlapping chains of causal connectedness each of which meets or exceeds the minimal level required for continuation of a causal series. This means, though, that between P_i and P_k themselves there may be only a very low level of causal connectedness even while there is continuity. It is also worth noting that while connectedness comes in degrees, continuity is an all-or-nothing affair. Finally, nothing in the definition of continuity rules out the possibility that there may be two contemporaneous sets P_k and $P_{k'}$ each of which is continuous with earlier P_i. That is, continuity can take a branching form. So if some type of continuity is the unity relation, this means that personal identity can, in principle, take a branching form: it is possible for persons to undergo fission. While many find this result profoundly unsettling, it should not come as a surprise given the Reductionist view that persons are mere conceptual fictions. As Ship of Theseus puzzle cases amply demonstrate, where an entity is constructed through the aggregation of elements based on considerations of utility, there can be multiple contenders for the role of the closest continuer of that entity, and no non-arbitrary way to decide among them.[15]

---

[15] In a case of a tie between contenders B and C for the role of closest continuer of A, it might thus be said to be conventionally indeterminate (neither conventionally true nor conventionally false) that B is A, and likewise that C is A. Dummett (1991: 326) says that it is the hallmark of what we are calling reductionism about Ks that there be bivalence failure for statements in the disputed class (that is, statements about the Ks). Cases of fission represent one way in which the Reductionist might comply with this requirement. But see Parfit (1984: 253–60) for a persuasive argument to the effect that these statements be considered not conventionally indeterminate but conventionally false. For Parfit, bivalence failure occurs

A slightly different form of the circularity objection may be raised against those Reductionists (such as Parfit) who see connections among first-person psychological states as playing an especially important part in the unity relation. As Campbell points out, while connections among psychological states may also play a significant role in the continued existence of animals that are not persons, it is distinctive of persons that 'their psychological lives are organized around first-person thinking; they are organized around autobiographical thought' (1994: 178). And while, according to this objection, it may be possible to give a purely causal account of the sorts of psychological connections typical of other animals, the kinds of connections that hold between first-person states are not causal in nature, and so cannot be described in impersonal terms. This is not, however, because the states that enter into such connections are formulated using the first person. When my intention takes the form, 'I should take an umbrella', the Reductionist can claim that since 'I' is a mere convenient designator, its occurrence in this context has no untoward ontological implications. Campbell's point is rather that the connections between such states are normative in nature, and that their normativity derives from their being connections between states of the same person. Suppose that prior to the intention about the umbrella there occurred the thoughts, 'I shall be walking home this evening' and 'Rain is forecast by late afternoon.' Suppose all three psychological states are elements of what the Reductionist would call a single causal series of psychophysical elements, so that the intention has causal connections 'of the right sort' with the two thoughts. It would be a mistake, Campbell claims, for the Reductionist to hold that these causal connections might be part of what makes this series one person. It is rather the other way around: these causal connections are 'of the right sort' because there is a normative relation between the two thoughts and the intention: given the two thoughts, the intention ought to occur. And the reason this normative relation holds is that these are all states of one person. If Smith had the first thought, and Jones the second, we would not think that Wallaby ought for that reason to form the intention.

While this is a new formulation of the circularity objection, the Reductionist reply will remain the same. The normative connections that hold among first-person states occurring in the same causal series derive from the Consequentialist grounds that stand behind construction of the causal series as a set of maximal causal connectedness. Indeed we can now see why connections among first-person states might play an important part in the unity relation. The ability of a system to form and use self-representations will clearly facilitate that system's self-scrutiny, self-control and self-revision capacities, and first-person psychological states are states that employ system self-representations. Causal connections among such states represent the exercise of these capacities. The normative dimension of these connections simply reflects the fact that such connections tend to promote overall maximization of welfare. (Later we shall discuss the role that autobiographical thinking might play in welfare-maximizing strategies.)

---

instead with statements of personal identity in the middle of his Combined Spectrum (1984: 236–43). We shall have more to say about this sort of bivalence failure in our discussion of *sorites* difficulties in the next chapter.

The Extreme Claim and foundationalism about egoistic concern

We began with an objection to Reductionism based on the Extreme Claim, the claim that if Reductionism were true then four central features of personhood – interest in one's own survival, egoistic concern for one's future states, holding persons responsible for their past deeds, and compensation for one's past burdens – would lack rational justification. Consideration of this objection led to an examination of several sorts of circularity objections against the ID thesis, but let us now return to objections based on the Extreme Claim. If this claim is true, then it could be argued that Reductionism is incoherent. For it might plausibly be claimed that it is central to our theory of personhood that the four features be rationally justifiable – that they are constitutive of personhood. If so, then if the Extreme Claim were true, the truth of Reductionism would entail that our theory of personhood is indefensible. But Reductionists hold that while there ultimately are no persons, our theory of personhood is nonetheless defensible. If the Extreme Claim were true, there would turn out to be no middle ground between Non-Reductionism and Eliminativism: either persons are ultimately real, or else all our person-regarding attitudes are rationally unjustifiable.

Thus a Reductionist must deny the Extreme Claim and hold instead a Moderate Claim, to the effect that if Reductionism is true, then mitigated forms of the four features may be grounded in facts about the impersonal entities and events that persons just consist in. For instance, Parfit holds the following view about egoistic concern: if Reductionism is true, then causal connectedness and continuity give some reason for egoistic concern, but (1) such concern allows of diminished degrees as the degree of connectedness decreases, and (2) such concern is not different in kind from concern for others.[16] And similar versions of the Moderate Claim can be formulated for each of the other three central features of personhood.[1] But Parfit also says that he knows of no argument that proves the Extreme Claim false and the Moderate Claim true (1984: 312). Moreover, it is widely held that coming to believe that persons are not ultimately real would lead to Extremism about egoistic concern, to the grasshopper's view that one should only be concerned for one's immediate welfare. We turn now to several attempts to support this intuition that the Extreme Claim is true.

Haksar's (1991) argument begins with a distinction between primary and secondary egoistic concern. Suppose I exhibit concern for the welfare of an agent solely because that agent's welfare is important to the fulfillment of certain of my plans or projects. In this case my concern for that agent's welfare is egoistic, but derivatively or secondarily so. Primary egoistic concern is exhibited when, for instance, I anticipate with dread some future suffering. When I dread root canal work, my concern is not typically centered on ways in which the experience will interfere with my carrying out some project. Haksar claims that secondary egoistic concern is parasitic on primary egoistic concern. This is presumably because I could not have concern for the welfare of what is required to promote my plans and projects unless I

---

[16]   Parfit (1984) introduces his Moderate Claim (about egoistic concern) at p. 311 without either of the two qualifications. His discussion of imprudence and paternalism at pp. 318–21 makes it clear that he would accept the two qualifications.

were already concerned with promoting the interests of my self – as that to which my plans and projects have value. But those who hold the Moderate Claim must assert that egoistic concern for my future well-being can be accounted for in terms of my present desire that my plans and projects be fulfilled: I want my life to go well so that the plans and projects I now value will reach fruition. On such an account, primary egoistic concern would derive from secondary egoistic concern, which is impossible. Hence on the Reductionist view egoistic concern is not rationally justified: it can only arise from what, according to Reductionism, is an illusion, that there is an enduring self. Haksar thus concludes that only the Extreme View is rationally defensible.

Stone's (1988) argument similarly attacks the Moderate Claim, according to which the fact that I bear a certain special relation (such as Parfit's Relation R) to a future person gives me some reason to be concerned about the welfare of that person. Stone claims that this relation will consist of two components: resemblance plus a causal connection.[17] He then asks why that future person's having those characteristics should make that person an object of my special concern. The Reductionist would respond that this matters because those characteristics resemble (or bear some other appropriate relation to) mine. But, says Stone, to call these present characteristics mine is to say that they are now had by the person who is identical to me. And this means that what makes these present characteristics confer special concern is synchronous identity: it is my identity with the person who has these characteristics that makes them matter. And synchronous identity is the same relation as diachronic identity. So only personal identity over time could confer special concern. Since Reductionism claims it is ultimately false that I am identical with any future person, Stone concludes that the Extreme Claim is true.

Haksar's and Stone's arguments share a common assumption, that any of my properties that have value for me can ultimately derive that value only from their being mine. I shall call this view foundationalism about egoistic concern.[m] In certain respects it resembles a certain widely held view of love; examining this view may shed light on the question of egoistic concern. People sometimes vacillate between wanting to be loved for the way that they are, and wanting to be loved just for being the particular person they are. On the first conception, I hope to be loved for my various virtues, talents and accomplishments; I would find repulsive a love that could survive utterly unchanged were I to become an irredeemably evil person. On the second conception, I want to be loved just for being *me*. I seek a love that is not conditional on my remaining a certain way, or on my changing in certain respects. I seek a love that is unconditional, that could not be threatened by the presence of rivals with qualities far more admirable than any I possess. Whereas on the first, conditional conception I wish to be loved because of my qualities, on the second, unconditional conception I want my qualities to be loved because they are mine. It is the latter conception of love that is the analogue, for love of another, of the view of self-love implicit in foundationalism about egoistic concern.

Now any Reductionist account (such as Parfit's or the Buddhist's) that makes particular persons potentially subject to fission (as in cases of a teletransporter

---

[17] In fact, resemblance enters into relatively few of the particular causal links between two R-related person-stages, but substituting other relations here will not affect the argument.

run amok) appears to be compatible with the conditional conception of love but incompatible with the unconditional conception. This becomes the basis for a line of objection to Reductionism first suggested by Bernard Williams (1973: 80–81): if my love could transfer straightforwardly to both products of the fission of my beloved, then it appears that what I exhibit is not the love of a person but a kind of connoisseurship. But the Reductionist can reply that love seems singularly unattractive on the unconditional conception as well – and this without the aid of the science fiction stories that Williams' objection requires. Why should I want to be the object of completely unconditional love, love that could survive my becoming an axe-murderer? Why wish for a love that would attach to someone who is not, in my estimation, worthy of being loved?

Those who claim to want an utterly unconditional love might actually have something different in mind. They may believe that human flourishing requires the sense that one is completely secure in the love of another. And this may be true at least of many persons. But if so, it would seem to be true for the reason that we hope there will always be someone who 'sees the spark of good within us', even when we have gone seriously astray in our own eyes. And this might be thought important to human flourishing because it might appear unlikely that we would make the effort to repair our diminished self-esteem without assurance from another that there is something worth repairing, that our nature holds at least potential value that is worthy of development. But if this is the motivation behind the desire for unconditional love, then what is wanted is still the sense that one is estimable in others' eyes. We are back, then, to the first conception of love, of wanting to be loved for one's qualities.

If this is indeed what we wish for when we want to be loved, then foundationalism about egoistic concern begins to seem quite puzzling. This is the claim that ultimately my properties (such as character traits, values, plans and projects) can be a source of egoistic concern for me only by virtue of being *mine* or promoting interests that are *mine*. This is the analogue, for self-love, of the unconditional conception of love (of another). If I can have egoistic concern for some future person's project only if it advances some goal I now have, and that goal in turn is of concern to me solely by virtue of its being mine, then egoistic concern appears to be structured like the unconditional formulation of love: one's properties are to be valued just because they are one's own.

Of course from foundationalism about egoistic concern, the Extreme Claim would follow. For since Reductionism denies the existence of persons as separately existing entities, if Reductionism is true then there is no separately existing entity through relation to which my properties might derive value. And the person as mere conceptual fiction will not satisfy the foundationalist's demand, since this fiction is partially constructed out of just those properties whose value to me foundationalism seeks to explain. Thus if Reductionism is true, foundationalism would mean that no relation to a future person can give me reason for egoistic concern about the states of that person. For if Reductionism is true, foundationalism would entail that nothing can be a reason for egoistic concern; all such concern is based on an illusion.

The question is why we should accept foundationalism about egoistic concern. Just as it seems odd that I should want to be loved by others not for my properties but just for being me, so it seems puzzling that the regard I have for myself should be unconditional, and utterly independent of anything that is true of me. Of course it is not puzzling, on a certain sort of evolutionary account, that we should be disposed to engage in behavior that advances certain of our body-based interests (see Parfit 1984: 308). But this does not yield a blanket reason for valuing any properties that happen to be mine.

Perhaps it is thought that unconditional self-regard, like unconditional love, is of instrumental value for human flourishing. Thus it might be claimed that one must first care about oneself in order to take an interest in any long-term projects one has. But as we saw with the instrumental defense of unconditional love, this tends to undermine the guiding assumption that only the self is of intrinsic value, that one's properties derive whatever value they possess through relation to the self. For any such instrumental defense of unconditional self-regard requires prior agreement on the value of such properties as are thought to constitute human flourishing. These properties cannot then be said to derive their value to the self just from their relation to the self.

Perhaps it is thought that if self-regard is not unconditional, an infinite regress threatens. Suppose that I care about completing some project, say, writing a book. Why? Perhaps because I value carefully working out my thoughts on the subject. But the question may then be raised why engaging in this sort of careful thinking should be of value to me. Perhaps this is in turn instrumental to some other project I am engaged in. But, it could be claimed, this regress cannot continue indefinitely: the value that any property holds for me must ultimately be grounded in some fact about me the value of which for me simply cannot be questioned. Otherwise, in the absence of some fact about me having intrinsic value, nothing else could be of any value whatever for me. And the only available candidate here seems to be that I am *me*.

To this the Buddhist Reductionist would respond by repeating the diagnosis of hypostatization that we saw them using in the last chapter. A self could not be of intrinsic value to itself, for that would be tantamount to its valuing itself, in violation of the anti-reflexivity principle. The phenomenon that is commonly described as valuing or esteeming oneself exhibits the same complexity that self-control and self-revision do. It is *qua* someone who values certain social goods that I may take pride in certain of my dispositions. It is *qua* someone with certain aspirations that I may derive a sense of self-worth from certain of my skills. It is true that if we are asked why we take pride in certain facts about ourselves, our responses may eventually terminate in a 'That's just the way I am.' But by this is not meant that the state in question is deemed estimable just by virtue of its being one that pertains to me. It is rather to say that the state in question is one among a number of options all of which are deemed equally worthy of esteem. Not only does the infinite regress argument fail to establish foundationalism about egoistic concern; examination of the argument's underlying assumption suggests that the position may be incoherent.

Another defense of foundationalism in support of the Extreme Claim

A slightly different argument for the Extreme Claim might be constructed on the basis of some remarks of Brennan's. He holds that our ordinary attitude toward persons vacillates between a 'type' theory and a 'token' theory of persons (1988: 324ff.). On the first view, what is of value about a person is multiply instantiable. A person's characteristic smile, for instance, might be produced by any of a number of persons with suitably similar bodies and behavioral repertoires. The second view, while not denying that distinct persons might have similar smiles, puts great emphasis on the ultimate uniqueness of a particular person's smile, for instance by pointing out that it is the manifestation of a behavioral repertoire associated with *this very* body. What he sets out to show is that what we want when we wish to survive is that we be the cause of those future states that we value, which is incompatible with the first, 'type' theory of persons. He presents two cases, the first being that of the terminally ill Beatrice and her adventitious replica, someone in a distant galaxy who is, entirely fortuitously, psychologically continuous with Beatrice as she now awaits her imminent death. The second is the case of Jones and the experience enhancer, a device that produces apparent memories of experiences that the subject has not in fact had. It so happens that when I use the experience enhancer and thereby come to seem to remember a hang-gliding adventure, my apparent memories are, quite coincidentally, qualitatively identical with Jones' veridical memories of his hang-gliding adventure over Senegal, even though Jones' experience played no role in the programming of the experience enhancer. Brennan says that according to the 'type' theorist, Beatrice should be consoled by the existence of her adventitious replica, and Jones should agree that were he to die, some of what matters in survival – that there be apparent experience-memories of his adventures – would be preserved. For the 'type' theorist presumably holds that what matters to me in survival is that certain interests be pursued, certain experiences be remembered from the inside, etc. But then it should be immaterial to me whether or not I play some causal role in bringing it about that these interests be pursued, or these experiences seem to be remembered. In this case, to be consoled at my death I would not even need assurance that my children, friends, and students will carry on my projects, etc. after I die. (Brennan thinks we do take some small consolation in these things.) The mere knowledge that some stranger somewhere has relevantly similar psychological states should suffice. Brennan thinks this is clearly mistaken: 'For the very severing of the causal connection severs the link that is crucial in considering *my* future survival' (1988: 324). I can think of myself as to some small extent surviving in my children, friends and students precisely because of the causal role I see myself as having played in those of their future states the anticipation of which consoles me.

What holds for interest in one's survival should presumably also hold for egoistic concern. That some future person has a nature I now approve of – doing political work I hold important, intending to write a book I wish to write – does not suffice to inspire special egoistic concern. For me to be especially concerned for their welfare, I must be able to feel that I am the cause of their having those properties. Otherwise, while I might feel a warm regard for them, I will not anticipate with dread some future suffering I foresee for them. Just as Beatrice is not consoled by the fact that after she dies someone in a distant galaxy will go on living a life very much like hers, so I do not feel special concern over the well-being of some unconnected stranger who happens to share many of my projects and ambitions.

So far, the argument has just been that a 'type' theorist is unable to account for the role of causal connection in our interest in survival and our egoistic concern. But is the Reductionist necessarily a 'type' theorist? Reductionism does open up the possibility of fission. And the psychological approach to personal identity does make it appear as if what is of value about a person is multiply instantiable. A Reductionist might nonetheless seek to explain why causal connection is important to survival and egoistic concern. The strategy of the argument will be to show that in doing so the Reductionist must presuppose foundationalism about egoistic concern, from which the Extreme Claim follows.

The Reductionist might claim that egoistic concern for the welfare of a person other than the present me requires an act of sympathetic identification whereby I imaginatively project myself into the life of that person. And causal connection helps lay down a path whereby I can see myself becoming them. What inspires egoistic concern for some person, in other words, is not so much what they are like as just that they be causally connected in such a way as to make it possible for me to see myself as being them. Causal connection would thus function as the Reductionist's *ersatz* enduring self, helping us project our present self-regard into the future. But then what about this end of the causal connection, the present me? Having egoistic concern for a person involves, among other things, placing special value on that person's properties: it is part of having prudential concern for my future that I want my future projects to go well, I bestow blanket approval on my future values and traits, etc. If I need to be able to imagine myself being the future person who has those properties in order for them to especially matter to me, what does this say about my special concern for my current properties? What it seems to mean is that I especially value them precisely because I see them too as *mine*. But Reductionism denies the existence of a self, and of any further fact through relation to which my properties could all be said to be *mine*. Instead it reduces this *me* to just those properties for the value of which to me we seek an explanation. And here the Reductionist cannot use causal connection as a surrogate self to explain why these properties especially matter to me. For here the question is not how I project myself into the properties of some future person; it is rather how I come to identify with my present properties in the first place. All that seems to be available at this point is just the fact that these properties are *mine*, that is, pertain to my self, a fact the Reductionist dismisses as trivial. And egoistic concern about one's present requires that one place special value on one's present properties. Hence Reductionism cannot explain egoistic concern about one's present. But egoistic concern about one's future requires egoistic concern about one's present, for prudential regard is a projection of current self-regard. Therefore because Reductionism cannot explain current self-regard, if Reductionism is true we can have no reason for egoistic concern about our own future.

This objection convicts the Reductionist of illicitly presupposing foundationalism about egoistic concern by getting the Reductionist to explain the importance that causal connection has for egoistic concern in a particular way: as what is required for identification with and appropriation of future states. This makes it appear as if the Reductionist thinks identification with and appropriation of one's present properties are unproblematic. A Reductionist reply to this objection will require some other explanation of the importance of causal connection. The strategy to be used here is the Consequentialist one discussed earlier. Identification with and appropriation of the states – past, present and future – in a causal series is justified on the grounds that this better promotes maximization of overall welfare than the available alternatives. Present properties do not have a privileged status in this account. I identify with and care about my future states because my having learned to do so better insures that there will be fewer pains among them. I identify with my present preferences and projects because these should be seen as resulting from a process of self-revision that likewise better promotes maximization. I identify with my past states because doing so facilitates appropriation of my present properties, which is necessary if self-revision is to be ongoing. It is adoption of the personhood stance as a whole – coming to treat a causal series as a unified system of identification and appropriation – that is justified. This justification is impersonal: pain is bad, and adoption of this stance helps minimize pain. There is no one point within the system through which all justification flows. The causal connection between present properties and future states is just one feature of the system. It is by virtue of many such features that the system promotes maximization.

A brief digression is now in order concerning the Moderate Claim, the claim that if Reductionism is true, then causal connectedness and continuity give some reason for egoistic concern, but (1) such concern allows of diminished degrees as the degree of connectedness decreases, and (2) such concern is not different in kind from concern for others. I claimed above that a Reductionist should hold such a view. It might be wondered what justifies the clause concerning diminished degrees of egoistic concern. Indeed it might seem as if only foundationalism about egoistic concern could justify this part of the claim. The justification would be that egoistic concern requires that one be able to approve of the character and the projects of its object, and only a high degree of connectedness can guarantee that some future part of this causal series will possess the sort of character and projects that I would now approve of. More distant and less connected portions are more likely to appear alien and less deserving of my special concern. And since 'ought' implies 'can', I cannot be said to be rationally obligated to have special concern for future parts of the series with little or no connectedness to the present part.[18]

There is, however, a different way for the Reductionist to justify the diminished degrees clause, one that does not invoke foundationalism. For systems with the capacities of self-scrutiny, self-control and self-revision, the strategy of doing what now seems best tends to promote welfare. But this tendency is enhanced when the strategy is amended to recommend doing what is likely to seem best both to present and to future portions of the series. One should, that is, take into account not only the interests one now has, but also the interests one is likely to have in the future. Now for highly connected future portions of the causal series, adopting this strategy does not involve any insuperable difficulties. In particular, any such portion is likely to have a character, values and projects like those of the present portion, and consequently be inclined to promote many of those things that now seem best. While acts stemming from my present aims may require modification when I take into account interests and projects I am likely to have in the future, the fact that those future interests and projects are seen to grow out of values I currently hold makes calculating and implementing the requisite modifications a manageable task. So egoistic concern

---

[18] Since Moderates believe continuity also confers some reason for egoistic concern, such concern will still be rationally justified even toward the more remote stretches of the causal series. But as clause (2) suggests, such concern will be more like the concern for the welfare of others that morality requires. For passages that suggest the foundationalist justification of clause (1), see Parfit (1984: 301, 319).

toward highly connected portions is part of a rational strategy. But with more remote stretches of the series, where there is continuity but little connectedness, things are different. The fact that the system undergoes self-revision opens up the possibility that for such portions of the series, little of what now seems best will any longer seem best. And since the system is self-revising, this in turn means that what now seems best may not in fact be best. But to seek now to determine what will then seem best is to induce a Tristram Shandy-like paralysis of infinitely spiraling attempts at self-prediction.[19] The reasonable strategy would then be to base decisions about what to do on what now seems best, tempered by consideration of interests and projects that highly connected portions of the series can be expected to have, plus consideration of interests that any sentient system will have (such as an interest in avoiding pain). This is just the Moderate policy of having egoistic concern for the continuity-related series, but with a discount rate for diminished degrees of connectedness. The Moderate Claim represents a compromise between the utility-promoting tendency of doing what now seems best, and the utility-promoting tendency of periodically subjecting to revision one's values and commitments.

We have seen that the Reductionist will give a Consequentialist justification of egoistic concern. Becoming a Reductionist means coming to see this strictly Consequentialist justification of egoistic concern. Overall utility is best served by the practice of each causal series coming to adopt an attitude of identification with and appropriation of the states in that series. Brennan is thus wrong to suggest that a Reductionist is unable to account for the indexical element in egoistic concern. I strive especially to avoid future suffering in *this* causal series not because its states are somehow connected to my self, and not merely because I value the type of person likely to be found in this series in the future, but because its states are those the welfare of which present strivings stand the best chance of affecting. One reason Beatrice is not consoled in the knowledge of her adventitious replica is that this replica would be just as she now is no matter how differently Beatrice had conducted her life up to the present. The practice of identifying with and appropriating the states of adventitious replicas could not promote overall welfare. I might be somewhat comforted by the thought that after my premature death an adventitious replica will carry on with my plans and projects, for I value these plans and projects, and am inclined to be favorably disposed toward those who seek to carry them out. But the lack of causal connection means that the Consequentialist justification for egoistic concern will not extend to the adventitious replica.

The Reductionist holds that the practice of thinking of ourselves as enduring persons about whose states one should have prudential concern can be expected to have significant utility. Suppose that I, realizing that the action I now contemplate will result in future pain for me, am deterred through anticipating that I shall experience pain. Now there is no further fact that makes it the case that the person who will feel that pain will be me; this fact just consists in the obtaining of certain causal relations between certain purely impersonal present and future entities and events. I do nonetheless have a special reason for refraining from the action, namely the fact that

---

[19]   See Dennett (1985: 111–13) for a useful discussion of the hazards of self-prediction.

this is (typically) the best way to insure that that future pain does not occur. Because pain is bad, we all have a reason to try to prevent its occurrence. And in general I am better positioned than anyone else to prevent my own future pains. Existential dread turns out to be unjustifiable, but a moderate degree of concern over one's anticipated future pain does have considerable utility.[20]

While egoistic concern survives under Reductionism, it does not survive completely unaltered. For my concern over my own future well-being no longer seems different in kind from my concern over the well-being of others (especially those others with whom I have formed special attachments). The aim of such concern is always just to promote the good in those lives whose future we can affect. That some project is *my* project does not give me an additional reason to promote it, or to promote the well-being of some future person who will be in a position to further it. Any interest I have in this project or derivatively in its agent must ultimately stem from the value of the project itself. Whatever added interest derives from my sympathetic identification with that future person is purely instrumental in nature. Ultimately that person is not me – for ultimately no one is me. The egocentric 'I' has been replaced by the indexical '*this* (causal series)'. There is no entity the existence of which confers special value on the events making up the series.

This also means that egoistic concern loses the element of attachment or clinging that, on the Buddhist analysis, is the root cause of suffering. And it may explain Parfit's claim that becoming a Reductionist lessens his fear of death. When egoistic concern is supported by covert belief in a self, my death seems to be the erasure of all that gives my life value and significance. By contrast, the moderate form of egoistic concern that survives becoming a Reductionist does not require the prospect of ever-new projects to sustain the illusion of a value-conferring self. I am thus able to face squarely the fact of my own mortality without being plunged into existential despair, that is, without it coming to seem that all prudential concern is pointless. If I know I shall die tomorrow, it would be pointless to prepare a special dessert for my enjoyment next week. But this need not undermine the enjoyment I shall derive from eating it tonight, and thus the reason I have for preparing it this afternoon.

Here we see an instance of the deflationary tendency that reductionisms generally induce: egoistic concern survives, in deflated form, one's coming to accept Reductionism. It remains the case that I have reason to take special responsibility for the welfare of my future self.[n] It is likewise true that I have reason to be especially concerned about the welfare of those others with whom I have intimate bonds. In both cases the reason has to do with my being particularly well situated to affect the welfare of these persons: I know well their needs and proclivities, and my actions will in any event impinge on their welfare. To the extent that cultivating the ability to sympathetically identify with future self or intimate other helps one promote their well-being, the emotions that stem from this ability are likewise justified.[o] But the

---

[20] A similar strategy is suggested by Jackson (1991) in response to the 'nearest and dearest' objection to consequentialism, to the effect that consequentialism counsels that we neglect intimate others whenever by doing so we can bring about greater overall good. He claims that in certain cases 'one ought to be *consequentially motivated* although one should not consciously reason consequentially' (1991: 469). And the greatest overall good turns out to result from a motivational structure that has us forming special attachments of care and concern with intimate others.

instrumentalist rationale that is at work here serves as a reminder that one should also strive to extend sympathetic identification to the stranger.[P] Future self and intimate other have a special claim on my efforts only because of my location, and not by virtue of some special connection to the elusive *me*. When I can promote the welfare of strangers without markedly diminishing my contribution to the well-being of future self and intimate other, I should do so. Some will wonder, though, whether one could maintain the appropriate person-regarding attitudes, even in their mitigated form, if one came to believe that Reductionism is true. It is out of such misgivings that the dual-aspect view grows, and we turn now to objections to Reductionism grounded in that view.

An objection based on a Kantian dual-aspect view

Korsgaard's (1989) criticism of Parfit's Reductionism does not include endorsement of the Extreme Claim. Instead she champions a kind of Kantian dual-aspect theory, and asserts that by illegitimately privileging one of the two stances we may take toward ourselves, Reductionism undermines the sense of agency necessary for action, leading to what we might call a Micawberite outlook on our future – the spectatorial attitude of waiting to see 'what turns up'. Now the claim that Reductionism leads to Micawberism is different from the Extreme Claim. But an investigation into Micawberism and its roots may also lead us to the source of some of the intuitions behind the Extreme Claim, so looking more closely at this critique of Reductionism may help clear up any remaining questions on that score.

Korsgaard utilizes the Kantian notion of two distinct standpoints or perspectives: the standpoint of theoretical reason, from which we seek to explain and predict the behavior of natural phenomena (including ourselves); and the standpoint of practical reason, the perspective from which we consider what we ought to do. Each perspective is, she claims, equally legitimate and equally necessary, so that neither may be subsumed by the other. The Reductionist account of persons may well be perfectly sound metaphysics, and thus quite adequately justified from the standpoint of theoretical reason. Difficulties arise, however, when normative consequences are claimed for it, since this involves encroachment on the terrain of practical reason. The Reductionist account of persons is incompatible with the view of ourselves she claims we necessarily adopt when we take on the perspective of practical reason. From this latter 'authorial' perspective, 'We think of living our lives, and even of having our experiences, as something that we *do*' (1989: 121), and not merely as events that befall us, as she takes Reductionism to imply.

The Reductionist might claim that it is a mere conventional truth that we accept when we see ourselves authorially, as agents distinct from our acts, and that the utility of this conventional truth is explicable in the completely impersonal terms of ultimate truth.[21] But Korsgaard would reply that to see our sense of our own agency as just the result of linguistic convenience would be to undermine our sense of ourselves as the

---

[21] Korsgaard herself discusses (1989: 109–14) some of the key factors that would go into a Reductionist account of our sense of unified agency, such as the constraints imposed on action by the fact that I have but one body the parts of which require careful coordination.

authors of our life narratives. For the force of this Reductionist 'mere conventional truth' is to suggest that certain elements of our sense of agency may lack the requisite metaphysical grounding and rest solely on the illusion of a further fact, an illusion that cannot be sustained in the light of Reductionist truths. Among the threatened elements are, she believes: my tendency to see myself as standing above my desires and choosing among them on the basis of reasons I have for acting (1989: 111); my ability to endorse and identify with certain of my desires and not with others (121); and my ability to see myself as 'a law to myself' (111). To lose these perspectives on our agency is, Korsgaard suggests, to lose elements necessary to genuinely being an agent and not just a conduit of causation. Because of Reductionism's imperialist tendencies – because it seeks to subsume the standpoint of practical reason – she claims it leads to the tendency to see my life, including my actions, as no more than a succession of experiences. Any concern I might then exhibit toward my future could only take the Micawberite form of anxiety about 'what will turn up'. The self-concept implicit in our stance of active engagement would then prove genuinely incompatible with the Reductionist vision of persons. Korsgaard claims that this incompatibility can only be resolved by isolating each conception within its own separate, irreducible sphere.

Central to this argument is the claim that a 'thick' Kantian sense of agency, one that involves seeing ourselves as standing over and above our desires and other psychological states, is necessary for purposeful action. What reason is there to believe this? At several points, as when she quotes Mill's complaint about the many who blindly follow custom (1989: 122), Korsgaard comes close to suggesting it is not at all necessary, but rather just an ideal that Kantians believe we should aspire to. In the passage she quotes, Mill is complaining that the majority of his contemporaries do not actively construct their own sense of agency through identification with various projects and life-plans, through second-order desires to have certain first-order desires and not others. Yet Mill is not claiming that these are un-persons lacking in any sense of purposeful agency; otherwise his complaint (which was addressed to them) would be pointless. So why is this thick sense of agency necessary, and not just a piece of bourgeois self-advertisement?

Korsgaard comes closest to giving an argument for this claim when she states, '[I]t is only from the practical point of view that actions and choices can be distinguished from mere "behavior" determined by biological and psychological laws' (1989: 120). Both here and in an earlier footnote (111, n.21) she explicitly connects this claim with the problem of free will. This suggests that the argument for the necessity of a thick sense of agency may be this: in order to see ourselves as purposeful agents, we must be prepared to acknowledge responsible authorship of our actions; this in turn requires that we see them as stemming from a character that we have actively shaped. But this we cannot do unless we view ourselves as possessing a self that transcends any of our particular desires, values, projects and life-plans, a self that is so positioned as to be able to endorse any or all of our pro-attitudes. Hence, the argument concludes, a sense of purposeful agency requires belief in just the sort of conception of ourselves that Reductionism denies. Now I should be reluctant to claim that this is precisely the argument Korsgaard had in mind. Galen Strawson (1986) does make just this type of argument, however, and in a way that neatly dovetails with all that Korsgaard says on the subject.

Strawson's overall task is to show both that believing one is free is a necessary condition of being free, and that while we do believe ourselves to be free, this belief involves a self-conception that is incompatible with what we know to be true of ourselves. While Strawson does not explicitly endorse a Kantian 'dual aspect' resolution of the resulting tension, he seems to believe we may continue to act on the basis of a self-concept we know to be metaphysically unacceptable. Strawson sees himself not as laying out the metaphysical conditions for the possibility of freedom, but rather as exploring the phenomenology of our commitments when we think of ourselves as free and act on that basis. From these explorations there emerges an argument for the claim that purposeful action requires the thick sense of agency that is allegedly incompatible with Reductionism. Moreover, the same argument may be used to support the Extreme Claim, namely by establishing foundationalism about egoistic concern.

According to Strawson, the incompatibility between our conception of ourselves as free, and our knowledge about the facts concerning ourselves, comes about precisely because the freedom we attribute to ourselves is of the responsibility-entailing sort that requires us to acknowledge full authorship of our actions. Hence in order for any action of mine to be free, I must be truly responsible for those of my beliefs, desires, dispositions, policies, decision-making procedures and the like that resulted in my choosing to perform the action. But since each of these was ultimately determined by factors (of either heredity or the environment) that were set before I was born and over which I therefore had no control, I cannot be said to be truly responsible for an action just in virtue of the fact that it flows from my present nature. Still, we do think of ourselves as free in the sense of being truly responsible for our actions. We therefore conceive of ourselves as having a self that (1) is single *qua* mental, (2) transcends all particular mental contents, but (3) nonetheless has content or character in the form of particular plans, desires, intentions and the like.[22]

Strawson argues that to think of itself as free, a being must be fully self-conscious in the sense of being able to think of its mental states (such as its beliefs and desires) as all its own. This requires that it think of itself as single just *qua* mental – as the subject that has various mental states, including the thought of itself as that which has these states. This in turn means that it must think of itself as transcending any particular mental state, and thus as transcending the content of any particular mental state. For suppose I were to think of the subject of my mental states as some one particular mental state, say the one that is currently occurring. Since this state is transitory, it cannot have been the subject of my prior mental states. Suppose I then think that the true subject is not this particular mental state, but instead the series of mental states as a whole. But a series composed of discrete mental states is not the sort of thing that could be said to be aware of the particular mental state that is currently occurring. I must think of the self as transcending all my mental states, and thus as transcending their contents as well. In particular, Strawson claims, I must think of my self as transcending any value or pro-attitude that happens to be contained within any of my mental states. I must nonetheless think of the self as possessing content, for it is

---

[22] This is at odds in various respects with the 'Pearl' view that Strawson (1997: 424) endorses. For instance, this attributes diachronic identity and at least a minimal degree of agency to the self, properties that the Pearl view denies the self has.

to serve as the author of those of my actions for which I am truly responsible, and this requires that it have some normative character on the basis of which it chooses actions. A bare subject of consciousness is not the sort of thing that would do as the core of my free, responsible agency. Still, each of the particular contents of my character seems thoroughly contingent: determined by my heredity and environment, and revisable in the light of further experience. Thus those normative components of my character that determine and confer value on my choices can do so only insofar as they pertain to my self. Since Reductionism denies the existence of a transcendent self of this nature, Strawson concludes that it undermines one's sense of oneself 'as a truly self-determining planner and performer of action' (1986: 119).[23] This argument thus supports Korsgaard's claim that Reductionism threatens our ability to see ourselves as any more than mere passive observers of our life-narratives.

But the argument does more: it also supports foundationalism about egoistic concern, which emerges from the tension between the demand that the self transcend all particular mental contents, and the requirement that the self be contentful. Coming to believe that Reductionism is true of oneself would mean, according to foundationalism, the loss of that which confers special value on the states of my future self. Strawson describes well the thought process that may occur concerning those of one's pro-attitudes and aspects of one's character that one endorses: 'if *per impossible* I were to be able to choose my character, then these are the features I would choose' (1986: 112). He then adds in a footnote, 'It is hardly surprising that the subjunctive conditional as it were confirms the central, acceptable *status quo*; for the "I" that features in the conditional is in a sense actually constituted, as something with pro-attitudes that imagines choosing its pro-attitudes, by the very pro-attitudes that it imagines choosing' (112, n.26). Recognizing the inherent instability of this subjunctive conditional, we are then led to resolve the conflict by supposing that it is just the fact that the self possesses this character and these pro-attitudes that confers validity on them. Thus a bare, transcendent self comes to seem the fount of a special sort of value, the sort that gives rise to egoistic concern. It now appears as if I have special concern for myself not because I have certain properties that make me worthy of special esteem; rather, my properties, and derivatively what is endorsed by these properties, are deserving of special concern just because these properties are *mine*.

How might the Reductionist respond? Strawson's argument contains the central claim that genuine freedom requires self-determination, that my character be subject to self-revision. The Reductionist might be tempted to retreat to a weaker conception of freedom, one according to which it is enough that the action 'come from within' the agent, regardless of how the agent came to have the particular beliefs, desires, dispositions, etc. from which the action flowed. But this temptation should be resisted, since we do expect agents to take responsibility not just for their actions but also for their own character. So my miserable childhood resulted in a predisposition to

---

[23]   Fully conforming onself to the lessons of Reductionism would also, according to Strawson, mean the loss of all desires (1986: 119), and the loss of full self-consciousness (1986: 155, n.19), resulting in a state that might be attainable by humans but that is nonetheless inhuman and unimaginable to us (1986: 120). Strawson repeats (1986: 118) the common error of supposing that Buddhist enlightenment means the extirpation of all desires, and not merely of all self-involving desires.

behavior that causes trouble for myself and others? Others tell me to stop kvetching. I agree, and set about trying to reform and improve my character. Being responsible for my actions means being responsible for being the sort of person who would perform those sorts of actions. Any account of freedom that omits this is justly criticized as too weak.

What does require scrutiny, though, is the step that leads from the stronger notion of a responsibility-entailing freedom that requires self-determination, to the notion of the agent-self as transcendent yet contentful. For while self-determination does require an 'I' with content, it is not clear that it requires belief in a transcendent self. If I am to be capable of revising my own character, then I require a stock of beliefs and desires on the basis of which I may critically evaluate and seek to reform various of my dispositions and tendencies. But if this is truly self-revision, then that stock of beliefs and desires must itself form part of my character, hence be among those standing dispositions and tendencies I am called upon to monitor. It may now seem as if, were they to constitute a part of the 'I' that performs self-revision, then the anti-reflexivity principle would be violated. But what this picture omits is the possibility that a given stock of beliefs and desires might serve as basis for a particular bout of self-criticism, yet some among these stand under subsequent scrutiny on the basis of a distinct (though perhaps overlapping) stock of beliefs and desires. This is the 'shifting coalitions' strategy of self-revision that was discussed above. On one occasion my anal-compulsive disposition might lead to extirpation of the desire to smoke. Yet subsequently a wish to be more accommodating to others might lead to an effort to curb my anality. At one time the anal disposition belongs to the coalition making up the 'executive', later it falls out of this shifting coalition. It is hypostatization that induces the illusion of a constant subject over and above the shifting content. Just as universal fallibilism does not require that we take up a God's-eye point of view, so the demand for self-revision does not require a transcendent self.

I suggest that this is the (implicit) thought process behind the intuition that Reductionism leads to Extremism. Because Reductionism denies the existence of a transcendent self, reducing the person to a series of impersonal entities and events, it appears to remove that which gives special status to my life-plans and projects, my character and values, the special status conveyed by the table-pounding 'because they're *mine*'. We then fail to see how, in the absence of what is thought to confer such special status, there could be reason for special concern over the fate of the future person who will reap the results of my character and values, plans and projects. From this perspective the Moderate Claim – that connectedness gives some reason for special concern – seems to lack appropriate anchoring. So the Reductionist can counteract these intuitions by showing how this perspective rests on a mistake, how self-monitoring and self-revision can be accomplished by a causal series of impersonal entities and events.

The notion that Reductionism leads to Micawberism has slightly different roots. This stems, I would suggest, from the conviction that without the sense of a transcendent, contentful self, one cannot see oneself as an autonomous agent, seeing oneself instead as a mere conduit of causation. That is, it stems from the denial that free responsible agents could believe themselves to be constituted by shifting coalitions of volitions – that the Reductionist account of persons could not be transparent. The Reductionist reply to this charge would thus be that the sense of self induced by hypostatization is not necessary in order for agents to carry out the sort of self-monitoring and self-revision required for full responsibility. In this respect the Reductionist will accuse the critic of underestimating the capacities of the sophisticated systems we are – of denying that we might prove capable of ironic engagement. We are, after all, able to cultivate our own happiness out of a desire to make those around us happy by appearing to be happy ourselves. Why should knowing that the participant attitude has purely impersonal grounding undermine our ability to adopt it? For consider our situation as epistemic agents. Scrutiny of the history of science tells us that much of what we now accept as established scientific theory will some day be considered false. Of course we don't yet know which of our theories will be rejected, but we can say with some degree of assurance that many will. Yet recognition of this fact has not brought about the utter paralysis of all scientific inquiry. Instead we proceed to investigate on the basis of theories that now seem well attested – knowing that our investigations will eventually undermine some of those theories. Such a procedure is not irrational. We know we cannot proceed without accepting some theory or other. Our history tells us that membership in the body of accepted theories changes over time. But it also tells us that such change comes about only when we proceed on the basis of those theories that seem well attested. And it tells us that proceeding in this way has led to marked improvements in our lives. Universal fallibilism does not induce the paralysis of skepticism. It just means keeping an open mind about our epistemic commitments – provisionally accepting them for purposes of inquiry, but periodically reviewing them for possible revision. The Reductionist would recommend that in our capacity as responsible agents, we should take the same stance toward our value commitments.

Another attempt at a Kantian objection

'Has Kant Refuted Parfit?' is Blackburn's (1997) appropriately titled and carefully nuanced exploration of two Kantian approaches to rejecting Reductionism. The first involves the dual-aspect view that we have just been investigating, while the second makes use of themes from the Transcendental Deduction in order to call into question the atomistic conception of psychological states that Parfit's approach seems to require. Blackburn acknowledges that the first strategy appears unpromising:

> It seems to lead, in Kant's thought, to a hopelessly transcendental self: a thing whose judging operations are responsible for time itself, and whose noumenal freedom is compatible with the sway of determinism over the entire world that we know. If this is the end-product, then it naturally seems better to avoid such strands in Kant, and retreat to the safer ground of connecting empirical self-consciousness with the exercise of other spatial capacities. [1997: 191]

And as we have just seen, efforts like Galen Strawson's to avoid Kant's metaphysical excesses while preserving something of the dual-aspect approach are readily answered by the Reductionist: the priority of a unified subject that is characteristic of the agent perspective can be labeled as no more than a sort of necessary illusion required for effective welfare-maximizing agency.

Still, Blackburn thinks there is something to the first approach. Not so the second. The strategy there is to try to show that experience, understood as consciousness of enduring objects, presupposes synthesis by an enduring subject, hence that the subject cannot be reductively analyzed into discrete experiences on pain of circularity. The basic point is the one Kant puts in terms of the requirement that all perceptions be accompanible by 'I think' if they are to be understood as experiences of an objective order. The idea is that successively given perceptions cannot be understood as experiences of one object rather than distinct but similar objects unless the perceptions can themselves be understood as each representing a point of view from some determinate location in the world, so that successive perceptions may be seen as tracing an experiential route through the world. So, the claim is, successive perceptions must be understood as all given to a single subject with determinate spatial location at each moment and whose location at successive moments is governed by the speed limit applicable to the relevant sort of body. The difficulty Blackburn sees in this approach is that it yields only an impoverished notion of an enduring subject, something a Reductionist can easily accommodate. For all that this seems to require is that successive perceptions be understood as deriving from faculties located on a continuous space-time path, perhaps the route of a single body, but also possibly the route of a succession of bodies, as in a relay race. Any given act of synthesis under a concept must, it is true, bring several distinct perceptions together. But even here the ability to think of them as all given to the same subject represents just one rather efficient way of meeting the demand that they be seen as deriving from determinate locations along a single experiential route. There may be other ways of meeting this demand. And even if there weren't, this looks like just the sort of merely pragmatic and thus superficial constraint that the Reductionist is happy to exploit. If a challenge to the ID thesis is to be mounted on the basis of Kant's thoughts concerning the unity of the subject, we will need to look elsewhere.[24]

So Blackburn takes us back to the terrain covered by Korsgaard and Galen Strawson. But he distances himself from dual-aspect theorists like Korsgaard, who he thinks concede too much to the 'sideways-on' perspective of theoretical reason, the perspective from which ontological questions are raised and answered. Korsgaard (1986: 120–21), for instance, appears quite happy to concede that Reductionism is justified from that perspective, and is merely inadequate to the demands of the separate but equal perspective of practical reason. The difficulty Blackburn sees with this is perhaps foreshadowed in Korsgaard's calling the unity of the subject a 'practical necessity', a 'pragmatic unity'. To put things this way is, Blackburn suggests, to make the unity of the subject appear to be no more than a kind of necessary illusion generated by the demands of action. To think of it this way is, of course, to adopt the perspective of theoretical reason. But it is difficult to resist such a move, to avoid privileging that perspective and to preserve a genuinely autonomous

---

[24] Cassam (1989) is more sanguine about this argument. He does say at one point that 'the notion of an experiential route through the world will simply provide [the Reductionist] with further ammunition, insofar as this notion is an abstraction from the full-fledged notion of a subject of experience' (1989: 88). But he goes on to argue that the notion of an experiential route will indeed require the full-fledged notion. The 'experiential-route' reading of the argument of the Transcendental Deduction derives from Peter Strawson (1966).

sphere of practical reason. As a corrective, Blackburn suggests that we take seriously Kant's point that thinking and judging are likewise actions. So the deliverances of theoretical reasoning are built on a foundation that they are ill-equipped to adequately represent. While Blackburn does not himself claim that the perspective of theoretical reason should consequently be seen as subordinate to that of practical reason, it is not clear that he would disagree with such a reversal of our rankings.

Trying to understand the person from the sideways-on perspective leads, according to Blackburn, to a distorting objectification of the self. And this in turn renders the formal unity of the active subject invisible. When we try to theorize our agency as a purely empirical phenomenon, we approach it with the question of prediction in mind: what will happen? This quickly leads to the dissolution of the subject into a variety of faculties and mediating causal connections. My now deciding whether to promote some interest I will only have in the future becomes a matter of a set of present dispositions bringing about a pro-attitude toward some causally connected successor state based on its supposed consonance (because of the causal connections) with currently held values. Once this account has been purged of its implicit (and illegitimate) homuncularism, we can see that the deliberative question (What should I do?) has been replaced by the very different question of prediction. And when we try to preserve some sense of deliberative agency in this picture, those values on the basis of which we choose end up being entered twice: once on the side of the deliberative agent, once on the side of the objects being deliberated about.

The unity of the subject revealed through agency is a purely formal unity that cannot be reduced to relations of resemblance or causation between person-constituents or person-stages. Blackburn brings this out through considering what it is to imagine oneself in some alien circumstance. In doing this it is not as if we carefully construct an appropriately resembling character, or the intervening links that explain the very different character. We simply identify with and appropriate the inner states of the protagonist. The 'I' of the imagined scene is no more than its invisible horizon. Likewise when we ask how it would be for me, it is not as if we introduce some set of tastes and preferences and then work out how a character so disposed would respond. The tastes and preferences are what I view the imagined scene through in answering this question; this is just what it means to work out how it would be for *me*.

In this connection, Blackburn also cites approvingly Williams' diagnosis of the belief in a Cartesian Ego as stemming from a form of hypostatization. Since the invisible horizon is present no matter what the circumstances of the imagined situation, we may be inclined to supply some one transcendent entity that is there quite independently of any contingencies of one's existence. When this train of thought is revealed for the mistake that it is, 'all is saved': the unity of the subject remains to be explained after the metaphysical excesses of the noumenal self are stripped away. Blackburn can agree with the Reductionist in rejecting Galen Strawson's analysis (which claimed that we require the notion of a transcendent self), yet still insist that there is a purely formal unity of the subject that Reductionism is incapable of accounting for. Particularly persuasive is his example of imagining one's own funeral. One can take up the stance of the spectator, observing the corpse and the reactions of the mourners; or one can imagine lying lifeless and insensate in the midst of the proceedings. But one cannot do both simultaneously; one cannot make oneself a character in the narrative that one imagines. To imagine a situation just is to take up the location specified by the scene's horizon; the unity of the subject is exhausted in this taking up.

Blackburn uses this to cast doubt on the coherence of a Reductionism that allows the possibility of fission. Rovane (1990) sought to defend Parfit's claim that in fission there is what matters in survival without personal identity. She claimed that fission could yield at least most of what matters in survival provided that persons undergoing fission knew this in advance and were thus able to form the appropriately adjusted first-person attitudes. Indeed I might then be able to realize two incompatible aspirations – say, writing my book, and taking up New Zealand sheep farming – by forming the quasi-intention that each fission product carry out just one. In this way I might achieve something that is in some respects better than ordinary survival. Blackburn responds that precisely because I cannot simultaneously hold together under one unified subject the states of both fission products, my attitude toward at least one can be no better than the warm regard I might hold toward the child or the student who advances a project I hold dear. I cannot anticipate at once both staring at the computer screen searching for the right phrasing, and attentively grooming my border collies. It will be one way or the other for me, and I must choose. And any choice of one fission product over the other must be arbitrary. So even if it should turn out that each will do their assigned task, this can only serve as some small consolation to me. Fission cannot give me any of what I want most in survival; at best it can give only the consolation that comes from knowing that others (perhaps closely connected others) will take up one's projects. Reductionists are blind to this truth because they mistake psychological connectedness for the formal unity of the subject. This is what comes of granting pride of place to the perspective of theoretical reason.

The Reductionist response to this will proceed in two stages. The first stage begins with the suggestion that the invisibility and unity of the subject of agency in acts of future-directed first-person imagining and intending have more to do with contingencies surrounding how we ordinarily learn to identify with and appropriate earlier and later states, than it does with any deep necessities about us as agents. In discussions of these matters, it is often forgotten that these are skills that we once had to master. The child does not generally heed the first parental 'You'll be sorry', and not because the prediction concerning future negative consequences is disbelieved. And when the predicted consequences do befall the child, its first response is typically one of outrage that the parent would allow such a thing to happen. The child must learn to identify with and appropriate future states in the series – developing the skills of anticipation, first-person imagination, and deliberation – and to identify with and appropriate past stages in the series – learning to take responsibility for earlier choices. These are hard lessons to learn, but because they are hard, and because they come early, their learning runs deep. Now because persons do not ordinarily undergo fission, when learning the skill of deliberating about the future we learn that only one of the imagined resultant states can be actualized (namely the one that occurs along the path of maximal causal connectedness from the present decision node). This fact, and the attendant causal regularities on which our present personhood conventions are based, are all relied upon in our mastery of this and related skills. It is for this reason that the effort to form appropriate quasi-intentions toward the products of fission seems so alien. In a world in which fission was known to occur regularly and in predictable ways, other lessons would doubtless be learned. We would then need to take into account the fact that two distinct states may be actualized. And this in turn would introduce the necessity of keeping track of the distinct future selves about whose fortunes one is deliberating, and of working out the intervening path through which the causal series flows. Invisibility and formal unity of the subject would go by the board. It does not follow that one could not learn to genuinely identify with and appropriate the states of both products of one's fission.

It might be objected that any particular act of future-directed first-person imagination must still conform to the demand for formal unity of the subject, the demand that is expressed in the Kantian doctrine of the transcendental unity of apperception. In deliberating about whether to emigrate to New Zealand, I must envision the circumstance of attentively grooming border collies as an experience had by me, the deliberator. And of course it is impossible to triangulate by so unifying this with the simultaneous experience of staring at the computer screen. But a Reductionist could agree that when deliberating about a future that contains a fission, one should not try to simultaneously imagine in the first-person way how it will be in both branches. For, the Reductionist will claim, the transcendental unity of apperception represents a strictly pragmatic constraint on systems of self-control and self-revision: that within such a system the capacity for the flow of information about the system be maximized. Given what was said above concerning the characteristics of such systems, the importance of maximizing information-sharing should be clear. What stands in the way of triangulating is the fact that system-internal information does not flow freely between the two fission products. It does, though, flow up and down each of the branching causal paths. I can imagine how it will be in the one, and then in the other. What keeps me from envisioning both simultaneously in the first-person way is that the two are not in a relation that allows free mutual exchange of information. Since the source of this constraint is strictly pragmatic, this inability to fully unify both does not show that fission must be a personal disaster. One could learn to survive twice over.

So ends the first stage of the Reductionist reply. At this point Blackburn might object that the Reductionist's talk of 'merely pragmatic' constraints is just another expression of the imperialistic tendencies of theoretical reason, something that must be resisted if any place is to be retained for real human agency. The difficulty lies in spelling out how this resistance is to be achieved. The Reductionist has offered an explanation of the phenomena surrounding the unity of the acting subject that is couched in terms of demands on a self-controlling system. No reason has been given to suppose that this explanation is false. If it is true, then these phenomena will turn out to be consistent with the truth of Reductionism, so that the Kantian may not use them to cast doubt on the project. Of course it might be alleged that belief in Reductionism erodes our ability to take up the stance of the agent subject. But this assumes that we are indeed incapable of what I earlier called ironic engagement. And even if this were true, it would only suggest yet again that the stance of the unified active subject is a kind of illusion fostered by practical necessities. So it looks like the only recourse is to subordinate theoretical reason to practical reason: to insist that theoretical understanding is ultimately just a tool of human practice, so that any attempt to use theoretical reason to understand agency must fail. A genuine dual-aspect view being unattainable, we should seek an account in which our best theory of what we should do meshes smoothly with our best theory of what we are – with the former theory being given more weight in cases of conflict between the two.

The second stage of the Reductionist reply will consist in a defense of their privileging of theoretical reason over practical. But this is tantamount to a defense of realism – which is no small task. In matters as large as this, perhaps the best we can do is to make explicit the intuitions that motivate the project, and explore the consequences for overall consistency. We have already encountered a clear instance of Buddhist Reductionism's realist commitments in the motivation behind its mereological reductionism: wholes are thought to be ultimately unreal just because our belief in their existence can be traced to conceptual construction. In the next chapter we shall examine this issue in greater detail, looking at the arguments offered in favor of mereological reductionism as well as its consequences for our final ontology. If the position should turn out to be unsupportable, that might give us some reason to abandon the realist stance underlying Reductionism, and adopt a more pragmatist stance in its place. But the intuitions supporting realism are strong: that something is conceptually constructed strikes most of us as a reason not to include it in our ultimate ontology. So the burden properly rests with the anti-realist: a robustly realist Buddhist Reductionism should be our preferred position until such time as we discover reasons why the overall position is unworkable.

Notes

[a] Following Collins (1982: 187–89) it has become common among Buddhologists to interpret 'neither the same nor different' as involving equivocation on 'same': neither qualitatively identical nor numerically distinct. But unlike English, Sanskrit (or in this case Pāli) does not allow equivocation on 'same'. Instead the expression must be understood as involving denial of both numerical identity and numerical distinctness. Of course the resulting failure of bivalence (the principle that a given proposition must be either true or false) appears paradoxical. But as Dummett (1991) has taught us, the anti-realist trades in bivalence failures. And a reductionism is a kind of local anti-realism.

[b] What Nāgasena actually says here is that all the past and present psychophysical elements are collected together through association with this body. The author of *Milindapañha* thus appears to be presupposing the early Buddhist view that it is one body that exists continuously from birth until death. Classical Abhidharma rejects this view, instead analyzing the enduring body into a causal series of coexisting sets of contiguous parts: this collection of cells going out of existence but giving rise to a successor set, etc. While *Milindapañha* is not an Abhidharma text, it does use some key elements of Abhidharma analysis. It is thus possible that by 'this body' the author merely means to indicate a particular causal series of bodily elements.

[c] See, e.g., AKB 2 and Yaśomitra's comments, AKB 12 (Pruden 76), VM 8.

[d] Williams is thus mistaken when he claims (1998: 140) that on the Buddhist Reductionist hypothesis pains do not allow of individuation. This is his third reason for denying that there can be subjectless pains. The first was that on an adverbial analysis of pain statements, pains will necessarily require a subject, while the second was that if pains are to be thought of as events, then since events are changes and changes require subjects, pains will once again require subjects. As Parfit makes clear (1984: 211), a Reductionist will prefer to think of the psychological elements of the reduction as events rather than as states (as an adverbial analysis would have it). But the claim that events are changes in subjects is controversial: what is the subject of the event of the early frost?

[e] At VM XVII.172, Buddhaghosha gives an interesting response to the objection that pleasure and pain require an experiencer. He points out that the syntax of the sentence 'The tree bears fruit' would seem to

suggest the existence both of the fruit and of a separate bearer, the tree. Yet 'tree' is a convenient designator for a causal series of impermanent tree-parts: roots, branches, twigs, leaves, flowers, and fruit. So the appearance of a separate bearer is just a linguistically induced illusion. When we say 'The tree bears fruit', we are simply singling out for special notice one sort of impermanent element from among the many that make up this causal series, and locating it as one constituent of this series. Likewise when we say that a person experiences pleasure, we are simply singling out one among the many impersonal psychophysical elements constituting the causal series conveniently designated a 'person'.

ᶠ See S.II.178ff.: 'All beings are in beginningless rebirth, deluded by ignorance ....'

ᵍ While it has become common to translate *saṃvṛti-satya* as 'conventional truth', still to some Buddhologists it may sound quite un-Buddhist to call our use of the personhood concept a convention, where by 'convention' is meant a social practice that prevails and persists in a society due to some set of contingent social arrangements. This is, however, one consequence of the assimilation of our term 'person' (*sattva*) to such terms as 'army' and 'city', which are clearly of use to us only because of a contingent set of human practices. (See VM Ch.xiv.) Presumably, we would not want to claim that our belief in the existence of chariots and houses (as entities existing separately from their constituent parts) is the direct product of 'beginningless ignorance', that is, that for each of infinitely many past lives we have held these beliefs. Surely the occurrence of such beliefs is the result of our having been socialized into a society that found it useful to employ such convenient designators. And since 'person' is regularly classified along with 'army' and 'chariot' as a convenient designator, the same should hold for our belief in the existence of persons.

Candrakīrti gives an account of the notion of conventional truth that also supports this interpretation: '*Saṃvṛti* means the arising together of things with one another through mutual relations. It has the characteristic of [the relation between] term and referent, knowledge and the known, etc. *Loka-saṃvṛti* means convention according to the world. World-conventional truth is truth ensconcing the world. All without remainder that is the common practice with respect to term and referent, knowledge and the known, etc., just that is said to be world-conventional truth. Nor do these conventional practices arise absolutely' (commenting on MMK 24.8, Pandeya 493) And while Candrakīrti is not himself a Reductionist, it is important to his project that his explication of this concept reflect the understanding of the Buddhist Reductionist.

It is possible to reconcile a conventionalist account of our belief in persons with the claim that it stems from 'beginningless ignorance'. Those wishing to uphold Buddhist orthodoxy on the question of rebirth might say that what gets perpetuated through the rebirth process is not belief in persons *per se*, but rather a propensity to hypostatize such convenient designators as prove useful in a given social setting. Since 'person' will likely prove useful in all possible births (whereas 'chariot' will not), this would explain how a belief acquired through conventional socialization processes could have existed in all prior births. The ignorance that is to be overcome through enlightenment is thus not our belief in the existence of the person, but rather our disposition toward hypostatization with respect to convenient designators.

ʰ A similar dispute between the Buddhist Reductionist and a Nyāya Non-Reductionist is described at AKB 472–73 (Kapstein 1987: 261–63). Of course Vasubandhu does not there invoke the notion of quasi-memory. He simply demonstrates how the fact that we only remember our own past experiences can be accounted for in terms of a set of causal relations among present and past psychophysical elements. In bypassing the notion of quasi-memory, he also succeeds in avoiding a weakness in the quasi-memory approach. While the concept of quasi-memory does not presuppose identity of experiencing and quasi-remembering subject, it does invoke the notion of a subject who has the experience, and of a subject who seems to remember. And it is natural to suppose that such subjects are persons (or person-stages), so that the account is still not completely impersonal. (This may be why Schechtman assumed that the Reductionist must be a punctualist.) Analysis of the unity relation in terms of the concept of quasi-memory can thus only be a first step in providing a fully Reductionist account. Vasubandhu proceeds directly to the attempt to give a subjectless account of such psychological connections as memory, without going through this intermediate step. For a discussion of how a Reductionist might proceed from the intermediate stage to complete the task of giving a thoroughly impersonal account, see Parfit (1984: 225–26).

ⁱ The Buddhist Reductionist will claim that my current body parts are numerically distinct from the ones I had earlier, consisting as they do of new matter. Of course if 'kidney' is a mere convenient designator, then it might be (conventionally) true that I have the same kidney for my entire life. Still, the ultimate body parts, whatever those are, will go out of existence and get replaced over time.

^j Even the Buddhist Reductionist acknowledges this – in spite of belief in rebirth. For the Buddhist, parinirvāṇa represents the permanent cessation of the causal series that is conveniently designated a person. So this event represents what would be called at the level of conventional truth the extinction of the person (their 'last death'). Of course it is virtually taboo in the tradition to refer to parinirvāṇa as the extinction of the person. But this is because that description tends to reinvoke precisely the frustration, alienation and despair that Reductionism is meant to allay.

^k This formulation is based on the Buddhist Reductionist assumption (first introduced and defended by the Sautrāntikas) that time is divisible into atomic moments, and that existing things only exist for a moment and are then replaced by new existents. Thus the members of P_i cease existing at the end of t_i, typically being replaced by new but related entities and events at t_{i+1}. On the alternative assumption that at least some psychophysical elements endure for more than a moment, the threshold level n will have to be adjusted to take into account the degree of overlap among the members of P_i and P_k.

^l Buddhist Reductionists do not claim that diminished degrees of connectedness entail diminished degrees of responsibility, compensation, or justifiable egoistic concern. This, I would suggest, stems from their acceptance of the karma–rebirth ideology. While belief in rebirth is compatible with Reductionism, the karma–rebirth ideological complex as a whole requires a strong form of retributivism that is incompatible with Reductionism. The complex requires retributivism because otherwise it cannot perform its ideological function of justifying a rigidly stratified social order (e.g., a caste system). If the members of such an order cannot be made to feel that each wholly and fully deserves their place in the hierarchy due to their very own deeds in prior lives, then some might be inclined to question their assignment. The ideological complex also serves to redirect dissatisfaction with one's present lot toward efforts to improve one's rebirth prospects: acquiescence in the social order is said to help ensure rebirth in better circumstances. So if one's egoistic concern for one's future lives reflected the diminished degree of connectedness that holds across rebirths, then even if one believed that acquiescence leads to good karmic fruit, it could still be rational to act against the present oppressive social order. Given that Indian Buddhism does not accept the legitimacy of the caste system, one might wonder why it ever accepted the karma–rebirth ideology. Perhaps this should be thought of as a deal with the devil (a Māran Compact), a price that institutionalized Buddhist Reductionism had to pay to survive in a highly stratified social order.

^m An especially clear expression of this view is to be found in *Bṛhadāraraṇyaka Upaniṣad* II.iv.5: 'Not for love of all is all dear, but for love of self all is dear.'

ⁿ Kolm (1986) refers to a sort of 'Buddhist egoism', by which he means the tendency of the Buddhist enlightenment-seeker to concentrate on eradicating their own suffering, and not that of others. Kolm says such egoism is 'purely instrumental' (1986: 253). For while I can work directly to end my suffering by eradicating my own sense of self, any efforts I make to end others' suffering are at best only indirect and are always prone to misconstrual in ways that make such efforts appear to affirm their selves. While I have a reason to work to end all suffering, I am more likely to succeed in ending my own.

^o The *arahant* (the person who has attained Buddhist enlightenment) has often been portrayed as devoid of all desires and emotions. (Stone and Haksar follow this tradition.) Recent scholarship has begun to question this interpretation of the *arahant*. Bastow (1986: 111–12) suggests that the *arahant* is described in thoroughly impersonal terms only to avoid association with the karmic realm, in which all desires and emotions are tainted by the false belief in a self and the associated tendency to cling. Katz (1982) makes the same point; see especially pp. 151–72, 185–202. Matthews (1983) makes a similar suggestion about the role of volition and desire in the psychology of the aspirant to enlightenment; see especially pp. 74–85. These readings of the classical literature are supported by Tambiah's (1987) account of modern Thai *arahants*.

^p For disciplines designed to extend the Buddhist enlightenment-seeker's concern to strangers, see VM IX.40–87.

CHAPTER FOUR

Wholes, Parts and Supervenience

So far we have seen the Reductionist argue (in Chapter 2) against the Non-Reductionist view that the person is a separately existing entity (a self), and (in Chapter 3) against the Eliminativist view that the person-convention should be replaced by some other way of aggregating psychophysical elements. In the last chapter we also looked at Reductionist responses to a variety of objections, some of which might be said to have been motivated by a 'further-fact' variety of Non-Reductionism. To the extent that the Reductionist responses are deemed adequate, it would appear that the Kantian dual-aspect view lacks support. But there still remains what to many has seemed an attractive form of Non-Reductionism. Suppose we agree with the Reductionist that there are no separately existing selves, and we also agree on the desirability of a single-aspect view, wherein our best theory about what we are meshes neatly with our best theory about what we ought to do. Is it not still possible that a more respectable ontological status might be found for persons than that of mere conceptual fiction? Specifically, might it not be the case that when sufficiently many psychophysical elements interact in a sufficiently complex way, there arise genuinely novel properties, properties the occurrence of which could not have been predicted from our knowledge of the constituent psychophysical elements alone? This view – that persons non-reductively supervene on the psychophysical elements – seems attractive precisely because it holds out the hope that we can make do without occult entities while still honoring our common-sense commitment to the existence of persons. For if person-properties are truly novel in the sense just specified, this suggests that there is genuine explanatory work to be done by a theory of persons – that such a theory is more than a mere instrument for explaining and predicting the behavior of psychophysical elements, that such a theory will have a place in our final picture of the world. Following Quine's dictum that to be is to be the value of a bound variable, we should then say that persons belong in our ontology. How, though, might persons be said to exist if they are not separately existing entities? Comes the response: as wholes that are constituted by psychophysical elements. Persons mereologically but non-reductively supervene on psychophysical elements.

In this chapter we shall examine this proposal and the Reductionist response. Our examination will take a somewhat roundabout path. We shall begin with a Buddhist Reductionist argument for their mereological reductionism, their claim that wholes are mere conceptual fictions. This will set the stage for the introduction of non-reductive supervenience as a possible middle path between non-reductionism and reductionism. We shall investigate just what this might mean, and how a case might be made for the claim that this is the correct analysis of the relation between person and elements. And then, after looking at some related work in recent philosophy of mind, we shall see how a Buddhist Reductionist might respond to this proposal.

The Buddhist Reductionist argument for mereological reductionism

One significant difference between the Buddhist formulation of Reductionism and Parfit's is that the former involves the explicit endorsement of the claim that wholes (partite entities) are ultimately unreal, while the latter takes no position on the question whether wholes other than persons are just as real as the parts of which they are constituted. The Buddhist Reductionist argues that since all wholes are conceptual constructions, the person, as a causal series of sets of psychophysical elements (that is, a whole made up of spatially and temporally distributed parts), must likewise be a mere conceptual fiction. Parfit simply deploys a variety of *sorites* arguments to rule out the possibility that the person is a whole constituted by its parts (1984: 229–43). Parfit's argumentative strategy seems *prima facie* preferable: we might be more likely to give up persons if we thought we could still retain tables and chairs and the like. The Buddhist Reductionist will insist, however, that an adequate defense of Reductionism requires a thoroughgoing mereological reductionism. To see why, we shall look at the argument Buddhist Reductionists gave for the claim that only impartite things are ultimately real, and then investigate some of the challenges that that position has prompted. The argument is as follows:

For any partite entity p composed of non-overlapping impartite entities $a_1, a_2, a_3, \ldots a_n$ such that $R(a_1, a_2, a_3, \ldots a_n)$, there are just four possibilities:

1   The whole p and the parts $a_1, a_2, a_3, \ldots a_n$ are both real. If so, then it must be the case that either:
    a p is identical with $a_1, a_2, a_3, \ldots a_n$ when $R(a_1, a_2, a_3, \ldots a_n)$;
    or:
    b p is distinct from $a_1, a_2, a_3, \ldots a_n$ when $R(a_1, a_2, a_3, \ldots a_n)$.
2   The whole p is real while the parts $a_1, a_2, a_3, \ldots a_n$ are unreal.
3   Neither the whole p nor the parts $a_1, a_2, a_3, \ldots a_n$ are real.
4   The whole p is unreal and only the parts $a_1, a_2, a_3, \ldots a_n$ are real.

The strategy is to prove (4) true by elimination. Hypothesis (2) is easily dispensed with, since this has the consequence that there is only one real thing, the universe. While some have embraced this sort of absolute monism, it has the apparently insuperable difficulty that we cannot then explain the success of practices based on drawing distinctions. Hypothesis (3) is also readily eliminated, since it has the absurd consequence that nothing whatever exists. Hypothesis (1a) can be ruled out using the indiscernibility of identicals. For instance, p has the property of being one while $a_1, a_2, a_3, \ldots a_n$ have the property of being many. Likewise p might have the property of being seen by me, while it is not the case that $a_1, a_2, a_3, \ldots a_n$ have this property. For instance, under ideal observation conditions I might be said to see the tree, yet it is not the case that I see all its parts, such as its roots. Finally, p might be said to survive the replacement of one of its parts, while $a_1, a_2, a_3, \ldots a_n$ do not have this property.[a]

This leaves hypothesis (1b). The difficulty with this is that there does not seem to be any empirical evidence in its favor. For this requires that in addition to whatever evidence there is that the parts exist, there be independent evidence for the existence of the presumably distinct whole. And any sensory experience that might be described as, for instance, seeing the chariot can also be described as seeing one or more of its parts. Likewise what we might think of as an effect of the chariot, such as transporting its driver across the battlefield, can be accounted for entirely in terms of the effects of the parts: the yoke being acted on by motive force transmitted from the horse's legs, causes the connected frame to move laterally, which in turn causes lateral motion of the axle, which in turn causes rotation of the attached wheels, etc. Now the proponent of (1b) may point out that this decomposition of the chariot's effects will hold only when parts a_1, a_2, a_3, ... a_n are in relation R, which fact might be taken as evidence for the separate existence of the whole. The Buddhist Reductionist will respond, however, that R is itself decomposable into a set of properties of a_1, a_2, a_3, ... a_n, so that when all the facts about the parts are taken into account the effect of the chariot is wholly accounted for. The principle of lightness thus dictates that we prefer hypothesis (4) over (1b). Strictly speaking there are no chariots – or horses, cars, desks, or trees either. This conclusion will, of course, strike many as outrageous. But the Buddhist Reductionist will quickly add that such things may be said to be conventionally real: 'chariot' is a convenient designator of these parts when related to one another in such a way as to perform the function(s) specified for the concept, hence the common-sense conviction that chariots are real is conventionally true.

The sinkhole objection and a Buddhist Reductionist response: a semantics for vague terms

There is much that might be said about this argument. One common response is to point out that if we accept the conclusion, but it should turn out that there are no genuinely impartite entities, then it follows that nothing whatever is ultimately real, which is absurd.[1] Since this response makes use of the threat that all existence might drain down a reductionist sinkhole, we shall call this the sinkhole objection. The Buddhist Reductionist response to this objection is a classic instance of 'One person's *modus tollens* is another's *modus ponens*.' Since we know that something must be ultimately real, and no reason has been given to doubt the soundness of the argument, we are entitled to conclude that there must be genuinely impartite entities. If pressed by the opponent to give concrete examples, the Buddhist Reductionist might point to particular mental events such as the occurrence of a pain sensation or of a simple desire like thirst. If the opponent is a physicalist who maintains that such events are reducible without remainder to the neurophysical, the Buddhist Reductionist will then propose one or another of two possible physicalist ontologies. The first claims that macro-physical objects are ultimately constituted by atomic property-particulars: a particular hardness, a particular smoothness, a particular color-and-shape, etc. If the opponent can convincingly demonstrate that all efforts at giving such an analysis are doomed to failure,[2] the Buddhist Reductionist will then retreat to a straightforward atomism, according to which the ultimate reals are indivisible physical particles. The opponent can be expected to point to past disappointments in our efforts to find such

---

[1] A particularly clear recent formulation of this objection is Block (1990: 168, n.9).

[2] As some have maintained in response to efforts by Russell and others to construct a pure sense-data language.

things: what we now call the atom (the name stems from the Greek term for something partless) turns out to be partite. What reason is there to suppose that the current candidate, the quark, will not eventually be revealed to likewise be made of parts? The Buddhist Reductionist will respond by once again pointing to their seemingly sound argument, plus the fact that obviously something must be ultimately real. These facts should together give us confidence that there are indeed genuinely impartite physical entities.

An alternative response to the sinkhole objection would be that the Buddhist Reductionist stance of mereological reductionism yields the best possible response to the *sorites* difficulties induced by the presence of vague terms in our language, and that this response requires that there be genuinely impartite entities. But this response is not one that was given by any Buddhist. Indeed it is striking that *sorites*-induced difficulties play no role whatever in the arguments used by Buddhists to support mereological reductionism.[b] So what follows should be considered no more than a possible response on the part of someone sympathetic to Buddhist Reductionism. This will begin with a brief survey of the sorts of difficulties posed by the presence of vague terms. I shall then sketch how Buddhist Reductionism would allow us to respond to these difficulties, and compare this to the other approaches to *sorites* difficulties currently on offer. The claim will be that the Buddhist formulation of mereological reductionism has distinct advantages over the rival views in this regard.

By a vague term I shall here mean a term that allows of borderline cases, cases where it is indeterminate whether the term applies or not. While ambiguous terms, as well as expressions that are insufficiently precise for the purpose at hand, are also sometimes called 'vague', these do not engender the sorts of logical and semantic difficulties that result from our use of terms that allow of borderline cases. Of the various sorts of terms that are vague in this sense, our focus will be on sortals or kind terms, since these are most directly relevant to the ontological status of partite entities. This will include virtually all terms for object-kinds or substances in our ordinary ontology: natural-kind terms such as 'cat' and 'elm', artifact terms such as 'house' and 'chariot', terms of aggregation such as 'forest', 'heap' and 'mob', and so on. With all such terms it is always possible to construct cases in which it is indeterminate whether a given object is included in the extension of the term, or whether two objects a and b, both in the extension of term 'K', are identical or distinct Ks. Following Unger (1979), for instance, we may ask at which point, in the removal of randomly chosen molecules from what is clearly acknowledged to be a cat, the term 'cat' ceases to be applicable. No answer is likely to be forthcoming, yet we know that long before this process is completed the predicate will cease to apply: there is a gray area of indeterminacy, to one side of which the object is clearly a cat and to the other side of which it is definitely not a cat.[3] This leads to the semantic difficulty of apparent truth-value gaps – seemingly well-formed sentences such as 'a is a cat' that are neither

---

[3] Biological kind-terms such as 'cat' are thought by many realists about substances to pose an especially difficult challenge to mereological reductionism. So it might be thought that the predicate will cease to apply at that point where the life of the cat in question ceases. But as the *sorites* difficulties surrounding the term 'living' show, there is unlikely to be a single point in the process of molecule-by-molecule removal where the cat in question ceases to be a living thing. Moreover, there are possible routes through this process that culminate in a living thing not properly called a cat.

true nor false – in violation of the principle of bivalence. And perhaps more seriously, it also seems to lead to a violation of the logical law of excluded middle. If in a particular case it is neither true nor false that *a* is a cat, it is then not the case that: either *a* is a cat or it is not the case that *a* is a cat; that is, we must affirm something of the form 'not(*p* or not *p*)'. But the principle of bivalence and the law of excluded middle are central to classical semantics and logic, which are in turn extremely well entrenched in our thinking and our practice. So the presence of such terms in our language appears intolerable.[4]

The Buddhist Reductionist response to the problem of vague kind-terms will crucially involve their doctrine of two truths, conventional and ultimate. They will point out that the vast majority of our kind-terms are vague (in the relevant sense) precisely because they are constructed so as to apply to partite entities. That there are borderline cases where it is indeterminate whether a set of entities may be called a chariot is a straightforward consequence of the fact that 'chariot' is a convenient designator for a set of related entities filling a complex functional role. Such terms are *tolerant* in Wright's sense: there is a degree of change (in the case of sortals for partite entities, change in composition) too small to make a difference in their application (1997: 156). So the removal of a single tree from a forest can never make it the case that it is no longer correctly called a forest. And since the ultimate truth consists only of sentences that do not use such convenient designators, it follows that the ultimate truth will behave classically in its logic and semantics; the indeterminacies introduced by terms like 'forest' will simply not arise, so there will be no bivalence failure and no violation of excluded middle (or of non-contradiction).[c]

Sentences using such terms may, however, be conventionally true, so the semantic and logical difficulties created by vague terms will show up there. This is not a particular embarrassment, however. For the conventional truth is meant to reflect how the world will seem to us given our needs, interests and cognitive limitations. And the tolerance of a term like 'tree' – which is what leads to it being indeterminate when a sapling becomes a tree – is readily understood as an artifact of limits on our discriminative powers, and of our interest in having a common term that is readily mastered and used. The relation between conventional and ultimate truth may then be seen as akin to that between physics and engineering. The so-called idealizations of physics – the frictionless plane, the point mass and the like – may be thought of as representing how physical systems in fact behave, whereas the 'don't-cares' of

---

[4]   Such terms also give rise to *sorites* paradoxes, seemingly sound arguments leading from premises we would all acknowledge as true (such as that someone with 100,000 hairs on their head is not bald, and that the loss of a single hair does not turn a hirsute person into a bald person), to a conclusion we all agree is false (e.g., that someone with no hairs on their head is not bald). Parfit exploits the vagueness of 'person' to construct *sorites* arguments against the 'further-fact' version of Non-Reductionism. His seeming reluctance to embrace a more thoroughgoing mereological reductionism would seem to be what lies behind his failure to apply the argument-form more broadly. A *sorites* paradox, of course, gives rise to an apparent violation of the law of non-contradiction, which is sometimes thought to be more serious than a breach of excluded middle. Since the series can be run in either direction, we can deduce that a given case both does and does not warrant the predicate: someone with *n* hairs both is and is not bald. We will focus on the issue of failure of excluded middle, however, since any approach that resolves that difficulty is likely to give relief on the score of non-contradiction as well.

practical engineering – such as a margin of error that reflects factors deemed not worth calculating given the cost of obtaining the data – are just how physical systems will seem to us under the constraints of everyday practice. That our engineering principles lead to success does not show that physical systems contain margins of error; there is no physical object whose mass is a certain amount plus or minus five milligrams. Engineering is physics filtered through our interests and our limitations, and that is where margins of error come from. Likewise the world contains no zones of indeterminacy or truth-value gaps; it has a determinate microstructure. Bivalence failure and violations of excluded middle arise only through compromises imposed on our dealings with that structure in response to the vicissitudes of everyday life.[d]

Of the other possible ways of handling *sorites* difficulties, most see vagueness as a strictly semantic phenomenon. There is, however, one approach that affirms that vagueness is not merely semantic but is instead metaphysical: at least some of the vague kind-terms of ordinary language denote genuinely vague objects in the world, objects whose boundaries are indeed fuzzy. This claim is often greeted with simple incredulity.[5] Evans (1978), however, gives an argument that is meant to rule out this possibility. The argument, roughly, is that if we suppose there to be vague objects, then a given precisification b of the ostensibly vague object a will have the property of being indeterminately identical with a.[6] But a does not have the property of being indeterminately identical with itself. Hence there is a property that b has and a lacks, namely the property of being such that it is indeterminately identical with a, hence it is false, and not indeterminate, that a and b are identical.

This argument has been widely criticized,[7] and I am not sure that it succeeds on its own. But it does raise some interesting questions concerning self-identity for vague objects that deserve further exploration. What I shall seek to show is that the defender of metaphysical vagueness can give no satisfactory account of how a vague object might be (synchronically) identical to itself. Now in its derivation of the contradiction that a and b both are and are not indeterminately identical, the argument makes use of the claim that they are indeterminately identical. The defender of metaphysical vagueness might object that there can be no indeterminate identity. Thus it might be claimed that since b lacks the area of indeterminacy distinctive of a, it is determinately not identical with a. But if the defender of vague objects takes this tack, it will then turn out that self-identity must likewise be determinate, even in the case of vague objects. And it is not clear how this could be true. To say of something that it is self-identical is to say that it is exactly congruent with itself – that it includes just those parts that are its own, and excludes all others. But a vague object would have a

---

    [5]   Dummett (1997: 111), for instance, says that the notion that things might actually be vague 'is not properly intelligible', but gives no reasons.

    [6]   The notion of a precisification of a vague predicate plays an important role in supervaluation theory. The basic idea is that for all penumbral cases in which the extension of the predicate is indeterminate we specify, arbitrarily, some value among the range of permitted values. So if it were indeterminate whether a given hair were a part of the cat Emily, there would be two classes of precisifications for 'Emily': those on which the hair is a part of Emily, and those on which the hair is not. See, e.g., Fine (1997: 125ff.) for a formal account.

    [7]   See, e.g., Chatterjee (1994: 66–79). See also Keefe and Smith (1997: 52–57) for a general discussion and further references.

region of indeterminacy wherein entities are neither determinately included in nor determinately excluded from the object's parts. So self-identity for a vague object would have to involve this region's exactly mapping onto itself. And this is arguably incompatible with the fact of higher-order vagueness – that it is indeterminate just where the region of indeterminacy begins and ends. It is not clear what it would mean to say that a vague object's zone of indeterminacy is exactly congruent with itself. For not only is it indeterminate where this region begins and leaves off, it is likewise indeterminate where this second-order indeterminacy starts to manifest itself. Consider, for instance, some particular cat as a candidate vague object. There must be entities that are quite determinately parts of the cat, such as molecules making up its currently functioning heart tissue. There are also entities that are quite determinately not parts of the cat, such as the constituents of Alpha Centauri's plasma. Then there are those entities that are in the zone of indeterminacy for the cat, such as perhaps a hair that is almost completely detached from its root but is kept from falling out by the hairs surrounding it. To say that there is second-order vagueness to the cat is to say that while some elements are determinately included in the zone of indeterminacy, others are not. Suppose that this hair is in the penumbral region of the zone of indeterminacy, where it is indeterminate whether it falls in the zone of indeterminacy. When we say that the cat is determinately self-identical, this seems to mean that the cat must always map onto itself in such a way as to have this hair come out penumbral. But second-order vagueness consists in it being indeterminate where this penumbral region begins and ends, so there must be possible cases where the hair is not penumbral after all, but is determinately indeterminate or else determinately either part of the cat or not part of the cat. So it is not clear what it would mean to say that a vague object is determinately self-identical. And to Quine's dictum, 'No entity without identity', we might well add, 'No identity without self-identity'. For we seem to lack purchase on the concept of identity if we are unable to say of something that it is identical with itself.

Now Evans' argument depends equally on the claim that *a* is (determinately) self-identical, so the champion of vague objects might be tempted at this point to claim that self-identity comes in distinct flavors for different sorts of objects: determinate self-identity for objects with precise boundaries, and indeterminate self-identity for vague objects. But this move has a decidedly *ad hoc* ring to it. For any two vague objects stipulated as distinct, the kind of identity that fails to hold is presumably determinate identity, and similarly for distinct entities with precise boundaries. And indeterminate identity was ruled out as a possible relation between a vague object and a precisification of that object. So the only work that seems left for indeterminate identity is to stand as the kind of identity involved in the self-identity of vague objects.

It is, moreover, far from clear what indeterminate self-identity would amount to. Presumably this should mean that it is neither true nor false that the object is identical with itself. How might this be? In the case of the cat, the only possible source of indeterminacy of truth-value would have to come from whatever entities are in its zone of indeterminacy, such as that hair. Could this be the source of its being neither true nor false that the cat is identical with itself? The considerations of the preceding paragraph might make it seem so, but we must recall that the claim here is that it is of the nature of the cat itself that this hair is neither determinately its own nor determinately distinct. The hypothesis under examination is that vagueness is metaphysical, not that it is semantic. So it should be true of the cat that this hair is neither determinately its own nor determinately distinct. And if this is true of the cat, then this fact cannot be the source of its supposed indeterminate self-identity; being the source of indeterminate self-identity would require not that it be true of the cat but that it be indeterminate. In short, there is no coherent account to be given of self-identity with respect to vague objects.[8]

Of the alternative accounts that treat vagueness not metaphysically but as a strictly semantic phenomenon, there are three major approaches: supervaluationism, multi-valued logic approaches, and the epistemic theory. Supervaluationism concedes that the presence of vague predicates in the language incurs bivalence failure, but seeks to rule out violations of excluded middle. This is done by claiming that the truth-value of a sentence containing a vague term is to be determined by supervaluation over precisifications of that sentence: a sentence is true (or 'super-true') if it is true on all precisifications, false if false on all precisifications, and indeterminate otherwise. Take the sentence 'either a is a cat or a is not a cat', where a denotes some collection of molecules obtained by the random removal of molecules from a cat in such a way that it is indeterminate whether a is a cat. Then since on every precisification of a either a is a cat or a is not a cat, the disjunction will turn out to be true, and no violation of excluded middle occurs. Now questions can be raised concerning the adequacy of this approach to the phenomenon of higher-order vagueness.[9] But there is another worry that is nicely illustrated by an example of Wright's (1997: 157). On the supervaluation approach it is as if vagueness represents a kind of intellectual laziness, as when two countries agree that there is a border between them but have not settled just where it is. In such a case there is no question but that there is a decisive single step to be taken that crosses the border; it has just not been established where that step occurs. To the supervaluationist, vague terms seem likewise to result from semantic indecision. This is just what is suggested by their notion of a permissible range of precisifications: any of these could have represented where we might have chosen to draw the line; we just haven't bothered to do so. As Wright and others have pointed out, this view is incompatible with the pragmatics of vague terms, which suggest that their tolerance, and hence their possession of a zone of indeterminacy (with its own higher-order indeterminacy), is fundamental to the semantics of such expressions. The Buddhist Reductionist approach fares decidedly better in this regard. Like supervaluationism, it insulates the logical laws of excluded middle and non-contradiction from violation. But it does so while allowing that the tolerance of vague expressions is crucial to their functioning in everyday discourse.

Where supervaluationism gives up bivalence in order to preserve classical logic, multi-valued logic approaches add additional truth-values in order to ensure that every proposition gets one, and then make corresponding adjustments to classical

---

[8] The view that metaphysical vagueness is coherent stems, I suspect, from a failure to keep meta-physical and semantic considerations sufficiently distinct. This would not be a problem for an anti-realist, but the view that there are vague objects is usually put forward by realists. And for the realist it is difficult to see how bivalence failure could be anything but semantic. But this will be the subject of further discussion in Chapter 8.

[9] For a useful and fair survey of these difficulties see Keefe and Smith (1997: 34–35).

logic. The basic idea is that borderline sentences such as '*a* is a cat' if neither true nor false may take some other truth-value, such as 'indeterminate' (for three-valued logics), or some degree n of truth where $0 < n < 1$ (for infinite-valued logics). This accords with our intuition that such sentences do succeed in saying something, just not something that is fully true or fully false. Most multi-valued approaches preserve truth-functionality for the sentential connectives, but such classical laws as excluded middle cannot be retained. So for instance disjunction is typically treated in infinite-valued systems as yielding the maximum of the values of the disjuncts: where p has a truth-value of 0.67 and q a value of 0.48, p v q will have a truth-value of 0.67. And since negation is typically treated as flipping truth-values (that is, the value of $\sim p$ equals 1 minus the value of p), it follows that for a sentence p whose truth-value is between 0 and 1, p v $\sim p$ will turn out less than fully true. As Machina (1997: 186) points out, however, no sentence of this form will ever have a truth-value of less than 0.50, so that we do have a 'law of the more-or-less excluded middle'.

One reason to prefer the infinite-valued approach to the three-valued approach is that the latter requires that there be sharp boundaries between each of the three truth-values, which seems inconsistent with the fact that the transition from clear cases to borderline cases is always gradual. An infinite-valued approach likewise allows us to speak of comparative differences among borderline cases: if this heap of molecules is more cat-like than that one, then 'This is a cat' may be said to be more nearly true (has a higher truth-value) than 'That is a cat.' But the problem of higher-order vagueness still haunts the infinite-valued approach. For there remain the abrupt transitions from truth-value 1 to values less than 1, and from truth-value 0 to values greater than 0, and this seems incompatible with the fact that it is indeterminate where the zone of indeterminacy for a vague term begins and ends. There is also the question whether it is consistent with the tolerance of vague terms that precise numbers be assigned to borderline cases: does it really make sense to say of this collection of molecules that it is true to degree 0.67 that it is a cat, and of that collection that it is true only to degree 0.48? While we might agree that the first collection is more cat-like than the second, how would we know just what numbers to assign?

Regarding this last problem, Edgington (1997) has some useful things to say. While championing an infinite-valued approach, she also concedes that the precision introduced by the quantification of degrees of truth is misleading. She thus proposes that we think of the numbers as an idealization, that is, as a tool that may prove useful for certain purposes in certain contexts, but that should not be taken as anything more than an only roughly isomorphic model. So while quantification lets us express comparative differences among borderline cases, there will always be limits on the precision with which we can represent those comparisons – and these limits will themselves change with differences of context. The numbers likewise enable us to represent the difference between significant and insignificant differences in tolerant predicates – to show how *sorites* reasoning involving such predicates leads from truth to falsity. But again, this should be thought of as just a useful way of modeling the structure of our thought, not as a way of representing what actually happens. In general, she claims, the relation between the representation and the reality is itself vague. This means specifically that where clear truth, or clear-cut application of the predicate, leaves off and indeterminacy begins is itself left vague. That the numbers suggest a clear border between 1 and values less than 1 is just an artifact of this mode of representation; where that border occurs in the model will vary depending on context and interests. On this version of the infinite-valued approach, at least, it appears that higher-order vagueness can be accommodated.

This requires, however, that a distinction be drawn between all-or-nothing truth and the truth represented in the model by the value 1. Edgington uses the term 'verity' to refer to the sort of truth that may come in degrees, and she makes clear that this is not intended to replace classical truth, the importance of which she sees as beyond dispute. This makes explicit what was already implicit in her calling the use of numbers merely an idealization. 'An idealization of what?' we might ask. 'The ultimate truth', a Buddhist Reductionist would suggest. That is, in order to accommodate the facts about our behavior and about higher-order vagueness, the infinite-valued approach requires the distinction between two levels of truth. Edgington's degrees of verity are how we deal with a reality too fine-grained for fully adequate representation given the demands of ordinary practice. Truth, the all-or-nothing concept, has application only when our representations are couched in a language that fully reflects the fine-grained structure, that refers only to impartite entities and the relations they enter into. This also explains how 'clear truth' could itself be vague (which it must be if the boundary between it and borderline cases is to be indeterminate). By 'clear truth' what is meant is the verity of value 1, and this is just conventional truth, something whose application is always subject to adjustment given various contextual factors. That this is so should no longer disturb us once we realize that this vague 'clear truth' is only a useful approximation to the real, all-or-nothing thing, something about which there is no indeterminacy whatever (and hence no bivalence failure and no violation of excluded middle). The only way to make sense of the infinite-valued approach to vagueness, I contend, is to interpret it in terms of the Buddhist Reductionist device of the two truths and its attendant mereological reductionism.

What about Platonically?

The remaining approach to vagueness, the epistemic approach, is in agreement with the two semantic approaches we have just examined that *sorites* phenomena originate not in objects with fuzzy boundaries but rather in our application of predicates to a world of precisely bounded objects. The difficulty, according to the epistemic approach, is just that we are ignorant of where the boundaries of those predicates lie. There is a fact of the matter concerning at just which removal of which molecule 'cat' is no longer predicable of that collection of molecules. This is just something that we can never know. So there is no need for adjustments in our logic or semantics. Bivalence is preserved, since '*a* is a cat' is either true or false (we will just never know which). And no violations of excluded middle are generated, since one or the other of '*a* is a cat' and 'It is not the case that *a* is a cat' must be true (we will just never know which). *Sorites* difficulties are just the result of our ignorance, and *sorites* arguments are demonstrably invalid.

The claim that there is a fact of the matter concerning at just which removal of just which tree the forest becomes a mere grove, is usually greeted with a stare of frank incredulity. But as Lewis points out in another context (1986), facial expressions are not refutations. And it has proven surprisingly difficult to show just what might be wrong with this approach. Williamson (1994) is particularly persuasive in his handling of the standard objections, including the claim that the epistemic approach cannot adequately deal with the phenomenon of higher-order vagueness. So it may prove impossible to decisively refute this approach. Still the sorts of considerations that are brought up in this defense make the view seem much less plausible than a semantic approach that utilizes the device of the two truths. Williamson claims that the fact of the matter concerning the point at which 'cat' ceases to be predicable is determined by facts about how speakers of the language use the term, and that these facts are simply too complex and multifarious for us to be able to compute the predicate's precise extension on any given occasion of use. But as Machina and Deutsch (2002) point out, these considerations support not epistemicism but the view that such predicates lack precise extensions. Williamson thus needs a positive argument in support of his epistemic approach. The strongest candidate for this role is the consideration that it preserves classical logic and semantics. But quite apart from the difficulties that Machina and Deutsch show with this argument, there is the fact that the Buddhist Reductionist approach described above has the same virtue without the vice of extreme counter-intuitiveness.

I conclude that a two-level account of truth represents the approach to vague terms most likely to preserve bivalence and classical logic. The Buddhist Reductionist could use this fact to answer the sinkhole objection. Their approach requires that the domain of discourse for the ultimate truth be impartite entities. To the extent that the preservation of bivalence and classical logic represent important desiderata, then, we should agree that there must be the kinds of impartite entities that the above argument requires.

Non-reductive mereological supervenience

One might respond to the above argument against wholes not by raising the sinkhole objection, but instead by accepting the refutations of hypotheses (1a) and (1b) as they stand, but insisting that these do not exhaust all the possibilities. Instead, it might be claimed, we should consider the possibility that at least for some wholes, the whole is neither ultimately identical with nor ultimately distinct from its constituent parts. The following might be said in support of the claim that this is not incoherent: for at least some cases, the whole has genuinely novel properties that cannot be accounted for in terms of the properties of the parts, so that the whole cannot be said to be identical with the parts. At the same time, since there is an asymmetrical dependence relation between the whole and its parts, the whole cannot be said to be distinct from the parts, since that would imply that the whole is on an equal ontological footing with the parts. So the whole can be said to be neither identical with nor distinct from the parts. Instead it should be said to bear a relation of non-reductive mereological supervenience (NMS) on its parts.

To say that s supervenes on b is to say that all the properties of s are determined (or fixed) by properties of b. The determination relation, which holds between properties, may be characterized in a number of ways. If no two things may be identical with respect to their P-properties yet differ in their P^*-properties, then P is said to determine P^*. Alternatively, the relation is said to hold when there can be no change in P^* without some change in P. The relation comes in different forms depending on the sort of necessity involved: logical/conceptual, metaphysical, or nomological. Regardless of the kind of necessity involved in determination, however, it is a defining feature of supervenience that the determination relation is asymmetrical.

Where it is also the case that P^*-indiscernible entities must be P-indiscernible, then the quite different symmetrical relation of necessary covariance of P and P^* holds. The supervenience relation leaves open the possibility that two things might be the same with respect to their P^*-properties yet differ with respect to their P-properties. For instance, if pain were thought to supervene on neurophysical states, then it might be held that two organisms could be in pain while in quite different neurophysical states. That is, it might be held that while pain supervenes on neurophysiological properties, pains may be realized differently in organisms with different neurophysiological constitutions. The resulting asymmetry in supervenience means that s (the supervening entity) and b (the base entity or entities) differ in ontological status, with b being said to be ontologically more basic than s. This is already implicit in the term 'determine': to say that the properties of entity s are determined by properties of b is to say that the former entity depends on the properties of the latter for its nature, including that part of its nature that makes s be the sort of thing that it essentially is. If all the properties of a pain, including that of its being a pain, are entirely fixed once all the properties of a central nervous system have been specified, but the opposite is not the case, then it looks as if the existence of a pain is dependent on the existence of entities with properties that are somehow more basic. This is not true in the case of necessary covariance. If mental states and brain states were (at some level of description) necessarily covariant, then depending on the kind of necessity involved, we might say one of two things. If the necessity were nomological, we should say that mind and brain are distinct things that causally interact. If the necessity were metaphysical or logical/conceptual, we should say that mind and brain are identical. But in neither case would we say that one is ontologically more basic than the other.

If the whole supervenes on its parts, then according to the proponent of the NMS view it would be misleading to say that the whole is distinct from its parts after the manner of hypothesis (1b), since that would entail parity of ontological status. This view also maintains that in at least some cases of mereological supervenience the whole is not reducible to its parts, and that in such cases the whole may also not be said to be identical with its parts. What is to count as evidence that one sort of thing is reducible to another sort of thing? I claimed in Chapter 1 that the occurrence of so-called bridge laws is not necessary, and may not be sufficient, for the reduction of entities treated of in one theory to entities treated of in another theory. This claim needs some defense. Nagel held that for genuine reduction between theories that treat of distinct kinds of entities, there must be bridge laws taking the form of biconditionals with predicates from the vocabulary of the one theory on the left, and predicates from that of the other theory on the right. That is, there must be laws of the form $P \leftrightarrow P^*$, where 'P' names properties distinctive of entities described by the first theory (e.g., being a quantum shift), and 'P^*' names properties distinctive of entities described by the second (e.g., that of being a covalent bond). For only then, he pointed out, is it possible for the laws of the reduced theory to be deduced from the laws of the reducing theory. But as Kim (1998: 25) points out, this presupposes a Hempelian D–N model of scientific explanation, a model that is now deemed inadequate by most philosophers of science. This should make us suspicious of the Nagelian account of reduction.

And we can do more than just raise suspicions concerning the presupposed model. Consider, as a paradigm instance of intertheoretic reduction, the case of the optical theory of light and the electromagnetic theory of radiation.[10] Suppose that as the two theories are developed, researchers begin to notice interesting correlations between the two sets of phenomena, and that these correlations can be expressed in the form of biconditionals of the right sorts. That this is not sufficient for reduction of one theory to the other is already suggested by the fact that so far it is not clear which is to be given the privileged 'reducing' status. Perhaps this might be settled by appeal to the supposedly wider applicability of the electromagnetic theory of radiation.[11] But there is still the difficulty that the correlations expressed in the biconditionals might stem from the fact that both theories are themselves derivable from some third, deeper theory. The correlation between a material's thermal conductivity and its electrical conductivity is a classic instance of this. Since this correlation is now understood to result from a single microstructure that underlies both sorts of phenomena, no one takes it to show that the theory of thermal conductivity is reducible to that of electrical conductivity, or vice versa. Most important of all, though, is the fact that bridge laws themselves do nothing to explain the correlations, and in the end this is what is wanted in order for reduction to go through. Otherwise, if the correlations remain an unexplained, brute given, then we shall have been given no reason not to suppose that the two sorts of phenomena are on an equal ontological footing, that the correlations represent causal interactions between distinct entities. In the case at hand, we say that the optical theory is reduced to the theory of electromagnetic radiation because we can explain the observed correlations through the simple device of identification: light rays just are a form of electromagnetic radiation, hence there is no mystery why the two phenomena should have appeared to be correlated.

Once we see that what is wanted for successful reduction is not bridge laws but explanation, we can also see why bridge laws may not be necessary for reduction either. Consider that part of aeronautical engineering concerned with wing design, and its relation to the theory of aerodynamics. The airplane wing is multiply realized: it may be constructed out of fabric and wood, or aluminum, or carbon composites; depending on such factors as the materials used and the characteristics of the propulsion system employed, it may have any of a variety of shapes. We are thus unlikely to obtain any bridge laws that would enable us to deduce the properties of airplane wings from the laws of physics. Any attempt at constructing such laws would yield formulas taking a disjunctive form, possibly infinitely disjunctive: $P \leftrightarrow (P^{*} \vee P^{**} \vee P^{***}...)$. And there is good reason to doubt that there are such things as disjunctive properties, let alone infinitely disjunctive properties.[12] Does this mean that we understand how airplanes fly not through our understanding of physics, but only through some autonomous theory of airplane wings? This conclusion seems unwarranted. For each possible wing configuration, it is just the principles of aerodynamics that explain why something of that configuration enables planes of a

---

[10] Adapted from the discussion of Sklar (1967: 118–21).

[11] Though it is not clear that researchers investigating the correlations would have held the theory of electromagnetic radiation to be wider in scope than the optical theory of light. That we do so today is partly the result of our view that light just is a form of electromagnetic radiation – that is, of our having accepted the reduction of the latter theory to the former.

[12] See Armstrong (1978b: 19–23).

certain sort to fly. The lift of the 747-E's wing just is the vertical force vector of classical aerodynamics. That there are no bridge laws connecting physics and the engineering principles of wing design does not preclude explanation of the latter in terms of the former. To insist on bridge laws for reduction is to insist on an inappropriately narrow sense of explanation – only allowing the sort of explanation that permits straightforward deduction of one theory from another. The deduction relation does hold in some cases of reduction, as of some parts of chemistry to physics: the principles of valency may be deduced from certain principles of quantum mechanics. And this is part of what we have in mind when we say that chemistry reduces to physics. But this is not to say that we do not possess a perfectly adequate understanding of the functioning of airplane wings just from our knowledge of the physics of aerodynamics. And given this understanding, it seems perfectly reasonable to claim that the airplane wing just consists in certain particles configured in such a way that the flow of gas particles at a given velocity will produce a vertical force of a certain magnitude. The wing lifts the airplane because particles with this configuration cause a force of such and such a magnitude given gas particle flow of a certain rate. As the Buddhist Reductionist would put it, 'airplane wing' is a mere convenient designator for particles in such a configuration.

It is explanation, not the availability of bridge laws, that is necessary for inter-theoretic reduction. Now it is true that there are many different sorts of explanation, and so far nothing has been said to specify the sort that is relevant to reduction. But reflection on the two cases of the light beam and the airplane wing suggests that it is causal explanation that is required here. We accept the reduction of light to electromagnetic radiation, and the wing to a certain configuration of particles, when we are satisfied that the effects of the first of these pairs is actually caused by the second. When we understand that the taking off of the airplane is just the effect of the forces generated by the motion of gas particles past the particles constituting the wing, we lose the temptation to think of the wing as something existing over and above those particles so configured. When we understand that the focusing of light passing through a lens is just the effect on a wavefront of entry into and exit from a medium with a different transmission velocity, we lose the temptation to think of light as anything other than a form of radiation. We can see why this should be if we concur with the Buddhist Reductionist that the mark of the real is causal efficacy.[e] For then to think of one sort of thing as distinct from another sort of thing, we shall need to be able to specify independent causal powers for each. If we cannot, then to persist in thinking of them as distinct existents is to countenance a kind of causal overdetermination that flagrantly violates the principle of lightness. Why suppose that there is really such a thing as a wing, when we know that it is the particles that are doing all the work?

So it is causal explanation that is required for reduction. This tells us what the proponent of NMS must demonstrate in order to show that a given whole supervenes non-reductively on its parts: determination without explanation. It must be the case that the whole's having some property P^* cannot be explained in terms of the laws governing its parts and their P-properties, even though P determines P^*. P^* must be a genuinely emergent property, one whose occurrence cannot, even in principle, be predicted on the basis of facts about the parts, even when these are supplemented by aggregation principles, the truths of mathematics, and any other b-level-accessible truths.[13] It was once widely believed that there are abundant examples of such properties. But recent advances in such fields as solid state physics and biochemistry have somewhat eroded this confidence. For instance, it turns out that we can predict that combining two atoms of hydrogen with one atom of oxygen will yield a light-transparent medium, while combining atoms of hydrogen and carbon in a certain proportion will not. It is in persons, however, that our real interest lies. If we think of persons as wholes with psychophysical elements as their proper parts, can we say that persons non-reductively supervene on psychophysical elements?

Against the non-reductive supervenience of persons

While there can be little doubt that the Buddha espoused a form of Reductionism, there were some Buddhists who held an anti-Reductionist position. Since the name by which their view came to be known (*pudgalavāda*) simply means the doctrine of the person, we shall call them Personalists.[f] And while they did not formulate their view in terms of the notion of non-reductive supervenience, there are many suggestive elements in their defense of their view. First, Personalists agreed with Buddhist Reductionists that there is no separately existing self.[g] They also held that the person is named and conceptualized in dependence on the psychophysical elements,[h] and that it can be said to be neither identical with nor distinct from those elements.[i] Unlike the psychophysical elements, it is not ultimately real, but neither is it a mere conceptual fiction.[j] Instead it must be accorded a distinctive sort of reality, since it has properties that none of the psychophysical elements has, such as being the bearer of moral desert over distinct lives,[k] and being perceptible by all five senses.[l] Its relation to the psychophysical elements is likened to that of fire to fuel,[m] of a shadow to a tree,[n] and of secondary material properties to primary material properties.[o]

Now to say that persons are named and conceptualized in dependence on the psychophysical elements, and that the elements are ultimately real but the person is not, seems to suggest that there holds between person and elements the asymmetrical relation of ontological dependency that is characteristic of the determination relation. And the tree–shadow relation looks like a classic case of determination – that is, provided we broaden the first relatum to the tree–sun–ground configuration. For there can be no change in the shadow without some change in this configuration, but not vice versa. In addition, the fire-fuel relation might be construed as involving multiple realization: we might be inclined to say that the same fire can exist in dependence on wood or on oil. Likewise for the relation between such secondary properties as color and such primary properties as the shapes of atoms: we might hold that the same blue color can be realized by many different combinations of atomic shapes. Finally, the claims about the properties of bearing moral desert and being perceptible by all five

---

[13] Prediction is an appropriate requirement because nomological necessity is required to support prediction. The predictability need only be 'in principle' because the complexity of a micro-system might be such that calculating a macro-effect from complete knowledge of the relevant initial micro-states would simply take a finite calculator too long. Presumably such limitations on our cognitive abilities should not be taken to have consequences for the nature of mind-independent reality.

senses look like assertions about novel emergent properties. So Personalism might be considered as at least an anticipation of the NMS view of persons.

There is a fine line that must be walked to make out a case for NMS, however: s-level properties must have autonomous explanatory powers, yet not count as ultimately real. Just as Reductionism is meant to be a middle path between Non-Reductionism and Eliminativism, so NMS is intended as a middle path between Non-Reductionism and Reductionism. If NMS requires determination without explanation, then there would have to be facts about persons that could not be explained in terms of facts about the elements. Hence any explanatory work done by those facts about the person could not be pre-empted by facts about the elements, and so would have to be truly autonomous. At the same time, the person should not turn out to be ultimately real. The second requirement may be met by way of the asymmetry of the dependency relation. That a given s-property is, for instance, multiply realizable may convince us that it is in some sense 'higher-level', and so not ultimately real. What would intuitively be considered the same shadow may be cast by any number of different configurations of sun, tree and ground. This may suffice to persuade us that shadows are not as robustly real as are the sun, the tree and the ground. The difficulty is that it then becomes unclear what explanatory work remains to be done by shadows, once the relevant facts about the sun–tree–ground configuration have been brought in. The Personalist points out that just as a flame persists through change from wood to oil fuel, so a person might persist (in a case of rebirth) through change from human elements to bovine elements. Suppose we agree that this shows persons to be multiply realizable. And suppose further that we take this to have the ontological implication that persons are in some sense merely 'along for the ride', that it is the elements that are doing all the work here. In that case, how is the Personalist to convince us that person-properties have autonomous explanatory powers?

Of the two person-properties mentioned by the Personalist, that of bearing moral desert sounds more promising than that of being perceptible by all five senses. The Buddhist Reductionist readily disposes of the claim that the latter represents a genuinely emergent property, using the counter-example of milk, which could likewise be thought of as perceptible by all five senses.[P] On the property-particulars analysis of physical objects favored by some Buddhist Reductionists, a substance like milk consists of a set of co-occurring property-particulars such as a particular instance of whiteness or wetness (construed as mind-independent reals), each perceived by just one sense modality. On the atomist analysis preferred by other Buddhist Reductionists, milk may be exhaustively analyzed into an aggregate of atoms, the properties of which explain our sensory stimulations. So on neither analysis are the constituents of milk perceptible by all five senses. But, says the Buddhist Reductionist, on either analysis 'milk' turns out to be a convenient designator for a bundle of entities no one of which is perceptible by all five senses; it is only through the aggregating of these entities that there arises the appearance of some one substance with the novel property of being perceptible by all five senses. The occurrence of this property can be predicted based on properties of the more particular constituents plus principles of aggregation. So any fact that it might explain can in principle be explained on the basis of properties of the constituents. And the same will hold for the person-property of being perceptible by all five senses.

The property of moral desert sounds more promising – no doubt because of the notorious difficulty of accounting for moral or other normative properties in terms of the wholly impersonal elements out of which the person is supposedly constituted. Suppose I now have the property of deserving punishment due to some evil deed performed at an earlier time. The elements constituting the current psychophysical complex are wholly distinct from those that made up the complex that was present at the performance of the deed. So in order to account for this property I shall have to invoke some relation or other between certain presently obtaining properties and properties that obtained at the earlier time. The most plausible candidate properties here would seem to be such person-properties as the property of being the agent of the action, the property of seeming to remember performing the action, and the like. These seem like plausible candidates because we can imagine how some relation between such properties could account for my present culpability. But insofar as these are still person-properties, the Reductionist still owes us an account of how they come to play the normative role they do. This appears difficult to explain if these properties are in turn wholly constituted by the properties of impersonal entities and events. How might the occurrence of a particular desire, a certain set of neural firings, the activation of a certain memory trace, and the like, even when joined together by myriad causal connections, yield a complete explanation of my moral culpability? Since we fail to see any normative properties in any of the individual entities and events, and causal connection in itself appears devoid of normative character, it is difficult to resist the notion that culpability and the like are genuinely emergent at the higher level of complexity represented by person-properties. If this is so, then the explanatory work done by moral properties (e.g., in explaining actions of rewarding and punishing) cannot be accomplished at any level lower than that of the person. Hence the relation between person and elements is one of determination without explanation, that is, non-reductive mereological supervenience.

To see how a Reductionist might respond, it would be useful to look briefly at an analogous dispute in the philosophy of mind. With the collapse of the mind–brain identity thesis in the 1960s, many physicalists were attracted to an analysis that had the mental supervening on the neurophysical, and that understood mental states in functionalist terms. As Kim (1997) characterizes the subsequent history, non-reductive physicalism became the prevailing orthodoxy as a result. But Kim himself has long opposed non-reductive physicalism, claiming that the combination of functionalism and the supervenience relation instead supports a reductive physicalism. At one time his reasons had largely to do with the fact that multiple realization is still compatible with 'local reduction': while it is true that pain states might have different neurophysical realizations in bats and in humans, this is consistent with there being genuine psychophysical laws concerning human pain (or bat pain), in which case pain may be reduced to neurophysical states on a local or species-by-species basis.[14] But this is still based on the questionable assumption that successful reduction requires bridge laws.[15] More recently Kim (1998) has mounted a frontal

---

[14] For an instance of this approach see Kim (1993: 74).

[15] The resort to strictly 'local' reduction was Kim's way of trying to avoid the problem of disjunctive – possibly infinitely disjunctive – psychophysical laws that multiple realization brings in its wake; the need

assault on non-reductive physicalism, claiming that functionalization of the mental directly leads to reduction. The argument for this surprising claim is roughly as follows. Functional properties are second-order properties. Second-order properties are constructed by quantifying over first-order properties. Hence second-order properties are themselves causally inert, their appearance of causal relevance deriving wholly from the first-order properties out of which they are constructed. But second-order properties have explanatory relevance only to the extent that they figure in causal explanations. And they can figure in causal explanations only by appearing to have causal relevance. Therefore functional properties lack autonomous explanatory powers.

Consider dormitivity, which, while not a functional property, is second-order. That is, by 'dormitivity' what we intend to refer to is that causal power, whatever it may be, through which the sleeping pill or potion causes sleep. Like functional properties, dormitivity is multiply realizable: different sleeping pills and potions have dormitivity by virtue of quite different chemical compositions. But for any particular sleeping pill, it is the distinctive chemical composition of that pill that is causally relevant to the sleep induced by its ingestion. Now it is not incorrect to explain my good night's sleep by saying that I took a Seconal, and that Seconal is dormitive. So its dormitivity can figure in explanations. But these are causal explanations, which require backing through something possessing causal relevance. And it is not dormitivity but its realizers – the chemical properties of the pill, whatever they may be – that possess causal relevance.[16] Hence where dormitivity plays a role in explanations, it does so only by standing proxy for its realizers. Since it is the realizers that do the real causal work, it is they as well that do the real explanatory work. The Buddhist Reductionist would thus say that 'dormitivity' is a mere convenient designator.

Kim comes close to this way of putting it when he puts his point in terms of the claim that there are no second-order properties, only second-order designators. His reasoning is that we could not create new properties merely by quantifying over first-order properties. Since there are no second-order properties, they cannot be said to be the causes of anything. Second-order designators (that is, predicates) can figure in explanations. But these will be true only to the extent that the first-order properties quantified over are causally efficacious.

Lewis (1972) would deny that 'dormitivity' is second-order. On his analysis, the term rigidly designates those properties that cause sleep, so that it functions like an indexical: when asserted of Seconal it designates some one particular chemical property, when asserted of grandmother's sleep potion it designates some distinct property (perhaps a chemical property, but perhaps some other kind of property). On this analysis it would be a mistake to say that dormitivity is multiply realized,

---

for such laws was as yet unchallenged. The discussion of Kim (1993: 327–30) is particularly interesting on this point.

[16]   To suppose that both are causally relevant is to brook overdetermination. See Block (1990: 155–62) for a clear formulation of this and related points. He also brings up an important exception to the claim that second-order properties are causally inert, namely cases involving recognition of the property by an intelligent agent, as with the placebo effect: my knowing that Seconal is dormitive may itself play a role in my falling asleep.

since 'dormitivity' is no longer thought of as a kind-term. And on this analysis the dormitivity of the Seconal has genuine causal relevance, so that it may be said to play an autonomous explanatory role. Now it can be questioned whether Lewis' is the correct analysis of our use of dispositional terms like 'dormitivity'. But even if the analysis is correct, this would not help establish that dormitivity is an emergent property. For on this analysis, to explain my falling asleep by appealing to Seconal's dormitivity is just to indicate those chemical properties that brought about my sleep. The correlation between its dormitivity and its (relevant) chemical properties is no mystery, for these turn out to be the same thing.

'Dormitivity' would not ordinarily be classified as a functional term. The 'functional' label is usually reserved for terms referring to that which performs some specified task in a complex system, and sleep aids are not ordinarily thought of as complex systems. But dispositional terms like 'dormitivity', and functional terms such as 'carburetor', 'printer driver' and 'immune system', are (when understood as kind-terms) alike second-level designators. So if mental states are understood as functional in nature, then they will lack autonomous explanatory power, and the so-called special science of psychology will turn out to perform a purely systematizing role. Mental properties could not then be understood as genuinely emergent properties that non-reductively supervene on neurophysiological properties.

It would appear that a Reductionist might use a similar strategy to defeat the claim that person-properties are genuinely emergent: show that person-properties are functional or otherwise second-order, and then show that this drains them of all autonomous explanatory power. We shall pursue this strategy below, but first there is one major obstacle to overcome. The supervenience obtaining between person and elements is mereological supervenience. Kim claims, however, that the supervenience of the mental on the neurophysical is not a case of mereological (or 'macro–micro') supervenience. If this is right, then this strategy is not available to the Reductionist.

Kim's claim concerning mind–body supervenience comes in response to the following objection: mind–body supervenience is just a case of macro-micro supervenience, and in other cases of this relation (such as chemistry to microphysics) there is no problem of causal powers draining away from the macro-level, so a functional analysis of mental states should not have the consequence that the mental loses distinctive causal powers. Kim's response is, I believe, mistaken on two counts: functionalism does make the mental mereologically supervenient on the neurophysical, and Kim should not accept the opponent's claim that the mereologically supervenient may possess distinctive causal powers. Concerning the second point, it is of course true that water dissolves salt (something that neither hydrogen nor oxygen can do), just as it is true that the chariot (but not the wheels, not the axle, etc.) transports the driver. But the dissolving of the salt is nothing over and above the ionization of sodium and chlorine, something accomplished by hydrogen and oxygen atoms when suitably related – just as the transporting of the driver just is the result of the lateral motion of the chariot body caused by forces transmitted from the axle, etc. It is, of course, more convenient to speak of water dissolving salt, or of the chariot transporting the driver, than it is to speak of interactions among the atoms of hydrogen, etc., or of the wheels, axle, body, etc. And because this way of talking is more convenient, it is true – conventionally – that water dissolves salt and chariots transport their drivers. But conventional truth reflects not just how the world is but also what our needs, interests and cognitive limitations happen to be. It is ultimately false that water causes anything. And, we might add, water being ultimately unreal, it must also lack autonomous explanatory power.[17]

As for the first point, Kim's claim is that in the case of mereological supervenience, that which is said to have the supervening properties is typically at a higher level than that which is said to have the base properties, whereas in the case of the mental, supervening and base properties are both had by the same entity – a human or other sentient creature. While this claim has some initial plausibility, it does not stand up to detailed scrutiny. First, consider a case of mereological supervenience that appears to involve macro-level and micro-level entities, such as the relation of organic chemistry to micro-physics. Of course chemical properties are not type-identical with micro-physical properties; chemical properties are had by molecules, and the molecule is a macro-level entity. But 'molecule' is a convenient designator for a certain sort of array of particles. And so a term for a chemical property, such as 'valency', will turn out to be a convenient designator for the joint effects of certain of those particles' properties. Macro-level properties are just as second-order as dispositional or functional properties. If there seems to be a difference here, that is only because in the typical case of macro-level properties the quantification is often over the micro-level properties of a collection of disparate entities. Since properties are generally attributed to a single entity, we feel compelled to construct a macro-level entity to serve as their bearer.

It is also not clear that on a functionalist analysis, the bearer of psychological properties is the same thing as the bearer of the relevant neurophysical properties. That it may at first blush appear so is due to the inherently teleological character of functional analysis: pain is understood to be whatever serves the function of signaling tissue damage, and it is hard to see what else besides the system as a whole – the organism – it could serve this function for. But it is the aim of homuncular functionalism to discharge this teleology, first by replacing the sentient system with a set of homunculi, and then subjecting each of this first set of homunculi to functional analysis yielding less 'intelligent' homunculi, eventually reaching a level of purely mechanistic description that requires no further attribution of sentience. Any aura of teleology remaining at this level may then be discharged through appeal to processes of evolution by natural selection. Suppose, for instance, that the Implementationist

---

[17] The argument here relies on the claim that successful explanation must rest ultimately on causal connection. The non-reductive physicalist might assert instead that it is explanation that has conceptual priority: that causal laws are constrained by what counts as a good explanation. Van Gulick's (1992) defense of non-reductive physicalism appears to flirt with this at times. But to take such a line is to abandon realism. While this may be defensible, it seems incompatible with the motivation of most non-reductive physicalists.

Van Gulick also raises the sinkhole objection against Kim's claim that a functionalist analysis of the mental yields reduction: if so, then biological, chemical, and macrophysical properties are likewise epiphenomenal, which is absurd (1992: 173). The Buddhist Reductionist would respond that it only sounds absurd to say that, e.g., biological properties are causally inefficacious, because one has neglected to mention that this is true at the ultimate but not at the conventional level. It is conventionally true that influenza infection causes fever, hammer blows cause the denting of wooden desks, etc.

version of Connectionism is true.[18] Then what bears the properties on which supervene the properties of my belief that snow is white is a neural structure consisting of widely scattered but connected neurons. (Their connectedness results from whatever is the natural analogue of Connectionism's 'training-up' process; the brain has architecture that supports such a process because architecture of that sort was selected for.) On the other hand, it is I, or perhaps my mind, that bears the property of having this as a fixed and firm belief. The macro–micro relation that we saw in the case of a chemistry-to-physics reduction holds here as well.

I conclude that the case against autonomous explanatory powers for psychological predicates construed along functionalist lines does indeed generalize to (other instances of) mereological supervenience. We may thus return to the question whether Reductionists may avail themselves of this strategy in order to respond to the NMS challenge. Recall that the Personalist alleges that some person-properties, such as moral culpability, although supervening on properties of the psychophysical elements, have autonomous explanatory powers, and must be considered genuinely emergent. Can the Reductionist make a plausible case for properties like culpability being second-order? Much of the case for this claim was made earlier, in the discussion of self-revising systems, so my remarks here will be brief. My culpability presumably consists in my being deserving of punishment for my earlier misdeed. If we take a consequentialist line on punishment, then the point of punishing me would presumably be to lower the likelihood of myself (and possibly others) performing similar deeds in the future. So then I can be judged culpable only if there is a reasonably high probability that pain input into this causal series will alter the motivational structure that brought about the original misdeed and would otherwise lead to similar misdeeds in the future. This requires the propensity of a set of elements to perform the operations of identifying with and appropriating past and future elements in the series, that is, mastery of the person-convention. It likewise requires that the present set of elements be disposed to identify with and appropriate those elements making up the past misdeed. This in turn requires that the misdeed has resulted from a motivational structure that represents a relatively enduring feature of the series. It is also required that the system be pain-averse, and be capable of self-revision in response to pain. Culpability thus seems to be a disposition to exhibit a highly complex functional property under certain sorts of conditions: being likely to effect self-revision of relevant parts of the motivational structure in response to pain input cognitively linked in certain specific ways to past effective desires in the series.

If this sort of analysis is on the right track, then when my culpability results in some change, as for instance when my recognition of the wrongness of my misdeed results in my revising my motivational structure, there will be a vast array of elements involved: those involved in the self-monitoring system, various desires, those elements involved in the mental acts of identification and appropriation, and the like.

---

[18] See Lycan (1991). He takes Implementationism to yield a non-reductive form of physicalism: 'then the higher-level [intentional] structure exists and affords higher-level explanation whether or not any particular beholder cares for it' (1991: 282). What he overlooks is the fact that the kind of higher-level explanation in question – which yields 'higher-level generalizations' and makes sense of 'the system's apparently rational output' – reflects the cares and concerns of human beholders. It is our cognitive limits, for instance, that help make higher-level generalizations so immensely important.

It is the properties of these elements on which my culpability supervenes. This explains why we would use a convenient designator – a second-order designator – to describe my state. The elements involved are just too many and too multifarious to usefully discuss in any other way. And it is these elements and their properties that are doing all the work. So we can understand how, when they do their work, this could be expressed in terms of a judgment of culpability. The property has no autonomous explanatory role; it reductively supervenes on properties of the elements.

Buddhist Reductionists state that only that which bears its own essential nature (that is, that has an intrinsic nature) is ultimately real. By contrast, something that borrows its nature from other things is said to be merely conventionally real, that is, a conceptual fiction. The underlying reasoning here reveals the realist roots of Buddhist Reductionism. Something x whose nature is wholly extrinsic is the result of a process of aggregation. If all x's properties are borrowed from other things, then it must be a multiplicity of other things from which these properties derive. Otherwise, if it were just one thing y from which all the properties were borrowed, then there would be no temptation to suppose that x and y are distinct. We are likely to suppose that x is some distinct entity only when its nature is constructed out of the properties of two or more different things. And such construction of aggregates is a mark of the mental. It is we who bundle things together in pursuit of cognitive economy and in ways otherwise reflective of our interests. So if our aim is to find out the nature of mind-independent reality – how things are apart from their being apprehended and conceptualized – then we must operate with an ontology of things that bear their own essential natures. Hence if person-properties are second-order, functional, and multiply realizable, they can have no place in our ultimate ontology.[19] They are conventionally real, for they play important roles in our way of life. But to include them in our final ontology is just to count twice over what is already there. And to seek out some third, intermediate status for them is to fall prey to the same bad arithmetic.

Notes

[a] Interestingly, Buddhist Reductionists do not raise this point about wholes. This is no doubt due to the fact that their rivals the Naiyāyikas, the champions of real wholes, held that a whole ceases to exist upon the loss or replacement of one of its parts. For more on this see the next three endnotes.

[b] In point of fact, the Indian tradition as a whole has no Chariot of Devadatta problem to parallel the Ship of Theseus puzzle. Instead, in the texts of early Buddhism there is the expectation that we will simply agree that chariots are ultimately unreal, once it is pointed out that a chariot is an assemblage of parts. In later Abhidharma texts we can discern the argument discussed above against the existence of wholes in general, but this argument makes no use of the boundary-setting difficulties that the admission of partite entities presents us with. I would suggest, though, that this is not because Indian philosophers were simply ignorant of *sorites* phenomena. Rather, those Indian philosophers, the Naiyāyikas, who championed the existence of wholes went to extraordinary lengths precisely to insulate their doctrine of complex substances from problems of indeterminacy. Thus Nyāya maintains that the addition or subtraction of a part from a given substance results in the destruction of that substance and the coming into existence of a new substance. And likewise for change in the arrangement of the parts, and for such qualitative changes as

[19] Kim says that the heart of functionalism about the mental, particularly multiple-realization functionalism about the mental, is that 'mental states have no "intrinsic essence"' (1993: 332).

change of color, taste, odor, texture, and the like. (See Ramaiah [1978: 61–90].) This position obviously rules out many of the sorts of spectra of indeterminacy that would otherwise plague the champion of complex substances. I know of no Nyāya text explicitly linking this position with the intention to avoid such difficulties. But I find it hard to imagine what else might motivate the adoption of such a counter-intuitive view, particularly on the part of the eminently sensible Naiyāyikas. In any event, the Buddhist Reductionist was not given the opportunity to exploit *sorites* difficulties in arguing against persons and other such wholes; those difficulties had been anticipated by the opponent.

^c When Nāgasena tells Milinda that it is neither true nor false that adult and infant Milinda are the same person, he is best thought of as speaking of the ultimate truth. But the apparent bivalence failure in this case should be seen as purely rhetorical, calling attention to the fact that sentences containing 'person' are ultimately ill formed, so that the question of their truth simply does not arise. On my way of seeing things this is not, then, a genuine instance of a truth-value gap. Tye (1994: 189) would count this as a case of a truth-value gap, but he distinguishes such cases of failure of reference or presupposition from cases of vagueness by claiming that only in the latter case is something said that is neither true nor false. The difference here seems to be purely terminological.

Following my suggestion here means that if the Buddhist Reductionist is to meet Dummett's requirement of a reductionism that it claims there to be cases of bivalence failure in our use of the terms in the disputed class, this must occur at the level of conventional truth. Specifically concerning personal identity, Parfit may well be right that in a case where I undergo fission, neither of the resulting persons should be said to be me – that this represents the best possible extension of our use of 'person' in the circumstances, given the pragmatic constraints governing the term. So such cases would not give rise to truth-value gaps at the conventional level. Cases at the middle of Parfit's Combined Spectrum would, however, result in statements for which bivalence fails. Likewise in the construction of a series of maximal causal connectedness (that is, a 'person' series), there will be cases where the pragmatic demands behind this construction would be equally well served were a given element included in or excluded from the series. It will then be conventionally indeterminate whether that element is a part of the person supervening on that series. (Of course in the overwhelming majority of cases it will be completely determinate whether a given element does or does not belong to the series.) Buddhist Reductionists did not actually invoke this sort of genuine bivalence failure at the conventional level; but this is no doubt because, as the previous endnote suggests, they were not pressed to. The suggested extension is, I believe, fully consistent with their views.

^d The Nyāya route around *sorites* difficulties – the claim that the addition or deletion of a single part results in the creation of a new substance – comes at a price. We ordinarily take a far more relaxed attitude toward substantial change, holding that it is the same tree even after shedding all its leaves and replacing them with new ones. Nyāya owes us some account of this gap between our practice and their theory. The obvious place to seek such an account is in something like the Buddhist device of the two truths. Thus they might claim that while it is ultimately true that over time there are many trees, since each such tree consists of parts virtually all of which belonged to the predecessor tree, it is conventionally true that there is but one tree. This is so, they might explain, because conventional truth reflects the exigencies of practice, and when distinct trees bear this intimate relation it is far easier to lump them all together under the concept of a substance that endures replacement of parts.

But were Nyāya to proffer such an explanation, they would then be hard put to resist the synchronic reduction of partite substances. If the one enduring tree should be seen as conceptually constructed, for pragmatic reasons, out of many ephemeral trees, why should not the ephemeral tree be likewise seen as conceptually constructed out of coexisting tree-parts? Of course Nyāya will have much to say in response to this question, but at least then the real issues concerning the existence of substances shall have been joined.

^e That this was the Yogācāra–Sautrāntika view is well known. Cf. e.g., Dharmakīrti at NB I.14: '*Arthakriyāsāmārthyalakṣaṇatvād vastunaḥ*'. But the causal efficacy criterion of reality was also held by earlier Ābhidhārmikas. See, for instance, AKB on AK I.12c: '*dhṛtyādikarmasasmṛiddhā*'. There Vasubandhu makes clear that the existence of the four elements is proven by their respective actions (*karma*), which are to be distinguished from their essential characteristics (*svabhāva*). The distinction

between a *dharma*'s essential nature and its action or function is also used in Theravāda Abhidharma works. See, e.g., VM XIV.

ᶠ These include the Vātsīputriyas and the Sammitiyas, although it is not entirely clear whether the latter were not a sub-sect of the former. For surveys of the available historical data on Pudgalavādin schools, see Dutt (1971); also see Warder (1970: 275–76).

The exact nature of the Pudgalavādin position on persons is not easy to reconstruct, since the only extant non-hostile presentation, the *Sammitīya Nikāya Śāstra* (or *Āśrayaprajñāpti Śāstra*), survives only in Chinese translation. Of accounts in hostile sources, that in the Pāli *Kathāvatthu* is by far the longest and most detailed, but it disagrees in certain important respects both with such other hostile sources as *Abhidharmakoṣabhāṣya* and *Tattvasaṃgraha*, as well as with *Sammitīya Nikāya Śāstra*. Most significantly for our purposes, on the *Kathāvatthu* account Pudgalavādins hold that persons are ultimately real, whereas our other sources have them conferring on persons a kind of reality that is neither ultimate nor merely conventional. I would claim, however, that other features of the position described in *Kathāvatthu* have the result of effectively canceling out this difference, so that this and our other sources represent essentially just notional variants on a single view.

ᵍ See, e.g., TSP 337.

ʰ See, e.g., KV I.1.171–72; also *Sammitīya Nikāya Śāstra* 174.

ⁱ See, e.g., KV I.1.138–41; also *Sammitīya Nikāya Śāstra* 175–76, 183; also TSP 337.

ʲ See, e.g., AKB 461 (Duerlinger 139) ; TSP 337; *Sammitīya Nikāya Śāstra* 182–83. KV I.1.1 does assert that the person is ultimately real. But this account also makes clear that the person is causally isolated from the psychophysical elements. Now Abhidharma generally accepts the principle that only the ultimately real is causally efficacious. And it seems reasonable to attribute a causal closure principle to Abhidharma, which would make every ultimate real capable of causal interaction with any other ultimate real. If this is correct, then the KV account turns out to be just a notional variant of the position that the person is neither ultimately real nor a mere conceptual fiction but instead has an ontological status somehow intermediate between the two.

ᵏ See, e.g., TSP 336; also *Sammitīya Nikāya Śāstra* 177–78. But in KV I.1.212 the Pudgalavādin exhibits vacillation over whether the doer of the deed and the reaper of the (karmic) fruit may be said to be identical.

ˡ AKB 463 (Duerlinger 143–44).

ᵐ AKB 462 (Duerlinger 140). The example is also mentioned at *Sammitīya Nikāya Śāstra* 182.

ⁿ See KV I.1.189.

ᵒ AKB 469 (Duerlinger 157). The relation between the *mahābhūta* (primary material properties) and the *bhautika* (secondary material properties) is a vexed one in Abhidharma. The former consist of the four elements: earth, air, water and fire. While these are said to take the form of atoms, they are also generally identified with their respective defining tangible properties: solidity, agitation, cohesion and heat. The *bhautika* are made up of such sensible properties as color, shape and odor. These are said to be secondary or derivative (*upadāya*) in the sense that they do not occur apart from the occurrence of the four *mahābhūta*. It is also not usually suggested that these take the form of atoms. Yet they are uniformly classified as ultimately real, on an ontological par with the *mahābhūta*. That the Pudgalavādins used the *mahābhūta–bhautika* relation to explain the relation between person and elements suggests that they thought of the former as somewhat like the distinction between primary and secondary material properties found in figures like Descartes and Locke, with secondary properties being the cognition-dependent effects of combinations of primary properties. But on this point the Abhidharma texts are silent.

ᵖ See AKB 463 (Duerlinger 144).

CHAPTER FIVE

Ironic Engagement

Reductionists claim that their view has two important ethical consequences: first, that coming to be a Reductionist leads to the cessation of existential suffering (the despair that stems from the realization of our mortality); and second, that it follows from Reductionism that we are obligated to act so as to promote the welfare of others. We have already touched briefly on both of these points. In this chapter we shall look more closely at the arguments in their favor. Both points turn on the claim that Reductionism, as a middle path between Non-Reductionism and Eliminativism, makes room for mitigated forms of the person-regarding attitudes. This makes both vulnerable to the objection that Reductionism induces a kind of distancing or alienation that undermines important features of our person-regarding attitudes. Such Reductionist-grounded attitudes would, according to the critic, be in disequilibrium, that is, unable to withstand knowledge of their own causes.[1] If the critic is right about this, then Reductionism is self-defeating or pragmatically inconsistent: it recommends that we act in ways that would make us worse off by its own terms. This is obviously a serious charge, and calls for some investigation. But first we should review and clarify the arguments for Reductionism's alleged ethical consequences.

The ethical consequences of Buddhist Reductionism

According to the Reductionist, the personhood convention prevails because it is more conducive to overall welfare than the readily available alternatives, such as punctualism and the *Weltgeist* convention. We have learned to think of ourselves and others as persons – elements have been organized so as to identify with and appropriate past and future elements in series of maximal causal connectedness – because this results in less overall pain than when we think of ourselves and others in the punctualist grasshopper way, or in the collective *Weltgeist* way. This does not mean, however, that the personhood convention is the ideally optimific strategy. For it leads to a distinctive sort of pain – existential suffering – that does not arise under the punctualism convention or the *Weltgeist* convention. Only when we think of ourselves as persons does the question arise what meaning my life can have in the long run, given that in the long run there shall be no *me*.[a] The punctualist *p*-person does not exist long enough for this question to have any force; and under the *Weltgeist* convention what matters is the continued existence of the *we*, something about which there is seldom much doubt. So utility would be better served if there were some way to combine the virtues of the personhood convention (such as the avoidance of gross imprudence, and the gains in welfare achieved through individual initiative) with a

---

[1] For the terms 'equilibrium' and 'disequilibrium' see Nozick (1981: 348–52).

strategy for avoiding existential suffering. Reductionism is said to represent this ideally maximizing strategy: while it is better to consider ourselves persons, it is best to understand 'person' to be a mere convenient designator.[b]

This is so because coming to be a person involves learning to see one's life (the events in the causal series) as a kind of self-authored narrative.[2] Identification with and appropriation of past and future states of the series are most efficiently accomplished through getting the elements to use the convenient designator 'my life' to unify the series' constituent events. This is effective because of the narrative constraints on what is to count as a life: demands for such things as discernible characters with relatively stable dispositions, a central character with links to a variety of subsidiary characters, and a story-line that connects individual acts to larger episodes, and individual episodes to larger unities, by way of an at least implicit *telos*.[3] When a system comes to deploy this concept under these constraints, its capacities for self-scrutiny, self-control and self-revision are clearly enhanced. For instance, the combined demands for a stable central character and an underlying *telos* serve as an effective way to organize the process of self-revision. To comply with these demands I must identify those relatively stable patterns in my behavior that importantly affect the future of this series and my interactions with other characters, I must be able to arrange these in such a way as to show some overarching unity of purpose, and I must be prepared to alter those dispositions that do not serve or no longer serve that purpose. Identification of the relevant behavioral patterns is a form of directed, self-scrutinizing information-gathering that enhances self-control. And the demand for an underlying *telos* is an effective way to organize the process of self-revision. We saw in Chapter 3 that systems of self-scrutiny, self-control and self-revision are better Consequentialist maximizers than systems lacking these capacities. Coming to see the events of the series as a story, in which I play the lead role and also write the script, is an effective strategy for constructing such systems.

---

[2]   Schechtman (1996: 93–135) provides a useful discussion of the process of narrative self-constitution. What I would dispute is her claim that this represents an alternative to Reductionist and other accounts of personal identity, with their exclusive focus on the unity relation. She usefully points to the puzzling ambiguity of 'personal identity', which for philosophers has meant the diachronic identity of persons, but for everyone else seems to mean, roughly, a person's most important traits ('who a person really is'). She then argues that the philosophers' quest for the unity relation rests on a mistaken reading of the question of personal identity, and that the narrative self-constitution view represents the best answer to a better under-standing of the question, personal identity understood as a question of characterization. A Reductionist can, however, forge a connection between the diachronic identity understanding and the characterization under-standing, for the Reductionist account of the unity relation makes crucial use of the notion of a person as a self-revising system. And the problem for any self-revising system is to determine which elements of the system are to be taken as stable and enduring features. So a Reductionist account of diachronic identity leads to the raising of the characterization question. And the Reductionist should, I think, agree with Schechtman that the narrative self-constitution view is a promising approach to answering that question.

[3]   There is, of course, room for debate concerning how tight the narrative unity constraint should be. Some will claim that the Victorian novel should be our model here, while others will hold that a life-narrative need be no more unified than a collection of short stories. The Reductionist need not be committed to any particular position in this debate in advance of the relevant empirical considerations. And these considerations might include facts about individual lives, or about shared forms of life, so that the optimific degree of narrative unification might vary across lives or cultures.

At the same time, the demand that a life appear to display some sort of unifying *telos* sets the stage for suffering. For this is the demand that my life be made up of projects that contribute to the meaning, value and purpose of this life. And how can this life be seen as meaningful when in the long run its central character will disappear from the stage? For whom else if not for *me* can this life be said to have purpose? (Of course the proponent of the *Weltgeist* convention will insist that I should instead identify with a collective *we* that will survive my death; but this option has already been ruled out at this point.) All my projects, and my commitments to particular others, seem to dissolve in pointlessness in the face of the utter contingency of my life.

Coming to see 'person' and 'my life' as mere convenient designators alleviates this suffering, for this makes transparent the process whereby persons are constructed. Not only does this show that persons are constructed, and hence not ultimately real, it also makes apparent the point behind the construction, namely to minimize the occurrence of pain impersonally conceived. So not only does coming to be a Reductionist remove the temptation to suppose that there is ultimately a *me* for whom the events of this life could have meaning, it also reveals why it may be useful to continue to act as though persons do exist. Suffering is thereby shown to be the result of a perfectly understandable cognitive error: we have been taking too seriously what is really just a useful piece of conceptual shorthand, like the average US taxpayer. It would be a mistake to inquire into, say, the reproductive anatomy of the average US taxpayer; but this does not detract from the usefulness of the construct when it comes to predicting the results of some fiscal policy. It is likewise wrong, according to the Reductionist, for me to think there is ultimately someone for whom the events of this life could have meaning. Still the underlying rationale behind the personhood convention continues to hold: policies promoting the right kinds of self-scrutiny, self-control and self-revision tend to maximize overall utility. I can reap the rewards of such policies, yet avoid suffering, by coming to recognize that while my life cannot have a point, there is a point to my having a life.

Parfit famously claims that in cases of fission, I can obtain much of what matters to me in survival even though neither of the resulting persons will be me (1984: 261–66). To this it is often objected that the existence of persons who resemble me and who will carry on with my projects and care for those I love can be of little consolation, given that these persons will not be me. The Buddhist Reductionist analysis of suffering helps us understand both Parfit's response and that of his opponent. My death appears bad just because it tends to undermine my sense that my life, and its projects and special commitments, can have meaning. Given this, the fact that in a case of fission my projects and special concerns will be continued will not seem to mitigate the badness of my death. It seems that the continuation of my projects and special concerns must be seen as events in my life in order to contribute to the sense of an underlying *telos* in that life. On the other hand, when we come to believe that the felt need for meaning is purely instrumental – that the demand for a narrative unity to our lives is just a way of ensuring that we are appropriately self-revising systems – then the fact that it will be other persons who carry on my life will no longer make a great difference. In ordinary survival, part of an effective maximizing strategy is to identify with and appropriate the future states of one person; in cases of fission, an effective strategy will require identifying with and appropriating states of two persons. If fission became common, we might invent some new concept that did for a fissioning life what 'the meaning of my life' does for us now. But the point would just be to make the maximizing strategy of identification and appropriation easier to implement in those changed circumstances.

Just as coming to be a Reductionist is said to alleviate suffering, so it is also said to dissolve the tension we commonly feel between the demands of others and the promotion of our own interests. It is widely held that temporally neutral self-interested conduct is supremely rational: it is always rational for me to choose to promote my interests, timelessly construed. At the same time, it is generally recognized that such conduct often conflicts with the demands of morality. Various attempts have been made to reconcile the seemingly conflicting requirements of morality and rationality. The karma–rebirth ideology, for instance, claims that the conflict is merely apparent, since immoral acts motivated by desire for selfish gain invariably cause the agent pain in subsequent lives; it is only ignorance of the causal laws governing karma and rebirth that makes some immoral acts appear rational. Such attempts at reconciliation are widely seen as implausible, however. Reductionists propose a very different way to dissolve the tension. Our common-sense view of what is rational stems, they claim, from taking too seriously what is really just a shortcut strategy for minimizing pain impersonally conceived. The fundamental obligation is to prevent pain, wherever it may occur. The personhood convention, with its associated view of what is rational, represents an effective strategy for preventing much avoidable pain. But where it is possible to prevent more pain by deviating from that strategy, we are obligated to do so.[4]

The Buddhist Reductionist formulates the argument for this claim in the following way:

> The continuant and the collective are unreal, like the row, the army, etc.
> There exists no one whose suffering this is, hence of whom will there be the owning of this?
> Ownerless sufferings are all devoid of distinction [between 'mine' and 'other'].
> Because it is suffering, it is to be prevented; how can this be restricted?
> If it were asked why suffering is to be prevented, it is agreed upon without exception by all [that it is].
> Thus if it is to be prevented, then also all [of it is to be prevented], if not then one's own case is also like that of [other] persons.
>
> If one says that that suffering [of other persons] does not harm me, hence it should not be protected against,
> Then since the sufferings of future bodies do not harm me, why should they be protected against?
> 'Because that is *me*'; if this is one's thought, that is a mistaken construction,
> For it is one who dies and another who is born.[c]

---

[4] The conflict between rationality and morality is thus like the commonly remarked-upon conflict between rule-utilitarian and act-utilitarian policies. Thus a rule utilitarian might, for instance, justify a stringent prohibition on lying, on the grounds that if it were left to us to decide whether or not to tell the truth in particular circumstances, we would prove bad at calculating the utilities of the outcomes. So although there will be individual cases where adherence to the rule against lying is not optimal, the overall effect of the policy is better than any alternative. The act utilitarian has greater confidence in our ability to fairly assess the consequences, and so would permit utility-maximizing lies.

The first section constitutes an argument for the claim that pain is ultimately – and hence impersonally – bad. The person, being an aggregate, is ultimately unreal. Hence if pain is ultimately real, it must be ownerless or impersonal. It is universally agreed that pain is bad ('to be prevented'), although this agreement is typically restricted to one's own case. Either pain is ultimately and impersonally bad, or no pain (including what is conventionally one's own) is ultimately bad. But it is absurd that no pain should be ultimately bad. Therefore pain is ultimately and impersonally bad.

The second section then uses this result to argue for the conclusion that we are equally obligated to act so as to prevent others' and our own pain. We all agree that each of us is obligated to act so as to maximize our own welfare, considered from a temporally neutral perspective. Flossing my teeth now is an inconvenience and can cause minor discomfort, but doing so helps prevent far greater future pain in the form of gum disease; so I ought to floss my teeth. On the other hand, many do not recognize an obligation to make similar small sacrifices to prevent the pain of the homeless and destitute stranger. This asymmetry is usually explained (and sometimes justified) on the grounds that the future person with gum disease will be me, while the stranger is not. But ultimately the future person is just a set of elements, and these are numerically distinct from those present elements that either will or will not floss. It is only conventionally true that that is me; this is a socially constructed fact.[d] And its social construction involves the ultimate fact that pain is bad; absent this fact, there could be no explaining the force of any convention. So my coming to identify with and appropriate the states of those future elements merely represents a strategy for minimizing pain impersonally construed. This strategy is justified on the grounds that I am ordinarily better situated to prevent future pain in this series than are others.[5] But it is also true that I am often well-situated to prevent others' pain. When this is the case, then the obligation I recognize to prevent my own future pain extends to others as well. It would be rational to persist in the practice of privileging self-interested concern only if it could be shown that this practice results in less overall suffering than any other. And we have ample reason to believe that this is false. We may continue to employ the useful fiction of the person in our interactions with one another.[e] But seeing this fiction for what it is, we now know not to let it blind us to the real needs of others for our assistance.

The alienation objection to the derivation of the ethical consequences

To this argument Paul Williams objects, '[T]o help others effectively requires *not* that we discount their individuality as the persons they are but actually to focus on that individuality most closely' (1998: 174). Williams goes on to tie this point to the notion of honoring a person's uniqueness, and this I think is a mistake: one can find solace in the fact that others are just like oneself in their woes. Still there is an important point here: we tend not to take much comfort in aid delivered impersonally, that is, in ways

---

[5] This account of self-interested concern requires that such egoism as we exhibit be the result of socialization into our prevailing personhood convention. Against this it is sometimes alleged that egoism is an innate disposition for our species. For a discussion of the empirical evidence supporting the claim that egoism is an acquired trait see Martin and Barresi (1995).

lacking in any suggestion of the intersection of two self-authored narratives. What we seem to want is that some particular someone care about us as a distinct particular someone. This means that the care be seen to proceed from a concern that is grounded in details of the two narratives. And this in turn means that the effective care-giver must convey to the recipient of their care both a sense of respect for the recipient's authorship, and the sense of an engaged authorship behind the act of care. Williams' objection might then be put as the point that a Reductionist would be hard pressed to convey either.

The Reductionist will reply that if effective assistance requires that one take up a particular stance toward the object of one's concern, then this shall simply be incorporated into the job description of the care-giver: in honoring our obligation to prevent suffering in others, one must act in ways typical of persons who are genuinely engaged in the sufferings of other persons. It thus emerges that the Buddhist Reductionist argument for altruism has the same consequence as its strategy for preventing existential suffering: after coming to be a Reductionist, one should continue to behave in accordance with the personhood convention, since such behavior is instrumental for promoting impersonal welfare. This is akin to the maximization strategy that some utilitarians use to answer the saintliness objection.[6] It is sometimes claimed that utilitarianism is an implausible moral theory in that it requires us to be moral saints, perfectly self-sacrificing creatures who consequently lack purely personal projects and caring commitments to particular others. For, goes the saintliness objection, if one's fundamental obligation were always to choose that action that best promotes the overall welfare, then it is likely that there will always be more optimific acts open to one than those that further a personal project or that confer special benefits on one's intimates. Since utilitarianism thus recommends an ideal that is all but unattainable for most humans, it is an implausible moral theory. While some utilitarians respond to this objection by simply biting the bullet, others accept the premiss that moral saintliness is generally unattainable, and reply by way of the maximization strategy. According to this strategy, it is a fact of human nature that we are best able to contribute to overall welfare if a significant portion of our efforts goes into pursuing personal projects and honoring commitments to particular others. For, it is claimed, those who are allowed to live lives of their own are more likely to be effective at assisting others in need. And their assistance is less likely to go astray if it is delivered chiefly to intimate others, persons whose needs and proclivities they are likely to know well. So utilitarianism, rather than insisting that we pursue the barren life of the moral saint, encourages us to forge rich and rewarding personal lives.

The maximization strategy and the Buddhist Reductionist approaches to suffering and to altruism share the feature that conformity to some part of our personhood convention is deemed instrumental for promoting overall welfare.[7] But the maximization strategy is subject to the important alienation objection, and this raises the question whether Reductionism does not face the same difficulty. The alienation objection is, roughly, that having a life is not the sort of thing one can choose as a means to further

---

[6] Scarre (1996: 182–204) gives a useful survey of the debate over the saintliness objection.

[7] This is assuming that having grounding projects and special relations with particular others is part of our understanding of what it means to be a person.

some separate end. It would, for instance, be most peculiar for someone to claim as their reason for bestowing love and affection on their spouse and children that this is the best way open to them to contribute to overall welfare. To claim this would seem to show a singular lack of understanding of just what love and affection are, and a person who said this might properly be described as alienated from their feelings of love and affection. The alienation objection has it that the utilitarianism of the maximization strategy, rather than promoting rich and rewarding personal lives, actually fosters alienation from our projects and important emotions. Such an outcome might be avoided if it were only a small elite of utilitarians who devised a maximization strategy for the non-utilitarian masses. But aside from the question how this elite are to live their lives, its nasty ring of authoritarianism makes such a proposal unacceptable to most. The only other option appears to be self-deception: somehow arrange it that after devising our own maximization strategies, we cease to believe our projects and intimate relations have only derivative value for us whenever we are actively engaged in those projects and relations. Perhaps this is possible; effective brainwashing or even neurosurgical techniques might be devised to induce the desired sort of compartmentalization. But to make utilitarianism so strongly self-effacing has seemed to many to be incompatible with its being a plausible theory about the nature of morality.

A similar objection could be raised to the Buddhist Reductionist proposals concerning suffering and altruism. The Buddhist Reductionist recommends that we come to fully recognize that Reductionism correctly describes ourselves.[f] They also claim that this will bring about the cessation of existential suffering, and motivate us to help others overcome suffering. But both these claims involve the prescription that we take up central elements of the personhood convention. For instance, the disposition to identify with and appropriate past and future elements of the causal series is necessary if one is to avoid the disutility of gross imprudence. And this, the Reductionist agrees, is best accomplished by viewing the events of the causal series as a life, something displaying the unities of a self-authored narrative. Likewise the ability to meet one's obligation to alleviate the suffering of others requires that one be able to show a genuinely personal concern for their suffering. And this seems to require that the care-giver be capable of exhibiting genuinely personal responses to the suffering of others. But this puts the Reductionist-inspired care-giver in precisely the position of the maximizing spouse and parent of the preceding paragraph: claiming a personal regard for the other that is undermined by its (in this case, Reductionist) rationale. Likewise the demand that we take up the narrative stance toward our lives appears incompatible with the belief that there are only causally connected, impersonal and ephemeral elements. If Reductionism is true, it may also be true that welfare is maximized by our feeling genuinely personal regard for others, and our viewing ourselves as the authors of our own life-narratives. But the belief that Reductionism is true seems to irreparably alienate us from all such person-involving attitudes.

Ironic engagement as a Buddhist Reductionist response to the alienation objection

A utilitarian might try to answer the alienation objection to the maximization strategy by denying that being strongly self-effacing is necessarily a defect in a moral theory.[8] This reply is not open to the Buddhist Reductionist. For the alienation objection to the Reductionist proposals is meant to show that Reductionism is not merely self-effacing but self-defeating: doing what it tells us to do would result in our being, by its very lights, worse off. This is so because Buddhist Reductionism tells us that we should conduct ourselves in certain ways through coming to believe certain things about ourselves. Thus it cannot be merely self-effacing. If belief in the Reductionist account of our nature alienates us from person-involving attitudes that are necessary to our welfare, then a life in conformity with the theory would be worse, by its standard of welfare, than many other accessible lives.

There are two other ways utilitarians might answer the alienation objection to their maximization strategy: by espousing a kind of indirect utilitarianism, and by claiming that direct utilitarianism need not be alienating. The indirect utilitarian holds that in choosing actions or courses of conduct, utilitarianism is not always the best decision procedure. Just as the sophisticated hedonist will aim not at pleasant experiences themselves but at that sort of life that objectively contains the most pleasure, so a sophisticated utilitarian should choose not acts that best maximize utility, but acts in conformity with a character and life-narrative that objectively best promote overall welfare.[8] So while a sophisticated utilitarian may well be cognizant of the fact that acts flowing out of their specific projects and commitments promote the impersonal good, this will not be their reason for choosing them. There is, consequently, no risk of alienation from one's personal projects and commitments.[9] A very different approach to the alienation objection retains a commitment to utilitarian decision procedures, but denies that in the case of following the maximization strategy, employing them results in alienation. For, it is claimed, when I reflect that my showing care and concern for particular others helps promote overall welfare, this should not be taken to mean that my reason for care and concern is the impersonal and hence alienating one of aiming to promote some transpersonal utility. What I aim for is to promote the well-being of the objects of my care and concern, thereby contributing to the overall welfare. The alienation objection assumes that the maximization strategy makes their well-being a mere means to the intrinsically valued overall welfare; this response claims that their well-being is instrumental to the overall welfare just by being one component of the overall welfare, so that I may choose to promote it in the unalienated way typically expressed as 'I care about them, and want them to be happy.'[10]

In Chapter 3 I have given a name to the Reductionist response to the alienation objection: 'ironic engagement'. The name suggests that it will parallel the indirect

---

[8]   See Railton (1984: 154–56) and Scarre (1996: 197) for brief discussions of this question, and further references.

[9]   See Railton (1984) for a subtle and nuanced defense of this strategy.

[10]   Scarre (1996: 197–204) favors this response to the alienation objection. He claims that the indirect utilitarian reply does after all commit us to a program of self-deception.

utilitarian response. For the name is meant to suggest that we are able to enter into certain sorts of engaged attitudes despite a knowledge that would seem distancing (in the way irony is usually thought to be), and thus alienating. And the indirect utilitarian response claims that a sophisticated utilitarian can have as their aim their personal projects and commitments despite the knowledge that what value these possess comes from their instrumentality for overall welfare. At the same time, there are certain resonances between Buddhist Reductionism and the direct utilitarian response. In particular, that response relies on the point that overall welfare is not some transcendent object, that it just consists in the aggregate of such things as the well-being of one's intimates. And this is reminiscent of Buddhist mereological reductionism. So one might expect there to be parallels between this reply and the Reductionist's 'ironic engagement' response. In fact, there are analogies with both strategies, though in neither case is there a perfect parallel.

Consider the case of civic pride. Suppose I take pride in the city in which I was born and now live. I am, however, a reductionist about cities (an 'urbanist' for short): I know that the existence of a city just consists in the existence of certain buildings and infrastructure in a certain location, and certain people interacting in certain ways. I know that 'city' is a mere convenient designator for these more particular entities when related to one another in certain characteristic ways. I know that cities are only conventionally and not ultimately real. Does this knowledge undermine my civic pride? As Railton points out (1984: 146–47), alienation is not always a bad thing; some degree of alienation from my home town might, for instance, be useful in combating the excesses of civic chauvinism. For this purpose, however, the mild alienation induced by reminding myself that I might just as well have lived in Nutley, New Jersey, or by recalling the history of late medieval Italy, might suffice. The question is what effect my urbanism will have on my pride. The suggestion is that it must have a terminally corrosive effect, since one cannot take pride in something one believes to be ultimately unreal. But this need not be true. I am, after all, a reductionist about cities, not an eliminativist. That is, I believe our use of the convenient designator 'city' reflects the genuine utility achieved when these more particular elements are related to one another in these characteristically urban ways. Moreover, I may believe that this utility is greatly enhanced when the inhabitants of urban aggregates engage in various kinds of cooperative behavior, and that such behavior is more likely to occur if they feel a sense of attachment to their location. So I may conclude that it is better, all things considered, that city dwellers feel pride in their city; and since I am a city dweller, I should feel pride in my city.

But what then? So far it seems all I have is a reason to feel a certain way about the place where I happen to live that has nothing whatever to do with that place. So any feeling I managed to summon up as a result would not be the genuine article, would it? The sophisticated urbanist would agree that such a direct strategy is unlikely to succeed. There is, though, a better way. I should reflect on what it is about this place that I particularly enjoy and appreciate, and begin to dwell on these features. Then I should share the fruits of these reflections with my neighbors, some of whom will no doubt respond with their own suggestions of valuable features to add to my list. Of course various defects will also come to light in these conversations. But the upshot of our discussions may well be that we set about on a campaign of civic improvement – an activity that will itself enhance our sense of civic pride. All of this is, I think, perfectly consistent with my urbanism. And it is hard to see how the feeling I come to have in the end is not the genuine article.

When, for instance, I enthusiastically describe the charms of the place to a visitor, my aim is not to enhance the experiences of all who dwell here. My aim is just to express my pride in the city. True, my pride came about because of my desire that the experiences of the inhabitants be improved. But that hardly makes that desire the motive behind all acts expressive of my pride. To think so is to commit the genetic fallacy. Indeed I can be perfectly clear how it is that I came to feel civic pride, yet still have the genuine article. The knowledge will induce a degree of ironic distance – enough to ward off the dangers of civic chauvinism. So as I wax poetic in singing the city's praises to the visitor, I shall also comment wryly on the somewhat hyperbolical character of my account. Still I do wax poetic; I want to share my love of the city with others. I am ironically engaged.

Comes the rejoinder: that the knowledge and the feeling can coexist does not show that they are logically compatible. For the feeling might be an atavism that simply resists rational correction.[11] This is, after all, pride we are discussing, and pride involves the sense that one is somehow ennobled through one's relation to the thing in which one takes pride. How can the urbanist rationally maintain that they derive value from their relation to a fiction? How can one feel pride toward something one believes not to exist? The urbanist replies that to take pride in something is to be disposed to do things such as praising it, defending it against its detractors, seeking to correct its flaws, and the like. This is what feeling proud – feeling ennobled by one's relation to the object – ultimately amounts to. And while the city is ultimately unreal, there is a reason for me to have these dispositions toward what 'city' conveniently designates: doing so tends to further enhance the experiences of urban dwellers like myself. My pride survives the disclosure that its object is only conventionally and not ultimately real, precisely because the object is thereby shown to just consist in more particular entities arranged in particular ways. There is no need here for a transcendent object, The City. So in cultivating my own sense of civic pride I need not try to deceive or distract myself concerning the ontological status of the object. The civic pride of the sophisticated urbanist is in equilibrium.

The Buddhist Reductionist will say similar things about those person-regarding attitudes considered instrumental to welfare impersonally construed. First, these attitudes allow of indirect cultivation. Just as 'Get a life!' is not gratuitous advice when directed at those who chronically complain about trivial matters, so the recommendation that I show special concern toward my projects and those with whom I have particular connections is one we can effectively act on. At the outset, my efforts at stamp collecting or friendship may feel artificial. But if I persevere, I shall eventually find that one becomes an avid stamp collector or a true friend through practice and habituation. The activity begins to take on a life of its own, so that what

---

[11]   This would be a natural place for the sociobiologist (or, as they now prefer to be called, evolutionary psychologist) to tell a just-so story about conditions in the ancestral environment that gave a reproductive advantage to those with a genetically linked mental module for collective territoriality. The upshot would no doubt be that our genetic endowment makes civic booster clubs perfectly understandable, but (unfortunately) makes equally understandable such things as campaigns of ethnic cleansing, and that we must formulate policies with these things in mind.

was initially valued only extrinsically now has intrinsic value for me – I genuinely care about my friend's welfare, and about the sorts of things that philatelists care about. If this kind of concern does not develop, the problem is likely to lie in my choice of object, and I should try befriending other acquaintances, and taking up bowling. Of course the sophisticated Reductionist will most likely already be in firm possession of the standard array of person-regarding attitudes upon coming to be a Reductionist, and so will not need to cultivate these attitudes. This is so because it is existential suffering that (according to the Buddhist Reductionist) motivates one to become a Reductionist, and existential suffering arises out of just these attitudes. What becoming a Reductionist does is give one a new reason to have such attitudes (in mitigated form), namely the fact that they tend to promote overall welfare impersonally construed. What the possibility of indirect cultivation shows is that their being instrumental for this new end need not undermine the holding of these attitudes.

Second, the Buddhist Reductionist will claim that the Reductionist's person-regarding attitudes are in equilibrium. Consider, for instance, Williams' advice to the would-be practitioner of enlightened compassion to exhibit a concern for the recipient of one's care that comes from the heart. Of course Reductionism denies the ultimate existence of any such thing as a heart. Still it is conventionally true that genuine compassion issues from the heart. This is because effective care-giving must take into account the particularities of its object, and this is more likely to occur when the care-giver is not impelled by an ulterior motive but is instead personally moved by the plight of the recipient. The new motive one acquires on becoming a Reductionist, to promote overall welfare impersonally construed, is consistent with effective caring of this sort. For this motive is not ulterior relative to the welfare of the recipient. Rather, what it aims at just consists in such more particular things as this person's welfare. So there is no self-deception for the Reductionist who heeds Williams' advice: to promote impersonal welfare is just to do things like showing a personal care for particular others; heartfelt compassion is just caring that is effectively focused on the needs of the recipient, that does not treat the recipient as a mere means to some private end of the care-giver. While the ultimate truth may be put as the denial that there is a heart, it is possible to know this and yet practice what would conventionally be called a caring that comes from the heart.

This, then, is the Buddhist Reductionist response to the alienation objection. Just as Reductionism is said to constitute a middle path in the area of ontology, so its proposal for ironic engagement may be seen as a middle path in ethics. At one extreme stands the cult of authenticity, with its demand that our acts be rooted in an essence that is beyond the reach of rational criticism: that my projects be of value to me just because they are mine, and that care for others derive from an act of pure will (which is another way of putting the demand that love be unconditional). At the other extreme stands a nihilistic detachment, insisting that since there is no authentic self, a paralysis-inducing alienation is inescapable and all action is just bad faith. The Buddhist Reductionist sees both views as selling us short, as denying that we can, as it were, walk and chew gum at the same time. The Buddhist Reductionist holds that, like the sophisticated urbanist, we can induce and maintain belief in a useful fiction while knowing it for what it is. We can be genuinely engaged persons while still preserving the sense of irony necessary to escape the suffering that is the usual fate of persons. We are smart enough to do two things at once.

Notes

ᵃ I am here interpreting *duḥkha* to mean not 'pain' but the very special sort of suffering that comes from the realization of one's own radical contingency. There are those who take the First Noble Truth to mean that each moment of sentient existence is necessarily painful. And it is true that one finds in the tradition the claim that even seemingly pleasant experiences are in fact characterized by *duḥkha*. On my interpretation, though, this truth amounts to the claim that for any reflective person, the happiness-seeking project that is constitutive of personhood will inevitably be undermined by the realization of one's own mortality, so that one's life comes to be predominately characterized by suffering in the form of frustration, alienation and despair. On this interpretation, a life may contain many experiences of unalloyed pleasure and happiness, yet still warrant the characterization of suffering. Vasubandhu argues in support of this claim at AKB VI.3. As for the claim that *duḥkha* is best understood as existential suffering, this is supported by the story of the four signs that supposedly led the young Gautama to renounce the world: an old person, a sick person, a corpse and a renunciant.

ᵇ The Abhidharma distinction between *punya* and *kuśala* reflects this point. Actions that are *punya* or meritorious are those that bring about pleasant karmic fruit. Actions that are *kuśala* or good are those that are conducive to nirvana. (See AKB IV.45–46ab.) Given that the laws of karma are said to reward actions conforming to conventional morality with pleasant fruit, it turns out that acting in accordance with conventional morality is meritorious, that is, leads to pleasant rebirth. Agents are often encouraged to take advantage of this fact by coming to identify with and appropriate the states of their future births. But this course of action, by encouraging attachment and clinging to the future states of the series, also sets the stage for existential suffering. Thus it is that acts that are *punya* or meritorious can be *akuśala* or evil.

On certain occasions, the Buddha is said to have exhorted his audience to do the meritorious rather than the good. The tradition explains this as an exercise of his *upāya* or pedagogical skill. On these occasions, it is claimed, the audience was made up of individuals who were constitutionally incapable of understanding and appreciating the teachings of non-self and the path to nirvana. These individuals were also ignorant of the truths of karma and rebirth, but the Buddha knew them to be capable of understanding and appreciating these truths. Moreover, by living a life devoted to performing meritorious actions, they would improve the odds of being reborn in a state more conducive to following the path to nirvana. The Buddha's exhortations were thus intended to help advance them on the path to nirvana. On these occasions, the *kuśala* and the *punya* happened to coincide.

But for a very different account of the relation between these two terms see Keown (1992: 116–28). It will be clear that I reject Keown's overall characterization of Buddhist ethics as, not a form of Consequentialism, but instead a virtue ethics akin to Aristotle's. I would agree that an account of the virtues plays a central role in Buddhist ethics – but as part of an aretaic Consequentialism, not an aretaic eudaemonism. The fundamental difficulty I see with the latter understanding of the Buddhist Reductionist project is that it requires some substantive theory of human nature in which to ground claims about the virtues' tendencies to promote human flourishing. This requirement strikes me as incompatible with the view that persons are only conventionally real and thus socially constructed. Aretaic Consequentialism, by contrast, views virtues as devices for minimizing pain impersonally construed, and thus needs no thick account of human nature. What I find valuable about Keown's approach is its insistence that nirvana be understood as a positive state of human fulfillment. This is a welcome corrective to a long line of authors who claim that nothing much can be said about nirvana since it transcends ordinary human understanding.

On my understanding of Buddhist Reductionism, its ethics would consist of two parts: an account of conduct that is conducive to nirvana, and an account of the mode of existence of the enlightened person. Given the relation between the good and the meritorious described above, the discussion of conventional morality will fall in the former. Since this part of Buddhist ethics is addressed to those who are not yet enlightened, it will be formulated in terms of the conventional truth. It could thus take any one of a number of forms: act utilitarianism, rule utilitarianism, or even a form of deontology. This is so because adherence to conventional morality is here seen as merely instrumental to attaining the insight required for nirvana: what matters in the early stages of the Path is just that one conform one's behavior to those causal laws that govern the dispelling of ignorance about the self, and adherence to the dictates of conventional morality will in time cause a weakening of one's egoistic habits of mind. In practice the Buddhist tradition has tended to cast its discussion of conventional morality in terms of a stock set of virtues. This is in keeping with the aretaic cast of Indian ethics generally. But it is particularly appropriate for the Buddhist Reductionist project, with its overarching notion that everyday conduct may be best governed by habits that represent convenient shortcuts: not ideally optimific, but more likely to promote welfare than is deliberation, given the constraints of worldly practice. As for the second part of a Buddhist Reductionist ethics, the account of life in nirvana will likewise take an aretaic form, but of a more reflective sort. Since enlightened persons understand the ultimate grounding of the conventional virtues, they are less likely to go astray if given license to deviate from conventional morality on those occasions when doing so produces greater welfare. The enlightened person, guided by an understanding of the badness of pain impersonally construed, will thus practice perfected forms of the conventional virtues.

c   BCA 8.101–3, 8.97–8. This is, of course, a Madhyamaka text, and Madhyamaka rejects Reductionism, so the presence of this argument here seems puzzling. I shall have much to say about this below. But at this point it can be said that the placement of the argument in the penultimate Chapter 8 on the perfection of meditation (*dhyāna*) rather than the final Chapter 9 on the perfection of wisdom (*prajñā*) might be used to relieve the puzzlement. For this might be taken to show that Śāntideva is still at this point discussing preliminary techniques which must first be mastered before approaching the final understanding of emptiness (which will undermine Reductionism).

This creates a new difficulty, in that the compassion of the *bodhisattva* (or of the *arhat* – see VM IX.40–87) becomes instrumental for enlightenment, rather than the result of enlightenment that it is said by the tradition to be. This is a difficulty, however, only if a clear means/end distinction may be drawn with respect to the attainment and practice of enlightenment. And there is evidence that this is not so at least for the orthodox Indian (Hindu) tradition's discussion of liberation (*mukti*). See, e.g., Fort (1996: 144) for evidence that in Advaita Vedānta, no clear line is drawn between the traits of the attained *jīvanmukta* and the traits cultivation of which is deemed conducive to this status. Brown (1996: 161) makes the same point with respect to the *Mahābhārata*. Given that the *arhat* and the *bodhisattva* represent the Buddhist tradition's versions of the ideal of the *jīvanmukta*, perhaps Śāntideva likewise means compassion to serve as both instrumental for and a result of enlightenment.

d   Some caution is required in understanding the Buddhist Reductionist notion of 'conventional' (*loka-saṃvṛti*) in terms of the concept of social construction. Classical Indian culture lacks the modern obsession with cultural variation in human practices, an obsession that deeply colors what it means for us to call something socially constructed. But at BCA 8.115, Śāntideva does say that the belief that this body belongs to a self results from practice; presumably he has in mind a socially inculcated practice.

e   Although immediately after calling the belief that this body is mine as the result of a practice, Śāntideva claims that we might through practice come to see others as likewise parts of ourselves. This suggests that he thinks we might need to revise our concept of the person (perhaps in the direction of the *Weltgeist* alternative?) if we are to successfully overcome the egoistic tendencies that stem from our taking the current conception too seriously.

f   The Buddhist takes this to be no simple matter. Reflection on the sorts of philosophical considerations we have examined is deemed necessary to this task, but not sufficient. In order to fully realize that there is no more to myself than a causal series of impersonal elements, I must engage in the systematic examination of those elements as they actually occur in this causal stream. What is called Buddhist meditation is a collection of techniques for carrying out such examination. The Buddhist tradition has been fairly consistent in holding that both philosophical reflection and meditation are required for enlightenment.

g   Such an indirect strategy may be used to dissolve not only the paradox of hedonism but also the paradox of liberation. Consider, for instance, the form of the latter paradox that applies to the ideal of liberation (*mokṣa*) as articulated in the *Bhagavad Gītā*: one should seek liberation since it is the ideal state for humans, but liberation can be attained only through the cessation of all selfish desires. The indirect strategy of *karma yoga* has one aim not directly at desirelessness, but at developing the disposition to perform all actions out of a sense of duty.

CHAPTER SIX

Establishing Emptiness

J.L. Austin famously claimed that in every philosophical work there are two parts: the part where the author makes some outrageous claim, and the part where the author takes it back. In the first part of this book I sought to defend a Buddhist formulation of Reductionism about persons. I shall now, in this second part of the book, claim that Reductionism is nonetheless wrong in important respects. But this is not additional evidence in support of Austin's characterization. For one thing, the reasons that I shall give for rejecting Reductionism rest on a kind of global anti-realism that many readers will consider far more outrageous than anything claimed in the first part of the book. More importantly, the view of persons that I shall now defend does not involve the blanket rejection of Reductionism, so I shall not be taking back all that was said in the first part. Thirdly, the argument of this work might also be seen as having the following disjunctive structure:

1. Either realism is true or global anti-realism is true.
2. If realism is true, then we ought to be Reductionists and hold that persons are empty.
3. If global anti-realism is true, then all things are empty.
4. Therefore persons are empty.

(I shall begin to explain later in this chapter what it means to say that something is 'empty'.) While the conclusion of this argument-structure does not reflect my real aspirations (since I hope to show that all things are indeed empty), it might be the best that I can realistically hope for. In that case, once again I would not be taking back what I claimed in the first part. In this chapter I shall be discussing some of the principal arguments that Buddhist critics of Reductionism deployed in their development of a distinctive form of anti-realism. In subsequent chapters I shall present some of the consequences of this view in the areas of epistemology, semantics and ethics. But before we can embark on any of this I need to make clear how I shall be using the contentious terms 'realism' and 'anti-realism'.

Realism and anti-realism

While the disjunctive strategy described above does not represent my intentions, I do hold (2). So it might be said that my defense of Reductionism in the first part of this book had the truth of realism as a suppressed premiss. By 'realism' I mean roughly the following view: (i) there is one true description of the world; (ii) with truth understood as the property that a statement possesses when the state of affairs that it expresses in fact obtains; and (iii) with the understanding as well that the states of affairs the obtaining of which makes up the world are independent of whatever relevant concepts we employ. The realist understands the world as 'what is there anyway', and this 'anyway' is meant to express a certain sort of mind-independence that is central to the realist conception of objectivity. But there are at least two different ways in which a state of affairs might be independent of mind, and we must be careful to keep them separate. Consider the view (popular among early modern philosophers) that certain material properties like color and smell are secondary properties. On one formulation of that view, such things as red and blue are dependent on consciousness in the same way that pain is thought to be: they occur only when they are cognized. This view contrasts such properties with what are called primary properties, such as extension and shape, which it claims may occur even when they are not being apprehended. On this view, red and blue could be said to be mind-dependent, and shape and extension to be mind-independent. Now a subjective idealist like Berkeley claims that all material properties are actually mind-dependent in this sense. Thus when I have the experience of perceiving a tree, both the color and the shape that I cognize exist only in relation to my cognition (or in relation to the cognitions of other perceivers). But there is another sense in which the subjective idealist could say that both the color and the shape are mind-independent: it might be claimed that the occurrence of these properties is quite independent of any finite mind's having the concepts of color and shape. On this conception of mind-independence, the states of affairs that obtain might outrun our ability to conceptualize them. (Since Berkeley held such a view, he would count as a realist, as I am using the term.[1])

It is this second understanding of mind-independence that is central to the realist view of objectivity. The underlying intuition at work here is the thought that the concepts we employ might reflect interests and cognitive limitations that are distinctive of us as individuals, as members of a cultural group, or as humans; any such reflection of our interests and cognitive limitations may detract from the ability of representations employing such concepts to capture the nature of the world. Aristotle noted, concerning the pair consisting of the obtaining of the state of affairs that Socrates is white and the truth of the statement 'Socrates is white', that while there is reciprocal implication between them (the state of affairs obtains when and only when the statement is true), the causal relation only goes one way: it is the fact that Socrates is white that determines the truth of the statement 'Socrates is white', and not the other way around.[2] To obtain truth we must let the world determine the nature of our representations. To be sure, our representations will make use of concepts, which we could agree are in some sense mental contents that do not exist apart from the minds that employ them. What we must insure, says the realist, is that it is the world that dictates the shape these concepts take. We must take special care to guard against the possibility that in employing some concept in our descriptions of the world we are actually projecting or superimposing on the world some nature that is not found there but only in the minds of cognizers. We do so, claims the realist, by only employing concepts that represent ways the world might be like absent those means of representation. True statements reflect how the world is independent of the concepts we employ in describing it.

---

[1]   Dummett (1993: 464) agrees.

[2]   *Categories* 12.13b.14–22.

It is a realism of this sort that lies behind the mereological reductionism at the heart of Buddhist Reductionism. This can be seen in some of the details of the argument against the existence of partite entities that was discussed in Chapter 4. At key points the argument invokes the principle of lightness or parsimony, for instance when it points out that all the alleged effects of the whole can be explained in terms of facts about the parts. Implicit in this invocation is the thought that the world would not bring about the same effect twice over, that such apparent redundancy is more likely to be the result of conceptual superimposition. The argument also relies on the causal efficacy criterion for real entities, something that would likewise seem central to the realist picture. Moreover, there is the fact that by itself this argument could equally be used to support either mereological reductionism, or a naive mereological eliminativism that claims wholes are – quite simply – utterly unreal. But it is a realist impulse to seek that one true description that accounts for all the facts making up the world. And among these facts is the fact that we employ concepts for wholes.[3] It is the realist interrogation of the concepts we employ in representing the world that leads to the notion that it might be facts about our interests and our limitations that explain our use of such concepts (and in the end to the reductionist's qualified vindication of that use). Finally there is the fact that the Buddhist formulation of mereological reductionism makes possible an account of vague predicates that explains their utility while preserving bivalence (at the level of ultimate truth). Given the realist commitment to the idea of there being one true description of the world, preserving bivalence is an important desideratum.

Now if this is right, and mereological reductionism is defensible on realist assumptions, then I think a strong realist case can be made for the Buddhist formulation of Reductionism. In particular, the device of the two truths helps us understand how the Impersonal Description thesis could be true despite its clearly counter-intuitive nature. But I think we can go further still. The same tendencies that produced Buddhist Reductionism eventually led to the formulation of a radical nominalism according to which all that exist are radically ephemeral, unique, causally efficacious particulars. Now realists are innately suspicious of such things as universals, properties and resemblances, given that they look like just the sorts of things that would not be thought to exist were it not for our use of general concepts. The chief obstacle in the way of realists embracing such a radical nominalism has always been the difficulty of developing a nominalist semantics that explains our use of kind-terms without invoking such things as universals, properties or resemblances. Certain Buddhist nominalists claim to have overcome this difficulty. (See the Appendix for an account of the semantics that is said to make this possible.) If their claim is correct, then I think it could be argued that realists should embrace just such a radical nominalism. In that case ultimate reality would be not only fully impersonal,

---

[3] It might be thought that this fact is not mind-independent in the relevant sense. But note that while the state of affairs could not obtain if we did not employ any concepts, it could obtain even if we lacked the concept of a concept and so were unable to represent to ourselves our employment of concepts for wholes. And the question of mind-independence is the question whether the state of affairs could obtain in the absence of the concepts we employ in representing it. The mereological reductionist claims there could be no trees or tables without the relevant concepts. But if the only concept-users were singularly unreflective, there could be the employment of concepts absent any means of representing this fact.

but also made up entirely of genuinely unique particulars, hence strictly ineffable in nature. (I leave it to the reader to decide whether this should be considered a *reductio* on realism.)

I believe that realists ought to be Reductionists about persons. But since the disjunctive argument-strategy outlined above does not reflect my intentions, I shall not say any more in defense of that claim. What I shall now defend instead is the claim that realism is a necessary condition for Reductionism's being true. Could it be the case that Reductionism is true while at the same time it is not the case that there is just one description corresponding to how things are independently of how we conceive of them? If we agree that Buddhist Reductionism represents the best formulation of reductionism about persons, then I think the answer is No. This is because of the role that the notion of the ultimate truth plays in that formulation. Recall that for instance the distinction between Reductionism and Eliminativism cannot be drawn without using the distinction between conventional and ultimate truth. Likewise recall the central role that the distinction between the two truths plays in answering any number of important objections to Reductionism, especially to its Impersonal Description thesis. Now the notion of the ultimate truth is just the realist notion of an account of how things are independent of our modes of conceptualizing them. Without this notion, Reductionism could not be clearly distinguished from its rivals, let alone adequately defended.

The same conclusion can be supported by considering the role that *sorites* considerations play in the defense of Reductionism. As may be seen from Parfit's work, any plausible criterion of diachronic personal identity is subject to instances of bivalence failure: for any such criterion it is possible to construct scenarios where by its lights it is indeterminate whether the person who exists after the imagined change is numerically identical with the person before the change.[4] Why should such cases – where (to use Parfit's phrase) it is an 'empty question' whether person B is the same person as person A – be taken as supporting the Reductionist view? The thought at work here is that the world itself must be fully determinate, that every possible state of affairs must either obtain or not obtain, so that cases of apparent indeterminacy can only be accounted for in terms of facts about us and our conceptual apparatus. We are happy to concede that there are cases where it is an empty question whether a collection of grains of sand is a heap, or whether this heap of bricks is the same heap as the one that was over there earlier, precisely because we see 'heap' as a mere convenient designator for certain sorts of collections of things. And notice that this resolution depends on the further thought that if we only took the time and effort, we could instead describe all the more particular things (grains of sand, bricks) and their properties (size, spatio-temporal location), and thereby avoid the instances of indeterminacy. This notion of an 'im-heapish' description is an expression of the fundamental realist conviction that at the end of the day there is such a thing as

---

[4] Parfit (1984: 231–43) only considers two such criteria, but the argument can be generalized given that the target view is the 'further-fact' version of Non-Reductionism, according to which the continued existence of the partite entity of the person does not consist in the continued existence of some simple entity, the self, but in some further fact pertaining to the parts and their vicissitudes. That Buddhist Reductionists did not employ *sorites* considerations in their defense of the position does not detract from its importance to that defense. See pp. 78–85 for a discussion of the reasons for this omission and how it may be remedied.

how the world is, independently of our ways of conceptualizing it, and that truth consists in conformity to just this 'how the world is anyway'. The success of *sorites* considerations in supporting Reductionism requires the prior acceptance of realism.

I can now state what it is that I do intend to try to show. While I hold that a realist ought to be a Reductionist, I also believe that there are good reasons to reject realism. Specifically I believe that realism requires the assumption that the ultimately real things have intrinsic natures. And I shall shortly begin to discuss a number of arguments designed to show that this assumption is false. So if I am also correct in my claim that a Reductionist must be a realist, then the real difficulty with Reductionism will turn out to be that it rests on a false assumption about the ultimate nature of reality. I shall proceed as follows. This chapter will be taken up with an examination of some arguments against intrinsic natures, and the consequences of these arguments for realism. After that will come a brief foray into epistemology, specifically an investigation of the epistemological consequences of the denial of intrinsic natures. Then will come a chapter devoted to the vexed question of anti-realism and truth. I have already indicated that the position I shall be defending might be thought of as a kind of anti-realism (namely what I shall call 'Buddhist anti-realism').[a] But there are many different views that go by the name of anti-realism, and many of these have extremely controversial consequences for semantics, so some clarification will be in order. Finally there will be a chapter devoted to examining the consequences of this position for our understanding of what we are and how we should conduct ourselves – an examination of what it would mean for us to know ourselves to be empty persons.

The realist commitment to intrinsic natures

The doctrine of intrinsic natures is the claim that all and only ultimately real entities have intrinsic natures. To say of an entity that it has an intrinsic nature is to say that in addition to any extrinsic properties it may have, there are genuinely intrinsic properties that characterize it. Additionally the doctrine claims that every property that is intrinsic to an ultimately real entity is an essential property of that entity. By a property I shall here mean what corresponds to a monadic predicate, an expression that takes only one name as argument. (I thus distinguish between properties and relations, the latter being what correspond to predicates of adicity greater than one, e.g., '— is taller than —', '— is between — and —', etc.) Now the resources of our language enable us to form a great many predicates that may truly be asserted of a given particular. So I can say of my cat not only that she is black but also that she is presently under the table, that she is disliked by the dog downstairs, and even that she is such that 7+5=12. But only certain monadic predicates denote intrinsic properties, namely those containing no names, definite descriptions or other devices for referring to distinct entities. Intuitively an intrinsic property is one that characterizes an entity quite independently of the ways in which other entities are. Being black would thus count as an instance of an intrinsic property of my cat, while the other three properties mentioned above would not. Now the doctrine of intrinsic natures says that all of an ultimately real entity's intrinsic properties are essential to that entity. This means that such an entity cannot undergo qualitative change in any of its intrinsic properties. So if my cat were an ultimately real entity, then while it could undergo change with respect to the property of being under the table – having the property at some times and lacking it at others – it could not change with respect to the intrinsic property of being black. No intrinsic property of something ultimately real can be incidental; all such properties are essential. It is then said to have a nature that is intrinsic, whereas the nature of something that is merely conventionally real is strictly speaking not intrinsic but extrinsic.

Buddhist Reductionists use the contrast between the concepts of 'one's own' and 'borrowed from another' to explain the distinction between intrinsic and extrinsic natures.[b] Suppose that the ultimate constituents of material objects are (genuine) atoms of four kinds: earth, air, water and fire. Suppose also that heat is the intrinsic nature of the fire atom, while wetness is the intrinsic nature of water atoms.[c] Now a given volume of water, such as the water in a pot, while essentially wet, may change from being hot to being cold. So if heat is an intrinsic property, then by the doctrine of intrinsic natures the volume of water in the pot is not an ultimately real entity. This will not come as a surprise, since we already see the mass of water as an aggregation of water particles. But the fact that it undergoes qualitative change with respect to an intrinsic property gives an additional reason to consider it a mere conceptual fiction. This in turn means that all its properties are derived or 'borrowed' from whatever are its ultimate constituents. On the atomic hypothesis described above, the wetness of this water derives from the wetness of its constituent water atoms. But its heat, when it is hot, cannot derive from the water atoms, since that which is essentially wet is not essentially hot. Thus the hot water in the pot must be an aggregate of water and fire atoms. While the volume of water appeared to have both essential and incidental intrinsic properties (wetness and heat respectively), on analysis it turns out that neither property is genuinely 'its own'; both are 'borrowed' and thus ultimately extrinsic.

Similarly, my cat might change in color only because its blackness, seemingly an intrinsic but incidental property, turns out on the Buddhist Reductionist account to be 'borrowed' and hence not ultimately intrinsic. While her blackness may be said to be conventionally intrinsic, analysis reveals it to involve covert reference to those things through relation to which she is presently described as black. Of course we do not subscribe to the variety of atomism described above, and we might be inclined to question the claim that a seemingly incidental intrinsic property like heat turns out on analysis to be essential. We may instead think that the fundamental particles of physics, whatever they might be, could undergo change with respect to a quality like heat. But this is most likely because we have learned to think of heat as kinetic energy, which we think a particle could have to different degrees at different times. Now the degree of kinetic energy a particle is said to possess is determined by its motion. And the motion that a particle exhibits is an extrinsic property of that particle: its motion cannot be specified without reference to other particles or to a spatio-temporal frame of reference. On this conception of heat, then, that a particle has a given level of kinetic energy is not a fact about its own nature; it is instead an 'external' fact that depends on relations between the particle and other things.

A realist should, I claim, hold the view that whatever entities are ultimately real have intrinsic natures. This was the view of Buddhist Reductionists. Their reasons are clearly traceable to their mereological reductionism. If, as mereological reductionists maintain, all partite entities are reducible without remainder to their constituents, then every property of a partite entity may be explained in terms of the properties of its constituents. Thus no properties of partite entities are ultimately intrinsic. But now suppose that the properties of the entities $p_1, p_2, \ldots p_n$ that are the constituents of the whole W were likewise all extrinsic. In that case, any explanation that was forthcoming of the nature of W would be incomplete. It would require for its completion some account of how $p_1, p_2, \ldots p_n$ come to have whichever of their properties figure in the explanation of W's properties. Suppose we can reductively explain the properties of p_1 in terms of properties of $p_{n+1}, p_{n+2}, \ldots p_{n+k}$, but that the properties of the latter are likewise all extrinsic. In this case we have clearly embarked on an explanatory regress that will undermine all explanatory force unless it can be terminated. Successful termination requires that the entities figuring in the final *explanans* have only intrinsic natures. Only then will we be able to understand how W could come to 'borrow' properties from its parts, for only then will we be assured that the ultimate parts of W have properties that are genuinely 'their own' and so available for 'lending' to higher-order entities.

The Buddhist Reductionist also claims that ultimately intrinsic properties are essential to their bearers – that in the final analysis all qualitative change is of extrinsic properties. This also derives from their mereological reductionism. Recall that their realism makes them inherently suspicious of all aggregation. This attitude applies as much to the aggregation of properties as it does to the conjunction of entities thought of as separable parts. So when it turns out that the pot of water has two distinct intrinsic properties – heat and its absence – it is only natural that they should account for this in terms of the presence or absence of ultimate constituents that have heat as intrinsic nature. For the alternative is to see water atoms as things that have wetness as an intrinsic property, but may also either have or lack heat as another intrinsic property. And this bundling together of intrinsic properties looks to the mereological reductionist like the same sort of aggregative process that led to the conceptual construction of the chariot.

But one need not adopt the Buddhist Reductionist stance to endorse the ultimate denial of intrinsic incidental properties. For there is something deeply problematic about the idea that something might undergo change in any of its intrinsic properties. While we may be accustomed to distinguishing between a thing's essential properties and its incidental or contingent properties, this distinction may not make sense as applied to its intrinsic properties. For to call a property intrinsic is to say it is part of its bearer's nature. And it sounds distinctly odd to say that a certain thing both has and lacks a certain nature. How can it be said to both be and not be a certain way? It doesn't help to be told that this occurs at two distinct times. For just what is the 'it' that is to be the locus of both the presence and the absence of this nature? Why are we to suppose that there is here just one enduring thing? The Aristotelian answer is that the subject of qualitative change is specified by way of the essential intrinsic properties: the water, that which may be either hot or cold, is that which is essentially wet. But now we require some account of the relation between essential and incidental properties, between wetness and heat. The occurrence of wetness, we are told, determines a range of potentialities that must be filled in some way or other at each moment, so that the water will always be hot or warm or cold. But this invocation of potentiality will arouse realist suspicions that what we really have here is a case of conceptual construction. For here 'potentiality' looks like little more than a projection of our expectations given past experience of co-occurrences of wetness and heat or its absence. There is nothing in the experience itself to justify the judgment of an enduring substance underlying the qualitative change. Even if we (unlike the Buddhist Reductionist) chose to see the wetness and the heat as intrinsic properties of one thing, nothing on the side of the object would tell us that this is the same thing as what later has wetness and cold as intrinsic properties.

Now for reasons that have already been discussed, I believe that realists should be mereological reductionists. And the doctrine of intrinsic natures is a consequence of mereological reductionism. But this doctrine is compatible with a wide variety of views concerning the nature of the ultimate reals. Realism requires that their nature be independent of whatever conceptual resources we use to represent them. The doctrine of intrinsic natures requires that the nature of each be intrinsic and essential to that entity. The combination of these two views will mean that the world consists of a determinate number of atomic facts, all of which are logically independent of one another. But it is still open how many such facts, and of what sort, there are. There might, for instance, only be one such fact, namely the occurrence of pure Being (as maintained by the Eleatics). Or there might be a plurality of such facts but they are all mental in nature (as maintained by subjective idealists like Berkeley and Vasubandhu). Or again that there is just one such fact, the occurrence of pure Being, but this is mental in nature (as held by Advaita Vedānta). Realism tells us there is always a potential gap between the way the world is and how we represent the world. The doctrine of intrinsic natures tells us that this gap arises through our failure to fully analyze phenomena. But further argument is needed before we can say whether the ultimate reals fall into natural kinds or are rather genuinely unique and ineffable; whether they are physical or mental in nature or of both sorts; whether there are many of them or just one. If the intrinsic natures requirement can be met by so wide an array of ontological views – from an absolute monism to a radical nominalist idealist pluralism – then the realist should not be entitled to complain that the requirement is overly stringent.[5] So if it should turn out that the intrinsic natures requirement cannot effectively be made compatible with facts about the world that we all acknowledge, then this will indicate deep difficulties with realism. It is to just such an anti-realist argumentative strategy that we now turn.

The problematic relation between intrinsic nature and bearer

Suppose we were to agree that among the ultimate constituents of material objects are earth atoms, with solidity as their intrinsic nature. Just what is the relation between the earth atom and its solidity? This question does not arise if the atom and its nature are identical, but before investigating that hypothesis let us explore the possibility that they are in some sense distinct. The earth atom itself is said to be that which bears its essence or defining characteristic, while solidity is said to have the function of

---

[5]   It should be noted that this requirement does not itself exclude that form of common-sense realism that acknowledges partite entities like tables and trees as fully real. That such realists likewise accept the intrinsic natures requirement is shown by the fact that they respond to arguments for mereological reductionism by seeking to show that (some) partite entities have autonomous explanatory power.

characterizing this bearer, giving it its determinate nature. Since they have what appear to be separate functions, it seems to make sense to think of bearer and defining characteristic as at least conceptually separable, and so the question of their relation likewise seems legitimate.

If the bearer is that which is characterized, then is it in itself devoid of intrinsic nature? The difficulty with this hypothesis is that there can be no such thing as what lacks any nature of its own. To think otherwise is to imagine that there might be some such thing as 'prime matter', a kind of pure potentiality that lacks all determinacy, something that somehow *is* without being any one way or another. Some would claim that they can make perfectly good sense of this notion of a sort of 'pure stuff'. The difficulty is that in doing so they are covertly supplying their allegedly characterless bearer with a defining characteristic of its own, namely 'pure stuff-ness'. So if there is a separate bearer to be characterized, then it must be something that in itself has some determinate nature. But then in that case it is not clear that the bearer may be said to be characterized by the defining characteristic. For if the bearer already has a determinate nature apart from its being characterized by the defining characteristic, then the function of the defining characteristic – to give the bearer a determinate nature – would seem redundant. Moreover, if the bearer in itself has some determinate nature apart from its being characterized by the defining characteristic, then we may ask how it comes to possess this determinate nature. That is, if we begin by asking how the bearer b comes to have the defining characteristic D_1, and we are told that b in itself has some determinate nature, then since this is equivalent to saying that b already has some defining characteristic D_2, we may now ask how it is that b comes to be characterized by D_2. And here there are just two possibilities: D_2 characterizes a b that is itself without defining characteristic; or D_2 characterizes a b that already possesses some determinate nature. But the first possibility has already been ruled out on the grounds that the idea of a pure propertyless bearer is incoherent. And the second possibility is tantamount to claiming that D_2 characterizes a b that is already characterized by some D_3. So this possibility may be rejected on the grounds that it leads to a vicious infinite regress. The hypothesis that bearer and defining characteristic are in some sense separable does not stand up to detailed scrutiny.[d]

Suppose, then, that bearer and defining characteristic are in fact identical, that, e.g., an earth atom just is solidity. Now our ordinary notion of an entity has two aspects, that of the particular itself, and that of a nature that may be common to or shared with others. In the case of the atom, for instance, there is the fact of its being this particular atom, and then there is the nature of solidity that it has in common with other entities. And the bearer/defining characteristic distinction seems to correspond in some ways with this distinction between the particular and what is common, with the notion of the bearer serving to express the particularity, and the notion of the defining characteristic serving to express the shared nature. So if bearer and defining characteristic are in fact identical, it is incumbent on us to ask which of these two aspects the entity actually expresses. It might be, for instance, that the identity of bearer and defining characteristic privileges the bearer side, that the notion of defining characteristic is absorbed into the mere 'thisness' of the entity. But this would seem to take us back to the idea of the entity as a pure substrate devoid of any nature – an idea we have already seen to be incoherent. So the hypothesis of identity should instead be seen as privileging the aspect of a nature that is shared with others. The earth atom would then be seen not as a 'thing' that somehow 'has' solidity, but instead just as an instance or occurrence of the nature of solidity.

Now there are those who think it is always a mistake to suppose that a property like solidity could be particular in the way in which we think a rock or a tree is particular. According to their way of thinking, we may immediately reject the view that an earth atom just is solidity, since a property like solidity could never be particular in the way we think an earth atom is. Properties, they would say, are always universal, and so (in the case of physical properties) either ubiquitous or else having no spatial location whatever. To this the proponent of identifying the atom with its solidity will reply that there is nothing absurd in supposing that the brown color of the cow is just as particular as the cow – that this brown occurs only where this cow is. True, the desk and the dog may have what we would call exactly the same color. But this judgment may be explained either in terms of resemblances among the three color-particulars, or in terms of some one brownness universal that inheres in all three color-particulars. That is, our judgment that the cow and the desk are just 'the same color' expresses not numerical identity but qualitative identity: it is not that there is some one thing (the color) that is located in both, but rather two things (the color-particulars) are related through similarity (which can be understood as either the resemblance-relation or the relation of being inhered in by a common universal). So the identity of the atom with solidity cannot be rejected quite so quickly.

But while it is true that the notion of property-particulars is a coherent one, still the objection we have just considered raises an important point. If an earth atom just is a solidity-particular, how exactly is this solidity-particular to be individuated, given that every other earth atom will likewise be said to just be an exactly resembling solidity-particular?[6] The notion of a color-particular appeared to make sense only because we could rely on substances like the cow and the dog to individuate the resembling browns. But the hypothesis we are examining is, in effect, that ultimately there are no substances, only properties. On this hypothesis, the solidity that we attribute to some one atom a_m cannot be distinguished from the solidity attributed to a distinct atom a_n just on the basis of their residing in different atoms. For a_m and a_n just are the solidity. So to individuate the two atoms (and the solidities in which they consist), it seems we must turn to other properties, such as spatial location. Perhaps we can say that a_m and its solidity are located in region R_{17}, while a_n and its solidity are located in region R_{23}. But then how are region R_{17} and region R_{23} to be individuated? Not through reference to the respective earth atoms located in the two regions, for this would involve a vicious circularity. Instead it seems we must rely on some intrinsic difference between the two regions. Now if space is construed not relationally (as no more than the sum of certain relations among objects) but as an entity in its own right, then its defining characteristic could be said to be non-obstruction. So then region R_{17} and region R_{23}

---

[6] We are supposing that all atoms have the same size and shape. The view that space is not continuous but discrete, that there is a basic 'atomic' size than which there can be nothing smaller, and that all atoms are of that size, would serve as a guarantee of the atom's impartite nature. And if it were granted that all atoms are of the same 'atomic' size, it would be difficult to see how atoms could be of different shapes. But even if atoms did come in different sizes and shapes, there could still be some having the same size, shape and other essential properties, so the problem remains.

are to be individuated in terms of the two distinct non-obstruction property-particulars that characterize them. But recall that on the present hypothesis, R_{17} is identical with a non-obstruction property-particular, and likewise for R_{23}. The regions cannot be individuated by reference to the property-particulars that characterize them, for the regions just are those property-particulars. We are once again confronted with an infinite regress.[e]

The upshot is that it seems we cannot make sense of the notion of an entity that bears its own intrinsic nature. If bearer and essence are conceived as distinct, then there is no clear way to understand how the essence comes to characterize the bearer. And of course if the essence cannot be said to perform the function of characterizing the bearer, then it seems odd to call it an essential nature. It is equally odd to call something a bearer when we cannot understand how it could come to bear its nature. So the hypothesis of distinctness seems hopeless. If, on the other hand, bearer and essence are conceived as identical, then we have trouble accounting simultaneously for both the particularity of the entity and its having a nature that is shared with other entities. But the problems induced by the intrinsic natures requirement have only begun.

Intrinsic natures and change

It is a basic fact of our experience that things undergo alteration. Milk becomes curds; water freezes to form ice; leaves change color, fall to the ground and decay; people mature, grow old and die. Is the fact of alteration compatible with the claim that ultimately real entities have intrinsic natures? Some alterations involve what we would consider incidental properties of the entities, and in these cases there would seem to be no problem. We might say that it is not an essential property of the leaf that it be green, or be attached to the tree; so the leaf's turning yellow and falling is compatible with its continued existence as a leaf.[7] And this is important if we are going to preserve our ordinary way of describing the event. When we say that the leaf changes color and falls, we seem to be saying that it is the leaf that undergoes the alteration: first it is green and on the tree, then it – that very entity – is yellow and on the ground. So we seem to be committed to there being properties that make this thing continue to count as a leaf even when it is no longer green and on the tree, and that these properties continue to obtain through the alteration. Likewise when we say that water freezes we are expressing commitment to a particular view of water's essence. People once thought that all liquids are aggregates of water atoms, and all solids are aggregates of earth atoms. On that theory, being liquid is an essential property of what we call water, so that strictly speaking water cannot be said to freeze. If, on the other hand, we hold that water's essence is being made of H_2O, then since H_2O molecules can assume both the solid state and the liquid state, we can after all speak of water undergoing the alteration from liquid to solid ice. For then it is just an aggregate of molecules having the property of being H_2O that undergoes this change.

---

[7] We might, though, wonder whether there could be leaves that are always yellow (in a world in which chlorophyll is green) and are never attached to trees.

What, though, of the case where there seems to be alteration of essential nature? We would ordinarily consider milk and curds to be distinct substances: it is not curds that come from the cow's udder, nor would one try to make a *raita* or a smoothie if there were only milk on hand. And if these are distinct substances, they should have distinct essences. But in that case milk cannot be said to become curds: something whose essence it is to be (say) liquid and sweet cannot come to have the incompatible essential properties of being thickened and sour. On our ordinary understanding of what milk is, milk cannot serve as the subject of this alteration. The same difficulty arises when we speak of a child growing up. Who is it that undergoes this process? It would seem to be essential to children that they be 'of tender years', and to grow up is to lose that property. An adult is someone to whom maturation has already happened, so they cannot be said to undergo the process either. Perhaps we might pin the process on the teenager. But then we will have to ask how the child came to be a teenager, and the search for a subject of that alteration will lead to the same difficulties.[f]

Of course none of this is thought to pose a real problem, for we handle these cases in just the same way we handle the case of water freezing – by positing an underlying substance that survives the alteration. So we think of milk as made up of H_2O plus a variety of organic compounds, and see the milk–curds transition as involving merely structural changes in some of those compounds. And we think of childhood and adulthood as stages or phases in the history of an enduring substance, the person. In either case the properties thought essential to the distinct things – sweetness and sourness, youth and maturity – get demoted to the status of the superficial. In this way, alterations of this sort – where something is said to become something else – are assimilated to cases of merely incidental alteration, as with the change of the leaf's color and location.

Such assimilation has its limits, though, for it will not work in the case of things that are thought to be ultimately real. Consider the case of the fundamental subatomic particle that is destroyed in a near-light-speed collision. Its destruction is confirmed through the detection of an energy burst in the vicinity of the collision. Can we say that the particle became that energy burst? A particle necessarily has some determinate mass and location (or in the case of a fundamental particle, either determinate location or determinate velocity), while an energy burst has neither mass nor determinate location. So a particle is not the sort of thing that can come to be an energy burst. If we wish to speak of this destruction as a kind of alteration, what is the subject of that alteration? The existence of mass-energy conservation laws might tempt us to suppose that there is some underlying stuff that at certain times has the superficial properties of matter, and at other times has the superficial properties of energy. But what might be the intrinsic nature of this stuff? It is no help to be told that it is of such a nature as either to manifest itself as matter or to manifest itself as energy, for this is not yet to tell us what it itself is like. And unless we wish to retreat to the Eleatic notion of pure Being (or its Advaita Vedānta cousin, Brahman), we shall need some assurance that there is something that this stuff is like. If it is to be a physical sort of stuff, but it is not like matter and also not like energy, what could it possibly be like?

The solution is to see this not as a case of alteration of one underlying substance, but as just the destruction of one existent and the creation of another existent. The particle goes out of existence, but then as a result of that and in accordance with the conservation law, a burst of energy comes into existence. The same pattern will hold good for anything else we might think of as a fundamental real and that appears to undergo substantial alteration. Consider, for instance, the sort of Reductionist who thinks of our basic psychological states as themselves ultimately real entities that are among the elements making up the causal series. Then the experience we would ordinarily describe as shock turning to rage, they might redescribe as a case of shock going out of existence but causing rage to come into existence in accordance with a basic psychological law. The general lesson to be learned from this is that given the sorts of alterations we actually encounter, at least some of the ultimately real entities must be thought of as coming into and going out of existence (presumably in accordance with causal laws). And of course to say that these are ultimately real entities is precisely to say that their coming into and going out of existence cannot be thought of as merely the transformation of an underlying substance.

We must now consider what would be involved in the coming into existence of such an ultimately real entity. Presumably this will occur due to the obtaining of the relevant causes and conditions. If the entity in question were a fire atom, these might be said to include the presence of fuel and air, and the striking of the match. Their result is the existence of something whose intrinsic nature is to be hot. So this means that the atom is characterized by heat due to these causes and conditions. But how is it that the causes and conditions bring it about that the atom is characterized by heat? Is it that the heat is already present among them prior to the coming into existence of the atom? If that were so then the production of the fire atom would be pointless: if the heat that characterizes fire were already present, why would anyone ever bother to light a fire? So the heat must instead be considered a product of the causes and conditions, something the occurrence of which they collectively bring about. But in that case the atom obtains the property of being hot from causes and conditions that are distinct from it. That is, the atom has this property only in dependence on those distinct causes and conditions. And this would mean that heat is not the intrinsic nature of the fire atom. While heat may be essential to fire (there are no cold fires), it cannot be intrinsic to fire if it is the product of distinct causes and conditions. Just as the chariot borrows its structural properties from the components that cause it to have a certain size, shape and rigidity, so the fire atom should be said to borrow its heat from whatever caused it to have that property. And while (some of) the chariot's structural properties are essential to the chariot, they are not intrinsic, for precisely the reason that they are borrowed and so decomposable under analysis. If the fire atom is not to be consigned to the same status as the chariot, if the fire atom is to count as ultimately real, then it cannot originate in dependence on causes and conditions. Thus ultimately real entities cannot come into existence; they must be eternal. Yet everything that we encounter in the world seems to be impermanent. So once again the assumption that things have intrinsic natures seems to have led us to a conclusion very much at odds with our experience.[8]

The argument so far purports to show that ultimately real entities, insofar as they bear intrinsic natures, would necessarily be eternal. That this conclusion conflicts with our experience of impermanence will be taken as evidence that the notion of an ultimately real entity is incoherent. But before coming to that, a question must be raised concerning a key step in the argument: why, precisely, should the fact that heat is a product of causes and conditions be taken to show that it is not an intrinsic property of its bearer? Suppose we agree that the structural properties of the chariot are not intrinsic, and that this is due to the fact that the chariot's having these properties is brought about by the properties of its parts. Insofar as the parts may be said to be the (material) cause of the chariot, we may then say that the reason the structural properties are not intrinsic to the chariot is that the chariot has them in dependence on a distinct cause. But this seems quite different from the case of the heat of fire. In the latter case the assemblage of causes and conditions does not exist simultaneously with the fire, so they cannot be thought of (collectively or individually) as the fire's material cause.[h] It is natural to think of the chariot as 'borrowing' its structural features from its parts, given that chariot and parts necessarily coexist and that the chariot consists of the parts. But this metaphor seems inappropriate in the case of fire, where the causes and conditions responsible for the production of the heat need no longer obtain when the fire has come into existence. That both cases involve causal connections appears irrelevant, since causation comes in many distinct forms. Does the argument not rest on an illegitimate conflation of two quite different senses of 'depend'?[i]

Intrinsic natures and the causal relation

To answer this question, we shall need to look more closely at the sort of causal relation that might be thought to figure in the production of something considered ultimately real. We have already argued that the kind of causal relation that obtains between the chariot and its parts is thoroughly intentional or conceptually constructed in nature – that it is not the sort of thing that could be said to obtain independently of our use of certain concepts. The argument we shall now examine seeks to establish that this is true of all varieties of causal relationship, even those between entities thought to be ultimately real. If this can be established, then it will be justifiable to conclude from the argument concerning fire's nature that causal dependence is incompatible with intrinsicality. For the intrinsic nature requirement, it must be remembered, is just an expression of the realist requirement that the ultimate facts be mind-independent, that they not be conceptually constructed. If the causal relationship involved in fire's having heat as essence is shown itself to be conceptually constructed, then heat cannot count as fire's intrinsic nature.

Suppose, then, that an ultimate real can be said to be an effect that originates from causes and conditions. In that case either the effect is identical with one or more of the entities that are among the causes and conditions, or it is distinct from all of them. But if the effect is identical with any of the causes and conditions, then it exists before it originates, which is absurd. So the effect must be distinct from the causes and conditions. In that case, it must be possible for whatever entities are among the causes and conditions to exist when the effect does not exist. So the fuel (that is, stuff made principally of hydrocarbons) and the air, for instance, exist before the fire originates. How is it, then, that upon their assembly these causes and conditions give rise to just the effect of the fire, and not some other effect like a pot? Both the fire and a pot are, after all, equally distinct from the fuel and air, yet we do not consider fuel and air to be among the causes and conditions of the pot. There must, we suppose, be some special connection between the assembly of these causes and conditions and the originating of fire; this would explain why fire, and not a pot, is the resulting effect. But what does this supposition amount to beyond the mere assertion that fuel, air, etc. give rise to fire (and not to pots)? Granted this is how our experience has gone, but what is wanted here is some explanation of this pattern.[j]

Perhaps the reason that the assemblage of fuel, air, etc. gives rise to fire (and not a pot) is that this assemblage possesses an inherent capacity, power or disposition just to produce fire. But now we must ask what it means to say that the assemblage has such a capacity, power or disposition. Perhaps the simplest answer would be that the nature of the effect is to be found, in unmanifest form, among the causes and conditions, and that their assembly makes this nature manifest.[k] But then the nature of a pot is not manifest among the causes and conditions of the fire, so what is to prevent us from saying that its nature is equally present, in unmanifest form, among them? To appeal to the fact that these causes and conditions regularly produce fire and not pots is to use the *explanandum* in explicating the *explanans*, which would clearly be circular. And if the nature of a pot is also present in unmanifest form among these causes and conditions, why is it that their assembly does not make this nature manifest as well?

Perhaps a more promising approach to explaining talk of capacities or powers would be in terms of counterfactual conditionals. On this approach, part of what it means to say of something m that it has the power to produce effect e under conditions C is that had m not existed then e would not have originated even had C obtained. But what fact could make this statement true? Certainly no actual fact, for in the circumstances of assertion we are imagining, m does exist. This is why we call the statement a counterfactual conditional. So if there is some fact that makes it true, that fact must be one that obtains in some possible world. And in fact there will be many possible worlds involved, namely all those in which m does not exist, conditions C do obtain, and e does not originate. Now questions can be raised as to just what a possible world is. The standard answer – a maximally consistent set of propositions – makes their existence dependent on the existence of propositions. And questions can be raised as to how propositions can be said to exist in a full-bloodedly realist sense, that is, how propositions can escape the taint of conceptual construction.[l] But let us waive those questions, and suppose that we have a clear understanding of what a proposition is, and what possible worlds are.[8] There remains one question that demands an answer. There are many possible worlds in which m does not exist, conditions C do obtain, but e does originate. Indeed there are possible worlds in which air, friction, etc. produce fire in the absence of hydrocarbons but in the presence of clay. At least there is no obvious contradiction involved in supposing that clay might burn. So why are those worlds not relevant in assessing the truth of the counterfactual? The standard answer is that those worlds are not as close to the actual world as the worlds in which in the absence of the (hydrocarbon) fuel there is no fire. Here closeness is measured by the degree of similarity in the natural laws that obtain. The worlds in which there is no fire in the absence of fuel share with the actual world the natural law that fire requires fuel. But what does it mean to say it is a law of nature (in the actual world) that fire requires fuel? What it means, apparently, is that the actual world is like those possible

---

[8] Lewis' (1986) actualism about possible worlds is intended as a way of explicating the notion of a possible world while avoiding commitment to propositions as extra-mental entities. Whether it succeeds in that aspiration may be questioned.

worlds in which there is never fire in the absence of fuel. Now of course we do not know that our world is like those worlds, since for all we now know clay might start burning tomorrow. But it would be a mistake to bring in questions about what we know here; what is at issue is just what the facts are. The relevant question to ask is, could it be a (to us as yet unknown) fact that the actual world is like those worlds? Notice that those worlds are specified as ones in which it *never* happens that there is fire in the absence of fuel. A possible world is a completed world, a world in which, so to speak, all the facts are in. For the actual world to be like those possible worlds, it would have to share this feature. And this, it can be argued, it cannot do.

Let us accept the standard view of possible worlds, according to which a possible world is a maximally consistent set of propositions. That is, for every proposition either it or its negation is a member of the set, and each member is consistent with all other members. Let us also accept the view of propositions according to which these are mind-independent objects timelessly inhabiting a 'third realm' that is neither physical nor a mere mental construction. (Perhaps propositions are joined there by the Platonist's mathematical objects.) While there are possible worlds in which nothing ever happens, the possible worlds relevant to the assessment of our counterfactual will include descriptions of sequences of events. And given that every proposition is either included in a possible world or excluded, the relevant worlds may be thought of as total histories, in that they will include specifications of all the events that ever happen in the world in question. So it is, for instance, true in some possible world that all life on earth is obliterated by an asteroid in 2183. To say this is just to say: there is at least one maximally consistent set of propositions containing the proposition expressed by the sentence, 'All life on earth is obliterated by an asteroid in 2183'; each proposition in the set is stipulated as true at that world, and thus this proposition is stipulated true at that world. Could the actual world be like that world? We can all agree that propositions about events in the actual world are not made true by stipulation. According to the realist, what makes a proposition true or false in the actual world is the facts. So for this proposition to be true in the actual world, it would have to be a fact that all life on earth is obliterated by an asteroid in 2183. And this is not a fact, for this state of affairs does not obtain. Of course it is equally not a fact that life on earth is not obliterated by an asteroid in 2183. Neither of these states of affairs obtains for the simple reason that it is not yet 2183. The actual world consists of all that has happened. But certain things have not happened yet, namely all those events that lie in the future. The actual world cannot be thought of as a maximally consistent set of propositions. Neither can it be thought of as what makes some such set true.[9]

We began by seeking to determine what it could mean to say that fuel, while distinct from fire, has the capacity, in the presence of certain other causes and

---

[9] Since this suggests that propositions about the future lack a truth-value, this may mean that there is bivalence failure with respect to future contingents. (The alternative would be to say that all propositions are (timelessly) true or false, but that no statement may be used to express a proposition prior to the occurrence of the state of affairs that makes that proposition true or false.) But this is not necessarily incompatible with the truth of the assertion, 'Either life on earth will be wiped out in 2183 or it will not.' In any event, the latter statement is not to be rejected on the grounds that it leads to fatalism. As Aristotle showed in *De Interpretatione* 9, the argument that this statement leads to fatalism rests on a modal fallacy: from 'necessarily (p or q)' to infer 'necessarily p or necessarily q'.

conditions, to produce fire. This was said to involve a counterfactual conditional concerning what happens in certain relevant possible worlds where that fuel is absent, with relevance understood in terms of similarity with respect to causal laws. The difficulty we then encountered was that while we understand what it means to claim that some causal law obtains in some set of possible worlds (all material conditionals of a certain form will then have the same truth-value), it is not clear what it would mean to extend that conception of a law of nature to the actual world. Thus we have not yet succeeded in discerning the meaning of the claim that fuel has the power to produce fire. The problem is that for it to be the case that some causal law obtains in the actual world, a set of propositions concerning actual future events must be true. And at the core of realism is the intuition that statements are made true by states of affairs that obtain independently of the concepts we employ; statements are made true or false just by what happens quite apart from what we think. On this understanding, contingent statements only come to be true when the states of affairs that they are about come to obtain. Those propositions about future events that must be true in order for a causal law to obtain cannot now be true (or false), since the events with which they are concerned have not yet happened.[10]

There are two strategies that a realist might pursue in order to preserve a realist sense for statements of causal law. One would be to claim that past, present and future facts all have a kind of timeless existence, so that propositions about future states of affairs may be said to now have truth-values. Now it is not clear how this view could accommodate facts about the passage of time, facts about how past, present and future differ when seen from our temporally situated vantage point.[m] The second proposal seeks to avoid that difficulty by acknowledging the reality of time's passage. What it claims is that at each moment there are three kinds of facts: those concerning what is now happening, those concerning what happened in the past, and those concerning what will happen. Only the first kind involve states of affairs that exist; the others involve states of affairs that have existed or that will exist. And the present fact that, say, an asteroid will strike in 2183, is a distinct fact from the fact that will exist in 2183, that the asteroid is now striking. At each moment there is a whole new set of facts. For instance today's fact that Richard Nixon was US president in 1972 is a different fact from yesterday's fact that Nixon was US president in 1972. But the facts concerning states of affairs that have come to obtain at some moment (those that count as 'present' at that moment) have a special status: facts existing at past and future times concerning a present state of affairs all depend for their existence on the present fact that that state of affairs now exists. So the presently existing fact that an asteroid

---

[10] It might be thought that a realist will have the same difficulty with statements about the past: since past states of affairs no longer exist, propositions about past behavior of fuel and fire must likewise lack truth-values. But a realist could plausibly claim that there is an asymmetry between past and future here: while the states of affairs that make statements about the past either true or false do not now exist and so no longer obtain, they have obtained; and a proposition once made true remains true.

I am in effect claiming that a realist must be anti-realist about the future, that is, must hold that future-tense statements lack a truth-value. But there is another sense in which realism about the future might, for all I have said here, be perfectly coherent: realism about the future might be construed as the view that future states of affairs will, when they come to obtain, exist mind-independently, and thus serve to make true statements to the effect that they do (presently) obtain.

will strike in 2183 is dependent on the fact that will exist in 2183 that an asteroid is presently striking.

The difficulty with the first proposal is that since, according to it, a fact and the true proposition that asserts its obtaining both exist timelessly, it cannot be the case that it is the fact that makes the proposition true. For a fact to play the role of truth-maker, there must be some time before which the proposition that is involved in asserting its occurrence was not true.[11] The second strategy avoids that problem, but at the price of an incredibly inflated ontology of facts: it requires that at each instant there be a totally new set of facts detailing the entire history of the universe. Now a realist might be willing to pay this price, but it is indicative of a deeper problem: it appears that all these extra 'facts' are really just propositions in disguise. The idea, once again, was that the proposition expressed by a present utterance of 'An asteroid will strike in 2183' is made true by a fact that exists at the moment of utterance, but that the existence of that fact in turn depends on the existence in 2183 of the fact that would then make true an utterance of 'An asteroid is now striking.'[12] The second claim is required in order to make it clear that while these are distinct facts they are also related facts, and thus that the truth of today's statement is indirectly tied to the fact that will exist in 2183. But what could it mean to say that today's fact depends for its existence on the fact of 2183? We might say that the fact that my pen is colored and the fact that my pen is green are distinct facts, and that the former fact depends for its existence on the latter fact. But even in this case there is the strong suspicion that we have just one fact here, that the appearance of plurality is an artifact of the concepts used to describe that fact (in this case, an artifact of the degree of specificity of those concepts). In the case of the asteroid facts, this suspicion is heightened by the claim that the one fact depends for its existence on the other. For if facts are things that exist in time (on this view only propositions are timeless), then how can a fact be said to exist in the present and yet depend for its existence on a fact that does not yet exist? The resort to a multitude of temporal facts looks like an effort at disguising what is really just the original proposal: what is here called 'today's fact' is actually the proposition that an asteroid strikes in 2183, as expressed by a future-tense statement; the 'fact' of 2183 is just the same proposition as expressed by a present-tense statement; the 'dependence' of the first on the second is just their identity: and the proposal is really just that the proposition is true now because it will be true then, since the fact will then exist. But once again, how, if it is facts that make propositions true, can a proposition be true when the state of affairs that it expresses will not obtain until sometime in the future?

The attempt to locate causal efficacy in an entity that is distinct from the effect has so far come up dry. There may be other ways besides the possible-worlds approach to trying to make sense of the notion of a causal law. But there is another consideration that suggests any such solution will be of no use in explaining what a productive capacity might be. Consider once again the aggregate A of causes and conditions (the *total* cause consisting of m and C), and the effect e that is said to be the product of

---

[11] This is because the makes-true relation requires an asymmetry between fact and true proposition – the asymmetry expressed by the realist's 'depends'. And this asymmetry cannot be furnished by variations across possible worlds: for all possible worlds, the fact exists just in case the proposition is true.

[12] Note that it is one and the same proposition that is expressed by both utterances. What varies in time, according to this proposal, is which fact makes the proposition true.

this aggregate. Now A, in bringing about e, is said to exercise a certain causal efficacy. When does this exercise take place? It clearly cannot occur after e has arisen, for then it would be superfluous. But neither can it be said to occur before e arises, since its exercise should yield the arising of e, something that has not yet taken place. Can there be some third time during which e might be said to be undergoing production? Not if e is to count as something that is ultimately real. This third time would have to be a time when the entity in question neither existed nor did not exist. And to say that e is ultimately real is to say that it bears an intrinsic nature. While realism can tolerate the claim that it may be indeterminate whether a heap exists or not, this is precisely because a heap is not something with an intrinsic nature. For the realist there can be no such cases of bivalence failure with respect to those things that are ultimately real. Hence there is no time when A can be said to exercise its supposed causal efficacy. This makes it appear dubious that there is any such thing as causal efficacy (or at least an ultimately real causal efficacy).[n]

It may seem as if the argument has overlooked two important possibilities. The first is that A and e occur simultaneously, and that A exercises its causal efficacy during the time when both it and e exist. The difficulty with this proposal is that if cause and effect are genuinely simultaneous in their occurrence, it is not clear which is cause and which effect. The second possibility involves supposing that A occurs at time t_1 and that e occurs at the subsequent time t_2. The proposal is that the causal efficacy of A is exercised throughout the duration t_1–t_2. This proposal reflects the quite sensible idea that while the cause precedes the effect, its nature as cause also involves the expression of that nature through the production of the effect, which in turn requires that the effect be existent. But while this idea may be sensible, it cannot be endorsed by the realist. For since A no longer exists at t_2, the exercise of its causal capacity during that part of the duration t_1–t_2 must involve conceptual construction: the effect having been produced, we retroactively impute causal efficacy to A at t_1.[13] While this may be what does indeed happen, it is not the sort of account of causal efficacy that the realist wants.[o]

The upshot of all this is that it appears impossible for the realist to give a satisfactory account of a causal relation that might be said to obtain among ultimately real entities. It now seems far more plausible that causation necessarily involves elements of intentionality or conceptual construction. This in turn gives support to the claim discussed above that an entity with an intrinsic nature – an ultimately real entity – cannot be said to originate in dependence on causes and conditions. For if causal dependence is itself conceptually constructed, then an entity's obtaining its essence in dependence on causes and conditions must likewise involve conceptual construction. And in that case the entity is not ultimately real; it is not something with an intrinsic nature.[p]

---

[13]   That A no longer exists at t_2 follows from the fact that A is the total assembly of causes and conditions thought responsible for the coming into existence of e. While some members of A might continue to exist when e has come into existence, other members no longer exist at t_2. Hence A no longer exists at t_2.

Emptiness and global anti-realism

If there is anything to the arguments we have been investigating, then it seems there cannot be things with intrinsic natures. The Buddhist anti-realist would put this as the claim that all things are *empty*, for by 'emptiness' they just mean the state of being devoid of intrinsic nature. Now a Buddhist Reductionist would agree that such things as chariots, forests and persons are empty in this sense. For it is a hallmark of all such conceptual fictions that they borrow their natures from the parts of which they are composed. But it is a long way from this claim to the claim that all things are empty. What might the latter claim mean? There appear to be just two possibilities: metaphysical nihilism, and global anti-realism. According to metaphysical nihilism, the ultimate nature of reality is such that nothing whatever exists. This might readily be taken as the consequence of universal emptiness given that there is good reason to believe the only ultimately real things must be things with intrinsic natures. If there are no such entities, then it seems to follow that there are no ultimately real things – that the ultimate truth is that nothing exists. According to global anti-realism, on the other hand, the very notion of an ultimate truth, of there being an ultimate nature of reality, is incoherent. This might be taken as the consequence of universal emptiness given that the notion of an ultimate truth depends on the claim that real things bear intrinsic natures. For if it turns out that nothing can bear an intrinsic nature, this might be seen as reflecting poorly on the underlying realist assumptions that generated the demand for intrinsic natures.

These are very different conclusions to draw from the doctrine of universal emptiness. For while metaphysical nihilism is based on the assumption that there is one true description of mind-independent reality, global anti-realism involves the rejection of this realist tenet. I have already indicated that I think the anti-realist conclusion is the one that should be drawn. I think as well, however, that even though it is false, the metaphysical nihilist conclusion still has a role to play when it comes to assessing the consequences of emptiness. But is it true that these are the only plausible views as to what emptiness might entail? Some have instead taken it to entail the claim that the real is strictly ineffable.[9] The idea seems to be that if no real entity may be said to have its own essence, then the reals must lack determinate natures, and so must somehow transcend all efforts at conceptualization. (To this is sometimes added the claim that the reals may nonetheless be apprehended through a kind of non-conceptual intuition.) Now this is clearly a form of realism, and so is distinct from the anti-realist view. And it holds that there are ultimately real entities, and so is distinct from metaphysical nihilism. The difficulty is that it cannot be a consequence of the doctrine of emptiness (unless that doctrine contains a contradiction), since it is incompatible with the doctrine. For to say that the reals are ineffable is to say that it is their nature to be ineffable, and so non-conceptualizable. And if the nature of a real is something that is beyond conceptualization, then that nature is mind-independent in the relevant sense, and so is intrinsic. The realist demand is just that real things have intrinsic natures; it does not require that those natures be such as can be adequately represented by our concepts. The doctrine of emptiness is sometimes put as the claim that everything we think of as real is actually a conceptual construct. It would be a mistake to conclude from this that what is really real must be beyond conceptualization. If the doctrine of emptiness is correct, then an ostensibly ultimate non-conceptualizable real would also be conceptually constructed.[r]

Metaphysical nihilism is clearly false. The thesis could not be formulated if nothing whatever existed. Of course it could be claimed that those entities involved in the formulation of the thesis are not ultimately real, that they are mere conceptual fictions. If realism is true, though, then the occurrence of conceptual fictions would require the existence of things that are ultimately real. Moreover, metaphysical nihilism presupposes realism, since it claims that there is such a thing as the ultimate nature of reality. But if metaphysical nihilism is so clearly a non-starter, why have I said that it is one of two plausible views as to what emptiness means? Because the alternative – global anti-realism – is extremely difficult to understand and accept. Buddhist anti-realists have typically relied on a *reductio* strategy that uses the absurdity of metaphysical nihilism in order to force one to reject realism: one concludes from the arguments against intrinsic natures that all things are empty, draws the nihilist conclusion, sees that this is absurd, and is thus forced to the radical step of giving up the underlying realist assumptions. The understanding that results from this process may be put in terms of the paradoxical-sounding claim 'The ultimate truth is that there is no ultimate truth'. This formulation helps bring out the soteriological significance of the doctrine of emptiness. Buddhist Reductionists claimed that coming to know the (thoroughly impersonal) ultimate truth about persons would end suffering by helping us overcome clinging. The Buddhist anti-realist holds that pursuit of the ultimate truth itself represents the last and most subtle form of clinging. Liberation is attained only after one comes to understand that the very idea of an ultimate truth is deeply incoherent.

The air of paradoxicality surrounding the claim 'The ultimate truth is that there is no ultimate truth', stems at least in part from the element of explicit self-reference built into the statement. But the air persists even when this element is removed. To claim that there can be no such thing as the ultimate truth is to court the question 'What is the truth-status of this claim?' If the claim cannot be ultimately true, the only option left would seem to be that it is conventionally true. Yet the notion of conventional truth appears not to make sense absent the contrast with ultimate truth. For we have understood conventional truth in terms of the idea of a kind of linguistic shorthand – namely for an ultimate truth that is too complex to grasp and convey. So perhaps the lesson to draw is that we should embrace a kind of semantic non-dualism, according to which statements can be neither ultimately true nor conventionally true; statements can only be said to be (non-dualistically) true. The next two chapters will be devoted to a careful exploration of this idea. But one thing to note in advance is that this may turn out to have an important bearing on our understanding of the claim that persons are empty. As was pointed out above, Buddhist Reductionists can agree that persons are empty. Since they understand the person to be a mere conceptual construction, they accept the claim that persons lack intrinsic natures. Buddhist Reductionists claim, however, that this is true only because it is also true that there are ultimately real entities making up the causal series that is conveniently designated by the term 'person'. When the Buddhist anti-realist claims that persons are empty, this claim is made against the background of the larger claim that all things are empty. That larger claim may make a difference to what the emptiness of persons comes to.

The semantic non-dualism of the Buddhist anti-realist may importantly affect our understanding of what we are.

Notes

[a] The Buddhists on whose views I base this position are the Mādhyamikas (members of the Madhyamaka school, founded by Nāgārjuna in approximately the 2nd century CE). As Tuck (1990) and others have pointed out, modern Buddhologists have made no end of proposals concerning how to identify Madhyamaka's philosophical allegiances: Nāgārjuna has been called everything from a nihilist (Wood, 1994) to a radical empiricist (Kalupahana, 1986: 81) to a post-modernist (Coward, 1990), and much in between. Seen against this background, my identification of Madhyamaka as a kind of anti-realism may arouse a certain degree of skepticism. But I do this not out of a concern to fit Nāgārjuna into some grand global-philosophical taxonomy, nor in order to enhance his prestige by linking him to some fashionable (?) view. I am interested rather in finding out what if any truth there is in anti-realism. And it strikes me both that many of the Madhyamaka arguments may be given an anti-realist reading, and that Mādhyamikas do not employ the same sorts of internalist and verificationist premises that are prominent in current formulations of anti-realism. Since these premises are widely seen as problematic, it seems to me worthwhile to explore the possibility that Madhyamaka resources make possible a more defensible form of anti-realism.

Of course there will always be those as well who insist that Madhyamaka cannot be profitably compared with any Western philosophical school or tendency, since Madhyamaka is not rational but mystical. But not only is such counsel based on an extremely narrow conception of the mystical; it also overlooks nearly a millennium of Madhyamaka debate with Indian realists (Buddhist Reductionists, but also Naiyāyikas and Sāṃkhyans) over the stock issues of metaphysics and epistemology. However else they may have seen themselves, the Mādhyamikas clearly thought that they were engaged in philosophical debate.

[b] 'Intrinsic nature' is my rendering of *svabhāva*, and 'extrinsic nature' is that of *parabhāva*. For a particularly clear exposition of this distinction see Candrakīrti's *Prasannapadā* comments on MMK 15.2cd (Pandeya 258), as well as his comments on MMK 13.4cd (Pandeya 235). Of course Candrakīrti is a Mādhyamika, and so he will himself reject the notion of *svabhāva*. But his representation of that doctrine here strikes me as quite fair.

[c] The Abhidharma conception of the four elements (the *mahābhūtas*) was more complex (see AKB 2.65ab, Pradhan 102–103, Pruden 308–309), but I am ignoring the details for purposes of expository clarity. There was also a controversy among Ābhidharmikas concerning whether, in the case of the *dharmas* or ultimately real entities, there is a distinction to be drawn between characteristic (*lakṣaṇa*) and the thing characterized (*lakṣya*). This question arose out of the dispute over whether a *dharma* has temporal thickness, whether it endures through distinct phases. If, as at least some Vaibhāṣikas maintained (in connection with their block universe conception of time), it could be said to endure, then a *dharma* must be thought of as something distinct from and underlying its properties. The Sautrāntikas, on the other hand, denied that *dharmas* endure through distinct phases, and so claimed that the existence of a *dharma* just is the occurrence of the intrinsic nature. The distinction between characteristic and thing characterized has, they maintained, no application in the case of the strictly momentary ultimate reals. And they are right that their doctrine of momentariness obviates the need for a notion of substantial entities as what underlie changes in attributes. But a *dharma* will still have, in addition to its intrinsic nature, certain contingent properties such as spatio-temporal location that we should be reluctant to identify with the *dharma* itself; hence there will still be a need to think of the *dharma* as that which bears both intrinsic nature and incidental properties. This oversight no doubt stems from a general Abhidharma tendency to posit a *dharma* for each predicate occurring in ultimately true sentences, hence for a tendency to suppose that for instance spatio-temporal predicates must either name ultimately real entities (something the Sautrāntikas deny) or else be mere convenient designators. But as the Sautrāntikas themselves pointed out on more than one occasion, this tendency leads to an infinite regress. So on this point it seems fair to side with the Vaibhāṣikas

and Theravādins and maintain the distinction between *lakṣaṇa* and *lakṣya*. On this controversy see AKB 2.46b (Pradhan 78f., Pruden 241–47), also Frauwallner (1995: 185–208), and Stcherbatsky (1970: 37–43).

^d The argument up to this point is that found in MMK 5.1–3. For the charge that there is an infinite regress if the defining characteristic should function on a bearer that is already supplied with defining characteristic, see Candrakīrti's *Prasannapadā* on 5.3: *kiṃ hi lakṣaṇavataḥ prasiddhasya bhāvasya punar lakṣaṇakṛtyaṃ syād ity anavasthātiprasaṅgaś caivaṃ syāt* (Pandeya 90).

^e This argument against identity of bearer and defining characteristic is a generalization of the argument Candrakīrti develops against the Yogācāra–Sautrāntika doctrine of the identity of means and object of cognition – the so-called 'head of Rāhu' argument – in *Prasannapadā* on MMK 1.2 (Pandeya 22). Bhāvaviveka develops a quite different argument for the same conclusion, as part of his argument against bearer and characteristic being either identical or distinct, at *Madhyamakahṛdaya* 3.75–76 (Iida 151–54).

^f The argument up to this point is that of MMK 13.4cd–6. It is of course open to the opponent to claim that all alteration is conceptually constructed on the basis of a series of ultimate reals, each of which simply manifests its own intrinsic nature and then ceases without undergoing alteration. (This is the strategy that is about to be proposed in the text.) The Mādhyamika will reply that still cessation must be construed as an alteration in which the entity abandons its intrinsic nature. This seems to have been the view of the Vaibhāṣikas and Theravādins, for whom a *dharma* endures through four phases. But the Sautrāntikas avoided this difficulty by maintaining that the occurrence of a *dharma* has no temporal thickness, so that its existence just is the occurrence of the intrinsic nature. It is in this way that the Sautrāntika doctrine of momentariness (*kṣaṇikavāda*) leads to the view that characteristic and characterized are identical. We have already seen one difficulty with the latter view; we shall shortly investigate another.

^g The argument here is that of MMK 15.2. See Candrakīrti's comment:

> *iha svo bhāvaḥ svabhāva iti yasya padārthasya yad ātmīyaṃ rūpaṃ tat tasya svabhāva iti vyapadiśyate / kiṃ ca kasyātmīyaṃ yady asyākṛtrimaṃ, yat tu kṛtrimaṃ na tat tasyātmīyaṃ tad yathāpām auṣṇyam / yac ca yasyāyattaṃ tad api tad ātmīyaṃ, tad yathā sve bhṛtyāḥ svāni dhanāni / yat tu yasya parāyat taṃ na tat tasyātmīyaṃ, tad yathā tāvat kālikāyācitakamasvatattnaṃ / yataś ca ivaṃ kṛtrimasya parasāpekṣasya ca svabhāvatvaṃ neṣṭaṃ, ata evauṣṇyam agner hetupratyayapratibaddhatvāt pūrvamabhūtvā paścād utpadena kṛtakatvāc ca na svabhāva iti yujyate / yataś ca itad evam atoyad evāgneḥ kālatraye 'py avyabhicāri nijaṃ rūpamakṛtrimaṃ, pūrva[ma]bhūtvā paścādyannabhavati, yac ca hetupratyayasāpekṣaṃ na bhavatyapāmauṣṇyavatpārāvāravaddīrghahtasvavaddvā, tat svabhāva iti vyapadiśyate // kiṃ khalu[agneḥ] tad itthaṃ svarūpam asti.* [Pandeya 258]

It is worth noting that the argument depends on the assumption that *dharma* and *svabhāva* are distinguishable as, respectively, property-possessor and intrinsic nature. A Sautrāntika would, of course, disagree.

^h In MMK 10, however, Nāgārjuna does raise an interesting question concerning the relation between fire and fuel. The opponent proposes that fire be seen as an example of something that is dependent on something else (namely fuel), yet has an intrinsic nature (namely heat). Nāgārjuna responds that for this to work, it must first be settled whether fire and fuel are identical or distinct. The difficulty with the hypothesis of distinctness is that it should then be possible for fire to exist in the absence of fuel. In this case, extinguishing fire by removing its fuel source would be futile, and fire would remain eternally alight.

ⁱ Hayes (1994: 316–19) makes a somewhat similar criticism of the argument of MMK 15.1–3. He, however, traces the problem to equivocation on *svabhāva*, which he thinks can mean either 'essence' or 'that which is causally independent'. He thus assumes that there is no argument from something's being an intrinsic nature to its not having arisen in dependence on causes and conditions; he takes Nāgārjuna to have simply failed to note the slide between these two different senses of the term *svabhāva*. I am proceeding on the contrary (and more charitable) assumption that there is an argument here. The question now is whether the sense in which the heat of fire is caused by its originating conditions is sufficiently like the sense of constitutive causation found in the case of the chariot as to show fire to be, like the chariot, a conceptual construction.

ʲ This is the argument of MMK 1.3. Both Candrakīrti and Bhāvaviveka end their comments on this verse with the introduction of the hypothesis that there is an action (*kriyā*) or causal force that mediates between the causes and conditions and the effect.

ᵏ This is the view known as *satkāryavāda*, the doctrine that the effect exists in its (material) cause, which was espoused by the Sāṃkhya school.

ˡ See Chatterjee (1996) for an attempt at an analysis of causal statements that avoids commitment to propositions through the use of Navya–Nyāya resources.

ᵐ This is the problem that the Sarvāstivādins never succeeded in solving. According to their 'block universe' theory of time, past, present and future existents are all equally real. To the question how the present then differs from past and future they proposed a variety of solutions, the most widely accepted of which was that a *dharma* exercises its efficacy in the present. (See Frauwallner (1995: 185–208) for a discussion of the history of this doctrine.) The difficulty is that the concept of the exercise of efficacy is the concept of an activity, that is, a process that takes place in time. As such, the concept requires prior grasp of the distinction between the present and the past and future. So it is not clear how this concept can be used to mark that distinction.

ⁿ This is the so-called argument of the three times, which is clearly to be found in MMK 1.5–7. Candrakīrti also sees this as the argument Nāgārjuna has in mind in MMK 1.4. But it is also possible to read that verse as anticipating the argument Śaṃkara will give against the *samavāya* relation: if between the cause *c* and the effect *e* there must be some mediating casual power *k*, then there must likewise be some mediating causal power *k'* between *c* and *k*, and some distinct mediating causal power *k''* between *k* and *e*, this being the beginning of an infinite regress. In MMK 7, Nāgārjuna gives a similar argument against the claim that a *dharma* could undergo arising, duration and cessation: the occurrence of the arising would require us to posit yet another arising, and so on.

ᵒ Garfield (1994) claims that in MMK 1, Nāgārjuna intends to refute only the claim that things originate in dependence on a cause (*hetu*), and not the claim that things originate in dependence on conditions (*pratyaya*). The first claim is said to involve the supposition that causation is more than mere Humean (*sic*) regularity, but is an ultimately real force that functions as the metaphysical glue of the universe. The second claim is identified as the far more modest view that dependent origination is thoroughly conventional, in that it is just regularity with explanatory utility – and hence that causation is always 'relative to human purposes and frameworks' (1994: 234). Now I agree that the Mādhyamika must subscribe to something like the latter account of causation. Indeed Bhāvaviveka's *Prajñāpradīpa* comments on MMK 1.3 say something quite similar: dependent origination is purely conventional, and our notion of a cause arises out of our expectation in the face of regularity. But Garfield's reading of this chapter is, I think, wrong. It forces him to invent a distinction between *hetu* and *pratyaya* that is not supported by the text or by any known Abhidharma work (where *hetu* is identified as the first of four kinds of *pratyaya*). It also forces him to read MMK 1.11–13 as objections, a reading not supported by the extant Sanskrit commentaries (which treat these verses as further arguments by Nāgārjuna against the notion of *pratyaya*).

What Garfield has, I think, failed to appreciate is the didactic structure of MMK. Nāgārjuna's aim in this work is purely negative: he seeks to demonstrate global bivalence failure at the level of ultimate truth, so as to induce first a nihilist response, then global anti-realism, and finally semantic non-dualism. (I take up this progression below, and in more detail in Chapter 8.) It is only at the final stage that a conventionalist view of causation may be safely reinstated. To introduce that view at the initial stage, alongside his argument that no realist account of causation is tenable, is to invite the response that causation is a conceptual construction superimposed on something – no doubt something ineffable – existing at the ultimate level of reality. This response is just another form of the realism he aims to extirpate.

ᵖ Much has been made by recent scholars of Madhyamaka of Nāgārjuna's assertion that dependent origination is equivalent to emptiness (MMK 24.18). For instance Garfield (in what may be an incautious remark) says of something that has been shown to be empty, 'The thing itself, apart from conventions of individuation, is nothing but an arbitrary slice of an indefinite spatiotemporal and causal manifold' (1994: 229). But on my reading of Madhyamaka, the equivalence is purely extensional: anything that is said to arise in dependence on causes and conditions is also devoid of intrinsic nature and is thus conceptually constructed. This reading is supported by Candrakīrti:

> *yo 'yaṃ pratītyasamutpādo hetupratyayā[na]pekṣy[āṅkura]vijñānādīnāṃ prādurbhāvaḥ*
> *sa svabhāvenānutpādaḥ / yaś ca svabhāvenānutpādo bhāvānāṃ sā śūnyatā // yā ceyaṃ*
> *svabhāvaśūnyatā sā prajñaptir upādāya / saiva śūnyatā upādāya prajñaptir iti*
> *vyavasthāpyate / cakrādīny upādāya rathāṅgāni rathaḥ prajñapyate / tasya yā svāṅgāny*
> *upādāya prajñapti sā svabhāvenānutpattiḥ, yā ca svabhāve[n]ānutpattiḥ sā śūnyatā.*
> [Pandeya 203–204]

In a Buddhist context in which it is assumed that all existents are dependently originated, this equivalence has the consequence that all existents are empty. But this does not give positive content to the ultimate truth, for instance by enabling us to say that ultimately real things participate in the ceaseless flux of dependent origination, or that their causal interrelatedness makes the ultimate reals mutually interpenetrating. To say that all things are empty is to say that there are no ultimately real things, hence that the domain of ultimate truth is empty. To anticipate, the ultimate truth is that there is no ultimate truth.

q See, e.g., Mohanty (1992: 278), Matilal (1990: 149), Murti (1955), Inada (1970: 24–26), and Ruegg (1977: 18–20).

r For instance the *svalakṣaṇa* that is said by Yogācāra-Sautrāntika to be ultimately real would turn out to be conceptually constructed and so merely conventionally real. Diṅnāga and Dharmakīrti sought to insulate this entity from the force of Madhyamaka arguments by making it a genuinely pure particular, something whose nature does not allow the distinction between bearer and property or that between essential and contingent properties. The Mādhyamika would point out two difficulties, however. First, the *svalakṣaṇa* is said to be causally efficacious. Second, it is not clear that coherent sense can be made of the claim that bearer and defining characteristic are identical.

CHAPTER SEVEN

Empty Knowledge

There are many different views that go by the name of anti-realism. They all share a common rejection of what I have called realism. And all are quite controversial. But beyond that there may be little that unites them. Our present task is to better understand Buddhist anti-realism, which I have so far presented as just the view that all things are devoid of intrinsic nature (the doctrine of emptiness).ª In this chapter I propose to begin that task by investigating some of the epistemological consequences of emptiness. Doing so should help us differentiate Buddhist anti-realism from other forms of anti-realism. It has recently become common to complain that anti-realists somehow conflate epistemological considerations with matters that properly belong to metaphysics and to semantics. Examining the epistemological consequences of emptiness should help us see to what extent Buddhist anti-realism might be guilty of such confusions. And this in turn should help us begin to see what might be distinctive about a formulation of anti-realism that begins with the doctrine of emptiness.

An epistemological objection: How can emptiness be known?

The central concerns of classical Indian epistemology are not the same as those we find in recent work in epistemology, where the key question has usually been how best to analyze '*S* knows that *p*.' Instead Indian epistemologists have seen their chief task as that of giving an account of the means of knowledge. By a 'means of knowledge' is meant some reliable process for bringing about mental episodes that represent how things are. All schools of Indian epistemology agree, for instance, that perception is a means of knowledge. Where there is substantial disagreement is over just how 'perception' is to be defined, that is, what the conditions are under which sensory stimulation is a reliable cause of cognitions that represent how the world is. There is likewise disagreement among the schools over how many other means of knowledge there are, and what their natures are, as well as what the proper object of each might be.[1] Still, all those who take this epistemological project seriously can unite in raising the following objection to Buddhist anti-realism. If all things are indeed empty, then anything that might be considered a means of knowledge must be empty, that is, lacking in intrinsic nature. Hence anything that might be considered a means of knowledge must lack whatever intrinsic nature is distinctive of a means of knowledge.

---

[1] Thus one school recognizes only perception, while all others also recognize inference, and some recognize additional processes such as verbal testimony, abductive inference, etc. One example of a dispute over the proper objects of a means of knowledge concerns whether universals may be perceived, or are cognized only through inference. There is also a dispute over whether each means of knowledge is restricted to some distinctive class of objects, or whether a given object may be cognized through different means of knowledge.

Hence ultimately there are no means of knowledge. By the same token, anything that might be considered the proper object of a means of knowledge must likewise lack the intrinsic nature distinctive of the object of a means of knowledge, so that ultimately there can be no objects of knowledge. Now if this is true, it follows that ultimately there are no means whereby the emptiness of all things can come to be cognized. It also follows that emptiness cannot be an object of knowledge. Therefore if the doctrine of emptiness were true, it could not be established. There is thus a pragmatic inconsistency involved in trying to show that all things are empty. If, for instance, the arguments for emptiness that were discussed in the last chapter were sound, then neither they nor any other arguments could be sound. While the doctrine of emptiness might be true for all that, it would be utterly futile to seek to demonstrate its truth.[b] (Since the inconsistency that is alleged here is purely pragmatic, we shall call this the self-stultification objection.)

Now Buddhist anti-realists do indeed seek to support their claim that all things are empty,[c] so some response to this objection is clearly in order. One way to respond would be to invoke the distinction between the two truths, and point out that while there might ultimately be neither means nor objects of knowledge, it might still be conventionally true that the doctrine of emptiness can be known to be true. That is, the doctrine itself might be conventionally true, and those instruments whereby it is established might themselves count as reliable means of knowledge relative to the standards of conventional truth. But while Buddhist anti-realists do say something like this, it is not their primary response to the objection. Instead they try to demonstrate that by the epistemologist's own standards, nothing can be shown to be a means of knowledge. Their basic strategy involves a kind of destructive trilemma: any attempted establishment of some procedure as a means of knowledge must be vitiated by infinite regress, or circularity, or arbitrariness. Suppose we sought to show that vision – understood as the operation of a normally functioning visual faculty on colors and shapes in the presence of adequate light, etc. – reliably leads to cognitions that represent how things are. How would we proceed? If we were to try to investigate vision using some other means of knowledge, then the question can be raised how our investigative tools are established as a means of knowledge. If these were in turn to be validated by some distinct means of knowledge, then we should quickly find ourselves embarked on an infinite regress. Yet the alternative strategy of first using them to validate vision, and then using vision to show that they are also a means of knowledge, would clearly be circular. If in light of this we were to claim that the establishment of vision as a means of knowledge does not require the employment of a distinct means of knowledge, this would *prima facie* conflict with the assumption behind the epistemological enterprise, that an entity's nature can only be known by using some means of knowledge. To say that this is true only of the objects of knowledge and not of the means of knowledge seems arbitrary. This conflict cannot be avoided by claiming that vision, in apprehending the nature of its object, also apprehends its own nature as a means of knowledge, for this would clearly violate the anti-reflexivity principle. Suppose we were to claim that vision and its object (color and shape) mutually establish one another: vision allows us to cognize the nature of the object, while the object in turn allows us to apprehend vision's validity as a means of knowledge. So for instance it might be thought that through vision I come to know the round shape of the object, and my success in using the object to fill a round hole assures me in turn of the validity of vision. But then how is this success ascertained? If by means of vision – by seeing that the hole is filled – then we are once again confronted with either circularity or an infinite regress. And if it is through some distinct means of knowledge, then we have reverted to the first possible strategy, which we have already seen to be inadequate. Thus the epistemologist is unable to establish that those processes considered to be means of knowledge are actually reliable means of cognizing objects.[d]

Indian realists responded to this attack on the epistemological enterprise by claiming that a given cognitive process may be both a means of knowledge and an object of knowledge. They agree that one and the same process cannot have both statuses simultaneously for a given cognizer, as that would require that the process that serves as means of cognizing an object also take itself as object, something that is ruled out by the anti-reflexivity principle. Still, the same visual process that gives us cognition of the roundness of the peg can subsequently be scrutinized. So if questions arise concerning the competency of the visual process to reliably inform us as to the shape of the peg, these can be settled through the investigation of the nature of the visual process itself. To the charge that this leads to an infinite regress, there is the interesting reply that while it might so lead, in practice it never does. It is true that in coming to cognize the nature of the visual process, I am relying on whatever means of knowledge I employ in that investigation. And questions might be raised about the competency of this means of knowledge to reliably inform us as to the nature of a cognitive process. If so, then I shall need to make this means of knowledge the object of some distinct investigative instrument. But this process never goes through more than a few iterations for a given cognitive occasion, and then our doubts tend to dissipate.[e]

This reply is interesting in that it seems to completely overlook the point that an instrument that is itself unvalidated cannot be used to validate a cognitive process. Perhaps, though, the point is not being overlooked but (implicitly) denied. That is, the Indian realist might (like those who today promote a program of 'naturalizing' epistemology) take the stance that justification is always piecemeal and local, and that justification in epistemology is no different in kind from that found in any other area of inquiry. True, all we ever obtain in this way is coherence. But if the scientific investigation of a use of an epistemic method yields results that are consistent with the results we obtain when we employ similar methods in the scientific investigation of other objects, that counts as evidence that it functions as a means of knowledge on that occasion. It is still possible that our body of beliefs – including our beliefs about the means of knowledge – contains mostly falsehoods. But our inability to rule out this possibility does not show that our use of this method on this occasion did not represent a means of knowledge. My inability to rule out skeptical hypotheses need not undermine a knowledge claim, since I might be justified even if I cannot establish to the satisfaction of all that I have justification. Only epistemological internalism (the view that a subject cannot be said to know unless they know that they know[2]) would

---

[2] Strictly speaking, internalism is the view that the 'justified' clause in the 'justified true belief' analysis of knowledge must be understood as the requirement that the subject have justification (and not merely that the subject be justified). The KK thesis represents the so-called 'strong' form of internalism. A weaker form claims roughly that the subject is justified only if the resources necessary to show justification are immediately accessible to the subject.

require that I be able to give the credentials of every instrument used in validating some epistemic procedure. And epistemological internalism is a controversial view, certainly not the sort of thing that a Buddhist anti-realist can safely assume in an argument against the epistemological enterprise.[f] It has not been shown that this way of proceeding cannot contribute to the success of that enterprise.

For reasons that will become clear later on, at this point I shall leave off discussing the historical debate between the Buddhist anti-realist and the Indian realist epistemologist. Instead we will now look at how that debate might be continued by current defenders of realism and anti-realism, beginning with an anti-realist response to the objection just posed by the Indian realist. During this part of the debate, their Indian counterparts will be waiting in the wings, to be brought back on stage at the appropriate time.

A coherentist response to the objection and its internalist presuppositions

At this juncture in the dispute, we can readily imagine an anti-realist responding as follows: this can only represent a Pyrrhic victory for the realist, since the coherentism at work in this defense of the epistemological enterprise will lead in the end to just the point that the anti-realist wants to make. Here is how. A realist epistemology would have it that a belief-forming process is reliable just to the extent that the cognitions it produces tend to represent the nature of the object. To discover which processes are reliable in this sense, we thus need some way of comparing the cognition resulting from a given process and the nature of that cognition's object. The difficulty is that realism requires that the comparison be with the nature of the object as it is apart from our ways of conceptualizing it. This immediately raises the suspicion that realism depends on the so-called 'myth of the given', the notion that an object can somehow be given to the cognizer in unmediated, non-conceptual form. But the real difficulty is that even if we could make sense of this idea of a sort of 'immaculate reception' of the object, this could not play the role that is called for in the realist's defense of epistemology.[3] In that defense, the comparison is to be between the cognition produced by the instrument in question and other cognitions produced by other instruments. And the comparison is to consist in examining the coherence of the one cognition with the others. But coherence is a relation that can only hold among items with propositional structure. So all the cognitions being compared must be such as can be represented using our concepts. The procedure that the realist envisions for testing epistemic processes can never bring about the direct confrontation between cognitions and an object whose nature potentially transcends our conceptual resources.

The realist will respond by first agreeing that there is no 'immaculate reception' of the object, no accessible cognition that represents the object without employing concepts.[g] So when we seek to validate some epistemic process by looking to see if the cognition it produces coheres with other cognitions, we are treating items with propositional structure. When I confirm my visual perception of round shape by

---

[3] The term is Alston's. See Alston (1996: 85–102) for a clear formulation of this argument as well as the realist reply.

inserting the peg in the hole, my confirming evidence comes in the form of a judgment based on tactile perception: 'the peg is in the hole.' Still, the fact that the validating procedure necessarily involves judgments does not show that the epistemic process is not being tested against the extra-conceptual facts. If my sense of touch is functioning properly, then my judgment that the peg is in the hole will reflect how things are in the world independent of the concepts I employ in representing the situation. That I employ concepts in representing the situation need not mean that all traces of the object's true nature have been lost sight of. There may be things about its nature that my concepts are unable to capture. Perhaps there are facets that will forever be inaccessible to the conceptual scheme of any finite cognizer. Still, even this would not mean that the concepts that we do employ distort the object's nature irremediably. There are limits to our ability to discriminate among shades of red, but this does not show that it is false to the real nature of a fire hydrant to call it red. Unless it could be shown that all conceptualization superimposes structure that is not present in the object itself, the fact that the validating procedure involves judgments with propositional structure need not mean that in that procedure epistemic processes are not being confronted with genuine facts. And, claims the realist, there is no reason to suppose that all conceptualization falsifies the object's nature.[h]

The anti-realist will reply that the difficulty is not that all concepts obscure the nature of mind-independent reality. It is rather that in any evidence we can have concerning the validity of an epistemic process, we are unable to separate out the respective contributions made by 'the world' and 'the mind'. We may think we know how these two factors can shape our judgments. We know, for instance, that someone who lacked our concept of a peg might represent the situation of the peg's being in the hole somewhat differently than we do. On the other hand, we might take our representing the situation in terms of something being located in something else to be the result of factors intrinsic to the situation itself, the result of how the world is quite apart from the concepts we employ. But while this distinction between 'world' and 'mind' has its uses, it cannot bear the load the realist wants it to carry. For the contributions of 'world' and 'mind' are inextricably intertwined, and thus in the final analysis cannot be held distinct. This was the real point of the earlier discussion concerning the unavailability of 'immaculate reception'. In the absence of some such method for determining the nature of the object as it is apart from all conceptualization, we have no way of verifying the claim that some feature of a representation is determined by 'the world' or by 'the mind'. Hence we do not ultimately know what it means to claim that a cognition represents things in accordance with how the facts are. This in turn means that the proposed procedure for validating epistemic processes cannot be said to show what it claims to: that certain processes produce cognitions that represent how things are. If we do not know what it means to say a cognition accurately represents mind-independent reality, then we cannot possess evidence that shows an epistemic process to reliably produce cognitions having that property.

The realist will protest that we can after all come to know what it would be like for the world to be a certain way quite apart from our mode of conceptualization. This might be accomplished through a sort of process of triangulation. Suppose we were to grant that there are a number of ways in which a given portion of the world might be represented, depending on our choice of conceptual framework. The anti-realist takes this to show the structure of knowledge to be such that there are no foundational judgments that could be taken as representing the nature of a mind-independent 'world'. But presumably there must be something common to all these different representations, otherwise they would not be taken as distinct ways of representing the same portion of the world. Just as we learn to accommodate differences in visual perspective by seeking what could be common to the different shapes perceived from distinct standpoints, so we can learn to find the mind-independent object in what is common to the different modes of conceptualization. Even if there should turn out to be little content remaining when we have subtracted all that is uncommon in the different representations, still we shall have achieved some conception of the world as 'what is there anyway' independent of any and all conceptual schemes. The anti-realist is thus wrong to suppose this an utterly empty notion.

The anti-realist will respond that this notion of an object whose nature stands behind all the distinct conceptual representations is necessarily empty. For what remains when we have subtracted what is uncommon is not merely 'little' content but no content. This is because the realist's notion of a mind-independent nature includes the idea of something that lies beyond our best efforts to grasp it. Now our conceptual capacities are acquired through our mastery of language, and ours is necessarily a public language. This means that our access to concepts is only by way of recognitional capacities that can be publicly manifested. If I am incapable of verifying the applicability of some predicate, then I cannot be said to have grasped the meaning of the concept it is used to express. And if no one is capable even in principle of recognizing its application conditions, then it cannot be said to express any determinate concept at all. While the realist notion of 'the world' might seem to us to have content, this is an illusion, resulting from hypostatization: we see that one way of representing the object is better than another, and that some third seems yet more free of our cognitive limitations, and then imagine that this process must terminate in some single absolute measure transcending all mere representations. While we do possess the concepts of 'the world' and 'the mind', these can only be applied where we have the ability to manifest our recognition of their obtaining. Our concept of 'the world' cannot be the realist's concept of 'what is there anyway'.

The realist rejoinder will be that while language is indeed shared, social and public, it gives us the resources whereby we may grasp recognition-transcendent meanings. For, the realist insists, we do after all know what it means to speak of how the object is independent of our or anyone's conceptual representation of it. We know that our grasp of the concept of, for example, water exceeds that of our ancestors (who thought of water as that one of four elements whose nature is liquidity). We can likewise envisage a future science that has replaced our understanding of the concept with one that is to us completely unimaginable. And just as our sensory experience of color must be forever unattainable to species like beetles that lack our visual apparatus, so we can imagine alien species attaining an understanding of water's nature that is beyond the capacity of any human to grasp. Indeed we can make sense of the notion that water's true nature might well be beyond the capacity of any merely finite intelligence to grasp. So even if it were true that the triangulation strategy yielded no positive content to our understanding of the nature of mind-independent objects (a point the realist might not willingly concede), this would not give us reason to deny the intelligibility of such a notion.

As often happens in realist/anti-realist discussions, this debate seems to have reached an impasse. I must confess that I fnd persuasive the anti-realist's point concerning the requirement that grasp of meaning be publicly manifested. Still there are powerful intuitions behind the realist's claim to be able to grasp verification-transcendent concepts. And so there is every likelihood of the debate degenerating into a battle of conflicting intuitions. Perhaps more importantly, our original aim was to see if the Buddhist formulation of anti-realism offered any advantages over the formulations that have figured in recent discussions, and the realist/anti-realist debate has been conducted in terms that are quite foreign to the original debate over establishing the means of knowledge. In particular it has become apparent that the anti-realist side relies on a kind of semantic internalism according to which meanings must be accessible to competent speakers. And while there might be much to recommend a moderate form of semantic internalism, it is still just as contentious a view as is epistemological internalism (as well as being just as foreign to the Indian context). The Buddhist anti-realist claims to be able to establish global anti-realism without reliance on any contentious doctrines. So perhaps we should look elsewhere for a way of resolving the dispute over the means of knowledge.

A contextualist response to the objection

Our problem was to understand how the anti-realist argument against an establishment of the means of knowledge (the 'anti-establishment' argument for short) functions as a response to the self-stultification objection. What we have explored is the possibility that the anti-establishment argument might show the apparently sensible view that there are means of knowledge to be incompatible with realism. And we saw that such a strategy will fail against a realist who is an epistemological and semantic externalist. An impasse results once we grant that these externalisms have some degree of intuitive plausibility. We can, however, recognize at least one positive consequence of the anti-establishment argument: it blocks a foundationalist route to realism. The realist cannot proceed by first determining that certain procedures are means of knowledge, and then employing them to show that things do have intrinsic natures. Of course the Indian realist epistemologist was not a foundationalist, if by 'foundationalism' we mean the Cartesian project of grounding our knowledge of the external world on truths thought to be more directly accessible to the cognizer.[i] But there is something they share with such foundationalists, namely the conviction that knowledge is a natural kind.[4] The Cartesian epistemologist reveals this conviction in the claim that knowledge naturally divides up into classes (such as knowledge of the external world) with determinate evidential relationships among them.[5] The

---

[4] It is a central claim of Williams (1991) that foundationalism and radical skepticism require the view that knowledge is a natural kind, and that this view is false.

[5] The Cartesian foundationalist holds that a judgment like 'Because I see it' does not ultimately justify the belief that I am sitting before the fire because both belong to the class of judgments about the external world. Such ultimate justification could only come from a proposition belonging to a class having stronger epistemic credentials than judgments about the external world. The Cartesian thus holds that there are invariant relations of epistemic priority among classes of knowledge-claims.

Indian epistemologist reveals it in the claim that certain processes are intrinsically capable of revealing the object. Both claims involve denying what the epistemological contextualist asserts, that what counts as justification is always determined contextually, through such factors as the type of inquiry, its environmental setting, and the aims of the inquirer. If this is correct, then there can be no relationships of epistemic priority among whole classes of propositions, given that a single proposition may enter into a variety of distinct justificatory relations depending on the epistemic context in which it figures. Likewise there can be no such thing as a means of knowledge *per se*, given that the justificatory role played by a means of knowledge derives in part from the context in which it occurs. Now the impasse that was reached above came about because a realist can plausibly deny foundationalism. Can the realist take an equally agnostic attitude toward the view that knowledge is a natural kind?

We can begin to answer this question by returning to the Indian debate. In addition to the anti-establishment argument, the Buddhist anti-realist has another argument against the epistemological project that might be more germane here.[j] This argument is meant to show that nothing bears the intrinsic nature of a means of knowledge. Consider some epistemic process P that is a particular instance of a class of procedures thought to be a means of knowledge. At what time may P justifiably be considered a means of knowledge with respect to some cognitive event c? Certainly not before cognition c has arisen. Something cannot be a cause if its effect is non-existent, and something is a means of knowledge only if it is the cause of a reliable cognition. (The realist, we must remember, has now embraced epistemological externalism.) But P likewise does not become a means of knowledge after c has arisen. For if the cognition has already come into existence when P occurs, then P cannot serve as its cause. This leaves just the third possibility, that P occurs simultaneously with c, in which case it is unclear which is cause and which effect. This argument is an obvious application of the argument of the three times discussed above (in Chapter 6). If nothing can be said to ultimately be a cause in any of the three times, then nothing can be a cause of reliable cognitions in the three times. But it is the nature of a means of knowledge to be a cause of reliable cognitions. Hence nothing bears the essential nature of a means of knowledge. Knowledge is not a natural kind.

Now this result is not yet sufficient to support the contextualist claim that there can be no context-invariant relations of justification among propositions. The realist might agree that 'means of knowledge' is not a natural-kind term, yet continue to maintain that the expression picks out a determinate kind quite independent of any contextual factors. For we could agree that the property of being either a cow or a goat is not a natural kind, yet still hold that the predicate 'either a cow or a goat' has a perfectly determinate extension. But to claim this we must hold that 'cow' and 'goat' are themselves natural-kind terms, that they have determinate extensions. So to avoid the contextualist conclusion, the realist must be able to claim that 'means of knowledge' likewise allows of reductionist analysis into natural-kind terms. And the arguments for emptiness discussed in the preceding chapter are designed to show that nothing is a natural kind. If those arguments have merit, then the contextualist conclusion is unavoidable: something can be a means of knowledge only by virtue of its role in some epistemic context.

Some caution is required in interpreting this result. This is not epistemological nihilism – or at least it need not be, provided we bear in mind the distinction between ultimate and conventional truth. The Buddhist anti-realist can claim that while nothing is ultimately a means of knowledge, it may still be conventionally true that a certain procedure serves as a means of knowledge on a given occasion. Conventional truth makes room for pragmatic constraints, for instance, and variations in these can lead to differences of epistemic status for a procedure across contexts. So depending on the aim and direction of inquiry (as well as other contextual factors), vision might well serve as a means of knowing that there is a fire before me. Indeed in most contexts we are likely to encounter in ordinary life, 'Because I see it' will serve to justify the judgment that there is a fire before me. What we must not forget is that both the 'ordinary' and the 'extraordinary' context are alike structured by pragmatic constraints and other background features. So when the presence of holographic images renders vision a problematic means of knowing that there is a fire before me, this need not induce general skepticism about all other cases in which I have relied on vision. In many contexts, vision is the cause of reliable cognitions. Of course it is not ultimately true that vision ever causes reliable cognitions, since no causal claim can be ultimately true. Still, it is conventionally true – given certain background interests and practices – that putting a lit match to kindling causes fire. And it can likewise be conventionally true that vision causes reliable cognition – given certain aims and a certain direction of inquiry. Certain procedures may still count (conventionally) as means of knowledge.

This gives the Buddhist anti-realist a credible response to the self-stultification objection. If all things are indeed empty, then nothing has the instrinsic nature of a means of knowledge, and so there are ultimately no means of knowledge and objects of knowledge. Still, emptiness can be known, namely by using instruments that function as valid means of knowledge within the context of inquiry in which they are employed.[k] Of course this means there can be no 'master argument' for emptiness, no one proof that conclusively establishes for all time and all cognizers that all things are empty. What functions as a means of knowledge in one context may fail to perform that function in others.[l] But this is not to say that emptiness cannot be known. To think otherwise is to suppose that a belief could count as knowledge only if it were immune to all possible challenges, hence that there can be justification that is context-invariant. And knowledge is not a natural kind: nothing bears the essential nature of a means of knowledge.

It is now possible to see the anti-establishment argument in a different light. It is tempting to see the argument as a kind of *tu quoque* response to the realist's self-stultification argument. On this *tu quoque* reading, it is aimed at showing that the epistemological project cannot be carried out on realist terms, that if realism were true there could be no means of knowledge. But this reading requires attributing epistemological internalism to the Buddhist anti-realist. Only internalism allows one to infer that there are no means of knowledge from the claim that the means of knowledge cannot be established or known. And such an attribution can be questioned on both strategic and historical grounds. But now we can see the argument as having a somewhat different aim: showing that something cannot be known to be a means of knowledge independently of all contextual considerations. The realist epistemologist seeks to know which are the means of knowledge in all possible epistemic contexts, and accordingly seeks invariant relations of epistemic priority. If such knowledge cannot be acquired even in this central case, this suggests that the underlying assumptions of the project need to be questioned, the most plausible candidate being the assumption that something can bear the intrinsic nature of a means of knowledge, that knowledge is a natural kind.

But this in turn casts the reply of the realist epistemologist in a somewhat different light. When the realist answers the infinite regress objection to the epistemological project by stating that while the regress of justification can iterate, it seldom goes past one or two stages, this reply has something of a contextualist ring to it. The realist epistemologist seems here to be suggesting that what counts as justification may vary from one context to another. And this in turn suggests that contextualism may after all be compatible with the views of the realist epistemologist. Do the anti-establishment argument and the argument of the three times hit their target, do they succeed in undermining the epistemological project of the realist, or could the realist concede that knowledge is not a natural kind?

The incompatibility of realism and contextualism

There is a clear sense in which the realist's project of seeking the means of knowledge could still be carried out on contextualist terms. It is possible to find significant (though not exceptionless) generalizations concerning reliable ways of acquiring beliefs, even granted that justification relations vary with interests and practices. To a certain extent this is what we do when we study the distinctive methodology of a particular discipline such as sociology or meteorology. What is not clear is that contextualist epistemology is compatible with realism. It is central to realism that the real be mind-independent in the sense of possessing a nature that potentially transcends the understanding of merely finite intelligences. This is equivalent to the claim that the real potentially transcends all our knowledge. And it may be questioned whether coherent sense can be made of this 'all our knowledge' on a contextualist understanding of knowledge. To say, as the contextualist does, that knowledge is not a natural kind, is to say that 'knowledge' is a family resemblance term, a term whose extension is fixed not by some determinate set of necessary and sufficient conditions but through a process of projecting from accepted applications along one or another axis of similarity. If 'knowledge' is like that stock example of a family resemblance term, 'game', then not only may there be nothing that all instances of knowledge have in common, but it may also prove impossible to say in advance what states might some day come to be considered kinds of knowledge.[6] While it seems natural to us to think of military exercises as properly called a 'war game', this use of 'game' might not have been readily anticipated at a time when the word was primarily used to refer to recreational activities. While a competent speaker might survey all the things that are currently called games, it would prove impossible to say much that is meaningful about all the things that will ever come to be considered games. And this need not be

---

[6] My thanks to the Carlin Gallery, Rue de Seine, Paris, for providing a locale that helped stimulate this insight.

because the word will undergo what must be considered a change in meaning. At least the use of 'game' to cover military exercises seemed to those who introduced it like a perfectly defensible projection from existing usage, and not a meaning change at all. The difficulty is just that changes in such factors as institutional arrangements and practices can lead to changed saliencies that in turn can make some novel application seem like a perfectly appropriate extension of currently accepted usage. Since we are not able to foresee all the ways in which our way of life might change, let alone all the ways those changes might affect our conceptual similarity space, we are singularly ill equipped to anticipate all the activities that might ever come to be called games.

A contextualist approach to justification yields similar results concerning knowledge: it is not clear that determinate meaning can be attached to the expression 'all our knowledge' if by that we mean all the things that will ever be considered knowledge. And the point here is not the trivial one that we cannot say in advance which propositions we will come to know in the future. It is rather that we cannot say what it is that we may come to consider reliable processes of cognizing what sorts of objects. We can recognize this in retrospect by looking at developments within a particular field of inquiry. At one time the electron was considered a purely theoretical posit, not the sort of thing that could ever be amenable to direct observation. But with changes in available technology and theory acceptance, and greater confidence in the reliability of certain instruments, it came to be considered perfectly sensible to speak of observing electrons. The contextualist claims that what counts as a means of knowledge in one context might not in some other, and this is just a diachronic instance of that general claim: seeing the needle move on some instrument might now count as a case of observing electrons, whereas it would not have so counted for inquirers of an earlier era (even for those conversant with the concept of the electron).

A standard way of fleshing out the realist claim concerning the object's knowledge-transcendence uses an analogy involving differences among creatures in their sense modalities. It would be presumptuous, claims the realist, for creatures lacking the sense of vision to suppose that they were fully informed about all the sensible properties of the physical world. We readily grasp this, since we have the sense modality that those creatures lack. What is not so easy for us to grasp is that there might be creatures with sense modalities that open up to them a range of physical properties just as unimaginable to us as colors would be to the unsighted. The realist claims it would be equally presumptuous for us to claim that there are no properties that we could not come to know in some way or other. But to the contextualist this has the ring of another sort of *hubris*, that involved in supposing we can anticipate all the ways in which what we now regard as our cognitive powers might come to be extended. This is not to say that humans are potentially omniscient. Consider the many possible future histories of human knowledge. It may well be that on each particular history there are always some facts that remain unknown. What is unclear is that there are any that remain unknown on every such possible history. Nor is it at all clear how this could be settled. So long as this is true, it is not clear what it could mean to say that the nature of the real is such as potentially transcends our best attempts at knowledge.

The anti-realist is sometimes accused of a kind of metaphysical narcissism: presuming to legislate a narrow set of confines within which the object must be located (namely that which is accessible to the human intellect).[7] Realists also charge some formulations of anti-realism with a kind of epistemological *hubris*, for instance those formulations that explicate truth in terms of warranted assertibility 'at the end of inquiry'. This is presumptuous, according to the realist, because it problematically assumes that all inquiry must necessarily converge on a single fixed point. Human inquiry might be such as to always allow of further refinements; or it might be such that there are many distinct possible ends of inquiry. Whatever the merits of this charge (about which more will be said in the next chapter), the contextualist would add that realism suffers from a kind of epistemological *hubris* all its own. When it speaks of the object as potentially transcending all our knowledge, it presumes to dictate confines beyond which human knowledge may not stray. This too is a kind of narcissism – not that of taking humanity as the measure of reality, but that of taking present inquiry as the measure of all possible future inquiry. If nothing is intrinsically a means of knowledge or an object of knowledge – if things only take on the status of one or the other in dependence on a variety of contextual factors – then given as well the facts about historical variation in contexts of inquiry, it is not clear how it could be true of reality that it potentially transcends all our knowledge. Which is not to say that the real is necessarily immanent to knowledge either. A contextualist can agree with the realist that epistemic accounts of truth are incoherent. For the contextualist, though, the incoherence stems from the implicit assumption (which an epistemic account of truth shares with realism) that knowledge is a natural kind about which meaningful generalizations can be made.

Buddhist anti-realism and skepticism

Something should be said at this point about the position of the Buddhist anti-realist *vis-à-vis* skepticism. I have been at some pains to indicate that the denial that anything bears the intrinsic nature of a means of knowledge is not tantamount to the denial that we are ever justified in taking ourselves to know certain things. It is one thing to deny that justification can be context-invariant; it is quite another to deny that anything ever justifies a belief. Yet with respect to the Buddhist anti-realist tradition the first has often been confused with the second: the tradition has often been described as a kind of skepticism,[m] and this in spite of explicit avowals by Buddhist anti-realists that there are – conventionally – means of knowledge.[n] It is worth considering why this might be. Suppose we agree that the needle's moving on a properly functioning detector is not intrinsically evidence for the existence of electrons, that it takes on this status only given the context of an occasion of inquiry within which certain propositions are held fixed. Where the question is whether some device works as an electron gun, there must already have been agreement on a substantial amount of microphysical theory, as well as on appropriate methods for detecting electrons. Absent such agreement, the question would simply not make sense. Now to say that the needle's motion is not intrinsically evidence for electrons is just to make this point – to say that the detector is only a means of knowledge relative to certain other things being taken as known.

---

[7] This charge receives an especially clear formulation in Johnston (1993).

A justificatory regress now seems to loom. But as has already been pointed out, unless we presuppose the KK thesis of epistemological internalism, this regress does not itself show that we lack knowledge when the conditions are met. So perhaps the invitation to skepticism lies elsewhere. One possibility is that the seeming justificatory regress appears to open up new error possibilities, new ways in which we might have gone wrong even before the present question was posed. Still, this can have skeptical consequences only if error possibilities are seen as cumulative: the more ways in which we might have gone wrong on the path to some present belief, the more likely it is that the present belief is unjustified. And this is something which we have been given no reason to believe, indeed something that the contextualist explicitly denies.

But raising the specter of there being ever more error possibilities *en route* to knowledge-claims does serve the skeptic's purpose. For this can help foster the impression that in those situations we consider paradigmatic of knowing, it is the crush of practical concerns that dictates our overlooking all the ways in which the assumptions underlying our inquiry might be erroneous. Michael Williams has argued that radical skepticism depends on a picture according to which there are two distinct and separable kinds of constraints at work in inquiry: pragmatic constraints and purely epistemic constraints (1991: 191ff.). The fact that we ordinarily ignore such possibilities as that we are brains in a vat, or are being systematically deceived by a malicious demon, is then attributed to the lowered epistemic standards we adopt under pressure from mere pragmatic or economic constraints. We can see this contrast at work in the Buddhist Reductionist distinction between the two truths: conventional truth is said to be 'merely transactional' in that it allows facts about our interests and cognitive limitations to enter into its standards of assertability, whereas the ultimate truth is deemed ultimate precisely because it presumably prescinds from all such strictly practical considerations. Once we have accepted this distinction, the way is then open to the skeptic to claim that the bizarre error-possibilities that are their stock in trade are indeed germane to the assessment of our epistemic situation, which is properly grasped only from a standpoint purified of transactional constraints. The contextualist claim that in a concrete context of inquiry certain propositions must hold fixed is now seen as no more than a concession to the practical exigencies of the marketplace. To properly assess our cognitive condition, the skeptic urges that we retreat to the study, where we can reflectively assess it attending exclusively to epistemic constraints.

At the end of the last chapter it was suggested that if the arguments rehearsed there for emptiness are sound, then the distinction between conventional and ultimate truth becomes problematic. If nothing bears an intrinsic nature, then there can be nothing for the ultimate truth to be about. This has the consequence of undermining any hard and fast distinction between pragmatic and purely epistemic constraints on inquiry. It thus becomes unclear whether there is such a thing as a standpoint of purely theoretical reflection detached from all practical considerations. If Williams' diagnosis of radical skepticism is correct, this in turn means that the skeptic is debarred from deploying such stock devices as malicious demons and brain-in-a-vat scenarios, unless some reason is forthcoming why they are relevant to the assessment of concrete contexts of inquiry. When I set about trying to discover why my car does not start, I do not ordinarily wonder whether a deceptive demon might be causing me to hallucinate the appearance of a car. If there is no such thing as the ultimate truth, then this failure cannot be explained as a mere concession to the demands of everyday life. If there is no such thing as the ultimate truth, then all inquiry is interested – is shaped by the aims reflected in our methodological practices. We must then ask what interests lie behind the questions asked in the context of philosophical reflection 'in the study' (questions like how we know we are not brains in a vat). The skeptic's questions presumably aim at discovering the purely epistemic constraints that undergird all methodological practices. The skeptic is thus presupposing that knowledge is a natural kind, that substantive generalizations about knowledge can be drawn across disciplinary contexts. If nothing is intrinsically a means of knowledge, then this intuitively appealing route to radical skepticism is blocked.

It is often claimed that the possibility of radical skepticism is a direct consequence of realism. Thus it should not be surprising that Buddhist anti-realism would have anti-skeptical consequences. Now some realists see the possibility of radical skepticism as something that can be safely bypassed, e.g., by adopting a thoroughgoing externalism. Others, though, agree with many anti-realists that the skeptical challenge represents a serious difficulty for realism, one that anti-realism presumably does not share. But realists are wont to charge that the alleged anti-realist triumph over radical skepticism is actually just a disguised capitulation. Consider, for instance, phenomenalism construed as a variety of local anti-realism about physical objects. According to the phenomenalist, external-world skepticism is undermined by the fact that talk about physical objects is really just talk about appearances (which are, of necessity, epistemically accessible). According to the realist, however, this is just a backhanded way of conceding the skeptic's point concerning the narrow confines of our knowledge; the phenomenalist is simply trying to make a virtue of the skeptic's necessity. Is the Buddhist anti-realist's anti-skeptical strategy open to this charge? The question whether anti-realism is just disguised skepticism is usually raised in connection with anti-realism's tendency to introduce epistemic elements into truth, thereby collapsing the distinction between the true and the knowable. And we have yet to examine where Buddhist anti-realism stands on the nature of truth; that will be the subject of the next chapter. Still, we can say at this point that contextualism has resources with which to distance itself from skepticism. The contextualist claims that in the context in which the question is raised whether a certain device will work as an electron gun, such propositions as those making up the relevant parts of microphysical theory stand fixed, that is, are not themselves open to evaluation. The realist might charge that this is implicitly conceding the skeptic's point that much of what we claim to know is based on unproven assumptions. The contextualist replies that without such fixed propositions there could be no inquiry at all, that these represent agreed-upon standards which have been found to be helpful in shaping and focusing inquiry in productive ways. To the realist this sounds all the more like skepticism in drag: to justify propositions by appealing to the useful results gained by accepting them seems tantamount to conceding that they cannot be justified in the normal way, by appealing to the evidence in their favor. But this charge rests on a questionable distinction between pragmatic and epistemic constraints on knowledge. In particular, it depends on the problematic idea that there could be inquiry that was somehow freed from all pragmatic constraints. If the ultimate truth is that there is no ultimate truth, this suggests that the idea of pure inquiry is an illusion, and thus that the realist charge is groundless. A contextualist epistemology will look like disguised skepticism only to those who still think something could bear the intrinsic nature of a means of knowledge.

If this is right, then Buddhist anti-realism constitutes a genuine middle path between the extremes of realism and radical skepticism. But this conclusion may be premature. It is possible that the Buddhist anti-realist falls in with other anti-realists in espousing an epistemic account of truth. In that case the realist's charge that the Buddhist anti-realist is a closet skeptic would gain in credibility. So we must now turn to an investigation of how truth fares if all things are devoid of intrinsic nature.

Notes

[a] One sometimes hears it claimed that Madhyamaka should not be thought of as a doctrine or philosophical system, since it holds no positions, theses, or views. It is true that Nāgārjuna argues in MMK 27 for the elimination of all *dṛṣṭi*, and this word is often translated as 'view'. Likewise he famously asserts in *Vigrahavyāvartanī* (VV) 29 that he has no thesis (*pratijñā*). But the *dṛṣṭi* that he argues against in MMK 27 are just those 'metaphysical views' that the Buddha claimed were undecidable, such as whether the world has a beginning in time. And in his use of 'thesis' in VV he clearly has in mind the Nyāya technical term for the conclusion of an inference, this being understood in the typical Nyāya way not as a proposition, but as an occurrent mental state that reflects the nature of mind-independent reality. Moreover, Nāgārjuna regularly speaks of the statement (*vacana*) that all things are devoid of intrinsic nature as something he asserts with the intention of negating intrinsic nature, and he discusses at some length how this statement might accomplish that task. See, e.g., VV 23. He thus appears to view the statement that all things are empty as a philosophically defensible position.

[b] This objection is stated by the opponent at VV 5–6.

[c] There is, however, a dispute among Mādhyamikas as to what form that support should take. Some claim that it can only take the form of *prasaṅga* or *reductio ad absurdum* arguments. Others claim that it is possible for a Mādhyamika to formulate arguments that employ premises commonly accepted by both the proponent (in this case the Mādhyamika) and the opponent (that is, the target audience). Now *reductio* arguments (or *tarka*) were considered by the realist Naiyāyikas not to be a genuine means of knowledge, since there is no mind-independent state of affairs to which the conclusion of such an argument corresponds; and much of Indian epistemology followed the lead of the Nyāya on this point. So on the view of the first sort of Mādhyamikas (called *Prāsaṅgikas* by Tibetan Buddhist doxographers), the Mādhyamika does not employ any means of knowledge in establishing emptiness. To attempt to establish emptiness using the means of knowledge known as inference would, they claim, commit the fallacy of attempting to prove that some property (emptiness) inheres in a subject that the Mādhyamika holds does not exist. Hence the Mādhyamika can only seek to refute the views of the realist opponent.

Those in the second camp (called *Svātantrikas* by the Tibetans), however, showed how by using the distinction between the two truths it is possible to turn a *reductio* argument into its contrapositive, an inference concerning a subject accepted by both sides. So the Mādhyamika will accept as conventionally real those entities posited by the opponent, and will then proceed to use various facts about those entities in order to prove that they have the property of emptiness, that is, that they lack ultimate reality. See Moriyama (1999) for a discussion of how this conversion to a contrapositive formulation is accomplished in Kamalaśila. Still, all Mādhyamikas would agree that the establishment of emptiness should not rely on any contentious philosophical doctrines. Thus the premises that may be employed in Madhyamaka arguments will be either theoretical commitments of the opponent (when their views are being subjected to *reductio*) or truisms of common sense ('things known to cowherds and women' in Candrakīrti's rather obnoxious phrase).

ᵈ This argument is to be found in VV 31–51. Of particular interest is Nāgārjuna's defense of the anti-reflexivity principle in VV 33–39. It is also worth noting here that this argument need not be taken as intended to support skepticism. For the argument might be seen not as casting doubt on the very idea of a means of knowledge, but rather as calling into question a realist understanding of the means of knowledge. Nāgārjuna seems himself to recognize the need for a Mādhyamika to employ some means of knowledge or other, for instance when he claims that the emptiness of all existents has been 'established by us in detail' (*iha cāsmābhiḥ pūrvam eva sarveṣāṃ bhāvānāṃ vistarataḥ śūnyatvam upapāditam* VV 59). But I shall have more to say below on the subject of skepticism and Madhyamaka.

ᵉ This is the Nyāya response to the Madhyamaka critique of their project, which is found at *Nyāya Sūtra* 2.1.8–20. The reply to the regress of justifications objection is found in Vātsyāyana's *Bhāṣya* on *Nyāya Sutra* 2.1.20 (Gangopadhyaya 88–89).

ᶠ Indeed I argue in Siderits (2000) that classical Indian epistemology as a whole is marked by the common acceptance of externalism. In particular, those who espouse the position that veridical cognitions are intrinsically veridical (the *svataḥprāmāṇyavādins*) are not claiming that possession of knowledge brings with it the awareness that one's cognitive state is veridical (which is the internalist's 'KK' thesis: to know one must know that one knows). They are rather claiming that a cognitive state with the right causal ancestry is properly described as a case of knowledge directly upon its occurrence and in the absence of any attempt on the part of the subject to verify it.

ᵍ Nyāya would agree, despite their recognition of a kind of non-conceptual cognition in the form of *nirvikalpaka* (non-conceptual) perception. For this is not itself cognitively accessible, in that its content can only be expressed in perceptual cognitions that have conceptual structure (*vikalpaka pratyakṣa*). This fact has recently led Chakrabarti (2000) to advocate that the system abandon this apparently pointless posit. But it can be argued that the basic principle Nyāya invokes in defense of the posit – no cognition of a relational complex without prior cognition of the relata – is crucial to their realist account of perception. For when they concede that all cognitively accessible perception contains conceptual structure, the posit of *nirvikalpaka* perception enables them to reply to the Buddhist rejoinder that their concession turns the perceptual process into a form of conceptual construction and thus not something that is ultimately veridical. To the Buddhist, of course, all aggregation is a form of mental construction, and as such is epistemically suspect. But the Naiyāyika can reply that the aggregation involved in a perceptual judgment is merely the assembly of elements already cognized in *nirvikalpaka* perception, and is thus guided by cognitive access to elements that the Buddhist must concede are not tainted by the odor of mental construction. It is of course crucial to the success of this strategy that among the elements supposedly grasped in *nirvikalpaka* perception are such relations as inherence and contact. Chakrabarti will deny that such things ever occur in an unqualified state, and this is no doubt true. But the Nyāya intuition here is that the relation itself, as distinct from its occurrence in relational complexes, must be thought to play a causal role in the perception of a relational complex. Otherwise we would have no reason to see the relational complex as anything more than another bit of mental construction.

ʰ The Yogācāra–Sautrāntika school does in fact claim that all conceptualization falsifies the object; they hold that the reals are all absolutely unique, while conceptualization necessarily involves superimposition of generality. Thus they draw a fundamental distinction between perception – which they view as inexpressible but veridical – and inference – which is said to be expressible, but which also distorts the object's nature through mental construction. This school nonetheless subscribes to a form of realism. Their *apoha* semantics (see Appendix) is meant to explain how the causal capacities of the unique reals make it (conventionally) correct to call some things cows and others goats. So they too must grant that while this particular entity is not ultimately a cow, there is something in its nature that makes it correct to call it a cow and incorrect to call it a goat.

ⁱ Of course it is possible to see Abhidharma reductionism as a kind of foundationalism, insofar as it seeks to ground our knowledge of conventional truths in facts about the ultimate nature of reality. But knowledge of these facts is typically more difficult for cognizers to attain, so Ābhidhārmikas would not be inclined to see their reductionist program as disclosing anything concerning relations of epistemic priority. Even where the issue of the existence of the physical world is joined (in the debate with Yogācāra), the discussion is couched in metaphysical terms, not epistemological. While Sautrāntika representationalism may have suggested the hypothesis of mind-only to the Yogācārins, the latter do not argue from the representationalist view that we lack direct access to the external object to the conclusion that its existence is unknowable. Instead they support their idealism through such things as appeals to the principle of lightness and an infinite-regress argument against atomism.

ʲ See Aryadeva's *Catuḥśataka* 9.12.

ᵏ Indeed a Buddhist anti-realist might claim orthodox support for this sort of contextualism in the doctrine of the Buddha's *upāya*, that pedagogical skill whereby he was able to tailor his discourse to the needs and capacities of his audience. This is, however, a very different construal of *upāya* than that which led the Ābhidhārmikas to the distinction between the two truths.

ˡ This would help account for the fact that Nāgārjuna employs such a wide variety of arguments in MMK (and other Indian Mādhyamikas follow his lead in this). Different aims of inquiry will give rise to differing methodologies, which may in turn lead to new ways of formulating and defending realism. And since 'methodology', like 'means of knowledge', is not the name of a natural kind, the Buddhist anti-realist cannot anticipate all possible challenges to the doctrine of emptiness. Of course it is likely that there will be discernible patterns in the different strategies that the Mādhyamika employs. But it is unlikely that any one argument or even set of arguments will suffice to establish the claim of emptiness in all possible contexts.

ᵐ For example, in Matilal (1986: 46–68) and Mohanty (1992: 278). (But more recently Mohanty (2000b: 144) has acknowledged the possibility that Nāgārjuna might instead be an anti-realist.) Garfield (1990) likewise calls Nāgārjuna a kind of skeptic, though in this case it is Pyrrhonian skepticism that he has in mind. And this, it can be argued, is quite different from the radical skepticism that emerges in the modern tradition after Descartes. Radical skepticism presupposes foundationalism, whereas Pyrrhonian skeptics would presumably reject it. I believe that there are other grounds on which to reject the assimilation of Madhyamaka to the Pyrrhonian sort of skepticism, but these have more to do with the ethical views involved than with epistemological matters.

ⁿ For example, by Candrakīrti in his discussion of Yogācāra–Sautrāntika epistemology at *Prasannapadā* on MMK 1.3: *tad evaṃ pramāṇacatuṣṭayāt lokasyārthādhigamo vyavasthāpyate* (Pandeya 23). It is interesting that Candrakīrti here affirms the four means of knowledge acknowledged by Nyāya, whereas Bhāvaviveka only affirms the two accepted by Yogācāra–Sautrāntika.

CHAPTER EIGHT

The Turn of the True

In the last two chapters we looked at some of the metaphysical and epistemological consequences of the doctrine of emptiness. It is now time to examine its consequences for semantics, particularly the theory of truth. Disputes over the nature of truth are central to the current controversy between realists and anti-realists. And there is a sense in which this holds as well for the debate between Buddhist anti-realists and their opponents. Still, the character of the Buddhist debate is rather different from that of the current dispute. Indeed some would say that the differences are so great that it should be questioned whether the champions of the doctrine of emptiness are properly called anti-realists. Part of the aim of the present chapter is to defend my terminological choice to call the doctrine of emptiness a kind of anti-realism. But my chief aim is to work out what I take to be the consequences of the doctrine of emptiness for the set of semantic issues that are central to the present dispute between realists and anti-realists. I shall do so by first laying out what Buddhist anti-realists have to say about the nature of truth, and then trying to extrapolate from that basis in order to arrive at some answers to the current crop of disputed questions. This extrapolation will involve a lengthy foray into the theory of linguistic meaning; for it turns out that important clues to the nature of truth emerge when we try to get clear about what linguistic meaning consists in. What I shall claim in the end is that Buddhist anti-realism constitutes a kind of middle path between the extremes of deflationism about truth and epistemologized truth. The argument for the claim will be that this is what follows when we apply some basic results of the doctrine of emptiness to the dispute over linguistic meaning.

The Buddhist anti-realist view of truth

I have already given some indication of the form in which the issue of truth arises for Buddhist anti-realism. The doctrine of emptiness has, I have claimed, the consequence that the ultimate truth is that there is no ultimate truth. Recall that for Buddhist Reductionism a statement can be ultimately true only through correspondence to what is ultimately real. And in that context 'correspondence' must be understood in the strongest possible sense: any entity the existence of which is either asserted or presupposed by a statement must belong to the ultimate ontology, lest the statement be deemed neither true nor false. Ultimate truth thus requires isomorphism between statement and state of affairs,[a] at least with respect to entities and the terms used to refer to them.[b] So if nothing bears an intrinsic nature, then since nothing would then belong to an ultimate ontology as conceived by the realist, it follows that no statement can be ultimately true. For the Buddhist Reductionist, bivalence failure was a local phenomenon, confined to talk of persons and other partite entities. For the Buddhist anti-realist, bivalence failure is global: for any statement s purporting to describe how things ultimately are, neither *s* nor its negation not-*s*, the conjunction of *s* and not-*s*, nor the negation of the conjunction of *s* and not-*s* may be asserted.[c]

In Chapter 4 I suggested that Buddhist Reductionism could readily accommodate cases of bivalence failure associated with *sorites* difficulties without abandoning classical logic and semantics, namely by ensconcing classical logic and semantics at the ultimate level while embracing a degree-theoretic approach to truth at the conventional level. The idea was to insulate ultimate truth from logical and semantic deviancy by screening out all terms referring to partite entities. At the same time the semantic and logical behavior of such terms could be handled at the conventional level by adoption of an infinite-valued approach to truth. The major difficulty facing such an approach to the semantics of vague terms – that assigning truth-values any more fine-grained than the two-valued 1 and 0 seems highly artificial – could then be overcome by suggesting that we view the numbers as mere approximations to the genuine truth. Since conventional truth always involves accommodations to human interests and cognitive limitations, it should be no surprise that in that context the use of degree-theoretic machinery should represent merely a useful device.

This solution falls apart when bivalence failure goes global. Now it must be pointed out that the bivalence failure that Buddhist anti-realists discuss is not the sort engendered by predicates whose application involves a range of indeterminacy (the sort of bivalence failure that according to Dummett is criterial for anti-realism). There is a long history in the Buddhist tradition of using bivalence failure as a rhetorical device for signaling failure of reference at the ultimate level, and hence, by the semantic rules of ultimate truth, semantic ill-formedness. Still, the upshot is the same. Suppose I construct a range of cases showing that the expression 'same light' exhibits indeterminacy under certain conditions. Since this suggests that in some cases there is no fact of the matter as to whether a certain light is the same light as a certain earlier light, we are likely to conclude that lights are not members of our final ontology: a truly real entity, we suppose, could not lack diachronic identity conditions in any possible situation in which it exists. And this is the very conclusion that Buddhist Reductionists intend when they say that the lit lamp at the second watch is neither the same light as the lit lamp at the first watch, nor is it a distinct light.[d] So when a Buddhist anti-realist claims that, for instance, it can be neither asserted nor denied that consciousness is characterized by its alleged defining characteristic of cognizing,[e] the intent is to show that consciousness is not among the constituents of ultimate reality. And of course the Buddhist anti-realist seeks to show similar results for every conceivable candidate for membership in our final ontology.

If they are right about this, then it seems we can no longer see conventional truth as a mere useful approximation to the ultimate truth. For if nothing bears an intrinsic nature, then there can be no such thing as a statement's capturing the structure of the world as it is independent of our conceptual activity. We earlier discussed conventional truth as a kind of warranted assertibility, where warrant was understood as conferred by conformity to the methodological standards of our conventionally agreed upon disciplinary practices.[f] Of course realists would be inclined to balk at the notion that truth might be understood as just warranted assertibility: to say this is to accede to the epistemologizing of truth, since this amounts to denying the possibility of verification-transcendent truths. But this understanding of conventional truth is acceptable to the Buddhist Reductionist realist precisely because conventional truth is seen by them as a mere useful approximation to the real thing, ultimate truth. If all things are, as the Buddhist anti-realist claims, empty, then we seem to be left with just truth as warranted assertibility. In recent discussions there has been some dispute as to whether taking an epistemic approach to truth is necessary or merely sufficient for being counted as an anti-realist. In either event, the global bivalence failure that results from the emptiness of all things seems to yield a kind of global anti-realism.[1]

There are three things that might be said against attributing this sort of anti-realism to the champions of the doctrine of emptiness (and hence for calling them 'anti-realists'). The first is that an epistemic account of truth is incoherent: to collapse truth into what is known – even what is known under the best of circumstances – is to lose sight of truth's normative role. In the absence of any textual evidence in its favor, this interpretation of the doctrine violates the principle of charity, since it saddles the upholders of emptiness with a highly implausible view. Second, it might be alleged that the view that truth is warranted assertibility is incompatible with the anti-essentialism implicit in the doctrine of emptiness. We have already seen that emptiness can be used to cast doubt on the notion that knowledge is a natural kind. Since any substantive theory of truth, such as the view that truth is just warranted assertibility, is built on the presupposition that there is a determinate essence shared in by all true statements, it might plausibly be claimed that emptiness is incompatible with any substantive theory of truth.[2] Third, it might be pointed out that the juxtaposition of conventional and ultimate truth is heavily implicated in our understanding of conventional truth. That is, it might be claimed that our notion of the conventional truth depends at least in part on an implicit contrast with the ultimate truth. So if the very idea of the ultimate truth must be rejected, then whatever conception of truth remains cannot be conventional truth as understood by the Buddhist Reductionist.

---

[1] Tillemans (1999: 199), using the distinction between substitutional and objectual interpretations of the quantifiers (see Marcus 1993), has suggested that the doctrine of emptiness be understood as follows: at the conventional level the quantifiers are to be given a substitutional reading, while at the ultimate level they receive an objectual reading. Since the champions of emptiness claim that the domain of ultimate truth is empty, it follows that any predication will be ultimately false. (I have more to say below about this way of trying to avoid contradictions.) Since there is thus no ultimate reference base, statements made at the conventional level cannot be given the usual substitutional reading, according to which the truth-value of an atomic statement is determined by the assignment of names to particulars (e.g., by way of a causal theory of reference). The theory thus avoids commitment not just to ontologically suspect entities (such as universals and kinds) but to entities of any sort whatever. The difficulty is that the truth of the atomic sentences, as well as all others, then looks to be purely conventional in a more problematic sense – wholly arbitrary, a matter of pure stipulation. Since this result is clearly unsatisfactory, we are still owed some account of what it means for a conventionally true statement to be true. The resort to a substitutional reading of the quantifiers merely defers this problem without offering any guidance on how it is to be resolved. While it may be problematic to equate truth with warranted assertibility, to say that global bivalence failure leads to such a view at least manifests awareness that there is a problem here.

[2] Note that this applies equally to the correspondence theory of truth. To the extent that realism requires seeing truth as correspondence, this would mean that the doctrine of emptiness is also incompatible with realism. This line of thinking thus leads to the suggestion that the doctrine of emptiness requires a deflationist view of truth. I consider this hypothesis below.

Now I must concede that there is some truth to each of these criticisms. I shall nonetheless persist in referring to those who champion the doctrine of emptiness as Buddhist anti-realists. For there is (*pace* the first criticism) some evidence that they do hold a view about truth somewhat akin to what is today called anti-realism. There is, for instance, their claim that while the Buddha sometimes taught a doctrine of the self, and at other times the doctrine of non-self, neither view was truly taught by the Buddha.[8] The reference here is to the Buddha's supposed skill as a teacher, which led him to adapt his message to the capacities of his audience (always bearing in mind the goal of helping them overcome suffering). Thus he would use talk of an enduring self when instructing an audience as yet unfamiliar with the processes of karma and rebirth, given that belief in a self is all but required at this initial stage of understanding, and assuming as well that such understanding is necessary to winning liberation from karma and rebirth. Now a Buddhist Reductionist would claim that teachings of this sort represent merely conventional truth, while the Buddha's teaching of the doctrine of non-self represents the ultimate truth. But the Buddhist anti-realist rejects that interpretation when they say that the Buddha did not truly teach either view. To say this is to say that neither is ultimately true, that both represent no more than pedagogical devices that prove helpful for attaining our goals in their respective contexts. The suggestion is thus that there is no fact of the matter concerning whether or not a self exists, and that the truth of any assertion on this matter just consists in the warrant possessed by the speaker in a context (where warrant can be conferred by pragmatic considerations[h]). Truth, it seems, is not correspondence with the facts but just warranted assertibility.

There is, nonetheless, something deeply problematic about this position; the three criticisms described above all have some merit. The resolution I shall propose will be dialectical in nature: while anti-realism represents a genuine advance over realism, there is something wrong as well as something right about it. To locate its place in the dialectical progression, I shall take advantage of the soteriological concerns of the Buddhist, and distinguish between teaching contexts – in which the enlightened person seeks to help others attain enlightenment – and lifeworld contexts – in which the enlightened person lives out their own life consistent with the understanding gleaned through their enlightenment. In the following progression of views, (3) represents the stance taken up in teaching contexts, while (4) represents that to be adopted in lifeworld contexts:

1. Common-sense realism, including belief in the existence of persons.
2. Buddhist Reductionism (understood as a variety of realism): persons are mere conceptual fictions and are ultimately unreal, hence the claim that persons exist is conventionally true but ultimately without semantic value.
3. Buddhist anti-realism: there is no ultimate fact of the matter concerning the existence of persons, hence no statement concerning their existence (including statements about their supposedly impersonal constitutents) is ultimately true; belief in the very possibility of ultimate truth represents an obstacle to liberation which must itself be overcome if the cessation of suffering is to be attained.
4. Semantic non-dualism: it is (non-dualistically) true that we are persons.

Position (4) is to be distinguished from position (1) in terms of the fact that the former is informed by recognition of what is right (as well as what is wrong) about anti-realism. Thus while (4) might look like a kind of deflationism about truth (the view that the concept of truth is of little theoretical interest), the fact that it is arrived at by way of position (3) will turn out to make an important difference.

To make any of this at all clear I shall first need to say something about the current controversy over truth between realists and anti-realists. Our entry into this dispute will be by way of an examination of current approaches to the following question: how do we best understand the ability of competent speakers of a language to understand the meanings of novel sentences? We will look at atomist and holist accounts of semantic competence, and see what these might tell us about the nature of truth. We will then explore what impact the doctrine of emptiness might have on the dispute between realists and anti-realists over truth. The hope is that we will then be better positioned to see how one might accept the designation 'anti-realist' while acknowledging that anti-realism is not fully correct.

A framework for investigating the nature of truth

There is now widespread consensus that an adequate theory of truth must meet at least the following material adequacy condition: it must entail every sentence of the form:

(T) Statement s is true if and only if p

where s is a statement-making sentence of the object language, and p is a translation of s in the metalanguage.[3] (Here the metalanguage is understood to include the object language plus certain semantic and set-theoretical terms.) Thus the following would be an instance of schema (T), that is, a T-sentence:

(1) 'The sky is blue' is true iff the sky is blue.

The question is what more, if anything, can be said about the property shared in by all true statements. A realist would claim that the consensus around the T-schema is explained by the fact that truth consists in a relation of correspondence between a statement and an existing state of affairs. Thus 'The sky is blue' is true just because it

---

[3] It might be thought that this can hold only if we take the truth-predicate to be classical or bivalent. Williamson (1994: 187–98) claims to show that the T-schema yields contradictions when conjoined with any account of truth that rejects bivalence. I claimed earlier that a Buddhist Reductionist should adopt a degree-theoretic account of truth for the domain of conventional truth (that part of our discourse that employs vague predicates). So if Williamson is right, then the Buddhist Reductionist could not join this 'widespread consensus'. But as Machina and Deutsch (2002) have shown, Williamson's argument in effect begs the question by presupposing bivalence. Indeed a degree-theoretic analog of the classical T-schema can be constructed by interpreting the biconditional in accordance with degree-theoretic semantics. In that case an instance of the T-schema will assert that the (degree-theoretic) truth-values of the quoted sentence on the left and the truth-conditions on the right are the same: 1, 0, or some number between these two. Kent Machina helped me see this.

picks out, from among all the states of affairs that might obtain, the fact that the sky is blue. Of course it is crucial to the realist that correspondence be understood as a relation between a linguistic item and something that obtains in the world independent of our linguistic and conceptual practices. An apparent difficulty is posed by the sentence, 'The word "sky" has three letters', which yields the T-sentence,

(2) 'The word "sky" has three letters' is true iff the word 'sky' has three letters.

Here the statement to the right of the biconditional seems to be about our linguistic practices. But the realist would point out that this orthographic state of affairs would obtain even if no one ever noticed, remarked on, or even conceptualized it. It is thus a sufficiently robust fact to stand as that which makes any assertion of the sentence in question true. This brings out the essential asymmetry in the realist notion of correspondence: while not all versions of the correspondence theory involve the notion of copying, it is necessary to the theory that there obtain something like the relation of original to copy (or representation) between state of affairs and statement if the latter is to be said to correspond to the former.[4]

An anti-realist would explain the apparent consensus around the T-schema by pointing out that in the usual example, what comes after the biconditional is typically just the assertibility conditions for the sentence. That is, our sample T-sentences tell us that the statement in question is true just in case the conditions obtain that would justify us in asserting that statement. The statement 'Snow is white' would be true just in case we had the evidence that would warrant our making the statement, namely (in this case) the observation that snow is white. Hence truth is not to be understood as correspondence to mind-independent reality, but rather just as warranted assertibility.[5] As has already been remarked, given certain plausible assumptions about meaning and knowledge, this will mean that there cannot be truths that in principle transcend our ability to come to verify them. And this in turn will mean that certain T-sentences will not be entailed by an adequate theory of truth, namely those involving verification-transcendent truth-conditions. But as we shall see, not all anti-realists endorse the resulting rejection of bivalence.

Deflationists (or disquotationalists, as they are sometimes called) would claim that the consensus around the T-schema reflects the fact that little more can be said about the alleged property of truth than just that all the T-sentences hold. Certainly there cannot, on their view, be any such thing as a substantive theory of truth. Truth, according to the deflationist, is not a property at all, but rather just a disquotational device: saying of a statement that it is true is just another way of accomplishing

---

[4] I would thus question the distinction Kirkham (1992: 119) draws between correspondence as 'congruence' and correspondence as 'correlation'. The latter is said to involve no more than a correlation between the truth-bearer (e.g., a statement) as a whole and a state of affairs: the former is true when and only when the latter obtains. It does not involve any relations of structural isomorphism between the two relata. But this appears to be just what is captured in the T-schema. To call this a kind of correspondence is to conflate the correspondence theory with deflationism. On this point see also Davidson's (1984: 48) discussion of why Tarski's theory is, after all, not deflationist but rather a rehabilitation of correspondence.

[5] The coherence and pragmatist theories of truth may then be seen as attempts at spelling out what in general supplies such warrant: coherence with the body of accepted beliefs, or utility, or the like.

what would ordinarily be done by asserting it. The truth-predicate facilitates certain procedures that we would be hard-pressed to perform in its absence, such as when we say that every member of a set of sentences is true, or when we note that the truth of a given sentence follows from the truth of certain other sentences. But there is no more to truth *per se* than what is captured in the truism reflected in the T-schema: a statement is true just in case things are as it says they are.

It is an interesting question whether the deflationist is a closeted anti-realist. The argument in favor of this identification is that in denying that there is any substantive property of truth, the deflationist is depriving realism of the crucial notion of truth as correspondence. The difference between the deflationist and the anti-realist would then be purely terminological: the anti-realist opts for a revised, epistemologized notion of truth, while the deflationist chooses instead to treat the issues involved in the realism/anti-realism dispute as purely semantic and epistemological. Against this interpretation there is the fact that many deflationists subscribe to the principle of bivalence.[6] But as Putnam (1994: 498) points out, they tend to view bivalence as a linguistic convention. Certainly on the deflationist view the truth of

(3) Either Oswald acted alone in assassinating Kennedy or Oswald did not act alone in assassinating Kennedy

does not consist in it being a real fact that he did act alone (if he did), or it being a real fact that he did not act alone (if he did not). The truth of (3) can be explained wholly in terms of our having chosen to treat statement-making sentences as either true or false. Any other kind of account would require a substantive theory of truth. Bivalence is central to realism precisely because on a realist conception of truth bivalence is metaphysically grounded. (I shall have more to say on this point below.) If all this is correct, then deflationism might best be seen as a variety of anti-realism, namely the variety that sees the question of truth as irrelevant to resolving the alleged antinomies of realism.[7]

If these differing views about the nature of truth can all be supported using the same evidence, how is the dispute to be resolved? Recently a major site of contention in the controversy between realists and anti-realists has been semantics for natural languages. The basic question at issue is what would constitute an adequate account of a competent speaker's understanding of such a language. One major constraint on any answer to this question is that mastery of a natural language confers the ability to grasp the meanings of a very large number of, quite possibly infinitely many, sentences, based on what are clearly only finite resources. How is this ability to be represented? One answer that has received some support is that to understand the sentences of a language is just to grasp the T-sentences for that language. Of course there will be just as many of these as there are sentences formulatable in the language, so this would not seem to help solve the 'infinite capacity, finite resources' problem. But following the lead of Davidson, who built on the tools Tarski devised for

---

[6] See, e.g., Horwich (1990: 80).

[7] Horwich would presumably reject this characterization of at least his own version of deflationism. But see Horwich (1990: 57–58) for his account of the 'essence' of anti-realism. And see Putnam (1994: 497) for a discussion of the relevant commitments of deflationists in semantics and epistemology.

constructing truth-theories for formal languages, we might give structural descriptions of sentences that show how the truth-conditions for complex sentences depend on those for the simpler sentences out of which they are built up. There are, as might be expected, many hurdles to be overcome in filling out the details of such a program. But before these may even be addressed, there is a more basic difficulty that must be resolved. How is the following sentence to be ruled out as an instance of the T-schema, and thus as representing part of our linguistic competence?

> (4) 'The sky is blue' is true iff grass is green.

With the connective 'if and only if' understood extensionally, as the material biconditional, (4) is true. It will be complained that what stands to the right of the biconditional is not a correct translation of the quoted sentence in the object-language. But of course our notion of a correct translation is just the notion of a translation that preserves meaning, and it is this notion that we are trying to understand. Those who recognize the notion of analytic truth will likewise complain that (4) is not analytically true. But then the concept of analyticity also involves the notion of linguistic meaning: a statement is said to be analytically true if it is true solely by virtue of the meanings of its constituent terms. And this is once again just the notion we seek to understand. Similarly for the allegation that (4) is not necessarily true: the concept of alethic necessity is likewise a semantic concept, so its employment in this context would undermine any attempt at achieving a genuine advance in our understanding of linguistic competence.

There are two ways to resolve the difficulty of ruling out (4), reflecting the two possible approaches to understanding semantic competence, atomist and holist. The atomist approach sees the mastery of sentence meaning as decomposable into the mastery of the semantics of sub-sentential units (such as names, first-order predicates, second-order predicates and sentential connectives). The hope is that by introducing axioms specifying the reference of names and the satisfaction conditions of predicates, grounds can be given for rejecting sentences like (4). Suppose our semantic theory contained axioms to the effect that 'sky' refers to the sky, 'grass' refers to grass, that 'is blue' is satisfied by blue objects, and 'is green' is satisfied by green objects.[8] Then given certain observations, we could rule out (4) and obtain instead

> (1) 'The sky is blue' is true iff the sky is blue

and

> (5) 'Grass is green' is true iff grass is green.

---

[8] Of course this was not Tarski's way of expressing satisfaction conditions, which was in effect to list all the objects that satisfy the predicate. But Tarski sought to define the truth-predicate in a way that avoided the use of other semantic notions, which he regarded as of dubious scientific respectability. When Tarski's methods are applied to the problem of explaining natural language competency, the result is an infinite sequence that gives the satisfaction conditions for a predicate, and this runs afoul of the 'infinite resources, finite capacity' constraint. Atomist semantics is thus drawn to a solution that relies on our ability to detect properties.

The holist approach, by contrast, eschews treating sub-sentential components as having semantic values independent of their occurrence in sentences. Instead it suggests that we construct our theory of sentence meaning holistically: we should build up our stock of T-sentences for the language in question by considering all the sentences affirmed by competent speakers. Now competent speakers of English will affirm both 'The sky is blue' and 'Grass is green', so the facts about these sentences do not yet give us grounds for ruling out (4). But competent speakers also affirm such sentences as 'Grass grows after rain', 'The sky is filled with stars', 'The sapphire is blue' and 'The emerald is green.' Given these and other facts about speaker behavior, the best hypothesis turns out to be that (1) and (5) represent theorems of a semantic theory for English, while (4) does not.[9] When we consider the entire body of evidence concerning speaker behavior, (1) and (5) better fit the facts than (4).

In what follows we will explore each of these two approaches to semantics in turn, seeking to determine what consequences they might have for the dispute over truth. To anticipate the results, I shall claim that either approach to accounting for linguistic competence, when supplemented by key elements of the anti-essentialism of Buddhist anti-realism, yields substantial support for an anti-realist view of truth. We will thus be spared the necessity of having to settle the dispute between atomist and holist in order to see what lessons natural language semantics might have for truth. If the anti-essentialist arguments presented in the previous two chapters are basically sound, then an adequate account of our linguistic capacities will require something like the anti-realist conception of truth.

Truth under atomist theories of meaning

We begin with the atomist's understanding of what it is that we master when we gain linguistic competency. The atomist approach to generating those T-sentences that are intended to represent our understanding of the meanings of sentences employs what are commonly thought of as word meanings. This raises a new worry: what constraints are there on our assignment of semantic values to individual words or terms? If the only constraints derive from which sentences are held to be true (as the holist claims), then we shall be unable to rule out an interpretation according to which T-sentence (1) has the truth-conditions we would ordinarily assign to (4). For as

---

[9] For an account of the details whereby this is accomplished see Siderits (1991: 44–50). It might be thought that this holist solution effectively smuggles word-meanings in through the back door, so that it does not actually differ from the atomist approach. The suspicion is that what we discover when we look at other sentences affirmed by competent speakers is that 'grass' refers to grass, etc. The holist will agree that what we discover when we compare how the presence and absence, from certain sentence-frames, of the sub-sentential component 'grass' affects speaker assent, could be represented as: ' "grass" refers to grass.' But, claims the holist, this fact about the semantic behavior of speakers does not show that speakers' knowledge can be represented by using this as an axiom. And to so represent their knowledge would be to falsely imply that linguistic competency is acquired by first mastering the semantic values of a stock of sub-sentential components. In this connection it is noteworthy that the method of presence and absence referred to above was designed to explain how a child first acquires linguistic competency through exposure to whole sentences. On this point see also Davidson (1985: 215–25).

Putnam (1981: 32–35, 217–18) has shown, it is possible to have (1) and (5) come out true while 'sky' is interpreted as referring to grass and 'is blue' is interpreted as satisfied by all and only green objects. The atomist needs to show how we are to rule out such deviant interpretations of reference and satisfaction for the terms of the language in question. One answer that has appealed to many realists is to fix the reference of terms through causal connection with their referents. So it might be claimed that the reference of 'sky' is fixed through a chain of causal connections stretching back to an original baptism by ostension whereby the term was first introduced into the language. On this sort of account, by 'sky' we intend to refer to whatever object was ostended at the end of this causal chain. Accounts of this basic sort have been developed for names, natural-kind terms, and indexicals. All depend on the idea that causal connections serve to fix the semantic values of certain terms by tying them to entities and properties that are mind-independently real.[10] These accounts are thus prone to one major difficulty. As we saw in Chapter 6, there are apparently insuperable barriers to construing causation in the realist way, as a relation that obtains independently of the concepts we employ.

Given these difficulties, it seems unlikely that causation can be used to support a realist atomist semantics. And this in turn makes unlikely any straightforward argument from our agreement on the T-sentences to a correspondence theory of truth. The realist hope was that sentence-meaning might be explained in terms of realistically construed reference and satisfaction conditions for sub-sentential components, so that what stands to the right of the biconditional in the T-sentences is tied to mind-independent, structured states of affairs. In that case truth might be understood as isomorphism between the left and the right sides of the biconditional, hence as correspondence between statements and mind-independent states of affairs. But this hope is dashed if the tie between a term and its referent or satisfaction conditions is itself conceptually constructed. Such a vindication of realist truth would require causation to act as a kind of glue that somehow connects statements up to the world. And this will only work if causal connections are real glue, obtaining independently of the concepts we employ. Since by the arguments rehearsed above they are not, there is no guarantee that what stand to the right of the biconditional are mind-independent, structured states of affairs.

The alternative for an atomist is a verficationist semantics. Such an approach has a long history in the empiricist tradition, where it was used early on by Berkeley in support of subjective idealism. According to verificationists of this stripe, the meanings of at least some stock of linguistic items are fixed through empirical observation. But more recently, Dummett's espousal of a verificationist semantics has been motivated primarily by considerations in the philosophy of mathematics. In that area, the relevant kind of verification is not empirical observation but proof. Moreover, while Dummett agrees that any account of sentence-meaning must conform to the composition principle, he is less wedded than traditional empiricist verificationists have been to explicitly accounting for verification conditions for

---

[10]   Fodor's (1990) version of semantic atomism introduces a number of important complications to this picture, but it still relies crucially on causal connections.

sentences in reliance on whatever fixes the meanings of words.[11] In any event, a verificationist semantics will at least be committed to the claim that the meaning of a statement just consists in the conditions that would verify it for us, or that we would count as evidence in its favor.[12] Since the conditions that count as verifying 'The sky is blue' are just those we observe when we see that the sky is blue, it follows that what we grasp when we understand this sentence is just the ability to recognize these conditions when they do obtain. Hence (4) can be excluded and (1) included in our stock of T-sentences.

Dummett's argument for verificationist semantics rests on the fact that language use is a shared social practice the acquisition and mastery of which must be such as can be publicly manifested. This means that at least for some basic stock of sentences, understanding must consist in some practical ability that the language learner can demonstrate to others. And since what one learns when one comes to understand a sentence is what that sentence means, it follows that the meanings of at least these basic sentences must consist in that practical ability. Now if, as was suggested above, we take the stock of T-sentences for a language as the starting point for constructing a semantics for that language, then it would be natural to construe the practical ability in question as that of being able to recognize truth-conditions. The meaning of a sentence would thus be those conditions which, if they obtained, we would be able to recognize as verifying it. But this imposes a significant restriction on what can go on the right side of the biconditional, at least for the basic stock of sentences – not realist truth-conditions, but verification conditions. That is, meaning is to be unpacked out not in terms of what happens to obtain independently of our recognitional capacities, but instead only in terms of what we are capable of confirming through some effective procedure (such as empirical observation or proof construction). Meaning consists not in (realist) truth-conditions, but in verification conditions.

Now one way to see the consequences this has for the theory of truth is through its application to the meaning of sentences containing the predicate 'is true'. Our mastery of the use of this predicate through our coming to understand those among the basic stock of sentences in which it is employed must also consist in acquiring the capacity to recognize humanly accessible verification conditions. Hence any account of truth that makes of it a property that might transcend our ability to verify its presence will be ruled out by these constraints on semantics. This is the source of the anti-realist's

---

[11] Dummett might thus better be thought of as a molecularist rather than an atomist: while he is committed to the necessity that an account of the meanings of complex sentences be based on the meanings of some stock of simple sentences, he does not think of the meanings of these simple sentences as straightforwardly derived from the meanings of sub-sentential components. The reasons for the latter have to do with his recognition of the constraints imposed on a theory of meaning by the context principle: only in the context of a sentence does a word have meaning. Dummett does, though, like the atomist properly so-called, adamantly reject holism. There must, on his view, be some basic stock of sentences whose meanings are independent of the meanings of other sentences, since otherwise we could not begin to acquire mastery of a language. See Dummett (1991: 221–25) and (1973: 192–96).

[12] There is obviously a difference between a semantics that requires conclusive verification conditions and one that requires merely conditions the recognition of which would count as giving defeasible support. But since this difference will have no significant bearing on the issues under consideration, I shall ignore it here.

notorious epistemologizing of truth: truth must be tailored to our ability to detect confirming evidence. But there is another way in which a verificationist approach to semantics creates difficulties for a realist account of truth.[13] On this approach there will be meaningful statements that are undecidable: there will be some circumstances under which we would recognize conditions as verifying the statement, there will be others under which we would recognize conditions as falsifying it, but there are also some circumstances such that there could be no effective means for us to either verify or falsify the statement in question. Statements about the past and subjunctive conditionals are among Dummett's stock examples, but we might also include statements containing vague predicates. Consider, for instance, the statement:

> (6) The number of grains of sand on the shore of Lake Michigan at the moment this sentence is written is even.

It seems that we understand this sentence, and yet as things stand there is no effective means for deciding its truth-value. Indeed even if we could eliminate the vagueness in the concept of a grain of sand, and in the demarcation of a lake's shore, it still seems as if we could never succeed in determining the number of grains existing just at that moment: our counting procedures would require some substantial duration, during which the number will likely have changed significantly. Yet it still seems as if we understand what the sentence means. This suggests that its meaning must consist in its (realist) truth conditions, that is, conditions that would make it either true or false independent of our ability to detect them. But for Dummett the lesson to take from this is just the opposite: the meaning of the sentence must consist in something other than truth conditions, which are, for us, ungraspable; it must consist in its verification conditions. Now at this point it is tempting to invoke something like ideal verification or an omniscient cognizer, thereby rescuing the intuition that (6) is either determinately true or false. But this gambit merely reveals how slender is the evidence on which our commitment to the principle of bivalence rests. It is we, after all, who claim to understand (6). Any meaning it has must consist in conditions we are capable of verifying. As things stand, (6) lacks a truth-value. And to imagine some nano-technology that would enable us to count grains rapidly enough is just to alter the case by introducing verification conditions.

Since the principle of bivalence is a semantic principle, it may not be clear what its rejection has to do with the theory of truth. Indeed it might be said that at most it can tell us something about the extension of the predicate 'is true', but not about what it means. Perhaps it will come as something of a surprise to discover that apparently meaningful sentences lack truth-values under some circumstances, but this may just reflect the fact that the world is a messy place.[14] But we have already seen in Chapter 4 why realists cannot consistently maintain that truth-value gaps can be traced to instances of metaphysical indeterminacy. If the truth of a statement consists in its corresponding to a mind-independent state of affairs, then it is difficult to see how it could fail to be the case that either the constituents of the relevant state of affairs are arranged as the statement asserts, or they are not so arranged. (Statements involving

---

[13]   Here I follow Engel (1991: 134).

[14]   As, for instance, Vision (1988: 180) suggests.

reference failure or false presupposition may be treated as either false or as lacking meaning.) To say that a meaningful statement lacks a truth-value under certain circumstances is to say that there is no fact of the matter in that case. But if, as the realist claims, in other cases where the statement does have a truth-value, there is a fact of the matter, how can there fail to be a fact of the matter in the case of indeterminacy? Now in our earlier discussion of this question, in connection with the problem of vague predicates, it seemed as if a realist might accommodate instances of bivalence failure. But that was because the bivalence failure in question seemed only local – confined to sentences containing vague predicates. The considerations motivating the adoption of a verificationist semantics threaten to make the phenomenon far more widespread. But equally important, the Buddhist anti-realist critique of intrinsic natures suggests that there cannot be the sorts of entities required by the notion of ultimate truth. This means that there can be no statements the assertibility conditions of which fail to depend in part on facts concerning human interests, practices and limitations. And this in turn means that bivalence failure becomes genuinely global. Under such circumstances, correspondence truth cannot be made to work.[15]

There are two important objections that may be raised against an anti-realist account of truth based on a verificationist semantics. The first has to do with the 'epistemologizing' of truth.[16] The objection is that there is an inevitable circularity involved in analyzing truth in terms of justification or warranted assertibility: to call a belief justified is shorthand for calling it justified *as held true*; to attribute warranted assertibility to a statement is to say that its assertion would be warranted *as true*. An anti-realist might claim that by 'justification' is meant just conformity to the standards of justification accepted by some community of epistemic agents. But this not only raises the specter of relativism, it also unduly 'flattens' the notion of justification, draining it of its normative force. What, after all, is the point of seeking beliefs that conform to the accepted standards of justification? Some anti-realists (such as Peirce and, at one time, Putnam) have sought to avoid this problem by speaking instead of 'ideal justification'. This might be unpacked in terms of the idea of what inquirers would agree on at the end of inquiry, or in terms of what would be justified under ideal epistemic conditions. But once again there is the difficulty of determining what would constitute *ideal* epistemic conditions, if these were not understood as just those most conducive to discovering the truth. Likewise how is 'the end' of inquiry to be understood? As that at which all inquiry is aiming? The circularity involved here is patent. The alternative, historical understanding of 'end' – as that time when epistemic agents cease changing their beliefs – has equally obvious difficulties.

---

[15] According to Young (1995: 26–31), a verificationist semantics can have no substantive metaphysical consequences: anti-realism about truth and meaning is consistent with the existence of the kinds of mind-independent states of affairs that realism sees as the truth-makers; it merely denies that such things could play that role. It is not, however, entirely clear what it would mean to assert that such things do or might exist, if verificationist semantics is correct. In any event, Buddhist anti-realist arguments against intrinsic natures are meant to show that realist metaphysics are incoherent without relying on verificationist assumptions.

[16] This line of attack is common to many critics of anti-realism, but see Kirkham (1992: 49–54) for a particularly cogent formulation.

Imagine that a thousand years ago a virus rendered the human brain incapable of acquiring beliefs not accepted prior to that date, thereby plunging humanity into an everlasting epistemic Ice Age. Of course 'ideal justification' could be understood in terms of what an omniscient cognizer would possess. But this is just a way of reinstating the notion of a God's-eye view, a notion that (Putnam has often reminded us) seems just a way of trying to make realist truth appear intelligible in light of the verificationist critique. And (as shall be discussed in more detail below) it can also be questioned whether the notion of an omniscient cognizer is fully intelligible.

The second objection is to, not the anti-realist account of truth, but the verificationist semantics that is here being used to support it. Following Vision (1988: 160–61), we may put the objection in terms of a distinction between enabling and inhibiting explanations. As applied to the acquisition of the concept of truth, an inhibiting explanation 'confines truth's legitimate application to the circumstances under which it is presumed it must have been learned'. By contrast, an enabling explanation 'regards those circumstances as showing how we are *enabled* to frame our realist concept'. The realist alleges that the latter is the better account of our acquisition of the concept, since it better accords with our general ability to project concepts into novel situations in ways not at all presaged in the learning situation.

Now a Buddhist anti-realist might reply to this second objection by applying the general Buddhist stricture against hypostatization (see Chapter 2) to this realist claim that we somehow extrapolate from the content of the specific learning contexts to arrive at a verification-transcendent concept of truth. Specifically the reply would be that we are no more entitled to the use of such a concept than we are to the belief that there is some one woman more beautiful than all others. To learn to use the word 'beautiful' is among other things to learn to make comparative judgments, but this does not justify the transcendental deduction of Miss Universe. Likewise in learning to use the predicate 'true' we learn that verification conditions may be defeasible, hence that some warrants may trump others. It is readily understandable that we might then arrive at an absolute conception of truth-conditions as somehow transcending our cognitive access. But while we can understand how this might happen, the deployment of such a conception is not thereby legitimated.

At this point the dispute over the two competing styles of explanation appears to be at something of a standoff. While the anti-realist can show that the realist's expansive approach to human capacities can lead to error when applied in other areas, the realist may claim that optimism about our abilities is still warranted in this case. But the realist will then interject that the anti-realist predilection for inhibiting explanations has revisionary consequences – it requires us to revise our ordinary conception of truth, which is just the realist conception.[17] Now this is one place where the soteriological project of the Buddhist makes a difference. Buddhists claim that existential suffering comes about in part because we conceptualize the world in ways that significantly distort its nature. Consequently a Buddhist is unlikely to be impressed by the charge that some view they put forth has revisionary consequences.

---

[17]   See Kirkham (1992: 265) for a similar charge against those anti-realists who seek to defend the epistemologizing of truth on the grounds that such a conception would be an improvement over our present realist conception.

Indeed we should expect any Buddhist philosophical analysis of persons and their place in the world to have at least some revisionary consequences. Since the aim of such analysis is the extirpation of suffering, it should seek to bring out those ways in which we would be well advised to alter our understanding of our situation by employing more adequate concepts. And a Buddhist anti-realist would claim that the realist conception of truth is precisely one of those concepts that are implicated in existential suffering. So the charge of revisionism does not succeed in shifting the burden of proof onto the anti-realist.

To be effective, the Buddhist anti-realist response to the second objection would need to be supplemented by an account of how realism is implicated in existential suffering. That topic will be taken up in the next chapter. But assuming that something can be said along those lines, the response seems to me to be persuasive. The fact that some piece of philosophical analysis would, if correct, require revisions in our ordinary ways of talking and thinking is no objection to that analysis, if it can be shown that the revisions in question would lead to an improvement in our lot. Moreover, the hypostatization response goes some way toward explaining how we come by those intuitions that seem to give support to truth-conditional semantics (and thus to the realist conception of truth).

We can also imagine the anti-realist giving a similar line of response to the first objection. The strategy would be to agree that we have the intuition that epistemic warrants are subject to an independent norm, and that this norm might best be construed as realist truth, but then to claim that the intuition derives from an illegitimate move from the comparative ('better warranted') to the superlative ('ideally warranted', that is, verification-transcendently true). Here, however, I think the strategy would be less successful. Assuming that the Buddhist anti-realist espouses universal fallibilism, their strategy requires us to believe that there can always be a 'better' while there is no 'best'.[i] We can, I think, imagine how this might be. But even so, we might still wonder if inquiry is not better conducted under the regulation of an ideal norm – whether realist truth is not, that is, grounded in a kind of practical necessity. Now this consideration clearly cannot be decisive, for it leaves open the possibility that the anti-realist might explain the source of this practical necessity in terms of facts about our epistemic capacities, thus ushering in a higher-order anti-realism about truth. But it does suggest that the anti-realist will need to formulate a more persuasive response to the first objection. We shall need to return to this question in any event, for the first objection (unlike the second) applies equally to semantic atomist and semantic holist defenses of anti-realism. Any semantics that results in an 'epistemologized' account of truth will have to face up to the question of truth's normative nature. This problem aside, the anti-realist has made a strong case against the realist conception of truth, based on the assumption of semantic atomism. If an equally strong case can be made based on the assumption of semantic holism, then the anti-realist can avoid having to settle the issue between these two approaches to semantics for natural language.

Truth under holist theories of meaning

According to semantic holism, a theory of meaning for a natural language can only be constructed out of the totality of patterns of assent and dissent of speakers of the language: to understand the meaning of a given sentence we must look at how competent speakers use other sentences. As was noted above, according to the semantic holist we derive the T-sentence,

(5) 'Grass is green' is true iff grass is green

by noting how speakers behave with respect to utterances of not only 'Grass is green' but a multitude of other sentences. The sort of theory of meaning that results will be decidedly modest by comparison to the full-blooded theory of understanding that the atomist aims at.[18] Where the atomist seeks to explain the meaning of a statement in terms of what it is that a speaker understands when they grasp it, the holist thinks we can only aspire to a more modest account that tells us how to interpret the utterances of a language. A theory of interpretation is modest by comparison with a theory of understanding in that the former aims only at establishing correlations between the linguistic understanding of the users of the language under study and that of the interpreters; the latter aims at giving an account of what the understanding of the users consists in. Holists give a variety of arguments in support of their position that a modest theory of meaning is the best that we can hope for. But since we are not concerned to settle the issue between holists and atomists, we can leave these aside.

It might be thought that a modest semantics must be hostile to the realist conception of truth. If the most that a theory of meaning can give us is a theory of interpretation, then it would seem unable to deliver on the project of explaining truth in terms of a relation between sentences and mind-independent states of affairs. It might, that is, seem as if for the holist truth must be something wholly immanent, having nothing to do with the sort of confrontation with reality that correspondence requires. Now this suspicion will, I think, turn out to be justified. Still, the pronouncements of some holists suggest that their view yields, if not exactly correspondence, then at least a conception of truth sufficiently robust to satisfy most realist appetites. Quine, that most celebrated of holists, famously speaks of our utterances as responses to 'the impact of light rays and molecules upon our sensory surfaces' (1978: 68). This has been taken by many to suggest that what stands to the right of the biconditional in the T-sentences is truth-conditions that can be understood in scientific realist terms. And Davidson claims that on his approach 'we can be realists in all departments. We can accept objective truth conditions as the key to meaning, a realist view of truth, and we can insist that knowledge is of an objective world independent of our thought or language' (1986: 307). Quine and Davidson represent the two possible forms a holist approach to semantics and truth might take. Quine might be seen as following Tarski in seeking to construct a 'scientifically respectable' account of language and thought, one that eschews suspect semantic notions and is compatible with a purely physicalist ontology. Davidson takes a more

---

[18]   See Dummett (1975) for the distinction between a 'modest' and a 'full-blooded' theory of meaning.

liberal approach, accepting truth as a primitive in order to construct a theory of meaning for natural languages. Our task shall be to determine if either approach can give aid and comfort to the realist.

Given Quine's famously skeptical attitude toward meanings, it is hardly surprising that he should adopt an equally dismissive stance toward truth. His view is best described as deflationary, seeing the truth-predicate as no more than a disquotational device that allows us to perform 'semantic ascent'. I earlier suggested that deflationism might be seen as a closeted anti-realism. But that a deflationist Quine should advance the project of 'naturalizing' epistemology suggests just the opposite: a naturalized epistemology looks like the completion of the Buddhist Reductionist project using the resources of current science, and the Buddhist Reductionist project is clearly realist in its semantic and metaphysical commitments. That project was to show how everything about us – including the fact that it seems to us as if we are enduring subjects – could be explained in purely impersonal terms. A naturalized epistemology would enable us to explain, in wholly physicalist terms, how the impinging of molecules and light rays on surface receptors gives rise to the 'torrent of output' that makes up our verbal and epistemic behavior. Since the physicalist vocabulary of such an account is ostensibly free of any intentional terms, the account may be advertised as wholly impersonal. Success would thus mean that the appearance of subjectivity could be accounted for in wholly impersonal terms. The realist would take this as vindication of their view that the success we achieve when we accept certain statements and act on the resulting beliefs is to be explained through the relation they bear to mind-independent reality. While this relation might not be classic correspondence, it is robust enough to suggest that it is structured relationships between words and things in the world that make our statements true – which is enough for the realist to feel vindicated. But while Quine's pronouncements often encourage just this response, I shall argue that it is mistaken, and that the Quinean stance on semantics and epistemology has anti-realist consequences.[19]

Earlier I characterized T-sentences as including, to the right of the biconditional, a homophonic translation p of the sentence s of which, on the left side of the biconditional, truth is predicated. Why should p be considered a *translation* of s, when it looks to be just the same sentence stripped of quotation marks? Part of the answer is that s and p belong to different languages. For instance, in

(1) 'The sky is blue' is true iff the sky is blue

the statement inside quotation marks is a sentence of the object language, in this case English, while the sentence to the right of the biconditional belongs to the meta-language we shall call meta-E. If Tarski's methods are to be applied to natural languages (something Tarski himself thought could not be done), then the truth-predicate for sentences of English must be located in meta-E, so that sentence (1) is a sentence not of English but of meta-E. (Likewise if we wish to say that (1) is true, we must ascend to meta-meta-E.) This device of ascent to a meta-language insures against the introduction of inconsistency in the language by way of such semantic

---

[19] In my discussion of Quine I shall be following Putnam (1985).

paradoxes as the Liar (e.g., the sentence, 'This sentence is false'). But if *p* is a translation of *s*, how do we know that it is the correct translation? How can we be sure that 'The sky is blue' has the same meaning in meta-E as it does in English? This question might seem misplaced. That the translation is homophonic might seem to make it perfectly transparent. Moreover, Quinean doubts about the respectability of the very notion of meaning might be taken to suggest that it can safely be bypassed. Still, the question has a kind of legitimacy, and requires an answer.

We can see how this is by looking at the sort of situation where Quine thinks the notion of meaning does have work to do – the situation of radical translation. This is the situation in which the field linguist seeks to work out a translation manual for some native language without the help of intermediaries, such as informants fluent in both the native language and the linguist's home language. Suppose (to take Quine's famous example) the native informant utters *Gavagai* whenever a rabbit is observed. Should this be translated as 'Look, a rabbit!', or as 'Rabbithood again!', or as 'Lo, undetached rabbit-parts!'? What, that is, does the native refer to in making this utterance? Each of these three possible translations can be incorporated into a translation scheme that adequately accounts for all the speech-dispositions of the native speaker. Thus there is, Quine holds, no reason (at least no scientifically respectable reason) to prefer one over the others; they should be seen as mere notational variants. For the job of the field linguist is just to construct a theory that explains and predicts the speech-dispositions of the native speaker. (For Quine, 'meaning' can be nothing more than something that is contextually defined in the process of building such a theory.) The question, What is the native speaker referring to? thus turns out to be empty. Of course we may say that the native speaker is referring to what it is that we would refer to when we uttered, 'Look, a rabbit.' But to say this is not to say that the speaker refers to an enduring substance, the rabbit, as opposed to, say, an instance of rabbithood, or to a collection of parts related in the 'rabbit' way. It is only to say that the utterer of *Gavagai* performs the same sort of linguistic task that we perform when we utter, 'Look, a rabbit.' To say that the native utterance involves reference to a rabbit is not to remark on a relation between the utterance and the extra-linguistic world; it is just to remark on a relation between the native's speech-disposition and our own. Questions of reference make sense, Quine says, only relative to a background language.

What goes for reference goes for sentence meaning and truth as well. Suppose the field linguist's best hypothesis is that the native utterance *Gavak khole* should be translated as 'The rabbit is in the cage.' We might inscribe this hypothesis as,

(7) *Gavak khole* is true-in-L iff the rabbit is in the cage

(where 'true-in-L' is the truth-predicate for the native language L undergoing radical translation). It would be a mistake to think of (7) as giving the meaning of the native sentence. The sentences of a language can be said to have meaning only relative to some background language. And a proposed translation manual merely gives one preferred way, from among a large number of equally adequate ways, of correlating the speech-dispositions of speakers of the two languages. For the same reason, it would be a mistake to think of (7) as giving realist truth-conditions for the native sentence. The question of truth likewise arises only relative to some background language, whereas realist truth-conditions are supposed to be language-independent states of affairs in the world. It is a mistake to think there is some fact of the matter that through its obtaining makes the utterance of the native sentence true. Truth is always immanent. The ascription of truth-conditions to the sentences of the native language is just an economical way of stating the translation manual – which, it must be recalled, is itself nothing more than a theory whose job it is to help us explain and predict noises produced by the natives.

When we think of translation this way – as theory construction designed to aid in the prediction of behavior – then reference goes inscrutable and truth turns immanent. There is no answer to the question what the native refers to with the utterance *Gavagai*, nor to the question what fact would make utterances of *Gavak khole* true. These questions make sense only relative to some background language. But what about the linguist's home language? What about

(8) 'The rabbit is in the cage' is true iff the rabbit is in the cage

It may seem as if here we finally step off Neurath's boat onto solid ground. But this is an illusion, fostered by the fact that (8) seems to be a sentence of English, when it is actually a sentence of meta-E. It is possible to take the same stance with respect to (8) that we can take toward (7): viewing this as a proposal concerning how to correlate the noise-productions of different speakers. Of course this is not our normal stance toward (8). Normally we 'take our language at face value', we 'acquiesce in' the language. To do this is in effect to accept sentences like (8) and other instances of the T-schema as involving homophonic translation. But there is, for Quine, no fact of the matter as to whether this translation scheme is correct. To say that (8) is true would just be to ascend to meta-meta-E, where the question would arise whether sentences of meta-E (such as (8)) allow of homophonic translation. We 'acquiesce', in effect treating object language and meta-language as the same language, because accepting some translation scheme or other allows us to stay afloat and do the sorts of things that speech production and processing make possible. There is no fact of the matter that vindicates our choice. When we step back from our ordinary attitude of linguistic engagement, reference goes just as inscrutable for the home language as for the native's.

So far, it seems as if Quine's version of semantic holism leads to a kind of linguistic idealism according to which 'the world' is nothing but talk all the way down. This would make exceedingly mysterious the degree to which Quine has been taken (whether correctly or incorrectly is not our concern) as championing realism. But those who see Quine this way would point to something we have not yet brought into the picture – his project of naturalizing epistemology – as evidence of his realist commitments. The competency of a language speaker may be thought of as a single, highly complex disposition. One goal of a naturalized epistemology would be to give a physicalistic characterization of this disposition. Once this was done, it would then be possible to explain how, under certain specified circumstances, certain impingings of light rays and molecules on surface receptors give rise to productions of 'The rabbit is in the cage.' Some care is required in interpreting this result. This would not establish that those light rays and molecules, or the causes of those light rays and molecules, are what these words refer to. Once again, the question what these words refer to can only arise relative to some background language. Still, such an explanation would ratify the central realist intuition that it is extra-linguistic states of affairs that ultimately account for the success we meet with when we come to acquire the disposition to assent to 'The rabbit is in the cage' under the condition of such impingings. This is not correspondence truth. But on the realist reading of Quine, it is just his semantic holism that rules out correspondence truth. Once reference goes inscrutable, there cannot be the kinds of structural isomorphisms between statements and facts that correspondence requires. The basic motivation is the same, however: that of trying to explain the utility of our statement-making practices through appeal to how things are in extra-linguistic reality.[j]

There is, however, one fatal flaw in this position: the word–world tie goes by way of a disposition, something that is intentional twice over. To attribute to me the disposition to utter *Gavagai* under certain stimulus conditions is to say that in all relevantly similar possible worlds, whenever those conditions obtain, I produce that utterance. When we discussed this way of understanding capacities (in Chapter 6), we waived the question whether sense could be made by the realist of the notion of a proposition. But for a would-be Quinean realist there is a clear answer to that question: No. For Quine, propositions are just as suspect as meanings (to which they are, after all, intimately related). And it is not clear what sense can be made of the notion of a possible world if these are not to be elucidated in terms of sets of propositions. The attribution of a speech-disposition also employs the notion of a cause. And we have already seen why this notion cannot be put to the kinds of uses that the realist has in mind here. The causal relation is conceptually constructed, and so cannot serve as the metaphysical glue that the realist requires in order to tie our words to a mind-independent world. This way of trying to forge a link between a mind-independent world and our linguistic and epistemic practices cannot succeed.

If the Quinean project shows anything, it is that any account of the success of our epistemic and linguistic practices can only be immanent. The attraction of the correspondence theory for the realist lay in its promise to explain this success by way of the concept of truth. A semantic holist form of deflationism, in ruling this out, also undermines the possibility of accomplishing the same goal by way of a naturalized epistemology. Consider the image of Neurath's boat, in which there are the planks that make up the hull – which we shift about and repair from time to time – and there is also the sea. Now we may say that it is the interaction of the planks and the sea that keeps us afloat. We may even say that different arrangements of the planks enhance the interaction and thus help us better achieve our ends. What is misleading about this image is that it tempts us to suppose there could be the equivalent of a science of hydrology, something that tells us about the nature of the sea quite independent of our ceaseless sailing, and thus explains the success of our marine ventures in terms of purely hydrological facts. The counsel of naturalized epistemology – that we should use the methods of science to reflect upon and improve our epistemic and linguistic practices – may well be wise. But we should not expect that following this counsel will lead us to some ultimate account of why it enhances our overall success. We already know why it might be wise to embark upon a project of naturalized epistemology: it is better to believe that the sky is blue, since the sky is blue; and the scientific investigation of our visual processes helps us understand how some may instead come to believe that the sky is green. But the ultimate account that the realist hankers after cannot be had. There can only be local explanations: we should believe this and say that because these are what the facts are in this case. When deflationists insist that truth is not a substantive property, they mean in part that it cannot do the sort of explanatory work the realist wants it to do. If we wish to know why it is valuable to believe only true statements, we must ask about them one by one – and then the answers we get will seem quite trivial: it is better to believe that the sky is blue because the sky is blue. Of course we may, if we wish, go on to seek an explanation for the sky's being blue. But as we saw in the preceding chapter, nothing – including the methods of the sciences – is intrinsically a means of knowledge. So any answer we receive on this score will turn out to be contextually determined and interest-sensitive, local and piecemeal, in short, not the sort of thing that will satisfy the realist's cravings. We saw above why a realist who is a semantic atomist cannot look to the sciences for vindication of the realist project. A similar difficulty faces the realist who embraces semantic holism.

Davidson's version of semantic holism is less austere than Quine's, less concerned to eliminate all semantic notions on grounds of doubts about their 'scientific respectability'. For instance, where Quine speaks of radical translation, Davidson speaks of radical interpretation: the task for the field linguist is to work out both what the native's utterances mean and what beliefs to attribute to the native who assents to those utterances. His approach thus appears more amenable to giving a substantive account of truth, and so might seem like more promising terrain for the realist. Indeed Davidson claims that while Tarski's Convention T gives a material adequacy condition for any account of truth, 'there is more to truth than Convention T: there is whatever carries over from language to language' (1986: 309). What carries over turns out to be correspondence – though not, he hastens to add, the traditional view of correspondence. That view required isomorphism between statement and fact, something exceedingly difficult to make sense of in all but the simplest cases. It was also wedded to an epistemology that saw confrontation between belief and the facts as the test of truth, and the idea of such a confrontation we can now see is absurd. Since only a belief can justify another belief, we must instead see coherence as the test of truth. Such an approach will yield 'correspondence without confrontation' (1986: 307). And correspondence will run not through the simple picture of structural isomorphism, but through (a modified form of) Tarski's notion of satisfaction: a sentence is true iff it is satisfied by every function.[20] Davidson grants that this does not look much like the traditional notion of correspondence to the facts, but it does, he claims, make truth depend on a relation between language and the world – and in a way that avoids all the difficulties of the traditional notion (1985: 47–49). To the realist's ears this will sound far more promising than Quine's wholly immanent, language-relative, disquotational truth.

---

[20]   It is in the details of this conception of satisfaction that the consequences of Davidson's commitment to semantic holism become evident. He, like Quine and unlike Dummett, privileges the context principle over the composition principle. See Davidson (1985: 215–25), and Wallace (1979). But Davidson traces out the implications of the context principle further than Quine when he uses it to undermine the distinction between observation sentences and other sorts of sentences (1986: 313–14, 316).

The route to this rehabilitated correspondence account of truth is by way of a coherence theory of knowledge and truth. How this is supposed to work may perhaps best be seen by considering the situation of the field linguist attempting radical interpretation. The native assertion *Gavagai* is an observation-sentence: it is something that native speakers assent to only under certain observation conditions; under different conditions they dissent from the sentence. The first task of the radical interpreter is to work out what is the cause of assent to this observation sentence, and others like it. The difficulty is that this cause has two distinct components, neither of which the interpreter knows: the meaning of the utterance, and certain of the native speaker's beliefs, namely beliefs concerning those conditions that obtain in the world at the time of assent (as well as other beliefs concerning relations between this sentence and other sentences held true by the speaker). So characterized, the task of the radical interpreter sounds hopeless. The trick is turned, however, through a liberal application of the principle of charity: the best policy of the interpreter is to attribute to the native speaker beliefs that are, by the interpreter's lights, mostly true, and translate native utterances accordingly. Given the intimate connections between the meanings of sentences of the language and the beliefs of its speakers, an interpretation scheme for the language must end up attributing beliefs to its speakers, given their patterns of assent to observation sentences. A scheme that would make the majority of the speaker's beliefs come out false in the interpreter's eyes can be known to be incorrect. Of course there will be matters about which speaker and interpreter disagree. And these disagreements need not be confined to matters like the cause of disease, or the elements of an ideal diet; there may be disagreements about observation conditions, such as the presence of rabbits in the neighborhood on a particular occasion. What the interpreter may not do is interpret the native's words in such a way as to make disagreement the rule rather than the exception.

Why must the interpreter accept the principle of charity as a constraint on radical interpretation? Because the intimately connected activities of language use and belief formation are key components of rational agency. We form beliefs about the world and communicate our beliefs and intentions as part of a rational strategy to improve our chances of obtaining our ends. If I interpret your utterances in a way that makes most of your beliefs false by my lights, I thereby deny your capacity for rational agency. And if you lack that capacity, then the noises you produce should not be construed as meaningful utterances. To interpret is to take it on trust that we are dealing with a rational agent. Potential interlocutors necessarily share a wide area of agreement in beliefs.

It follows that most beliefs in a coherent total set of beliefs held by an agent are true. This follows because any such set will be systematically tied to the meanings of the sentences of the language the agent uses to formulate them, and the interpretation of that language must proceed by way of the assumption that most of these beliefs are true. This is how coherence is said to yield correspondence. When a belief coheres with a coherent total set, we are justified in believing that it is true, that is, that it corresponds with how things are. And this 'how things are' is to be understood in terms of 'an objective world independent of our thought and language', 'an objective world not of our making' (Davidson 1986: 310). But this last claim will be contested by those who wonder how coherence could ever yield anything but immanent truth.

There are two distinct ways in which this objection might be put. Someone who is an anti-realist on grounds of 'conceptual relativity'[21] might claim that since there is a variety of distinct, mutually incompatible conceptual schemes each of which serves adequately to organize experience, coherence cannot yield scheme-transcendent truth; coherence can at best yield truth internal to a conceptual scheme. This opponent agrees with Davidson that correspondence by confrontation is absurd, however, and that a belief can be justified only by another belief. So the lesson to be drawn, it will be claimed, is that the only conception of truth for which we can have any use is an immanent or 'internal' conception, and that talk of truth as correspondence to how things are in 'an objective world independent of our thought and language' is just so much empty, table-pounding, realist rhetoric. Davidson responds to this version of the objection by calling into question the intelligibility of the notion of alternative conceptual schemes. To attribute to language users a conceptual scheme truly at variance with our own would be to attribute to them hugely many false beliefs, thereby undermining the assumption that their behavior is meaningful. But if we cannot make sense of the idea of alternative conceptual schemes, then the very idea of a conceptual scheme turns out to be empty. We must reject the scheme–content dichotomy enshrined in the image of Neurath's boat. And when this goes, so also goes the notion of immanent or internal truth. Truth is primitive and perfectly transparent; truths are about just what they claim to be about – how things are in the world (1985: 198).

The second attack on Davidson's claim that coherence yields correspondence comes from a realist, someone who thinks the notion of verification-transcendent truth makes perfectly good sense. This objection is a variant on the common charge against coherence theories that a coherent set of propositions can still be false. Why couldn't it be, asks this opponent, that speaker and interpreter understand one another through shared but false beliefs? Granted what they share is true by the lights of the interpreter, but this does not rule out the possibility that both are deluded. It might be said that this possibility is ruled out by the fact that both achieve some degree of practical success using their system of shared beliefs. But success is here measured in terms of that very system, so belief in success might itself be among their false beliefs.

Davidson replies that shared delusion can, and sometimes does, happen. But, he says:

> [I]t cannot be the rule. For imagine for a moment an interpreter who is omniscient about the world, and about what does and would cause a speaker to assent to any sentence in his (potentially unlimited) repertoire. The omniscient interpreter, using the same method as the fallible interpreter, finds the fallible speaker largely consistent and correct. By his own standards, of course, but since these are objectively correct, the fallible speaker is seen to be largely correct and consistent by objective standards. We may also, if we want, let the omniscient interpreter

---

[21] This is Alston's term for a view he attributes to Putnam. See Alston (1996: 163–68). The attribution may be questioned, since it appears to depend on the view that sense may be made of the notion of a world that transcends all modes of conceptualization, a view at odds with Putnam's many strictures against the *Ding an sich.*

turn his attention to the fallible interpreter of the fallible speaker. It turns out that
the fallible interpreter can be wrong about some things, but not in general; and so
he cannot share universal error with the agent he is interpreting. [1986: 317]

This is an interesting response, and it would, I think, be effective if we were to grant
that the idea of an omniscient interpreter makes sense. But the idea does not make
sense to a Buddhist anti-realist. An anti-realist of any persuasion would challenge
the notion of an omniscient cognizer on the grounds that it is just a reinscription of
the notion of a God's-eye view that is central to realism. Davidson might respond by
claiming to have shown, by the considerations discussed in the preceding paragraph
but one, that anti-realism is incoherent. But a Buddhist anti-realist would pose a more
pointed challenge to the idea of an omniscient interpreter. Given what was said in
Chapter 7, it is not clear that coherent sense can be given to the notion of omniscience.
For this notion requires that there be such a thing as the totality of knowledge; an
omniscient interpreter is one who knows everything that could bear on interpretation,
that is, all possible knowledge. If knowledge is not a natural kind, if nothing bears the
intrinsic nature of a means of knowledge, then it is far from obvious what could be
meant by 'all possible knowledge'. If something is a piece of knowledge only if it is
the product of a means of knowledge, and something is a means of knowledge only
in a particular context, then it seems there can be no context-invariant sense of
'knowledge' that would allow formation of a totality across all possible epistemic
contexts. Certainly we know how someone could be well positioned to endorse
the results of a proposed radical interpretation: by being genuinely bilingual. The
bilingual interpreter will hold that the radical interpreter's beliefs are, for the most
part, true, so that the radical interpreter cannot share systematic error with the native
speakers being interpreted. But 'true' here is by the lights of the bilingual interpreter.
What the argument needs is truth by the lights of an omnilingual interpreter. And
what could omnilinguality consist in? What could it mean to speak of all possible
languages? This idea could be given determinate sense only if we could isolate
some intrinsic nature that all languages necessarily share. The prospects here seem
decidedly dim.

I conclude that Davidson's reply to this objection does not work. Another possible
strategy would be one that mirrored his reply to the anti-realist objection. It might be
claimed that if the scheme–content distinction goes by the boards, then with it will
go not only the notion that truth might be wholly immanent or internal, but also the
idea of transcendent truth used by the realist and the skeptic. While this might be
true, Davidson's reason for dismissing the scheme–content distinction relied on his
coherentism, which is precisely what is under assault by the opponent. But there is
another reason to reject the idea of a radically non-epistemic truth. As I indicated in
the last chapter, when we give up on the notion that knowledge is a natural kind, we
are no longer able to make clear sense of the claim that truth may transcend all
possible means of knowledge. Since nothing bears the essential nature of a means of
knowledge, it is not at all clear what it would mean to say that how things are might
outrun all possible inquiry, since this notion of 'all possible inquiry' is radically
underdetermined. Adopting this strategy would, however, mean conceding that talk of
truth as correspondence to how things are in 'an objective world independent of our
thought and language' is indeed empty rhetoric. If, as Davidson maintains, truth is

perfectly captured in the T-schema, then there is a sense in which a true statement may be said to correspond to how things are. But this 'corresponding to how things are' is just the feature that the anti-realist unpacks as warranted assertibility, and the deflationist as disquotation. The business about 'an objective world independent of our thought and language' seems like just so much idle machinery. Perhaps the only notion of 'world' that is available in this context is precisely one that relies on the suspect scheme–content distinction.[22] In that case, Davidson should agree that such a world is 'well lost'.

Davidson will respond that while the notion of 'the world' at work in skeptical arguments is problematic, there is still work for it to do once we replace the old 'building-block' notion of correspondence by confrontation with the Tarskian notion of truth through satisfaction. The skeptic typically relies on a picture of language according to which individual words are tied to particular things in the world through the reference relation, and a sentence is true when the things referred to by its component words stand to one another as the words say they do. But to take the context principle seriously is to see that this approach is hopeless. Take a reference scheme for a language, a scheme that assigns referents to all names in the language: 'Jones' refers to Jones, 'snow' refers to snow, etc. For any such scheme, there are many permutations of that scheme that yield all the same truth-values for the statements of the language. The skeptic relies on this image of language failing to mesh properly with the structure of the world. A semantic holist like Davidson will respond that what matters is just that our language as a whole turns with the world. That all the different permutations of reference scheme yield the same predictions concerning patterns of assent and dissent on the part of speakers should be no more surprising than that weight can be measured in pounds or grams, or temperature by the Fahrenheit or Celsius scales.[23] What matters is the pattern: how linguistic behavior with respect to a word varies with changes in linguistic context and extra-linguistic conditions. It is this pattern that an account of truth in terms of Tarskian satisfaction records. And it is this pattern that we exploit in arriving at knowledge about the world from the utterances of others. While individual pieces of language do not confront individual facts, the language as a whole does confront the world as a whole. Thus there is, Davidson will claim, an important sense in which a true sentence does say how things are in 'an objective world independent of our thought and language'.

While this is an interesting response, in the end it strikes me as no more satisfactory than the Quinean realist's resort to naturalized epistemology. It too in effect relies on viewing linguistic competency as a single complex disposition yielding behavior as output in response to input consisting in (Quine's version) 'light rays and molecules impinging on surface receptors', or (Davidson's version) 'an objective world independent of our thought and language'. Davidson's avoidance of the scientistic language of 'light rays and molecules' might seem like an advance. Still, the refusal to say what kinds of things the 'objective world' consists in only heightens the suspicion

---

[22]   This is Rorty's understanding of Davidson, first articulated in his 'The World Well Lost' (1972) and stated more carefully in his 'Pragmatism, Davidson, and Truth' (1986).

[23]   See Wallace (1977: 315), Davidson (1985: 224–25).

that this is, after all, the noumenal realm of the *Ding an sich*, something that was supposedly banished with the rejection of the scheme–content dichotomy. The true difficulty, though, is the one that undermined the Quinean realist version: it relies on the idea of a causal connection between 'the world' and language behavior. Since causation is conceptually constructed, such a connection cannot be used to establish a world that is 'independent of our thought and language'. A Davidsonian version of semantic holism is thus unable to give succor to the realist.

Buddhist anti-realism as semantic non-dualism

At this point it would be useful to take stock of what has been accomplished so far. I claimed at the outset that a *prima facie* case could be made for attributing an anti-realist view of truth – the view that truth is just warranted assertibility – to those Buddhists ('Buddhist anti-realists') who espouse the anti-essentialist position described in the preceding two chapters. But I also stated that such a view of truth would turn out not to be the final position of the Buddhist anti-realist. We then turned to a brief survey of the available approaches to natural language semantics. There I argued that each of the plausible candidate theories gives some support to the anti-realist view of truth (or to its close cousin the disquotational view). But there still remains the important objection that the anti-realist's 'epistemologizing' of truth is incompatible with truth's normative role. It is also worth noting that at certain key points the argument for such a view of truth made crucial use of considerations drawn from the anti-essentialist arsenal of Buddhist anti-realism (e.g., the claim that causation is conceptually constructed, and the claim that nothing bears the intrinsic nature of a means of knowledge). So the argument that was presented for anti-realist truth is to that extent a Buddhist anti-realist argument. And it should be pointed out that the key contribution here is precisely anti-essentialism. Unlike more recent forms of anti-realism, the Buddhist formulation does not rely for its support on verificationism or any form of semantic or epistemological internalism. It may well be that no variety of anti-realism can avoid 'epistemologizing' truth in the end. I would contend, however, that for the Buddhist variety this emerges as a mere byproduct of global anti-essentialism; it is not central to the view, as it must be to any formulation grounded in verificationism.

According to the Buddhist anti-realist, there can be no such thing as the ultimate truth: such truth would require a domain of entities with intrinsic natures, and nothing can bear an intrinsic nature. It follows that the only way in which a statement can be said to be true is conventionally – by having the sort of truth that consists in conformity with the conventionally determined dictates of common sense. According to realists such as Buddhist Reductionists, truth of this sort is 'merely conventional', it 'obscures' the nature of the world, because it is tailored to fit our cognitive abilities as well as our needs and interests. It might be thought at this point that the Buddhist Reductionist is too quick to derogate what they call the conventional truth. Suppose we agree with the Buddhist anti-realist that what the Buddhist Reductionist considers ultimate truth is not to be had. Why might not their 'merely conventional' truth still be considered fully realist? Granted, the use of convenient designators – terms for which there are no mind-independent entities to serve as referents – means that the truth of a conventionally true statement cannot consist in any simple isomorphism between sentence and state of affairs. Still, the realist might claim, there is an important sense in which such statements represent how the world is independently of the conventions we happen to employ: it is, after all, something other than those conventions that accounts for our ability to use them with fruitful results. Otherwise there could be no explaining the fact that the world does reward us with success when we properly employ concepts that we know may not carve up nature at its joints. While the scheme that we employ may not accurately represent all the structural features of the world, still we must suppose statements we make employing it to represent a world that is not of our making.[k]

We might expect an anti-realist to respond to this realist objection by questioning the scheme–content distinction that it presupposes: can genuine sense be made of this notion of a world that is independent of the concepts we happen to employ, if it is in principle impossible to distinguish between those features that we contribute and those that reflect the way that the world is anyway? But this response relies on contentious internalist views, and the Buddhist anti-realist would prefer to avoid any such entanglements. As we saw earlier, the Buddhist anti-realist would instead reply by invoking the point that causation is conceptually constructed. The realist reading of conventional truth relies on a picture according to which the world causes scheme-encoded cognitive states that in turn issue in successful behavior. The problem with this scheme–content distinction is not that because scheme and content are inextricably intertwined we cannot verify any claims concerning a mind-independent world as content-provider. The problem is just that any world that is said to cause our cognitive states must already be a conceptually constructed world. To identify 'the world' as cause of anything is already to locate it squarely within the domain of the intentional. The Buddhist anti-realist can agree with Putnam's verificationist anti-realist slogan, 'The mind and the world together make up the mind and the world' (1981: xi). But it is not verificationism that motivates the Buddhist anti-realist to deny we can make clear sense of the two as distinct notions.

While the Buddhist anti-realist may avoid commitment to verificationism, they are still open to the charge of having 'flattened' truth, that is, of having overlooked its normative dimension. If the only truth is conventional truth, then truth must be thoroughly conventional – a product of tacit agreements designed to further our interests and reflect our cognitive limitations. Now we have already seen how the Buddhist anti-realist will challenge the claim that there could be verification-transcendent truths: by questioning whether coherent sense can be made of the notion that there are determinate boundaries to what might count as a means of knowledge, and hence of the notion of verification-transcendence. Still, the anti-realist will have to concede that inquiry is better served by the realist conception of truth. It is not, after all, only individual epistemic agents who are sometimes in want of correction. The epistemic conventions of a community – that make up that community's common sense – can usually benefit from some alteration. To espouse a view according to which what counts as true is wholly immanent is to undermine any motivation for calling community standards into question. And we are better off today – epistemically as well as medically – because the old consensus on diagnosing disease (by trying to visualize the demon responsible) was successfully challenged. If we agree that there may always be room for improvement on our current ways of conceptualizing the world, then it seems we would do well to conceive of truth as resting on something beyond the reach of the practices of finite cognitive agents.[24]

The anti-realist can acknowledge the force of the considerations behind this objection without conceding that they comprise a case for realist truth. The argument is, it will be pointed out, purely pragmatic: we would do well to act as if truth were verification-transcendent. This the anti-realist will hardly take to be a vindication of such a conception of truth, given all the difficulties the anti-realist sees in that conception. Instead it will be seen as just a useful bit of advice for the practicing anti-realist. But it is not entirely clear what it would mean for the anti-realist to act on this advice. Would it consist in part in a readiness to assert the claim that truth is verification-transcendent? Since for the anti-realist there is no gap between warranted assertibility and truth, this puts the anti-realist in the odd position of holding as true the realist conception. And how, the realist will wonder, could one act as if truth were transcendent while explicitly holding it to be entirely immanent? Now there is a way the anti-realist can answer this question – by invoking the notion of ironic engagement that was introduced earlier. The anti-realist can claim that we are capable of taking up the common-sense realist stance toward truth while at the same time embracing the anti-realist critique of realism. The engaged ironist, it will be recalled, engages in the practices dictated by the role of a concept while simultaneously recognizing that the concept has merely pragmatic grounding. Still, the considerations we have been rehearsing bring out an inherent instability in the anti-realist conception of truth.

These reservations are reinforced by considerations drawn from the doctrine of emptiness. Our truth-bearers, statements, arise in dependence on causes and conditions.[25] It follows that they are conceptually constructed and hence devoid of intrinsic nature. If all statements are empty,[1] then there can be no intrinsic nature common to those statements the assertion of which would be warranted.[26] Ultimately there can be no such property as warranted assertibility. So the anti-realist account of truth cannot be ultimately true. If that account is true at all, it must be conventionally true, that is, true only within a determinate context and given certain institutions and practices. There can be no substantive theory of truth for the anti-realist. Of course this rules out any realist theory of truth, but this will be small consolation to the anti-realist, who now feels pressed from the deflationist side. Such pressure is heightened by the consideration that the expression 'conventional truth' derives its meaning in part through implicit contrast with the term 'ultimate truth'. If, as the Buddhist anti-realist claims to have shown, there can be no such thing as the ultimate truth, then it is at least somewhat misleading to put this as the claim that there is only conventional truth. If there can be no truth other than that which arises through accredited practices of inquiry, it seems wrong to suggest that such truth is a mere

---

[24]   See Price (forthcoming) for a similar defense of truth as a constraint on speakers separate from those of sincerity and subjective assertibility.

[25]   This would not be true of propositions as classically understood, since these are timelessly existent entities that cannot be said to arise. Here, then, is one place where our choice of truth-bearer makes a significant difference. The Buddhist choice of episodic events such as statements over eternal entities like propositions is based on their claim that an eternal entity would be incapable of causal efficacy.

[26]   Putnam (1994) gives a somewhat similar argument against a verificationist account of truth; see especially Lecture 3.

approximation arrived at through accommodation to our cognitive limitations – which is just what is suggested by the appellation 'conventional'. Instead it seems we should take truth to be the perfectly transparent property that everyone else takes it for: a statement is true when things are as it says they are.[m] This, of course, is the common-sense realism toward truth that is captured in the T-sentences, and that deflationists take themselves as championing. To say of a statement that it is true is just to pay it the compliment of concurring in its assertion. This stance may be summed up in the slogan, 'No Truth, but truths'. In the Buddhist context this might best be called semantic non-dualism: no ultimate truth, no conventional truth, just truths, that is, statements that tell it like it is. Perhaps it is semantic non-dualism and not anti-realism that is the proper conclusion to draw from the doctrine of emptiness.

There is, however, one major difficulty that the Buddhist anti-realist will see in adopting semantic non-dualism as their final view of truth. This view might be thought of as a kind of principled endorsement of common-sense realism with respect to truth. And the latter stance is properly thought of as a 'realism' because, while it does not espouse a correspondence account (not itself being a developed theory of truth), it does serve as an open invitation to just such an account. To adopt semantic non-dualism is thus to risk lapsing back into a stance that is allegedly implicated in hypostatization, clinging and suffering; it is to risk losing all the insights gained through, first Buddhist Reductionism, and then the doctrine of emptiness. The resolution of this difficulty should by now be clear: adopt a multi-layered, progressive approach that culminates in an ironically engaged semantic non-dualism. There is thus a hierarchy of accounts of truth, starting with (1) common-sense realism, which is superseded by (2) the correspondence theory of Buddhist Reductionism; the doctrine of emptiness then undermines this and other forms of realism, replacing it with (3) the anti-realist view, which in turn gets supplanted by (4) semantic non-dualism. And stage (4) differs from stage (1) by virtue of its being adopted in full cognizance of the progression through intervening stages (2) and (3), each of which is recognized as superior to its predecessor in the sequence. The semantic non-dualist thus recognizes that there are epistemic contexts in which each of these stances toward truth would be appropriate – but also that no stance, including that of semantic non-dualism, can be viewed as the final word on Truth (there being no such thing).

We have already discussed at some length the progressions from (1) to (2) and from (2) to (3). Both are motivated by a combination of soteriological and strictly philosophical considerations. (The soteriological concerns involved in the adoption of (3) will be more fully discussed in the next chapter.) But more needs to be said about how we are to arrive at (4). I earlier characterized the upshot of the doctrine of emptiness in terms of the slogan, 'The ultimate truth is that there is no ultimate truth.' The seeming paradoxicality enshrined in this utterance is brought out quite clearly when the anti-realist account of truth is applied to itself. If truth just consists in warranted assertibility, then ordinarily, in normal contexts, truth should be quite transparent. For normally the truth-conditions and the verification conditions for a sentence will not differ. In such contexts the truth of a sentence will amount to the same thing on either a realist or an anti-realist account: things being as the statement says they are. Application of the anti-realist account brings out truth's immanence only in contexts where truth-conditions and verification conditions appear to diverge, namely where the truth of the statement would seem to transcend our ability to verify it even in principle. And the same considerations that led us to embrace a contextualist epistemology also lead us to deny that clear sense can be made of the idea that a statement could be in principle unverifiable. As a result, there being no such extraordinary contexts, all epistemic contexts are in some sense 'normal', and anti-realism about truth has the consequence that truth is always quite transparent. This means that the anti-realist account of truth should be quite thoroughly self-effacing: if truth is transparent, then such statements such as 'Truth is just warranted assertibility' will turn out to lack warrant. To call truth transparent is to recommend that we leave off all efforts at characterizing it beyond what is captured in the T-sentences. Certainly this minimalist stance toward truth is incompatible with such anti-realist claims as that truth-conditions are always conceptually constructed. Perhaps there is no explicit contradiction that results when a theory is as strongly self-effacing as this. Still, there appears to be a pragmatic inconsistency here: we are to hold as true a theory that by its own lights we should not hold as true. And given that for the anti-realist truth just consists in our having good reason to concur, the distance between pragmatic inconsistency and contradiction seems vanishingly small.

This difficulty is resolved by taking on the stance of semantic non-dualism. The resolution is not effected by giving up the anti-realist insight that truth-conditions are conceptually constructed. Rather, the resolution comes through taking up a contextualist approach to truth. Semantic non-dualism is not a substantive theory of truth. It is a stance that one adopts upon having come to fully appreciate the difficulties inherent in any substantive theory of truth. This stance involves adopting the appropriate approach to truth in different contexts: in ordinary lifeworld contexts, the common-sense realist approach; in contexts where one aims at extirpating the gross suffering of clinging to persons, the Buddhist Reductionist approach of correspondence realism; in contexts where one aims at extirpating the subtle suffering of clinging to mind-independently real entities, the anti-realist approach. Since semantic non-dualism has nothing substantive to say about truth, there is no question of what happens when it is applied to itself. Not being a theory, it is not a strongly self-effacing theory.[n] The worst that can be said about it is that it might turn out to be bad advice.

The superseding of (3) by (4) is also motivated by the considerations behind the normativity objection. The doctrine of emptiness entails that there are no mind-independent truth-makers, hence that truth cannot be said to outrun possible justification. Yet further reflection upon the doctrine of emptiness shows that it is equally problematic to see truth as wholly immanent: to say this is to presuppose that determinate sense can be given to the notion of a limit to possible justification. At the same time it is clear that some epistemic conventions are better than others, hence that there is utility in seeing truth as transcendent. It is far from clear how to do justice to these three points within an anti-realist framework. This difficulty is avoided on the contextualist approach of semantic non-dualism. Under a contextualist epistemology, those propositions that define an epistemic context remain fixed and beyond question as long as the project of inquiry that they frame persists. This has the result of making truth appear transparent within any context of inquiry: because such propositions are beyond questioning in the epistemic context they frame, they come to constitute a 'world' that is independent of our epistemic behavior within that context; the aim of inquiry is then seen as that of arriving at beliefs that accord with how that world is.

Anti-realism has the effect of disrupting the appearance that the 'world' found within any given context of inquiry transcends all possible inquiry, thereby inducing its 'flattening' effect on truth. Semantic non-dualism serves as a reminder that there is no meta-context from the standpoint of which anti-realism could serve as the final truth, hence that the 'world' that is given within an epistemic context does after all transcend the limits of our knowledge. Of course the proviso must be added: 'the limits of our knowledge *within the context of that epistemic project*'. But since according to the contextualist there is no meta-context, no project of pure inquiry, and so no blanket generalizing over epistemic contexts, this proviso is quite innocuous. Then the fact that what is given and fixed in one context may be questioned in another does not undermine the role played by the 'world' of the first. For the ironically engaged inquirer, inquiry aspires to something that transcends its limits – even though all the while those limits and what lies beyond them are conceptually constructed in the process of inquiry. While all things are empty, truth is transparent – rivers are rivers and mountains are mountains.°

Semantic non-dualism and truth

The Buddhist anti-realist will thus espouse a semantic non-dualist account of truth's nature. There still remain important questions concerning how truth will behave on this account. I claimed earlier that on the semantic dualism of Buddhist Reductionism, ultimate truth behaves classically and bivalently, while a degree-theoretic or infinite-valued account should be used at the level of conventional truth. Since semantic non-dualism would seem to call for a unified treatment of truth, will it be one of these approaches, or some third approach, that is said to describe truth's logical properties? I think that a degree-theoretic account would best suit the overall aims of the Buddhist anti-realist. But before discussing this, something must be said about the Buddhist anti-realist stance toward the ultimate truth. The proof that all things are empty depends on demonstrating global bivalence failure at the ultimate level. It is by showing that any given proposition can be neither ultimately true nor ultimately false (nor, for that matter, ultimately both true and false, nor ultimately lacking in truth-value) that the Buddhist anti-realist aims to demonstrate the ultimate incoherence of the notion of ultimate truth. (This, it must be remembered, occurs in the anti-realist moment of the progression toward semantic non-dualism.) This strategy requires that truth be assumed to be bivalent. For the strategy is that of the classic *reductio*, of deriving a contradiction from the opponent's assumption, thereby demonstrating the falsity of that assumption.^{p} And the demonstration (by way of *modus tollens*) could not proceed were ultimate truth not assumed to be bivalent. On a degree-theoretic account of truth, if p has a truth-value less than 1 but greater than 0, then while p & $\sim p$ can never be true, it may also have a truth-value greater than 0 and so not be ('completely') false either. The falsity of the opponent's assumption can only be demonstrated if the derived contradiction is false, which requires bivalence. This is, of course, what the realist opponent holds, but it cannot be the view of the Buddhist anti-realist, since the Buddhist anti-realist denies there can be such a thing as the ultimate truth. The Buddhist anti-realist can at most be seen as holding that if there were such a thing as the ultimate truth, it would conform to the principle of bivalence. This would presumably be because of the sorts of considerations discussed in Chapter 4.

When it comes to the question whether truth behaves classically or multivalently, the Buddhist anti-realist does not have the luxury that the Buddhist Reductionist had, of inscribing different schemes at different levels; for the semantic non-dualist there is just truth. But there is a complication introduced by the contextualism of Buddhist anti-realism. Might it be that on their view there is no single unified treatment of truth to be had, that in some contexts truth is bivalent, in others it allows of gaps, in yet others there are three or even infinitely many truth-values? While there does not appear to be anything formally inconsistent about such a proposal, it seems to be somewhat at odds with the spirit of semantic non-dualism. Part of the appeal of this position was that it promised to give us a straightforward and relatively unified account of truth. If the scheme of truth-values differs across contexts, then so must our logic: the principle of excluded middle, for instance, requires the assumption that there are only two truth-values; a multi-valued logic can have at best a heavily modified form of the principle. And if logic varies across contexts, it seems that little if anything could meaningfully be said about two or more distinct contexts. Now the initial attraction of contextualism lay in its promise to block the generalizations across epistemic contexts that fuel radical skepticism. But this blockage cannot be total, lest the position become unstatable. While the contextualist can always invoke some new context as the location within which comparison of two or more distinct contexts occurs, the possibility that none share a common logic would seem to put severe constraints on what can be said across contexts. It would be better if there were a kind of logical *lingua franca*, a default logic that was available for use in those contexts that are meta-contextual.

The appropriate choice here would, I think, be the degree-theoretic account. This is best suited to the task of logical *lingua franca* because it is possible to see other truth-value schemes as idealizations of the infinite-valued approach. When, on the other hand, a logic of lower tonicity is taken as the standard choice, the infinite-valued approach looks like a degeneration. And where the alternatives seem degenerate, the customarily favored approach comes to seem intrinsically correct, whereas this need not be the case where the alternatives are seen as idealizations. But another reason to favor the degree-theoretic approach is that it comes closer to the common-sense realist view of truth that semantic non-dualism seeks to privilege. People do, after all, ordinarily say that a certain statement is not completely true, and that one statement is more true than another. While such locutions can always be translated into a bivalent format, something does get lost in the translation.

If the Buddhist anti-realist embraces a degree-theoretic approach to truth as their preferred stance for those contexts that function as meta-contexts, this will yield an interesting result concerning the logical consequence relation: it too will become something that is graded or allows of degrees. So, using the real numbers from 0 to 1 to represent degrees, a given statement may be said to follow from some other statements to degree 1, or to degree 0.8937, or only to degree 0.563, or to an otherwise unspecified 'very high' degree that is not yet the highest possible degree of 1. The classical consequence relation is, of course, an all-or-nothing affair. On that understanding of the relationship, to say that r is a consequence of p and q is to say that the argument

p
q
$\therefore r$

is deductively valid. And this in turn is taken to consist in the inconsistency of the conjunction of p and q with the negation of r, that is, the absence of any model in which p & q comes out true while r comes out false. But if falsity comes in degrees (if, that is, a sentence can have a truth-value greater than 0 and less than 1), then there are varying strengths of inconsistency, and so of the consequence relation as well. So instead of only looking at those models in which p & q has truth-value 1, we should look at those models in which this conjunction has a truth-value of relatively high degree; and the inconsistency of this conjunction with the negation of the conclusion will then consist in there being no model in which the truth-value of r is significantly lower than that of the lesser of the values of p and q. The conclusion of a deductively valid argument will then be said to follow from the premises to degree 1, while it is possible for the conclusion of an argument that is not deductively valid to be said to follow from the premises to a degree less than 1 and greater than 0.[27] (Where the consequence relation holds to degree 0, the negation of the conclusion follows from the premises to degree 1; in this case the conclusion quite unequivocally does not follow.)

If the consequence relation is graded, this may alter the way we see the alleged distinction between 'deductive' and 'inductive' arguments. Now Machina (1985) has, I think, shown that this distinction cannot be drawn on purely formal logical grounds. We can, of course, legitimately speak of certain sorts of generalizing epistemic procedures as inductive, and perhaps we could speak of arguments modeled on those procedures as 'inductive' in some derivative sense. But this seems to make the status of the argument hostage to the epistemic processes that led to its formulation. Consider the case of an argument that is not deductively valid: how are we to decide whether it is a (failed) deductive argument or a (possibly successful) inductive one? We might appeal to the intentions of the person who gave the argument. But these cannot always be trusted: the person may not understand the distinction, or they might be confused about it, thinking for instance that all and only arguments that 'go from the particular to the general' are inductive. We might instead look at the context in which the argument was given, and see if it is the sort of context in which a deductively valid argument would be called for. But in that case what we would be calling 'deductive' is not the argument itself, but the total context. And we would be once again appealing (this time implicitly) to the speaker's intentions – in this case those of the ideally rational speaker.

Now if we embrace a graded consequence relation, this might seem to yield a formal way of distinguishing between at least those arguments that are deductively valid and those arguments that are inductively strong but not deductively valid. And this might give at least some support to the claim that arguments are either deductive or inductive. The deductively valid arguments would then be those where the

---

[27] For more on the graded consequence relation see: Chakraborty (1988), Chatterjee (1994), as well as Chakraborty and Basu (1997).

consequence relation has degree 1, while the inductively strong would be those in which the consequence relation is less than degree 1 but greater than, say, 0.5. Indeed the possibility of this sort of graded consequence relation seems to hold out the hope of a unified logical treatment of all good arguments. But further investigation dashes these hopes, so that in the end we must continue to speak simply of those arguments that are deductively valid, and of those that are not. For there is just one logical relation involved in any good inference, the truth-preserving relation, and this is monotonic. It is the fact that in studying inferences we introduce epistemic factors that leads to there being the possibility of lesser degrees of inferential support for the conclusion.

We can see why this is so by considering what a graded consequence metric actually measures. Where the consequence relation holds to degree 1, there is no possible world in which the premisses are all true but the conclusion is false. Where it holds to degree 0, in every possible world in which the premisses are all true, the conclusion is false. Where it holds to degree 0.7, there are more relevant possible worlds in which the premisses are true and the conclusion is true, than there are relevant possible worlds in which the premisses are true and the conclusion is false. And which are the possible worlds that make up the first set? These, I suggest, are just those worlds in which there are laws of nature that justify the projection from the evidence presented in the premisses to the conclusion. In other words, an inference that is tight but does not follow a deductively valid pattern is one the pattern of which would be deductively valid if its premisses were supplemented by those assumptions about the laws of nature that would make the presented evidence cogent. And the strength of the inference reflects what proportion of the relevant possible worlds are ones in which those laws hold. The test of a logically good argument remains deductive validity. The tightness of an inference varies in inverse proportion with the restrictions that must be added to the premiss set to make its pattern a deductively valid argument. And how restrictive these are is a measure of how well we have performed our epistemic duty: how many of the relevant possible worlds that would invalidate the argument we have managed to rule out.

Now, that there is such a model of a graded consequence relation of degree less than 1 and greater than 0 may make it seem as if we are talking about what is after all a matter of logic – and thus that there is after all a deductive/inductive distinction to be drawn within logic. But this model depends on confining our attention to the relevant possible worlds, and we need to consider just what this 'relevance' consists in. Consider these two arguments:

(A) Every one of the thousands of crows I've seen has been black.
Every crow that has been reported on by reliable ornithologists has been black.
Every case that was thought to be an instance of a non-black crow has turned out to be an albino starling.
Therefore the next crow that comes along will be black.

(B) All ravens are black.
Poe is a raven.
Therefore Poe is black.

If in evaluating argument (A) we were to look at all possible worlds, there would be vastly more worlds in which it was false that the next crow to come along is black, than worlds in which it is true. We do not begin to get subsets with anything remotely like the right proportions for the model until we have restricted our attention to just those accessible possible worlds that reflect the epistemic situation of the audience, given the speech pragmatics of the statements making up the premises. For (A) these will be possible worlds in which there hold such nomological generalizations as that crows are birds, that a bird's color is not changed by observation, that ornithologists are not as a rule color-blind, and countless other considerations standing behind the projection rule that we here entertain. Our intuition that (A) is a tight inference is modeled by there being a higher proportion of these relevant worlds with a black next-sighted crow than without such a crow.[28] But here, in picking out the relevant worlds from all possible worlds, we are bringing in facts about ourselves and the epistemic and pragmatic constraints that affect our situation. And these are not matters of logic. Our ability to construct a model would tell us that the graded consequence relation is a logical relation only if the construction proceeded on the basis of consideration of facts of form alone; this is what it means to say that logic is a formal science. And this the construction manifestly does not do. There is no way to represent the logical form of the premises of (A) that will tell us which are the 'relevant' possible worlds. This is quite different from the situation with respect to (B), where we know perfectly well how to represent the logical form on which its deductive validity rests. So accepting a degree-theoretic account of truth, and with it a graded consequence relation, gives no support to the problematic claim that there are both deductive and inductive arguments.

It might be wondered whether as radical a break with classical logic as a graded consequence relation is called for once a degree-theoretic account of truth has been embraced. For, it might be said, the same results can be obtained using the classical consequence relation and an infinite-valued truth predicate. Consider the case where r is said to follow from p and q to a degree that is high but less than 1. This non-classical relation might be given the meta-level description: the truth-value of r in all relevant models is somewhat lower than the lesser of the values of p and q. And at this meta-level, it may be claimed, there is no need to invoke a non-classical consequence relation, so its introduction at any level is purely otiose.

Two things may be said in response. First, an infinite-valued consequence relation is not superfluous. Its existence is vouched for by such ordinary locutions as 'more

---

[28]   Of course even with such restrictions, the set **R** of relevant possible worlds in question will have infinitely many members. Likewise the set **S** that is the subset of **R** in which it is also a law of nature that all crows are black will be infinite in number. And so will the set **T** that is the subset of **R** in which it is not a law of nature that crows are black. So it may seem unclear in what sense **S** could be said to be larger than **T**. But there is a way to give meaning to the claim that one infinite set is larger than another: when the elements of the first are put in a one-to-one pairing with the elements of the second, there are elements of the first that are left over. Brendan Gillon (in conversation) has expressed reservations that even if this is allowed, it would make sense to speak of there being a mathematically expressible proportion between these sets, so that (b) might constitute, say, 73.92% of (a). But if this does not make sense, then it is no longer clear what a graded consequence relation might represent, and this approach to preserving a deductive/inductive distinction will likewise fail.

strictly follows from'. It makes possible a unified treatment of all argumentation. And once it is conceded that inconsistency comes in degrees, it must also be allowed that the consequence relation does as well. Second, the availability of a meta-level description that does without the degree-theoretic relation does not prove as much as might be thought. In particular it does not show that the classical account always trumps the non-classical.[29] There are contexts in which it will be useful to provide a classical semantics for such a decidedly deviant notion as a degree-theoretic 'follows from'. But it is equally possible to portray the classical consequence relation as no more than an idealization of the infinite-valued version, and there are contexts in which this would prove useful. Since there is no ultimately privileged context, this proves nothing about which form the consequence relation 'really' takes.[30]

This completes our survey of the semantic consequences of the doctrine of emptiness. The chief consequence is anti-realism about truth, the view that truth is just warranted assertibility. In its Buddhist anti-realist form this is mitigated somewhat by two factors. First, it is not built on the contentious base of verificationism. Second, it is supplanted in lifeworld contexts by a deflationist semantic non-dualism akin to the common-sense realist stance that takes truth as transparent. Of course ironic engagement guarantees that even when truth is so considered, there are resources with which to resist the slide into essentialism that threatens when we take the truth of what are currently our best theories to be the simple matter of their stating how things are. The ontological commitments that come with accepting the germ theory of disease lead to our taking 'bacteria' as a natural-kind term, hence to supposing there to be an essence that sets bacteria apart from other entities. Because of the anti-realist moment in the path that led to semantic non-dualism, the Buddhist anti-realist will understand this implicit essentialism to be the thoroughly contextualized product of certain human institutions and practices.[q] A second semantic consequence of emptiness is, I claim, the adoption of a degree-theoretic approach both to truth-values, and to truth's transmission via the consequence relation. While this was never explicitly affirmed by any Buddhist anti-realists, it accords well with their semantic non-dualism, as well as with their desire to avoid practices that invite hypostatization.[31]

There still remains an important question concerning the Buddhist anti-realist account of truth. In answering the question how so counter-intuitive an account could be credible, the Buddhist anti-realist claimed that suffering is fueled by essentialism not just about persons but about entities of all descriptions. It is not clear how that might be. Nor is it clear how this thoroughgoing anti-essentialism might affect the ethics of compassion that was discussed in connection with Buddhist Reductionism. This question takes on special importance now that semantic non-dualism has reintroduced a kind of essentialism (albeit a highly mitigated kind). If there is just

---

[29] 'Classical' with respect to the consequence relation. Since we are here presupposing a degree-theoretic account of truth, the logical connectives will not behave classically even where the consequence relation does.

[30] The points in this paragraph developed out of an extremely fruitful conversation with Amita Chatterjee, M.K. Chakraborty, S. Basu and T.K. Sarkar.

[31] The degree-theoretic approach to truth may be read in a way that sees the values of 0 and 1 as mere idealizations. Such an interpretation goes some way toward helping us see how, when it comes to theories, there might be 'better' without 'best'.

truth, then it seems we might say that persons do after all exist; indeed we might even say that persons have selves. What sort of Buddhist anti-realist ethics could this lead to? These are the sorts of questions that we shall take up in the next chapter.

Notes

[a] Or judgment. What count as truth-bearers in Buddhist semantics is a complex question. Since the distinction between conventional and ultimate truth was originally designed to aid in the interpretation of the Buddha's teachings, we may say that it is statements (that is, particular statement-making assertions) that were seen as the truth-bearers. (The facts corresponding to conventionally and ultimately true statements were then said to be conventionally and ultimately real respectively.) But this situation changes when Diṅnāga takes up the Nyāya project of determining the reliable means of knowledge. For Nyāya, the primary truth-bearer is not the statement but the judgment, a particular cognitive event that purports to represent how things are. But since for Nyāya the content of every judgment is verbally expressible, their position could equally be put as: it is statements that are true or false, while a judgment has the interesting property of veridicality just in case the statement that expresses its content were true. Diṅnāga, however, holds that there are veridical judgments that cannot be verbally expressed, namely those resulting directly from perceptual processes. Because the Yogācāra–Sautrāntika school of Buddhist epistemology follows him in this (though Dharmakīrti adds that the perceptual process must be non-defective for the judgment to be veridical), for them the class of judgments outstrips the class of statements, so that the truth of statements appears to become the derivative concept. What is clear, though, is that no one in the Indian tradition holds that propositions – understood as timelessly existing third-world entities – are what can be true or false.

[b] Most Ābhidhārmikas are implicitly committed to the existence not only of particular *dharmas* but also to the kinds to which they belong, hence to universals or at least real resemblances. But a radical nominalist such as the Yogācāra–Sautrāntika will deny that the state of affairs making the statement 'The cow is brown' true consists in anything other than the pure particular that is said to be a cow and brown. The school's semantics of *apoha* is designed to show how truth can be understood entirely in terms of reference to real particulars, and without any appeal to properties or relations. (See Appendix.) It must nonetheless be the case, on their account, that 'cow' and 'brown' are both causally connected to the same particular for the statement to be true. So the isomorphism constraint remains. Of course Yogācāra–Sautrāntika also denies that there are genuine names, and hence that a use of 'the cow' (accompanied by an act of ostension), or even 'that' or 'Bossie' names a particular. But most of their scruples about naming could be avoided with a form of causal theory of names.

[c] The tetralemma (*catuṣkoṭi*) form is a device that may be traced back in the Buddhist tradition to the Buddha's treatment of the so-called indeterminate questions (*avyākṛta*). It consists in the positing for investigation of four possible alternatives with respect to statement *s*, namely *s*, not-*s*, both *s* and not-*s*, and neither *s* nor not-*s*. Nāgārjuna sometimes uses the device in order to express his rejection of all contenders for ultimate truth on some topic, e.g., at MMK 12.9, 22.11, and arguably at MMK 1.1. More frequently, however, he will deny the first and second lemmas, assert that the third lemma cannot obtain, and say nothing concerning the fourth lemma. See, e.g., MMK 5.6, 8.7, 25.11–18. This constitutes strong evidence that the logic of his arguments is classical, that he accepts the principles of non-contradiction and excluded middle. See Ruegg (1977) for a history of the form, its role in Madhyamaka, and the variety of modern interpretations. Tillemans (1999) agrees with Ruegg that all the evidence points toward Madhyamaka adherence to classical logic: the rejection of all four lemmas is merely meant to underline the point that their shared assumption of an ultimate ontology must be rejected. Ruegg, however, adds that in some instances the fourth lemma is used apophatically as a way of gesturing toward what is best indicated by silence. While he insists that this is not tantamount to affirming an inexpressible ultimate, it is not clear what else this might be if it is not just another way of saying that the ultimate truth is that there is no ultimate truth.

[d] See *Milindapanha* 40, where 'light' is described as a convenient designator for a causal series of distinct flames. By the mereological reductionism of the Abhidharma, it follows that the light that occurs at

the end of this series can be said to be neither identical with nor distinct from the light that occurs at the beginning of the series (since any statement concerning the light will lack a truth-value at the ultimate level of truth). This is a stock instance of the bivalence failure characteristic of Buddhist Reductionism. See Chapter 4.

   e As does Nāgārjuna at MMK 5.7.

   f See Candrakīrti's comments on MMK 24.8: *sarva evāyam abhidhānābhidheyajñānajñeyādivyavahāro 'śeṣo lokasaṃvṛtisatyam ityucyate.* 'All that indeed without remainder that is the accepted practice with respect to term and referent, cognition and object of cognition, etc., that is said to be conventional truth.' Bhâvaviveka adds that conventional truth does not conflict with popular practice (*lokavyavahāra*).

   g See MMK 18.6: *ātmety api prajñapitam anātmety api deśitaṃ / buddhair nātmā na cānātmā kaś cid ity api deśitaṃ.* The second half of the line is read by some as claiming that the Buddha sometimes teaches the doctrine of neither self nor non-self. See, e.g., Garfield (1995: 49), and Ruegg (1977: 7), who follows Candrakīrti's interpretation of the verse. But *Akutobhayā* makes clear that the intent is to deny that the Buddha holds any statement about the existence or non-existence of the self to be ultimately true, hence that the Buddha's various teachings on this matter can only represent *upāya* or pedagogical skill.

   h Later Mādhyamikas such as Jñānagarbha speak of conventional truth as 'that which accords with how things appear (*yathādarśana*) to all from scholars to cowherds'. Here 'appearances' are understood as resulting from a variety of observational and inferential procedures. But there is a long history in Indian epistemology of taking efficacy as a criterion of the veridicality of cognition. Thus for both Nyāya and Yogācāra–Sautrāntika, the undistorted perceptual cognition of a novel sample of water cannot be said to be an instance of knowledge until such time as the cognition has led to confirmatory behavior such as having one's thirst satisfied. Given this, it should be possible to see pragmatic constraints as playing an important role in a Madhyamaka account of warrant.

   i This is a consequence of holding both that there is no ultimate truth, and that conventional truth must be divided into the categories of correct and mistaken conventional. On the latter distinction see verse 12 of Jñānagarbha's *Satyadvayavibhaga* in Eckel (1987: 79). Evidence that this distinction yields a hierarchy of theories each of which is better than its predecessor may be found throughout the work of Jñānaśri, but see also *Bodhicaryāvatāra* 9.4. I shall have more to say in the next chapter concerning this idea of a better with no best.

   j Tillemans (1999: 8) accuses Katsura of having wrongly attributed to Dharmakīrti a naive pragmatic theory of truth; he then goes on to argue that Dharmakīrti's theory of truth is best seen in terms of Kirkham's (1992: 119) notion of 'correspondence as correlation' (which is supposed to be a realist form of quasi-deflationism). Concerning the first claim, in fact Katsura (1984: 222) merely points out (correctly, I think) that Dharmakīrti subscribes to a pragmatic criterion of a cognition's veridicality; he nowhere claims that Dharmakīrti takes truth, or even a cognition's veridicality, to consist in its leading to practical success. Concerning the second claim matters are more complicated. While there are important similarities between Quine and the Yogācāra–Sautrāntika, Dharmakīrti is not a semantic holist. So if there are reasons for denying that he takes truth to be 'correspondence as congruence', that is, realist isomorphism, these are not the same as those applying in Quine's case. But there are no other reasons that I can see. Granted that according to Dharmakīrti when we correctly attribute a predicate to a particular, there is no corresponding property to be found inhering in the particular. Still, the point of *apoha* semantics is just to explain how the nature of the particular makes it the case that the predication can lead to successful action with respect to that particular. So while the isomorphism may lie concealed beneath the surface form of the judgment, it is nonetheless there in the case of a true judgment.

   k This is in effect the position of Yogācāra–Sautrāntika. Only perceptual cognitions may be said to be ultimately true, and this is only so because they are immediate and non-conceptual in nature. Thus the content of such a cognition cannot be expressed, and cannot itself play a role in any inferential processes. There are, then, no statements that may be said to be ultimately true. A perceptual cognition may give rise in turn to a perceptual judgment, which does involve subsumption of the particular under concepts, and is thus expressible and able to enter into inferential relations. But for precisely that reason, such judgments cannot be said to be ultimately true. Since they involve superimposing universals on the unique particulars (the *svalakṣaṇa*s), they cannot be said to be strictly isomorphous with how the reals are. Such judgments do, however, along with the inferences that spring from them, lead to successful practice. And this fact is to be explained in terms of facts about the particulars and their causal capacities. So perceptual and inferential judgments may be said to be conventionally true: while their use of concepts involves concessions to our cognitive limitations, there is still a sense in which they may be said to correctly represent 'how things are anyway'.

l See VV v.21. Of course here Nāgārjuna is not denying the existence of all statements, including his own. As he goes on to point out in v.22, his claim that all things are empty is real in the same sense as a chariot or a pot, namely, conventionally.

m That is, the 'that which accords with how things appear (*yathādarśana*) to all from scholars to cowherds' of Jñānagarbha.

n While Nāgārjuna agrees (VV v.23) that he has a statement that requires support, he also denies (VV v.29) that he has a 'thesis' (*pratijñā*). By this he means a component of a Nyāya-style inference. But insofar as this should be understood as a device that is intended to capture some aspect of reality, we may also understood 'thesis' here to mean a theory about how things ultimately are. So when he denies that he has a thesis, this may be understood as the denial that he has any theories to offer.

o Semantic non-dualism thus corresponds to the third phase described in the famous Zen saying: 'Before enlightenment, rivers were rivers and mountains were mountains; when I became enlightened, rivers were no longer rivers and mountains mountains; but after my enlightenment had deepened, rivers were once again rivers and mountains were mountains.' While the matter is hugely complex, I think it is possible to see important continuities between Madhyamaka and Ch'an or Zen.

p Tillemans (1999: 200) claims that for the Mādhyamika there is no contradiction generated by asserting, for any predicate *F*, both

(9) $\sim(\exists x)\ Fx$

and

(10) $\sim(\exists x)\ \sim Fx$.

There is no contradiction, he says, because any existentially quantified statement is false where the domain is empty, and for the Mādhyamika the domain of ultimate truth is empty. While this is quite correct, I think it is somewhat misleading to say that there is no contradiction here for the Mādhyamika. For assuming that the logic is classical, and absent a distinction between types of negation, (9) and (10) will yield respectively

(11) $(x)\ \sim Fx$

and

(12) $(x)\ Fx$.

This too need not lead to a contradiction if the domain is empty. But where the *F* in question is the existence-predicate (as at MMK 5.6–7), the very assertion that the domain is empty seems to contradict the substitution-instance of (12). And the existence-predicate will be necssary if we interpret the quantifiers as possibilist, which we shall need to do if the Mādhyamika is to make assertions about entities that they do not believe actually exist. It would be better, I think, to distinguish between what the Mādhyamika would say in the context of debate with a realist, and what Mādhyamikas might say among themselves. This I think is the best way to employ Tilleman's useful suggestion that we heed the distinction between the objectual or referential interpretation and the substitutional interpretation of the quantifiers. In the former context the logic is classical and the quantifiers are read objectually; contradictions are then generated, thus motivating us to find the hidden assumption that is responsible. In the latter context the realist assumption has been discarded, the quantifers are read substitutionally, and no statements of a form conjoining (9) and (10) can be derived.

q This is in effect the Svātantrika reply to the Prāsaṅgika charge that Svātantrikas are guilty of a covert essentialism, of reintroducing *svabhāva* at the conventional level. Both sides aim at a conventional truth-predicate that is, in accordance with ordinary usage, transparent. The Svātantrika point is that then we must also account for the conventional distinction between true and false theories, and the solution that best accords with our practice is to suppose that the terms of a true theory pick out determinate kinds.

CHAPTER NINE

Empty Persons

The Buddhist tradition is divided into two major branches, with what we have here called Buddhist Reductionism representing the first, and Buddhist anti-realism making up one major strand of the second.[a] Adherents of the second approach to Buddhist practice claim that theirs differs from the first through the positions it takes on two key points: (1) its thoroughgoing anti-essentialism, according to which not only persons but all existents are empty or devoid of intrinsic nature; and (2) its view that the ideal life is that of the *bodhisattva*, a fully enlightened being who desists from entering into final nirvana in order to help others overcome suffering. In the last three chapters we have looked at the first claim. It is now time to look at the second. What reason might there be for an enlightened person to devote the remainder of their sentient existence to the amelioration of others' suffering? And how might this compassion of the *bodhisattva* be connected to the realization that all things are empty, or devoid of intrinsic nature?

It might be wondered just how seriously we should take the ideal of the *bodhisattva*. It is quite clear, for instance, that many of the deeds ascribed to *bodhisattva*s in the literature of this branch of Buddhism are beyond the powers of ordinary humans. For example, it would be decidedly unrealistic for an individual to set about trying to construct a world being born into which would automatically insure the attainment of enlightenment. In cases where the *bodhisattva* is described in such terms, it is perhaps best to consider the account as a somewhat hyperbolical outpouring of devotionalism. Still, there are many places where the career of the *bodhisattva* is presented in a perfectly straightforward and sober fashion, as something to which we might quite sensibly aspire. And in such contexts it is also made clear that this aspiration is supremely rational; that such obstacles as make the *bodhisattva*'s path seem beyond the abilities of normal humans represent no more than ignorance on our part. Moreover, the ignorance involved here is, we are told, just what is overcome through knowledge of the emptiness of all existents. So it looks as if the connection between the positions taken on points (1) and (2) is very tight indeed.[1]

But a major question immediately presents itself. We saw in Chapter 5 that the Buddhist Reductionist account of persons has as a consequence that we are obligated

---

[1] The parallel with the case of the philosopher-king as described in *Republic* VI–VII is often pointed out. Plato appears to hold that one who has attained knowledge of the Good is compelled to, as it were, return to the cave, that is, desist from pure philosophical contemplation and put their knowledge to work in order to benefit others. But it may be questioned whether we should take the work's central political metaphor of the republic this seriously. Perhaps Plato really intends nothing more by this than that the rational part of the soul should take up the project of seeking to govern the spirited and appetitive faculties of the individual. In the case of the *bodhisattva*, on the other hand, there can be no doubt: they are to turn back from nirvana in order to help others attain it.

to strive to eliminate all suffering regardless of its location. This looks remarkably like an injunction to take up the career of a *bodhisattva*. Now the ideal of the *bodhisattva* is said to be new to the second branch of the Buddhist tradition; advocates of this approach claim that those who seek enlightenment by following the teachings of Buddhist Reductionism are less disposed to practice the great compassion of the *bodhisattva*, and more likely to pass into final nirvana (the cessation of the particular causal series constituting the enlightened person) without sharing the benefits of their enlightenment. Our earlier results make us wonder if this can be true. Buddhist anti-realists also claim that the obligation to embark on the career of the *bodhisattva* follows from the doctrine of emptiness. The fact that such an obligation seems to follow from the far more restricted anti-essentialism of Buddhist Reductionism – anti-essentialism just about persons and other wholes – makes us wonder as well about this second claim. In preceding chapters we looked at the metaphysical, epistemological and semantic consequences of Buddhist anti-realism. Does the view have any distinctive ethical consequences? If so, what might they be?

We can begin to answer these questions by considering the following Buddhist anti-realist claim: as a result of the thorough comprehension of emptiness, one overcomes the twin defects of attachment and fear, and is thereby enabled to desist from entering into final nirvana, instead abiding in the world so as to help the unenlightened overcome suffering.[b] Now the tradition has generally understood entrance into final nirvana to be the cessation of all future rebirths. So the claim being made here could be understood as the assertion that one who comprehends emptiness will undergo future rebirths (that is, abide in the world) for the sake of preventing the suffering of others. But we might interpret the reference to 'abiding in the world' less literally, taking it just to mean that one's conduct continues to be governed by the conventional semantic and epistemic practices prevailing in the world.[c] In this case the claim would be as follows. In the last chapter we discussed what was called a kind of 'acquiescence' in the conventional truth that follows from adopting semantic non-dualism: conventional truth ceases to be 'mere convention' and instead becomes transparent. The claim would be that the semantic non-dualist's acquiescence in conventional truth plays a role in facilitating the *bodhisattva*'s practice of compassion. More specifically, the claim would be that emptiness frees one from the attachment and fear that are obstacles to such acquiescence and hence to such practice. If this is an admissible interpretation, then perhaps we can begin to glimpse a path from the doctrine of emptiness to a distinctively Buddhist anti-realist view concerning the grounding of the ethics of the *bodhisattva*. But the conceptual connections involved here are as yet quite obscure, and require careful exploration.

The first point requiring elaboration involves the relation between Buddhist anti-realism and Buddhist Reductionism. The latter is, we know, explicitly realist in its metaphysical and semantic commitments. Historically, Buddhist anti-realism developed in reaction to the Reductionist reading of the Buddha's teachings. The critique of intrinsic natures was meant to undermine the notion of an ultimate ontology, and with it the idea that truth might be understood as correspondence to mind-independent reality. So if the arguments deployed in that critique are sound, then the Buddhist Reductionist account of persons seems to lack support: it cannot be the case that 'person' is a mere convenient designator for a causal series of impersonal, impermanent elements that are ultimately real, nor that pain impersonally construed is ultimately bad. This in turn suggests that the *bodhisattva*'s compassion cannot be accounted for through the argument discussed earlier – the argument that since suffering is equally bad regardless of location, the obligation to prevent pain applies transpersonally, that is, across distinct causal series. The Buddhist anti-realist would thus seem to owe us a new account of the *bodhisattva*'s compassion. The passage discussed in the last paragraph claimed that comprehending emptiness was useful for one who wishes to exercise compassion; it did not identify emptiness as what motivates compassion. If the Buddhist Reductionist's argument is to be discarded, how is compassion to be grounded?

In point of fact, the Buddhist anti-realist can appropriate the Buddhist Reductionist argument for compassion, albeit not precisely in its original form. This is possible because of their contextualism, and their notion that there is a progression of teachings concerning the person. As has already been pointed out, there are contexts in which the Buddha appears to affirm the existence of a self. All Buddhists agree that this is nothing more than an instance of the Buddha's pedagogical skill, intended only to prepare the audience for a fuller exploration of the subject. Buddhist anti-realists also agree with Buddhist Reductionists that the self cannot be ultimately real. They concur in the arguments meant to establish that a self could be neither identical with any of the psychophysical elements, nor distinct from the elements. The Buddhist anti-realist goes on to argue, however, that since the self is not ultimately real, the psychophysical elements are likewise not to be found in our ultimate ontology: the elements are identified as 'that which pertains to the self', and as such cannot be said to exist if the self does not exist.[2] Here the Buddhist anti-realist appears to be in agreement with the Non-Reductionist, who denied that the concept of impersonal pain made sense. According to the Non-Reductionist, such psychophysical elements as pains can only be understood as adjectival on persons, so that in the absence of a subject conceptually distinct from the elements there could be no such things as pains.[3]

The agreement is only apparent, however, for the Non-Reductionist holds that both the self and the psychophysical elements are ultimately real, while the Buddhist anti-realist intends to show that neither can be. Since nothing can bear an intrinsic nature, neither Reductionism nor Non-Reductionism can be ultimately true. Moreover, the Buddhist anti-realist will go on to claim that, conventionally, Reductionism represents an advance over Non-Reductionism. Given the common human aim of extirpating suffering, when we inquire into our nature we would do better to think of ourselves as conceptually constructed out of wholly impersonal psychophysical elements, than to think of ourselves as persons with enduring essences. So while there is no ultimate truth concerning persons (save that there is no ultimate truth about persons), Buddhist

---

[2] The argument here appears to depend on a problematic verificationism, in that it seems to equate the existence of the psychophysical elements with their being identified under a particular description. A better argument would seek to establish that the elements are conceptually constructed, on the grounds that they originate in dependence on causes. Since all conceptual construction involves at least implicit reference to persons as constructors, it would follow that the elements could not exist if the self does not exist. On this reading the mistake of the Buddhist Reductionist lay in their failure to see that causal relations are thoroughly intentional in nature.

[3] This view is famously championed by Strawson (1959). But see P. Williams (1998: 153–64) for a recent formulation aimed at the Reductionist account of persons.

Reductionism is still to be preferred over its rival theories. And since in this epistemic context we may be said to know that suffering is impersonally, intrinsically bad,[d] it follows that we are obligated to prevent suffering regardless of its location. The *bodhisattva* is compassionate because the *bodhisattva* has come to enlightenment through a realization of emptiness that is not wholly forgetful of the Reductionist stage on the path traveled.[e]

Buddhist anti-realism is thus not incompatible with our earlier account of why an enlightened person must recognize an obligation to help others overcome suffering. But this does not yet tell us how understanding emptiness might contribute to the practice of compassion. It is claimed that such an understanding combats the attachment and fear that would otherwise stand in the way of such practice. It seems clear what is meant by attachment here: the twin passions of desire and aversion, which fuel the happiness-seeking project and thus lead to suffering. But these are supposedly extirpated through coming to grasp the truth of Buddhist Reductionism: since there is ultimately no person to be found, and those things to which we ordinarily become attached turn out to be mere conceptual fictions, attachment no longer makes sense. Why should the further stage of understanding emptiness be thought necessary? Part of the answer, we are told, is that emptiness shows all things to be like the trunk of the banana plant or the onion: lacking in essence and so not ultimately real.[f] The suggestion is that the global anti-realism of the doctrine of emptiness is more effective than the merely local anti-realism of Buddhist Reductionism at preventing attachment. But it is not clear that the austere ultimate ontology of Buddhist Reductionism is rich with opportunities for forming attitudes of attachment to objects; so it is not clear why a more effective antidote would be needed. It would be more plausible to say that the notion of ultimate truth engenders a different and more subtle form of clinging.[g] On this reading, the insight associated with Buddhist Reductionism can itself serve as the basis for attachment – not to objects, but to the full and final truth as something that one possesses. From this perspective we can see the table-pounding gesture that typically accompanies assertions of realism as the act of self-assertion that it really is: there is a world that serves as final arbiter of all our judgments, and it bestows the prize on *my* side. To understand emptiness is then to abandon this last refuge of the desire to find some larger meaning in one's life. All meaning is necessarily local, provisional, occurring only in the context of some set of shared practices, and as such unable to confer on our lives the sort of dignity we hanker after.

But there is another, more straightforward way in which understanding emptiness disrupts attachment, and this turns out to play an important role in explaining the motivation for the *bodhisattva*'s compassion. Parfit has remarked (1984: 279) that he is able to temporarily stun his ordinary (that is, Non-Reductionist) stance toward his existence by rehearsing the arguments for Reductionism, but that that stance soon reasserts itself in everyday life. This difficulty was recognized by Buddhist Reductionists, who saw our belief in a self as deeply entrenched in a set of habits that both structure and are reinforced by ordinary lifeworld activity. Realizing that the intellectual understanding of non-self generated by mastery of the arguments in its favor was unlikely to suffice for disrupting such deep-seated patterns of behavior, they recommended in addition a set of meditational practices designed to bring home in a far more vivid way the fact that a person is a system without an enduring core.

But this approach works best if one can devote large amounts of time to the practice of meditation, and so is not well suited to persons outside a monastic setting. And the compassion of the *bodhisattva* depends on full recognition of the truth of Reductionism and its implications. Now the doctrine of emptiness – the doctrine that all things are empty of intrinsic nature – is sometimes put as the claim that everything is like a dream, or like the illusions generated by a magician who is himself a mere magical creation.[h] This analogy clearly has its limitations, in that if taken too literally it can lead to a problematic nihilism. But it also has its uses as a therapeutic device: as an intervention in affective behavior, it can serve to disrupt the formation of attachments by reminding us that the object of desire or aversion is quite literally insubstantial – that at the end of the day there is nothing of which it is composed. Now within the Buddhist tradition there is widespread recognition of a relation of mutual entailment between 'inner' and 'outer', the subjective and objective poles of experience.[i] In accordance with this, a disruption of attachment should lead to a diminished sense of self: if there are ultimately no things toward which I can reasonably feel desire or aversion, what then remains of this 'I', something that is, after all, conceptualized as the locus of attachment? So the doctrine of emptiness can serve to reinforce the truth of Reductionism, thereby facilitating the practice of compassion by reminding us that pains have no ultimate owner.

It is rather more difficult to see what is meant by the claim that fear is a potential obstacle to the practice of compassion. What sort of fear is intended here, and how might insight into emptiness help one overcome it? One clue is to be found in the fact that Buddhist anti-realism is said by its proponents to be a middle path between the extremes of realism – the belief that there are ultimately real existents – and nihilism – the view that nothing whatever exists.[j] Attachment may then be identified as the vice that arises from belief in real existence. Emptiness is an effective antidote for this vice, in that it shows the subject and object of attachment to be no more real than a dream, space, or the illusions created by a magician.[k] But this seems tantamount to nihilism, which inspires fear. If nothing whatever is ultimately real, not even those things to which one's existence is thought to be reducible, then clearly there can be nothing of any ultimate value – not even liberation from suffering. It is quite natural to respond to this loss of all potential sources of value with dread.

Fear, like attachment, can stand in the way of acting on one's obligation to help others overcome suffering. In the case of attachment the danger is that the underlying sense of self-importance will distract one from the equal disvalue of all suffering, so that one will revert to placing undue emphasis on the welfare of oneself and one's nearest and dearest. In the case of fear the danger is that one will fall into the paralysis of despondency: if there can be nothing of real value, why should one do something rather than nothing? As the advocates of emptiness never tire of telling us, if all things are empty then there is no distinction to be drawn between nirvana and the realm of suffering (both being equally empty).[l] In that case why should the *bodhisattva* strive to help others attain nirvana? Of course this attitude reveals an underlying disappointment that is inconsistent with the insight supposedly won through Reductionism. Fear and despondency make sense only on the assumption that there is an 'I' for whom entities and events might have had value.[m] But to one in the grips of a dread inspired by the abyss of nihilism, the counsel that there is after all no 'I' to feel afraid will likely prove deeply unhelpful.

While emptiness may inspire fear, it can also be its antidote. This comes about in the same way that anti-realism about truth can lead in turn to the semantic non-dualist view of truth as transparent. To say that all things are empty is not to say that all things are utterly non-existent. As we saw in Chapter 6, the doctrine of emptiness is not to be mistaken for metaphysical nihilism. It is indeed expected that we will at first take emptiness in this way. But the nihilist moment in our understanding of the consequences of emptiness is intended to serve as the basis for a *reductio* that rejects the realist assumption (shared by nihilism) of a reality that is free of conceptual construction. The middle path between realism and nihilism then turns out to be the position that all things contain elements of conceptual construction – and so are, while not real in the sense that the realist hankers after and the nihilist despairs of finding, real nonetheless. Chariots, houses, forests, trees, rivers, mountains, persons, psychophysical elements, atoms, quarks – all are real in the only way in which something could be real. Each has its own determinate nature by virtue of its functional role within some human practice. Each is of course empty – devoid of intrinsic nature, hence lacking in the reality of mind-independent reals. But since nothing could be real in that way, the appellation 'empty' attaches to everything there is. Only in contexts where the illusory ambitions of realism are still in play will 'empty' serve to mark a significant distinction. In ordinary lifeworld contexts, where it applies to everything, the term becomes semantically empty. That rivers and mountains are empty becomes the simple fact that there are rivers and mountains. That persons are empty becomes the simple fact that we are persons. With the world regained in this way, what is there to fear?

Coming to grips with Buddhist anti-realism can be usefully compared to what happens when a currency is taken off the gold standard. A paper currency that is readily convertible into gold may come to be seen as having value quite independently of its relation to something antecedently thought of as intrinsically valuable. To withdraw the backing of gold is to disrupt any attachment we may feel toward the currency by showing it to be without intrinsic value. This may in turn give rise to the fear that our currency will become just so much worthless paper. Such fears are shown to be misplaced when it turns out that the currency retains its former value after going off the gold standard. For we then learn that what gives a currency value is its role as a medium of exchange within that set of human institutions and practices known as an economy. Indeed we then come to see that gold is equally without intrinsic value, that its value has always rested on contingent facts about human interests and practices. But the insight that nothing has intrinsic value does not trigger the despair of economic nihilism. Instead we simply acquiesce in the practice of accepting the currency (and gold too, for that matter) as having economic value.

Of course there is now the danger that we will, as it were, once again become attached to the currency. When the fear that is inspired by emptiness is overcome through the ascent to semantic non-dualism, we revert to the practice of thinking of ourselves as persons, with all that it entails. One thing it entails is that we come to think of ourselves as having selves. Another is that it becomes meaningful to ask what the overall significance of our lives might be. But this need not lead to the kind of attachment that generates suffering. Here is one place where ironic engagement has an important role to play. Just as the knowledge that nothing has intrinsic economic value can keep us from again becoming obsessed with currency, so the insight that we are after all empty persons can ward off the habits that lead to existential dread. Knowing ourselves to be persons, we form the sorts of person-regarding attitudes that are required for effective care-giving. But knowing the persons we are to be empty, we know that what grounds our being persons is not some ultimate state of affairs but just the lifeworld context in which we help others overcome suffering. Existential dread cannot arise where a healthy sense of irony prevents our taking entirely seriously the existential question of life's meaning. This is another lesson to be learned from the case of the floating currency. Just as paper money derives its value from its role within a complex web of interactions, so the value that attaches to the lives we lead as persons derives from our circulation within a social economy. If the life of a person may be said to have a meaning, that meaning must be found within the sorts of lifeworld activities that constitute the context for our being persons; it must, in other words, emerge out of our interactions with others. To say this is not to say that a meaningful life must be one that is devoted to the good of the greater social whole. This is not the place to look for the source of the *bodhisattva*'s compassion.[n] It does mean, however, that the life of a person is not the sort of thing that can be said to have cosmic significance. So when we are inclined to wonder what our lives will have meant after we are gone, we will know that the question we ponder is of less than complete intelligibility.

So far we have been looking at ways in which Buddhist anti-realism might help overcome obstacles to a practice that is motivated by the Buddhist Reductionist argument for compassion. It now becomes clear that ironic engagement has a somewhat different meaning in the Buddhist anti-realist context than it did in the Buddhist Reductionist. The difference can be put in this way: as truth becomes more transparent, the concept of a person becomes more opaque. That is, for the Buddhist anti-realist who has fully embraced semantic non-dualism, the truth that we are persons becomes a simple and more substantive truth. Reductionist irony was focused directly on the concept of a person: ironic engagement was there a matter of simultaneously employing the concept and seeing through it to its pragmatic grounding in the impersonal ultimate truth. Anti-realist irony is aimed more broadly at our realist tendencies in general, at our predilection for supposing that an ultimate ontology is required to explain the success of our semantic and epistemic practices. And since for the global anti-realist there is nothing else that an ontology could be than the set of commitments expressed in our going theories, our acquiescence in the practice of being persons will result in a stance that is in many ways indistinguishable from the pre-reflective stance of ordinary life. Ironic engagement is here a matter of seeing through the ontological commitments implicit in all our semantic practices, not just those implicit in our use of the first-person pronoun. And in ordinary lifeworld contexts it becomes a matter just of using our full set of concepts without reifying them. So long as we do nothing that threatens to reawaken our realist tendencies, we can engage in the practice of being persons quite undisturbed. Where Buddhist Reductionism had us take a stance toward the person that is the equivalent of the representationalist's toward physical objects, the semantic non-dualism of Buddhist anti-realism gives us something more like direct realism.[4]

---

[4] So the ethical stance of the Buddhist anti-realist follows a trajectory similar to that of Putnam's

This has consequences for the *bodhisattva*'s exercise of compassion. One Buddhist anti-realist text describes an elaborate procedure for learning to exchange self and other, that is, seeing oneself from the first-person perspective of those unenlightened and suffering individuals one wishes to help. Here the aspiring *bodhisattva* is instructed to enter into the envy and hurt pride of the other 'with an intellect free of false construction'.° This is interesting for several reasons. First, it constitutes an implicit admission that those who seek enlightenment might be insensitive to the ways in which their advanced spiritual accomplishments, if perceptible to others, might cause jealousy and other unhelpful responses. Second, it blames our normal inability to see such responses on the same kind of cognitive error ('false construction') as what is said to lie behind our basic realist tendency to posit intrinsic natures. The suggestion is thus that one must become a truly empty person in order to effectively practice compassion. The insight afforded by Buddhist Reductionism may yield the requisite motivation for compassion. But the practice of compassion also requires certain skills that may not be available to one who has not realized the emptiness of all things. Being an empty person involves a certain sort of studied naivety: because no practice has ultimate grounding, one just is a person. It is this stance which makes it possible to enter fully into the perspective of the unenlightened other and thus see how one's conduct must be changed if one is to be truly helpful. As long as I continue to believe that something stands behind the appearance of my own subjectivity, I remain unable to discard it and enter fully into the subjectivity of another. As long as I see the first-person perspective as an illusion generated by something deeper, I cannot at once reflect that there is really no 'I' and also take up the first-person stance of the other. Only by abandoning the idea of something standing behind the illusory appearance, only by embracing the thought that absolutely everything might be illusion, only by accepting empty persons as persons, can I practice the 'supreme mystery' of exchanging identity of self and other.ᵖ

The metaphor of the floating currency can be extended in a way that sheds light on another part of the Buddhist anti-realist position. A stance against hypostatization is a theme that runs throughout the Buddhist philosophical tradition from its outset in the discourses of the Buddha. In Buddhist anti-realism this stance manifests itself in the view that while some theories may be said to be better than others, there is no best. We can begin to see how this might be by considering what happens when a protected economy begins to open up to external trade.⁵ Typically in a protected economy the currency is not backed by a precious metal such as gold; instead the currency's value is established by fixing the prices of a variety of staple commodities such as rice or bread, and other necessities like housing and transportation. Now when such an economy begins to increase its economic interactions with its neighbors, the currency may be subject to pressures – either inflationary or deflationary – that undermine the structure of fixed prices. And in some cases this may represent an improvement. It might be, for instance, that the population would be better off if the economy were to

---

'internal realism': from an explicit anti-realism to a quasi-deflationist form of naive semantic realism. For this final phase in the development of internal realism see Putnam (1994).

⁵ Nothing in what follows is meant to suggest that market mechanisms are superior to other ways of establishing price structures, or that trade liberalization inevitably brings about greater overall welfare.

shift away from rice production by importing rice from more efficient producers and employing the agricultural work force in industrial production. So price changes that resulted in less overall purchasing power for local rice farmers might lead to a genuine enhancement of overall welfare. In that case it could be said that the new offering price for rice is better than the old price, in that it is better suited to the satisfaction of human interests than was the old. But to say this is not to say that it somehow comes closer to reflecting the intrinsic value of rice. There is no such thing as the intrinsic value of rice, and so no price that would be the best price, in this or in any other economic circumstance.

This is so for the following reason. To say one price is better than another is just to say that with the prices of all other goods and services held relatively stable, the one price yields behavior bringing about greater overall welfare than the other. Other prices must be held constant in the comparison because changes in the prices of other commodities can affect the amount of satisfaction produced by rice, for instance by bringing about changes in eating habits and food preferences. So it is only within a given economic context – with the prices of other commodities, as well as consumption preferences, held fixed – that it makes sense to say that one price is better than another. And to say that a certain price is the ideal price is simply to assume that the prices of all other goods and services in that economic context are themselves ideal. Of course it could be argued that we should be comparing not individual prices for a particular commodity, but total patterns of pricing for all goods and services, and the preference-satisfaction values that they yield. Perhaps it would then turn out that there is one overall price structure that yields greater overall welfare than any other. In that case, it might be claimed, the price assigned to rice in that structure would be its ideal price. But this assumes that satisfaction values are commensurable across economic contexts – that, say, the satisfaction yielded for some group of people by eating rice and toast in one economic scenario could be said to be greater than the satisfaction they derived from millet and chapati in some other economic scenario. The problem with this assumption is not that it is unclear how it might be verified.[6] The problem, according to the Buddhist anti-realist, is that it requires that there be an intrinsic nature of satisfaction – that there be something that a given feeling of pleasure is like independent of all contextual factors. As we have seen, there is ample reason to reject the assumption that anything could bear an intrinsic nature. It is an illusion that there could be a total price structure that is ideal. There can thus be no such thing as the ideal price of rice, yet we can still say that one price is better than another.

Understanding how there can be a better with no best is important because it illustrates an anti-realist path around normative relativism. It is widely believed that a global anti-realist must be committed to relativism about evaluative claims. The thought is that if nothing bears an intrinsic nature, then nothing can be intrinsically good or evil, beautiful or ugly, etc.; hence that judgments on such matters are legitimate only within some determinate context in which appropriate normative standards are taken as antecedently fixed. And from this normative contextualism a

---

[6] It is indeed difficult to see how such a claim might possibly be verified. But we are operating on the assumption that Buddhist anti-realism does not rely on any form of the contentious doctrine of verificationism.

very strong form of normative relativism is thought to follow: depending on how broadly or narrowly normative contexts are defined, it will be claimed that, for instance, members of one society may not make ethical judgments about the behavior of members of another society, or that one individual may not ethically criticize the actions of another. Now normative contextualism does indeed follow, but normative relativism does not. Individual normative relativism does not follow because for the anti-realist an evaluative context is determined by a shared way of life. Where two individuals share a way of life, they necessarily share implicit commitment to a set of norms, so that normative disputes between them are always in principle adjudicable. And cultural relativism is likewise ruled out because normative evaluation across cultures requires widespread agreement on evaluative standards. Just as there could be no trade between two economies that did not agree about the relative values of a great number of commodities, so there could not be transcultural ethical criticism in the absence of a shared set of ethical norms. To engage in ethical criticism is to presuppose that the target of such criticism is at least capable of correction through being criticized. And we would make no such assumption about the members of a culture that seemed to lack the institution of morality. In the absence of a pattern of widespread agreement between two cultures on ethical matters, there would be no reason for members of one to suppose that the other culture had a practice answering to their own practice of morality, and hence that its members were open to correction through ethical critique.[7] Now not all transcultural normative criticism will be legitimate, since the enterprise of interpreting actions and norms across cultures is beset with all sorts of difficulties. Still, where there is genuine disagreement over the moral status of a given action, there should be better and worse ways of applying the agreed-upon norms to the case at hand, and hence a better-supported position in the dispute.[8] There can be a comparative even though there is no superlative.

This result is important to the project of Buddhist anti-realism because the *bodhisattva* needs to walk a middle path between the extremes of excessive tolerance and rigid dogmatism. The *bodhisattva*'s aim is to prevent the suffering of others. In some cases the *bodhisattva* will be able to further this aim by acting alone. But typically it will require the *bodhisattva* to get those who suffer to act in certain ways and refrain from acting in other ways. As we saw above, to be effective at this the *bodhisattva* must learn to take on the perspectives of the unenlightened. But all such identification with the other contains the risk of acquiescing in the very habits and preferences that create the conditions for suffering. The *bodhisattva* must retain the conviction (basic to Buddhism) that a life devoid of attachment and clinging is better than life as it is ordinarily lived – something that few who suffer are likely to believe. At the same time this conviction must not harden into a dogma to which the *bodhisattva* becomes attached. The *bodhisattva* must be able to effectively intervene in the lives of many individuals exhibiting a wide variety of patterns of

---

[7] The argument here is essentially a variant on Davidson's argument against conceptual relativism.

[8] As Mohanty points out (2000a: 279–80), there may be considerable difficulty involved in trying to individuate cultures. This consideration raises similar questions concerning whether cultural normative relativism can be coherently formulated. If we cannot say where one culture leaves off and another begins, it is not clear what it means to say there might be distinct cultures with normative practices that are incommensurable. I am indebted to Dan Arnold for first bringing this point to my attention.

beliefs, desires and aspirations, and this will require considerable flexibility on the *bodhisattva*'s part. Of perhaps greater importance, the *bodhisattva* must avoid even the slightest appearance of superiority in outlook or bearing, lest any proffered assistance invoke resentment on the recipient's part. And those of firm conviction about how to live one's life are not always best at avoiding seeming to know better than others. Understanding how, when it comes to normative matters, there can be better with no best will help the *bodhisattva* avoid the two dangers of being spineless and being overbearing. For this means that there can be no universal prescriptions for overcoming suffering, that any assistance must be carefully crafted to suit the particular context. And it also means that even the most helpful advice is not backed up by The Good, hence that its prescriber has nothing with which to pound the table. Indeed this means that even the most skillful *bodhisattva*'s performance can always be improved upon. In the task of improving our lives, no one has the final answer. The ultimate truth is just that there is no ultimate truth.

Finally, there is a good deal of deep delight and spontaneous laughter in the life of the *bodhisattva*, and this fact plays an important role in the exercise of compassion. Suffering is lightened through the sympathetic joy that the *bodhisattva* induces, and some will be inspired to embark on the practice that leads to such a state. While this side of the *bodhisattva*'s nature is well attested in the Buddhist anti-realist tradition, we are not told how this connects up with the fact that the *bodhisattva* is an empty person. We may speculate, however, that this comes about at least in part through something akin to the sense of liberation that is said to result from the acceptance of Reductionism. There it was claimed that liberation from belief in a self gave rise to a sense of freedom from all the cares and concerns that are its attendants, as well as to a sense of greater closeness to the lives of other persons. Given that Buddhist anti-realism dissolves the fear that is inspired by the possibility of nihilism, it must give rise to an equally deep sense of liberation. But there is something else as well. It has often been claimed, by figures as diverse as Plato, Aristotle and Marx, that the best life is one that involves the realization and expression of the human essence. Since the Buddhist Reductionist denies there is such a thing as a human essence, they cannot claim that one who has comprehended non-self lives well for that reason. Buddhist anti-realism does, however, make room for a mitigated essentialism in its semantic non-dualism. So it might be claimed that the *bodhisattva*'s conduct represents an expression of the essence of the person. And we might imagine that there is great joy to be derived from being what one essentially is: an empty person, that is, a person whose essence it is to be devoid of essence.

Notes

[a] The Abhidharma schools, such as Vaibhāṣika, Theravāda, and Sautrāntika, make up the first branch. The second consists of the Mahāyāna schools, chiefly Madhyamaka and Yogācāra. The Yogācāra–Sautrāntika school (the school of Diṅnāga) represents something of an anomaly in this classification, in that while it is officially Mahāyāna, it teaches a kind of Abhidharma, its position being the logical terminus of Buddhist Reductionism's trajectory. Its doctrine of *trisvabhāva* represents an attempt to split the difference between the realism of Reductionism and the anti-essentialism of Mahāyāna. It may be questioned whether this attempt is entirely successful. The basic difficulty is that while the *pariniṣpanna* is said to be ineffable, this does not preclude its having an essence. The term *svalakṣaṇa* itself expresses this difficulty.

ᵇ *satkitrāsāttvavnirmuktyā saṃsāre sidhyati sthitiḥ / mohena duḥkhenārthe śūnyatāyā idaṃ phalam,*
BCA 9.53.

ᶜ The *bodhisattva* does, after all, abide in *saṃsāra* in order to teach the *dharma* to the unenlightened. And such teaching, we are told, requires acquiescence in the conventions whereby worldly transactions are conducted. See, e.g., BCA 9.8.

ᵈ Note the essentialism involved here: in this context pains may be considered to have badness as an intrinsic nature. Prāsaṅgikas regularly complain of a covert essentialism in Svātantrika – a tendency to posit intrinsic natures at the conventional level. (See Della Santina (1986: 158ff.) and Cozort (1998: 239–43) for instances.) But this is just what is needed to make the present account of the *bodhisattva*'s compassion work. And it is justifiable given the Svātantrika distinction between better and worse theories at the conventional level. (See my (1994) for a fuller discussion of this point.) To say that Keplerian astronomy is better than Ptolemaic is in part to say that while a geocentric system may reflect how things appear to us and may have a limited degree of utility (as in celestial navigation), Kepler's heliocentric system more accurately reflects how things actually are. And this 'how things are' is to be taken realistically, in terms of mind-independent natures. Of course this essentialism is mitigated by its semantic non-dualist context. It is only given certain aims and methods of inquiry that Keplerian dynamics may be said to capture the real nature of planetary motion; there is no such thing as the nature of planetary motion independent of all epistemic contexts. Still, to acquiesce in the better theory is just to take its essentialist commitments at face value. To suppose, as Prāsaṅgikas do, that this must lead to attachment and clinging is to deny the possibility of ironic engagement – that we might acquiesce in the commitment while at the same time retaining the anti-realist lessons of the doctrine of emptiness.

ᵉ This means that the Buddhist anti-realist can accept the argument for altruism without being committed to the controversial implication that pain is ultimately, and so impersonally, bad. The Buddhist anti-realist does hold that we are better off if we adopt practices that lead to less overall pain. So a theory that leads to such practices is to be preferred to one that does not. But it would be a mistake to think there might be some transcendental ground of this fact about us.

ᶠ The figure of the banana plant is used at BCA 9.74, 9.150.

ᵍ This is suggested by BCA 9.154. But see also Candrakīrti's *Vṛtti* on *Catuḥśataka* 8.7: 'For it is just by means of the complete purging of all theories [about the ultimate nature of reality] that nirvāṇa is obtained.'

ʰ See, e.g., MMK 17.31–32; VV 23, 27; CŚ 7.24; BCA 9.150.

ⁱ See, for instance, not only MMK 18.4, but also Vasubandhu's *svavṛtti* on *Viṃśatikā* 10.

ʲ This common theme in Madhyamaka self-interpretation is first articulated at MMK 15.6–7.

ᵏ See BCA 9.150–54, VV 23, *Prasannapadā* on MMK 16.8 (Pandeya 295).

ˡ See, e.g., MMK 25.19–20.

ᵐ This is Śāntideva's proposed remedy for such fear; see BCA 9.56.

ⁿ It is tempting to see in Nāgārjuna's apparent equation of emptiness with dependent co-origination (at MMK 24.18–19) a way of grounding the *bodhisattva*'s compassion. The idea would be as follows. If emptiness is to be understood as dependent co-origination, then to say that all things are empty is to say that the identity of each existent is inextricably intertwined with the identities of all other existents. In that case the person cannot be thought of as an ultimately distinct individual, and the meaning of a person's life is necessarily bound up with that of the lives of others. Hence to see the emptiness of all is to see that one has an obligation to help others overcome suffering.

I see three difficulties with this suggestion. First, the conclusion does not follow from the premises. It might well be that a person's life can have value and significance only through its relation to the lives of other persons, but this would not mean that the only sorts of activities that could give a life value and significance involve assisting others. A life devoted to the oppression of others would gain whatever meaning it had through its relations to the lives of others. Second, I can find no textual support for this way of linking emptiness with the *bodhisattva*'s compassion; there is, on the other hand, ample textual support for the grounding of compassion in the impersonal badness of pain (as in the argument of BCA 8). Third, the suggestion involves reading a certain sort of metaphysical theory into the doctrine of emptiness, namely the Hua Yen view of the interpenetration of all *dharmas*. This strikes me as incompatible with the Madhyamaka stricture against metaphysical theories (as, e.g., at MMK 13.8). The argument from the impersonal badness of pain, on the other hand, need not employ any assumptions about the ultimate nature of reality. It can instead rest entirely on common-sense observations about what we do and do not find when we investigate ourselves and our practices.

° *bhāvayerṣyām ca mānaṃ ca nirvikalpena cetasā*, BCA 8.140.

ᴾ *paramaṃ guhyaṃ parātmaparivartanam*, BCA 8.120.

A Buddhist Nominalist Semantics

We have seen that Buddhist Reductionists view with suspicion anything that might be thought of as produced by a mental process of aggregation. This is what lies behind their rejection of forests, armies, chariots and persons as things to be included in our ultimate ontology. The same attitude eventually led the Buddhist Reductionist tradition to reject real universals as well. This in turn leads to the question how a kind-term like 'cow' functions. If there is no such thing as the universal cowness that all cows share, then how are we able to learn to use the word 'cow' as applying to all cows? Certain Buddhist Reductionists developed the answer that the meaning of a kind-term is the exclusion (*apoha*) of the other. So the meaning of 'cow' may be formulated as 'not non-cow'. This formula is the basis of the radical nominalist semantics of *apoha*.

'Nominalism' will here mean the view that in the case of a kind-term like 'cow', all that is common to the individuals called cows is the name 'cow'. The contrasting term 'realism' will here be used to mean the view that, in the case of the cow, inhering in each individual cow is the universal cowness, some one entity that all cows share in common.[1] Realists thus hold that at least some of our kind-terms pick out classes of particulars based on some one shared, objective character. A universal like cowness is thought to be some one entity that exists eternally and is somehow equally present in all its instances. Some Indian realists held that 'cow' denotes the universal cowness; others held that on each occasion of use it designates an individual as inhered in by the universal cowness. Nominalists deny that there are such things as universals; they maintain that the use of a single term to form a class out of many distinct particulars is entirely the result of human linguistic convention. According to the doctrine of *apoha*, the relevant convention is best expressed in terms of the fact that what all the particulars called cows have in common is just that they are not non-cows. More generally, words have meaning through the exclusion of the other (*anyāpoha*).

Conceptualism is sometimes thought to represent a third possible view of the matter, and *apoha* semantics has sometimes been identified as a sort of conceptualism. The conceptualist holds that what all cows have in common is just that they fall under the same concept, where concepts are thought of as mental contents of some sort or other. But if one holds that concepts are essentially linguistic in nature, so that

---

[1] A realist need not hold that cowness is a universal. A realist might instead hold that a natural kind such as the cow is built up out of a set of features, such as being four-legged, being ruminative, etc., and that this set is 'fuzzy': that there is no determinate set of features that every cow must have. What the realist must hold is that at least some features correspond to real universals. Such natural kinds as the cow might then be thought of as built up out of some set of universals. I shall continue to treat cowness as a plausible candidate for the status of universal, but this is just for the sake of having a common example at hand. In this I am following the practice of the classical Indian philosophers, who used 'cow' as their stock example in the dispute over universals even though they disagreed as to whether the cow is a natural kind.

one could acquire the cow concept only by learning to use the word 'cow', then conceptualism collapses into nominalism. Conceptualism might seem to represent a distinct position if one holds an abstraction theory of concept formation, according to which one forms the cow concept by abstracting away the distinctive features of particular cows and conjoining only the similarities. Such a form of conceptualism would claim, *contra* the nominalist, that our use of 'cow' is governed by objective features of individual cows (namely their real resemblances) and not just by linguistic conventions. And since it does not explicitly appeal to the realist's cowness universal in explaining our linguistic behavior, it appears to be distinct from realism as well. But to this it may be objected that two things may be said to resemble one another only if they share some common feature, that is, a universal. And if the conceptualist responds that our judgments concerning shared features are based on resemblances (and not vice versa, as the critic contends), then there is still the objection that the resemblance conceptualist must appeal to a resemblance universal to collect together all the distinct instances of resemblance their theory requires. Moreover, as we shall see below, the *apoha* theorist claims that our judgments of resemblance are themselves a result of our mastery of the use of kind-terms, and thus cannot ground such mastery. Hence while the *apoha* theory has sometimes been represented as a kind of resemblance-conceptualism, it is not clear that this would have been seen as a viable option by any of its proponents.

It is hardly surprising that Buddhist Reductionists should reject real universals as mental constructions, and that our tendency to see all the individual cows as sharing in a common character should be relegated to the level of mere conventional truth. What is ultimately real must, on this view, lack all shared properties; it must be strictly unique and unrepeatable. This means that only the unique particular is real. Such common-sense particulars as cows now have two strikes against them: not only are they partite, and thus not ultimately real by the strictures of mereological reductionism; also, to the extent that they are understood as having a nature in common with other members of their kind, they are likewise confined to the realm of the conventionally real. Even the impartite particulars (whatever they may be like) do not possess mind-independent shared natures. So if we thought that, for instance, earth atoms were genuinely impartite, we would still have to deny that the earth atom is ultimately real. True, there would be an ultimately real particular that somehow stands behind each successful predication of the term 'earth atom'. But anything that is a member of that kind can only be conventionally real, since membership in that kind is understood as stemming from having a shared nature. Thus Buddhist nominalism makes use of a two-tiered ontology: ultimately real particulars that are strictly unique and ineffable, and conventionally real particulars that sort into kinds based on their shared natures.[2] The trick, of course, is to explain our behavior with

---

[2] Buddhist nominalists also claim that the ineffable pure particular is cognized through perception (which they understand as non-conceptual), while cognition of common-sense particulars, since it is mediated by concepts, is always inferential in nature. It was this feature of Buddhist nominalism that led the Russian Buddhologist Th. Stcherbatsky in his (1962) to see strong affinities between their view and that of Kant. He sees the unique particular as analogous to the noumenon, understood as the immediate object of sensible intuition. And their common-sense particulars are seen as like Kant's phenomenal objects,

respect to the latter in terms of facts about the former. (In what follows we shall ignore the fact that cows are partite, and use them as our stock example of common-sense particulars having unique ultimate counterparts.)

Buddhist nominalists have in their favor the widely shared intuition that the real is always particular. Moreover, realism faces formidable obstacles. For instance, if the universal is truly distinct from all its instances and yet present in each, then it must be partite. In this case, it would seem that another universal must be invoked in order to explain how these scattered parts constitute a single entity, and the regress thus begun appears unstoppable. But the nominalist also faces notorious difficulties. If there is nothing common among the individual cows themselves that warrants our application of the term 'cow', then how do we ever learn to use the word? How do we agree among ourselves as to which particulars count as cows? And how am I able to use the word consistently from one occasion to the next? To make our use of kind-terms depend solely on human convention is to appear to make such use entirely arbitrary, thereby leaving inexplicable the success we meet with when we learn to use such terms. These difficulties are familiar ones for those familiar with the controversy between realists and nominalists in the Western tradition. Only now in the Buddhist Reductionist context the nominalist's standard difficulty – explaining how our use of kind-terms might be rule-governed – becomes a version of the problem of the two truths: explaining why acceptance of a statement that is only conventionally true and is ultimately false, might nonetheless have utility. We will recall that Buddhist Reductionists standardly make use of causal connections to solve this sort of problem when it arises in other areas, such as their treatment of partite entities. So we will not be surprised when causal connections of some sort are eventually invoked by the Buddhist nominalist.

According to the doctrine of *apoha*, to say of a particular that it is a cow is to say that it does not belong to the class of things that are appropriately called non-cows. This strategy is obviously designed to avoid positing any shared nature or resemblance among the individual cows; all they are said to have in common, apart from the absence of being non-cows, is the name 'cow'. And absences are not themselves real. What we think of as perceiving an absence is actually just the perceiving of a present particular, and then noticing that it fails to satisfy some expectation we have; to perceive the absence of a pot is just to perceive the ground when we are looking for a pot. Thus the absence of being non-cow is seen as a mere imposed property and cannot serve as the objective ground of the common class membership. The credentials of the doctrine of *apoha* as a pure nominalism are beyond dispute.

But this strategy would seem to rely on there being some discernible nature common to all the non-cows. For if there is not, then it would appear that one can tell what a non-cow is only by knowing what cows are, and we will have come full circle. This circularity is problematic, given that linguistically mediated cognition is efficacious. If there is not some nature the presence of which makes an individual a

---

constituted as these are in part by conceptual activity. Of course Buddhist nominalism knows nothing of Kant's transcendental apparatus. Still Stcherbatsky's analogies are interesting, and even useful up to a point.

cow and the absence of which makes it a non-cow, why when I ask my assistant to fetch a cow do I obtain a cow – something that gives milk – and not an ox or a lawn tractor? It is no help to be told that my assistant knows oxen and lawn tractors are non-cows. How can she know this unless she first knows what a cow is?

The *apoha* theorist responds by agreeing that cows do have a common nature, cowness. Buddhist nominalists are quite open in their practice of theft over honest toil; they readily affirm that the 'exclusion of the other' plays exactly the same role in their semantics that the universal plays in realist semantics. But the *apoha* theorist quickly adds that this shared nature is a linguistically induced fiction and is ultimately unreal. Thus this seeming concession does not appear to help. For it would seem that only what is ultimately real can, in the final analysis, explain efficacy. If each real particular is indeed genuinely unique (and thus strictly ineffable), then it is difficult to see why those particulars making up what are termed lawn tractors should be excluded from the extension of 'cow', while those making up the milk-givers are included.

A crucial component of the *apoha* theorist's response to this difficulty is the distinction between two kinds of negation, which we might call nominally bound negation and verbally bound negation. This terminology brings out the point of the classical Indian linguists (who first drew the distinction) that where a sentence contains a negation, the first type tends to be associated with the noun (or adjective), the second with the verb. There are thus two distinct ways to negate the sentence, 'That is polite', namely 'That is impolite' (nominally bound negation) and 'That is not polite' (verbally bound negation). And it should be noted that in the former case the negation serves as a positive characterization of the action in question, whereas in the latter case the emphasis appears to be on simply denying attribution of the predicate 'polite' to the action in question. But now we may see as well that when the two types of negation are conjoined, as in 'That is not impolite', the result is not what one would expect given the classical rule of double negation: this sentence is not equivalent to 'That is polite'. This is because in this case, the nominally bound negation behaves not classically (like exclusion negation) but like choice negation: besides those things that are said to be polite, and those things that are said to be impolite, there are also those things that may be said to be neither polite nor impolite (namely those actions where questions of politeness simply do not arise). Verbally bound negation, on the other hand, always behaves like the classical exclusion negation (never occasioning bivalence failure), so that the standard rule of double negation applies. But when the two forms of negation are conjoined, as in 'That is not impolite', the result is a refusal to characterize the referent of 'that' as impolite – which leaves it open whether it may be said to be polite, or is instead the sort of thing to which such predicates simply fail to apply.

With this distinction in hand, we are now prepared to investigate the *apoha* theorist's resolution of the difficulty mentioned two paragraphs back. Their answer begins by considering how we might represent the uniqueness of the ultimate particular. This uniqueness may be thought of as the fact that a given particular is wholly distinct in nature from every other. For a given particular s_n, we may then say that every other particular is non-s_n in nature, employing nominally bound negation on the particular (hereafter to be symbolized as '$-s_n$'). Now if we were to perform verbally bound negation on this expression, saying of something that it is not non-s_n ($\sim -s_n$), what we said would be true precisely of s_n and nothing else, so this gets us no closer to the semantics of kind-terms, which must be predicable of many particulars. However, perceptual contact with a particular causes the occurrence of a mental image. This mental image is itself a particular, and thus its apprehension in perception will not yield the basis for any generality. But given the right training, we can learn to employ a mental image p_n generated by a particular s_n in a somewhat different way. We can learn to perform the nominally bound negation of p_n in such a way that not all other mental images are excluded by (that is, appear incompatible with) this negation. Thus the nominally bound negation $-p_n$ may function like choice negation. As we saw above, the choice negation of the predicate 'polite' yields a complement class of those things that are impolite, but at the same time it leaves open the possibility of a non-empty set consisting of those things that are neither polite nor impolite. By the same token, we can learn to treat $-p_n$ in such a way that mental images p_{n+1}, p_{n+2}, etc., while distinct from p_n, are not in the exclusion class formed by $-p_n$. In this case, the expression '$\sim -p_n$' will be true of p_n, p_{n+1}, p_{n+2}, etc. That is, '$\sim -p_n$' functions as the name of a mentally constructed pseudo-universal. We have learned to form $-p_n$ in such a way as to overlook the differences among p_n, p_{n+1}, p_{n+2}, etc., so that each may be said not to be other than the rest.

Suppose, counterfactually, that cows were ultimate particulars. (The supposition is counterfactual because the cow, as an aggregate substance, could not be ultimately real.) And suppose that s_n, s_{n+1}, and s_{n+2} were correctly called cows. Now the representation p_n when apprehended perceptually is absolutely distinct from all other representations, including p_{n+1} and p_{n+2}. To learn to use 'cow', however, is to learn to treat some such representation as p_n in such a way that it does not exclude such other mental images as p_{n+1} and p_{n+2}. To have learnt to use the word is to have acquired the disposition to form this paradigm image upon hearing the word. I am then able to determine that the novel instance s_{n+3} is a cow by noting that the mental image p_{n+3} is not excluded by, is not incompatible with, p_n. I correctly call s_{n+3} a cow through overlooking the difference between s_n and s_{n+3}. I am likewise able to correctly say that s_m is not a cow (it is in fact a lawn tractor) by noting that the mental image p_m generated by it is excluded by or incompatible with p_n.

So much for the formal machinery of *apoha* theory, and its psychological model. At this point it would be reasonable to wonder whether the original difficulty has truly been addressed, or merely shoved back a step. How, we might ask, am I able to learn to form p_n in such a way as to ensure that precisely such mental images as p_{n+1} and p_{n+2} are not thereby excluded, if the *apoha* theorist is right in claiming that s_n, s_{n+1}, and s_{n+2} share neither a class character nor any real resemblances? We are told that this learning proceeds in accordance with a set of verbal conventions, but this seems unhelpful. These conventions can be employed only if there is some objective basis for intersubjective agreement concerning the formation of p_n. And what might this be if s_n, s_{n+1}, and s_{n+2} share neither a class character nor any real resemblances?

The *apoha* theorist's answer is that s_n, s_{n+1}, and s_{n+2} do share something, namely the capacity to give milk. But this is a misleading way of putting the point. Instead we should say that each of these particulars serves as cause of milk, that is, has the capacity to satisfy a desire for milk. If we are tempted to suppose that this amounts to a real resemblance among them, we should consider the plants *guḍūcī, dhātṛ, abhaya*, etc., each of which has the power to abate fever (see TS 723–26, PV III.73–74). These are distinct kinds of plants, so there can be no temptation to suppose they resemble one another in any way save in their antipyretic virtue. And we should refrain from judging that they have a real resemblance in this respect, since our interest in fever abatement would clearly be behind such a judgment. Just as with 'chariot' and 'forest', our interests make it the case that it would be lighter – less prolix, more parsimonious – to employ the one term 'antipyretic' rather than having distinct names for the power of each. And so, again just as with 'chariot' and 'forest', we end up projecting onto the world something that is not really there – a class character that gives rise to judgments of resemblance. There is an objective basis to the formation of p_n in such a way as to ensure that mental images p_{n+1} and p_{n+2} are not excluded: each of s_n, s_{n+1}, and s_{n+2} are able to satisfy our interest in obtaining milk. Our use of 'cow' expresses this interest. But such use also leads us to see particular cows as similar and sharing in a common class character, when they are in fact utterly distinct and incommensurable.

Having said all this, certain Buddhist nominalists were still concerned that the capacity to produce the same effect would be seen as a shared property. Thus two additional arguments are given for the ultimate distinctness of the instances of a kind-term. The first is that when we collect together a set of particulars on the basis of their each producing the same effect, this basis is better described as their each being distinct from what is incapable of producing that effect. The many cows should not be thought of as sharing the causal capacity to produce milk. Instead they should be thought of as sharing only distinctness from such things as lawn tractors, conduct with respect to which leaves unabated my desire for milk. The causal capacity – what serves as the basis for the convention governing formation of the paradigm mental image – may itself appear to be one shared feature. But this appearance is itself generated by the exclusion of the other.

The second strategy involves taking a straightforwardly empiricist line on so-called causal capacities. When we say that cows produce milk, we tend to imagine in each cow some power through the exercise of which milk somehow emerges. And since the product (the milk) seems to be the same in each case, although the particular cows might otherwise vary, we suppose that the power itself must be the same. This view is not empirically warranted, however. All we are given in experience is just positive and negative concomitance: this occurring, that occurs, while in the absence of this, that does not occur. The notion of a causal capacity or power is merely a convenient way of collecting together the various positive and negative correlations. That this way of talking proves convenient should not mislead us into thinking it reflects some objective feature of reality. There is ultimately no such thing as the power to produce milk. There are just particular cows, lawn tractors, and pots of milk.

The theory of *apoha* has consequences that resonate throughout the Buddhist nominalist tradition. The logician Dharmakīrti, for instance, uses it to explain why coextensive terms are not necessarily equivalent in meaning, thereby formulating a version of the sense–reference distinction. Although his discussion concerns kind-terms, the same approach is subsequently applied to singular terms, thus anticipating Frege's famous 'Hesperus–Phosphorus' argument. The semantics of *apoha* also gets employed later in the tradition to explain our ability to make true assertions concerning non-existent entities. For instance, we might ordinarily consider the sentence 'Devadatta, the son of a barren woman, does not speak' to be true. But contradictions are alleged to follow from this admission. For instance, since

Devadatta might equally well be said not to be silent, from which it appears to follow that he does speak, it would seem to be true that he both speaks and does not speak. Buddhist nominalists seek to defend our linguistic intuitions concerning the truth of the original sentence by developing an account of predication that blocks the problematic inference. Their resolution relies on a view of the role of conceptual constructions in *apoha* semantics that was first worked out in connection with a sort of master argument for the *apoha* theory. It was argued that no realist theory of word-meaning could account for the fact that we may assert of an entity both that it exists and that it does not exist. This phenomenon can, however, be explained by *apoha* semantics, according to which the referent of any referring expression is a conceptual construction, namely the exclusion of the other. Once this feature of the theory had been made fully explicit, Buddhist nominalists were motivated to try to work out a consistent logic for empty subject terms.[3]

It has become something of an orthodoxy that a consistent semantics must eschew the radical nominalist path and embrace either universals or resemblances. The doctrine of *apoha* constitutes an interesting and important challenge to this orthodoxy.

---

[3] For more on this, as well as a full bibliography of the primary and secondary literature on the theory of *apoha*, see the fourth chapter of my *Indian Philosophy of Language: Studies in Selected Issues* (1991).

Bibliography

Sanskrit texts (with key to abbreviations, and English translations)

AKB: *Abhidharmakośabhāṣyam of Vasubandhu*, ed. Prahlad Pradhan, Patna: Jayaswal Research Institute, 1975.
English translation of Louis de La Vallée Poussin's French translation: *Abhidharmakośabhasyam*, trans. Leo M. Pruden, Berkeley, CA: Asian Humanities Press, 1988.
English translation of Chapter 9: Duerlinger, James, trans. (1989), 'Refutation of the Theory of Selfhood: A Resolution of Questions about Persons', *Journal of Indian Philosophy*, **17**: 137–88.

BCA: *The Bodhicāryāvatāra of Śāntideva with the Commentary Pañjika of Prajñākaramati*, ed. P.L. Vaidya, Dharbanga: Mithila Institute, 1960.
The Bodhicāryāvatāra, trans. Kate Crosby and Andrew Skilton, London: Oxford University Press, 1993.

KV: *Kathavatthu: Abhidhammapitake Kathavatthupali*, ed. Bhikkhu Jagadisakassapo, Varanasi: Motilal Banarsidass, 1961.
Points of controversy; or, Subjects of discourse; being a translation of the Kathavatthu from the Abhidhammapitaka, trans. Shwe Zan Aung and C. Rhys Davids, London: Luzac, 1960.

M: *Milindapañho*, ed. R.D. Vadekar, Bombay: Bombay University Publications, 1972.
The Questions of King Milinda, trans. T.W. Rhys Davids, Delhi: Motilal Banarsidass, 1965.

MMK: *Mūlamadhyamakakārikā*, ed. Raghunath Pandeya as: *The Madhyamakaśāstram of Nāgārjuna*, with the Commentaries *Akutobhayā* by Nāgārjuna, *Madhyamakavṛtti* by Buddhapālita, *Prajñāpradīpavṛtti* by Bhāvaviveka, and *Prasannapadā* by Candrakīrti, Delhi: Motilal Banarsidass, 1988.
The Fundamental Wisdom of the Middle Way, trans. Jay L. Garfield, Oxford: Oxford University Press, 1995.

NB: *Vinītadeva's Nyāyabinduṭīkā*, reconstructed and translated by Mrinalkanti Gangopadhyaya, Calcutta: Indian Studies Past and Present, 1971.

S: *Saṃyutta Nikāya*, ed. Feer in 5 vols, London: Pali Text Society, 1884–98.
The Book of the kindred sayings (Samyutta-nikaya) or grouped suttas, trans. C. Rhys Davids, London: Luzac, 1950–56.

TS: *Tattvasaṅgraha of Śāntarakṣita*, edited with the *Pañjikā* (=TSP) by Embar Krishnamacharya, Baroda: Oriental Institute, 1984.
The Tattvasaṅgraha of Śāntarakṣita, with the Commentary of Kamalaśīla, trans. Ganganatha Jha, Delhi: Motilal Banarsidass, 1986.

VM: *Visuddhimagga of Buddhaghosâcariya*, ed. Henry Clarke Warren, rev. by Dharmananda Kosambi, Cambridge, MA: Harvard University Press, 1950.

The Path of Purification, trans. Bhikkhu Ñanamoli, Kandy, Sri Lanka: Buddhist Publication Society, 1991.

VV: *Vigrahavyāvartanī*, edited and translated in: *The dialectical method of Nagarjuna: (Vigrahavyavartani)*, eds E.H. Johnston and Arnold Kunst, trans. Kamaleswar Bhattacharya, Delhi: Motilal Banarsidass, 1978.

Recent Scholarship

Alexander, Ronald G. (1997), *The Self, Supervenience and Personal Identity*, Brookfield, VT and Aldershot, UK: Ashgate.

Allen, Douglas (1997), 'Social Constructions of Self: Some Asian, Marxist, and Feminist Critiques of Dominant Western Views of Self', in Allen, Douglas (ed.), *Culture and Self: Philosophical and Religious Perspectives, East and West*, Boulder, CO: Westview Press, pp. 3–26.

Alston, William P. (1996), *A Realist Conception of Truth*, Ithaca, NY: Cornell University Press.

Armstrong, D.M. (1978a), *Nominalism and Realism: Universals and Scientific Realism*, vol. I, London: Cambridge University Press.

Armstrong, D.M. (1978b), *A Theory of Universals: Universals and Scientific Realism*, vol. II, London: Cambridge University Press.

Bastow, David (1986), 'Self-Construction in Buddhism', *Ratio*, **27**: 97–113.

Basu, Ananyo (1997), 'Reducing Concern with Self: Parfit and the Ancient Buddhist Schools', in Allen, Douglas (ed.), *Culture and Self: Philosophical and Religious Perspectives, East and West*, Boulder, CO: Westview Press, pp. 97–110.

Bearn, Gordon C.F. (1997), *Waking to Wonder: Wittgenstein's Existential Investigations*, Albany, NY: SUNY Press.

Bhaskar, Bhagchandra Jain (ed.) (1971), *Āryadeva's Catuḥśatakaṃ, along with the Candrakīrti Vṛtti and Hindi translation*, Nagpur, India: Alok Prakashan.

Blackburn, Simon (1997), 'Has Kant Refuted Parfit?' in Dancy, Jonathan (ed.), *Reading Parfit*, Oxford: Basil Blackwell, pp. 180–201.

Block, Ned (1990), 'Can the Mind Change the World?' in Boolos, George (ed.), *Meaning and Method*, Cambridge: Cambridge University Press.

Brennan, Andrew (1988), *Conditions of Identity: A Study of Identity and Survival*, New York: Oxford University Press.

Brooks, D.H.M. (1994), 'How to Perform a Reduction', *Philosophy and Phenomenological Research*, **54**: 803–14.

Brown, C. Mackenzie (1996), 'Modes of Perfected Living in the Mahābhārata and the Purāñas', in Fort, Andrew and Patricia Mumme (eds), *Living Liberation in Hindu Thought*, Albany, NY: SUNY Press, pp. 157–83.

Campbell, John (1994), *Past, Space, and Self*, Cambridge, MA: MIT Press.

Cassam, Quassim (1989), 'Kant and Reductionism', *Review of Metaphysics*, **42**: 72–106.

Cassam, Quassim (1997), *Self and World*, Oxford: Oxford University Press.

Chakrabarti, Arindam (1982), 'The Nyāya Proofs for the Existence of the Soul', *Journal of Indian Philosophy*, **10**: 211–38.

Chakrabarti, Arindam (1992), 'I Touch What I Saw', *Philosophy and Phenomenological Research*, **52**: 103–16.

Chakrabarti, Arindam (2000), 'Against Immaculate Perception: Seven Reasons for Eliminating *Nirvikalpaka* Perception from Nyāya', *Philosophy East and West*, 50: 1–8.

Chakraborty, M.K. (1988), 'Use of Fuzzy Set Theory in introducing Graded Consequence in Multiple-valued Logic', in Gupta, M.M. and T. Yamakawa (eds), *Fuzzy Logic in Knowledge-based Systems, Decision and Control*, Amsterdam: Elsevier Science Publishers.

Chakraborty, M.K. and S. Basu (1997), 'Graded Consequence and Some Meta-logical Notions Generalized', *Fundamenta Informatica*, **32**: 299–311.

Chatterjee, Amita (1994), *Understanding Vagueness*, Delhi: Pragati Publishers.

Chatterjee, Amita (1996), 'Natural Laws, Accidental Generalizations and Vyāpti', in Chakrabarti, Arindam (ed.), *Epistemology, Meaning and Metaphysics after Matilal*, Special Issue of *Studies in Humanities and Social Sciences* (Simla, India: Indian Institute of Advanced Studies) 3 (2): 123–50.

Chatterjee, Amita (1997), 'Truth in Indian Philosophy', in Deutsch, Eliot and Ron Bontekoe (eds), *A Companion to World Philosophies*, Oxford: Blackwell, pp. 334–45.

Collins, Steven (1982), *Selfless Persons*, Cambridge: Cambridge University Press.

Coward, Harold (1990), *Derrida and Indian Philosophy*, Albany, NY: SUNY Press.

Cozort, Daniel (1998), *Unique Tenets of the Middle Way Consequence School*, Ithaca, NY: Snow Lion.

Davidson, Donald (1984), *Inquiries into Truth and Interpretation*, Oxford: Oxford University Press.

Davidson, Donald (1986), 'A Coherence Theory of Truth and Knowledge', in LePore, Enest (ed.), *Truth and Interpretation: perspectives on the philosophy of Donald Davidson*, Oxford: Blackwell, pp. 307–19.

Della Santina, Peter (1986), *Madhyamaka Schools in India*, Delhi: Motilal Banarsidass.

Dennett, Daniel (1978), *Brainstorms*, Cambridge, MA: Bradford.

Dennett, Daniel (1985), *Elbow Room: The Varieties of Free Will Worth Wanting*, Cambridge, MA: Bradford.

Dennett, Daniel (1991), *Consciousness Explained*, Boston, MA: Little, Brown and Co.

Dummett, Michael (1973), *Frege: Philosophy of Language*, London: Duckworth.

Dummett, Michael (1975), 'What is a Theory of Meaning?' in Guttenplan, Samuel (ed.), *Mind and Language*, Oxford: Oxford University Press, pp. 97–138.

Dummett, Michael (1991), *The Logical Basis of Metaphysics*, Cambridge, MA: Harvard University Press.

Dummett, Michael (1993),'Realism and Anti-Realism', *The Seas of Language*, Oxford: Oxford University Press, pp. 462–78.

Dummett, Michael (1997), 'Wang's Paradox', in Keefe, Rosanna and Peter Smith (eds), *Vagueness: A Reader*, Cambridge, MA: MIT Press, pp. 99–118.

Dutt, Nalinaksha (1971), 'The Sammitiyas and their Puggalavāda', *The Maha Bodhi*, **79**: 129–36.

Eckel, Malcolm David (1985a), 'The Concept of Reason in Jñānagarbha's Svātantrika Madhyamaka', in Matilal, B.K. (ed.), *Buddhist Logic and Epistemology*, Dordrecht: Reidel, pp. 253–78.

Eckel, Malcolm David (1985b), 'Bhāvaviveka's Critique of Yogācāra in Chapter XXV of the Prajñāpradīpa', in Lindtner, Christian (ed.), *Miscellanea Buddhica*, Indiske Studier V, Copenhagen: Akademisk Forlag, pp. 25–75.

Eckel, Malcolm David (1987), *Jñānagarbha's Commentary on the Distinction Between the Two Truths*, Albany, NY: SUNY Press.

Edgington, Dorothy (1997), 'Vagueness by degrees', in Keefe, Rosanna and Peter Smith (eds), *Vagueness: A Reader*, Cambridge, MA: MIT Press, pp. 294–316.

Engel, Pascal (1991), *The Norm of Truth*, Toronto: University of Toronto Press.

Evans, Gareth (1978), 'Can there be vague objects?' *Analysis*, **38**: 208.

Fine, Kit (1997), 'Vagueness, truth and logic', in Keefe, Rosanna and Peter Smith (eds), *Vagueness: A Reader*, Cambridge, MA: MIT Press, pp. 119–50.

Fodor, Jerry A. (1990), *A Theory of Content and Other Essays*, Boston, MA: MIT Press.

Fort, Andrew O. (1996), 'Liberation While Living in the *Jīvanmuktiviveka*', in Fort, Andrew and Patricia Mumme (eds), *Living Liberation in Hindu Thought*, Albany, NY: SUNY Press, pp. 135–55.

Frauwallner, Erich (1995), *Studies in Abhidharma Literature and the Origins of Buddhist Philosophical Systems*, trans. Sophie F. Kidd, Albany, NY: SUNY Press.

Garfield, Jay L. (1990), '*Epoche* and *Śūnyatā*: Scepticism East and West', *Philosophy East and West*, **40**: 285–308.

Garfield, Jay L. (1994), 'Dependent Arising and the Emptiness of Emptiness: Why did Nāgārjuna start with causation?', *Philosophy East and West*, **44**: 219–50.

Glover, Jonathan (1988), *I: The Philosophy and Psychology of Personal Identity*, London: Penguin.

Grice, H.P. (1975), 'Personal Identity', in Perry, John (ed.), *Personal Identity*, Los Angeles, CA: University of California Press, pp. 73–95.

Haksar, Vinit (1991), *Indivisible Selves and Moral Practice*, Edinburgh: Edinburgh University Press.

Hayes, Richard P. (1994), 'Nāgārjuna's Appeal', *Journal of Indian Philosophy*, **22**: 299–378.

Heller, Mark (1996), 'Against Metaphysical Vagueness', *Philosophical Perspectives*, **10**: 177–85.

Horgan, Terrence (1994), 'Robust Vagueness and the Forced-March Sorites Paradox', *Philosophical Perspectives*, **8**: 159–88.

Horwich, Paul (1990), *Truth*, Oxford: Blackwell.

Huntington, C.W. Jr (1983),'The System of Two Truths in the *Prasannapadā* and the *Madhyamakāvatāra*: A Study in Mādhyamika Soteriology', *Journal of Indian Philosophy*, **11**: 77–106.

Iida, Shotaro (1980), *Reason and Emptiness: A Study in Logic and Mysticism*, Tokyo: Hokuseido Press.

Inada, Kenneth K. (1970), *Nāgārjuna: A Translation of his* Mūlamadhyamakakārikā *With an Introductory Essay*, Tokyo: Hokuseido Press.

Jackson, Frank (1991), 'Decision-theoretic Consequentialism and the Nearest and Dearest Objection', *Ethics*, **101**: 461–82.

Jayatilleke, K.N. (1963), *Early Buddhist Theory of Knowledge*, London: George Allen and Unwin.

Johnston, Mark (1993), 'Verificationism as Philosophical Narcissism', *Philosophical Perspectives*, **7**: 307–30.

Kalupahana, David J. (1986), *Nāgārjuna: The Philosophy of the Middle Way*, Albany, NY: SUNY Press.

Kapstein, Matthew (1987), 'Self and Personal Identity in Indian Buddhist Scholasticism: A Philosophical Investigation', unpublished PhD dissertation, Brown University.

Kassapa, Bhikkhu Jagadosa (ed.) (1961), *Kathāvatthu*, Pali Publication Board, Bihar Government.

Katsura, Shorryu (1984), 'Dharmakīrti's Theory of Truth', *Journal of Indian Philosophy*, **12**: 215–35.

Katz, Nathan (1982), *Buddhist Images of Human Perfection*, Delhi: Motilal Banarsidass.

Keefe, Rosanna and Peter Smith (1997), 'Introduction: theories of vagueness', in Keefe, Rosanna and Peter Smith (eds), *Vagueness: A Reader*, Cambridge, MA: MIT Press, pp. 1–57.

Keown, Damien (1992), *The Nature of Buddhist Ethics*, New York: St. Martin's Press.

Keown, Damien (1996), 'Karma, Character, and Consequentialism', *Journal of Religious Ethics*, **24**: 329–50.

Kesarcodi-Watson, Ian (1994), *Approaches to Personhood in Indian Thought*, Delhi: Sri Satguru Publications.

Kim, Jaegwon (1993), *Supervenience and Mind*, New York: Cambridge University Press.

Kim, Jaegwon (1997), 'The Mind–Body Problem: Taking Stock after Forty Years', *Philosophical Perspectives*, **11**: 185–207.

Kim, Jaegwon (1998), *Mind in a Physical World: An Essay on the Mind–Body Problem and Mental Causation*, Cambridge, MA: MIT Press.

Kirkham, Richard L. (1992), *Theories of Truth*, Cambridge, MA: MIT Press.

Kolm, Serge-Christophe (1986), 'The Buddhist theory of "no-self"', in Elster, Jon (ed.), *The Multiple Self*, Cambridge: Cambridge University Press, pp. 233–55.

Korsgaard, Christine M. (1989), 'Personal Identity and the Unity of Agency: A Reply to Parfit', *Philosophy and Public Affairs*, **18**: 101–32.

Larson, Gerald James and Ram Shankar Bhattacharya (eds) (1987), *Encyclopedia of Indian Philosophies, vol. IV: Sāmkkhya*, Delhi: Motilal Banarsidass.

Lewis, David (1972), 'Psychophysical and Theoretical Identifications', *Australasian Journal of Philosophy*, **50**: 249–58.

Lewis, David (1986), *On the Plurality of Worlds*, Oxford: Basil Blackwell.

Lindtner, Christian (1981), 'Atiśa's Introduction to the Two Truths, and its Sources', *Journal of Indian Philosophy*, **9**: 161–214.

Loar, Brian (1992), 'Elimination versus Non-reductive Physicalism', in Charles, David and Kathleen Lennon (eds), *Reduction, Explanation and Realism*, Oxford: Clarendon Press.

Lopez, Donald S. Jr (1987), *A Study of Svātantrika*, Ithaca, NY: Snow Lion.

Lycan, William (1991), 'Homuncular Functionalism Meets PDP', in Ramsey, William, Stephen P. Stich and David E. Runelhart (eds), *Philosophy and Connectionist Theory*, Hillsdale, NJ: Lawrence Erlbaum Associates.

Machina, Kenton F. (1985), 'Induction and Deduction Revisited', *Nous*, **19**: 571–78.

Machina, Kenton F. (1997), 'Truth, belief and vagueness', in Keefe, Rosanna and Peter Smith (eds), *Vagueness: A Reader*, Cambridge, MA: MIT Press, pp. 174–203.

Machina, Kenton F. and Harry Deutsch (2002), 'Vagueness, Ignorance, and Margins for Error', *Acta Analytica*, forthcoming.

Marcus, Ruth Barcan (1993), *Modalities: Philosophical Essays*, Oxford: Oxford University Press.

Martin, Raymond (1987), 'Memory, Connecting, and What Matters in Survival', *Journal of Australasian Philosophy*, **65**: 82–97.

Martin, Raymond (1998), *Self-Concern: an experiential approach to what matters in survival*, Cambridge: Cambridge University Press.

Martin, Raymond and John Barresi (1995), 'Hazlitt on the future of the self', *Journal of the History of Ideas*, **56** (3): 463–81.

Mason, Elinor (1998), 'Can an Indirect Consequentialist Be a Real Friend?', *Ethics*, **108**: 386–93.

Matilal, B.K. (1986), *Perception: An Essay in Classical Indian Theories of Knowledge*, Oxford: Oxford University Press.

Matilal, B.K. (1990), *The Word and the World: India's Contribution to the Study of Language*, Delhi: Oxford University Press.

Matthews, Bruce (1983), *Craving and Salvation: A Study in Buddhist Soteriology*, SR 13, Waterloo, Ontario: Wilfrid Laurier University Press.

McDowell, John (1997), 'Reductionism and the First Person', in Dancy, Jonathan (ed.), *Reading Parfit*, Oxford: Basil Blackwell, pp. 230–50.

Mohanty, J.N. (1992), *Reason and Tradition in Indian Thought*, Oxford: Oxford University Press.

Mohanty, J.N. (2000a), 'My Philosophical Position/Reply to my Critics', in Gupta, Bina (ed.), *The Empirical and the Transcendental: A Fusion of Horizons*, Boulder, CO: Rowman and Littlefield, pp. 253–80.

Mohanty, J.N. (2000b), *Classical Indian Philosophy*, New York: Rowman and Littlefield.

Moriyama Seitetsu (1999), 'Kamalaśila's Proof of Non-Substantiality (*Niḥsvabhāva*) and the Contrapositive Formulation of the Reductio (*Prasaṅgaviparyaya*)', paper delivered at the XIIIth Congress of the International Association for Buddhist Studies, Lausanne, Switzerland, August 1999.

Murti, T.R.V. (1955), *The Central Philosophy of Buddhism*, London: Allen & Unwin.

Nagel, Thomas (1986), *The View From Nowhere*, New York: Oxford University Press.

Noonan, Harold (1989), *Personal Identity*, London: Routledge.

Nozick, Robert (1981), *Philosophical Explanations*, Cambridge, MA: Harvard University Press.

Oaklander, N.L. (1987), 'Parfit, Circularity and the Unity of Consciousness', *Mind*, **96**: 525–29.

Parfit, Derek (1984), *Reasons and Persons*, New York: Oxford University Press.

Parfit, Derek (1986), 'Comments', *Ethics*, **96**: 832–72.

Parfit, Derek (1995), 'The Unimportance of Identity', in Harris, Henry (ed.), *Identity*, Oxford: Oxford University Press.

Perret, Roy (1998), *Hindu Ethics*, Society for Asian and Comparative Philosophy, Monograph 17, Honolulu: University of Hawaii Press.

Perry, John (1975), 'Personal Identity, Memory, and the Problem of Circularity', in Perry, John (ed.), *Personal Identity*, Los Angeles, CA: University of California Press, pp. 135–55.

Price, Huw (forthcoming), 'Truth as Convenient Fiction'.

Putnam, Hilary (1981), *Reason, Truth and History*, Cambridge: Cambridge University Press.

Putnam, Hilary (1985), 'A Comparison of Something with Something Else', *New Literary History*, **17**: 61–79.

Putnam, Hilary (1992), *Renewing Philosophy*, Cambridge, MA: Harvard University Press.

Putnam, Hilary (1994), 'The Dewey Lectures 1994: Sense, Nonsense and the Senses: An Inquiry into the Powers of the Mind', *Journal of Philosophy*, **91**: 445–517.

Quine, W.V.O. (1960), *Word and Object*, Cambridge, MA: MIT Press.

Quine, W.V.O. (1975), 'The Nature of Natural Knowledge', in Guttenplan, Samuel (ed.), *Mind and Language*, Oxford: Oxford University Press, pp. 67–81.

Railton, Peter (1984), 'Alienation, Consequentialism, and the Demands of Morality', *Philosophy and Public Affairs*, **13**: 134–71.

Ramaiah, C (1978), *The Problem of Change and Identity in Indian Philosophy*, Trirupati: Śri Venkateswara University Press.

Robinson, John (1988), 'Personal Identity and Survival', *Journal of Philosophy*, **85** (6): 319–28.

Rorty, Richard (1972), 'The World Well Lost', *Journal of Philosophy*, **69**: 649–65.

Rorty, Richard (1986), 'Pragmatism, Davidson, and Truth', in LePore, Ernest (ed.), *Truth and Interpretation*, Oxford: Blackwell, pp. 333–55.

Rovane, Carol (1990), 'Branching Self-Consciousness', *Philosophical Review*, **99**: 355–95.

Ruegg, David Seyfort (1977), 'The Uses of the Four Positions of the Catuṣkoṭi and the Problem of the Description of Reality in Mahāyāna Buddhism', *Journal of Indian Philosophy*, **5**: 1–71.

Schechtman, Marya (1996), *The Constitution of Selves*, Ithaca, NY: Cornell University Press.

Scarre, Geoffrey (1996), *Utilitarianism*, London: Routledge.

Shoemaker, Sydney (1985), 'Critical Notice of *Reasons and Persons* by Derek Parfit', *Mind*, **94**: 443–53.

Shoemaker, Sydney and Richard Swinburne (1984), *Personal Identity*, Oxford: Basil Blackwell.

Siderits, Mark (1987), 'Beyond Compatibilism: A Buddhist Approach to Freedom and Determinism', *American Philosophical Quarterly*, **24**: 149–59.

Siderits, Mark (1991), *Indian Philosophy of Language: Studies in Selected Issues*, Dordrecht, The Netherlands: Kluwer Academic Publishers.

Siderits, Mark (1994), 'Matilal on Nāgārjuna', in Bilimoria, Purushottama and J.N. Mohanty (eds), *Relativism, Suffering and Beyond: Essays in Memory of Bimal Krishna Matilal*, Delhi: Oxford University Press, pp. 69–92.

Siderits, Mark (2000), 'Nyāya Realism, Buddhist Critique', in Gupta, Bina (ed.), *The*

Empirical and the Transcendental, Boulder, CO: Rowman and Littlefield, pp. 219–31.

Sinha, Jadunath (1958), *Indian Psychology: Cognition*, Calcutta: Sinha Publishing House.

Sklar, Lawrence (1967), 'Types of Inter-Theoretic Reduction', *British Journal for the Philosophy of Science*, **18**: 109–24.

Stcherbatsky, Th. (1962), *Buddhist Logic*, New York: Dover (reprint; first published in the *Bibilotheca Buddhica* series by the Academy of Sciences of the USSR, Leningrad, 1930).

Stcherbatsky, Th. (1970), *The Central Conception of Buddhism and the Meaning of the Word 'Dharma'*, Delhi: Motilal Banarsidass (reprint; first published by the Royal Asiatic Society, London, 1923).

Stone, Jim (1988), 'Parfit and the Buddha: Why There are no People', *Philosophy and Phenomenological Research*, **48**: 519–32.

Strawson, Galen (1986), *Freedom and Belief*, Oxford: Clarendon Press.

Strawson, Galen (1997), 'The Self', *Journal of Consciousness Studies*, 4: 405–28.

Strawson, Peter (1959), *Individuals*, London: Methuen.

Strawson, Peter (1966), *The Bounds of Sense*, London: Methuen.

Suber, Peter (1996), 'The Paradox of Liberation', unpublished manuscript.

Tambiah, Stanley J. (1987), 'The Buddhist *Arahant*: Classical Paradigm and Modern Thai Manifestation', in Hawley, John Stratton (ed.), *Saints and Virtues*, Berkeley, CA: University of California Press, pp. 111–26.

Tillemans, Tom J.F. (1999), *Scripture, Logic, Language: essays on Dharmakīrti and his Tibetan successors*, Boston, MA: Wisdom Publications.

Tuck, Andrew P. (1990), *Comparative Philosophy and the Philosophy of Scholarship: On the Western Interpretation of Nāgārjuna*, New York: Oxford University Press.

Tye, Michael (1994), 'Sorites Paradoxes and the Semantics of Vagueness', *Philosophical Perspectives 8: Logic and Language*, ed. James E. Tomberlin, Atascadero, CA: Ridgeview, pp. 189–206.

Unger, Peter (1979), 'There are no Ordinary Things', *Synthese*, **41**: 117–54.

Unger, Peter (1992), *Identity, Consciousness and Value*, New York: Oxford University Press.

Van Gulick, Robert (1992), 'Nonreductive Materialism and the Nature of Intertheoretical Constraint', in Beckermann, Ansgar, Hans Flohr and Jaegwon Kim (eds), *Emergence or Reduction?*, Berlin: Walter de Gruyter, pp. 157–79.

Venkataraman, R., trans. (1953), 'Sāmmitīya Nikāya Śāstra', *Viśvabhārati Annals V*, pp. 165–242.

Vision, Gerald (1988), *Modern Anti-Realism and Manufactured Truth*, London: Routledge.

Warder, A.K. (1970), *Indian Buddhism*, Delhi: Motilal Banarsidass.

Wallace, John (1979), 'Only in the Context of a Sentence Do Words Have Any Meaning', in French, Peter A., Theodore E. Uehling, and Howard K. Wettstein (eds), *Contemporary Perspectives in the Philosophy of Language*, Minneapolis, MN: University of Minnesota Press, pp. 305–25.

Williams, Bernard (1973), *Problems of the Self*, Cambridge: Cambridge University Press.

Williams, Bernard (1995), 'Identity and Identities', in Harris, Henry (ed.), *Identity*, Oxford: Clarendon Press, pp. 1–11.

Williams, Michael (1991) *Unnatural Doubts*, Oxford: Basil Blackwell.

Williams, Paul (1998), *Altruism and Reality: Studies in the Philosophy of the* Bodhicāryāvatāra, Curzon Critical Studies in Buddhism, Richmond, Surrey: Curzon Press.

Williamson, Timothy (1994), *Vagueness*, London: Routledge.

Wolf, Susan (1986), 'Self-Interest and Interest in Selves', *Ethics*, **96**: 704–20.

Wood, Thomas E. (1994), *Nāgārjunian Disputations: A Philosophical Journey through an Indian Looking-Glass*, Monographs of the Society for Asian and Comparative Philosophy, No. 11, Honolulu: University of Hawaii Press.

Wright, Crispin (1997), 'Language Mastery and the sorites paradox', in Keefe, Rosanna and Peter Smith (eds), *Vagueness: A Reader*, Cambridge, MA: MIT Press, pp. 151–73.

Young, James O. (1995), *Global Anti-realism*, Brookfield, VT and Aldershot, UK: Ashgate.

Index